THE INDUSTRIAL GEOGRAPHY OF ITALY

CROOM HELM INDUSTRIAL GEOGRAPHY SERIES
Edited by Ian Thompson, University of Glasgow

The Industrial Geography of Canada
Anthony Blackbourn and Robert G. Putnam

Industrialization in West Africa
J.O.C. Onyemelukwe

The Industrial Geography of Italy
Russell King

THE INDUSTRIAL GEOGRAPHY OF ITALY

Russell King

CROOM HELM
London & Sydney

© 1985 Russell King
Croom Helm Ltd, Provident House, Burrell Row,
Beckenham, Kent BR3 1AT

Croom Helm Australia Pty Ltd, Suite 4, 6th Floor
64-76 Kippax Street, Surry Hills, NSW 2010, Australia

British Library Cataloguing in Publication Data

King, Russell
    The industrial geography of Italy — (Croom Helm industrial geography series)
    1. Italy — Industries   2. Italy — Economic conditions — 1976
    I. Title
    338.0945   HC305
    ISBN 0-7099-1501-2

Printed and bound in Great Britain

CONTENTS

Ai geografi italiani

FIGURES

TABLES

INTRODUCTION

To the geographer, Italy presents an ambivalent picture. The Alps, the Po plains, the peninsula and the islands create an illusion of unity, neatly defined by sea and mountain-crest: a 'geographical expression', to quote Metternich's famous phrase. Yet this physical illusion must be tempered by political reality and a lack of internal cohesion. In 1848, year of European revolutions, Italy comprised seven sovereign states. Whereas other European countries have been unified states for hundreds of years, Italy was a latecomer to the European family of nation-states, completing its unification only in 1870. It thus came into the industrial revolution cautiously, fragmented and still paying homage to a series of foreign masters. Along with Germany, Austria and Switzerland, it broke the barriers constraining industrial expansion in a kind of 'second round' of European development. Not until after the First World War did absolute numbers engaged in agricultural employment begin to fall; not until after the Second World War were there more workers in industry than in farming. Italy has, rather uniquely, become one of the world's ten leading industrial powers while at the same time the proportion of the workforce engaged in agriculture remains higher than in any other Common Market country except Greece and Ireland.

Since 1945 Italy has made great strides towards compensating for early industrial deficiencies. In the post-war period the Italian economy has consistently had one of the highest growth rates of any industrial country. Its average annual growth rate of around 6 per cent during 1951-71 was bettered only by Japan amongst the world's major capitalist countries. Yet the Italian industrial experience contains a number of recently-manifest cautionary lessons which are of great potential relevance to other semi-industrialised or recently-industrialised countries. Rapid industrial growth has frequently been compromised by a painfully inefficient and cumbersome bureaucracy. In many fields policy-making structures are archaic. The process of industrial decision-making is at best labyrinthine, at worst corrupt. There are positive lessons to be learnt too. How to live with continuing inflation is one. Much can be learnt about the dynamics of enterprise by studying the small firms of Prato or the rural Veneto, or the merchants of medieval Florence, or a moribund modern giant like Montedison, or the loss-making nationalised industries of the IRI group. The Mezzogiorno provides one of the best object-lessons in European regional policy.

The way in which a lagging polity trails far behind an economy and a society in flux is symptomatic of a fundamental Italian malaise: imbalance and instability. There is an overconcentration of industry in the Italian 'industrial triangle' of Milan-Turin-Genoa. Polarisation between big and small producers seems to be worsening. Particularly alarming are certain persisting social imbalances. While the dynamism of the industrial economy, particularly in the 1950s and 1960s, led to rapidly rising living standards and the spread of the 'consumer society' to most parts of the country, social services have languished. For this, Italians paid the price in the 1970s and 1980s: overcrowded schools, universities and hospitals; unchecked urban growth and land speculation; a severe shortage of low-cost housing and urban recreational space; the menace of urban terrorism; and mass unemployment.

A study of Italian industrial geography, like that of most countries, admits three basic approaches: temporal, sectoral and regional. These have been used as the basic framework of this book. Part One: Background to Industrial Development in Italy, is essentially chronological. After a brief examination of the physical and human resource base, Italy's uniquely fluctuating historical pattern of industrialisation is traced. From a position of world industrial dominance in classical and medieval times (insofar as one can talk of 'industry' in these eras), Italy slumped to relative obscurity by the seventeenth century. Post-unification industrial development has been concentrated in two main periods: from the late 1890s until 1913; and since 1945. Part Two examines the major industrial sectors in turn: power and infrastructures, textiles, metallurgy and engineering and chemicals. For each, the analysis is in terms of origin, structure and spatial distribution. The third part of the book deals with regional contrasts. Here three major industrial vignettes are painted: for the North, Centre and South.

In writing this study I have used a wide range of published materials, mostly in English and Italian, drawn from a variety of disciplines in addition to geography. A glance at the Bibliography reveals the richness of Italian geographical literature and the diversity of non-Italian scholarly studies — particularly in the field of economic history — which are relevant to Italian industrial development. I have also benefited from the detailed statistical publications of the Italian *Istituto Centrale di Statistica,* henceforth referred to as ISTAT. Perhaps no other country in the world has such abundant and well-presented statistical and census material. Major sources such as the decennial censuses of population and industry have been supplemented in this study by the excellent annual publications *Annuario Statistico Italiano* and *Annuario di Statistiche Industriali*. At the time of completion of the manuscript (late 1984), only some provisional results of the 1981 Industrial Census were available. I have incorporated 1981 data in descriptive form in the text whenever possible, and in some of the maps of Chapters 6-8. Chapter 9 was aided by reference to an unpublished typescript in French on industrial development in northern Italy by Etienne Dalmasso.

A word of thanks must go to the staff of Leicester University Library, especially the Inter-Library Loan Department, who supplied me efficiently with requested material from outside Leicester. Readers will be able to judge for themselves the fine quality of the maps in this book. They are the work of Kate Moore and Ruth Rowell of the Cartography Unit in the Department of Geography, Leicester University. Pauline Dawes and Renie Groves typed the manuscript expertly and speedily, whilst Peter Sowden of Croom Helm deserves my special thanks for his quiet patience and encouragement.

It has been my good fortune to know Italy as a student, traveller and researcher for twenty years, visiting the country almost every year since 1965. To my many Italian friends and colleagues in universities and offices the length of the country, I extend a sincere vote of thanks for their friendly help and interest in my work, dedicating this book to them as a token of my esteem and appreciation.

Russell King
University of Leicester

PART ONE

BACKGROUND TO INDUSTRIAL DEVELOPMENT
IN ITALY

1 RESOURCES, NATURAL AND HUMAN

Introduction

It is still the fashion for most regionally-focused geography textbooks to start with a more or less detailed account of physical geography. This approach is eschewed here. Only the briefest topographical generalisations are made, sufficient to give the reader unfamiliar with Italy some idea of its broad physical structure. The main emphasis of this introductory chapter is on examining resources — physical, cultural, demographic — which have a direct bearing on industrial development.

In order to become familiar with commonly-used Italian regional names, we start by looking at Italy's administrative geography. Italy is now divided into 20 regions, 95 provinces and more than 8,000 communes. Numbers of these administrative units have tended to increase over time; in 1870, for instance, there were 73 provinces. Isernia in Molise and Oristano in Sardinia are the most recently created provinces.

The 20 regions are shown on Figure 1.1 and listed in Table 1.1 with their basic geographic and demographic characteristics. They bear some resemblance to the Roman divisions of Italy and are roughly comparable in size and significance to French and Spanish regional units like Brittany and Andalusia, except that Italian regions have evolved considerable administrative autonomy since the end of the war and especially since 1970. Five of the regions have special powers. These are either islands (Sicily, Sardinia) or frontier regions (Val d'Aosta, Trentino–Alto Adige, Friuli–Venezia Giulia) possessing special cultural or linguistic characteristics.

At the next level are the 95 provinces. These are more significant as geographical areas than as units of local government. Typically each province consists of a major town or city, from which the province takes its name, and a number of villages and smaller towns which make up the communes of the province. The commune is the basic unit of local government. Provinces are important in the study of the human and industrial geography of Italy because of the wealth of statistical data published by the government agency ISTAT at this level.

At a more macro scale, common usage divides Italy into a number of sectional arrangements. A simple North/South dichotomy is common in questions regarding the Mezzogiorno. ISTAT employs a threefold

1

Table 1.1: Italian Regions: Population, Area and Density

Region	Population, 1983 ('000)	Area (sq.km)	Density (persons per km²)
Piedmont	4,426	25,400	174
Val d'Aosta	114	3,260	35
Lombardy	8,856	23,850	371
Trentino-Alto Adige	864	13,610	64
Veneto	4,312	18,360	235
Friuli-Venezia Giulia	1,220	7,850	155
Liguria	1,793	5,420	331
Emilia-Romagna	3,929	22,120	178
Tuscany	3,563	22,990	155
Umbria	806	8,460	95
Marche	1,409	9,690	145
Latium	5,074	17,200	295
Abruzzi	1,232	10,790	114
Molise	326	4,440	73
Campania	5,475	13,600	403
Apulia	3,931	19,350	203
Basilicata	604	9,990	61
Calabria	2,060	15,080	137
Sicily	4,987	25,710	194
Sardinia	1,598	24,090	66
Italy	56,577	301,260	188

Source: *Compendio Statistico Italiano 1981,* Rome: ISTAT (1982), p.6; *Bollettino Mensile di Statistica, July 1984,* Rome: ISTAT (1984), p.166.

division into North, Centre and South, whilst the Constitution further divides the South into mainland and islands. Some rationale for these macro-divisions undoubtedly exists.[1] The North is given unity by the focal function of the great Po Plain, encircled by the sweep of the Alps and the northern Apennine slopes. The high productivity levels of both agriculture and industry furnish its inhabitants with a high standard of living. Close commercial and cultural links with Central and Western Europe enhance the 'northern' consciousness of its peoples. With the exception of the Ligurian coastal strip, the North possesses an un-Mediterranean climate with marked continentality, summer rainfall maxima and of course heavy snowfall on the Alps and high Apennines. The Centre, comprising Marche, Tuscany, Umbria and Latium, is essentially Mediterranean and still largely rural. Compared to the North, there is a marked absence of industrial advantages and traditions. Finally, the South, given a certain physical unity by climate, soils and geology, constitutes a special region because of its relative backwardness, the legacy of centuries of neglect. Campania, Abruzzi, Molise, Apulia, Basilicata and Calabria make up the mainland South, although Abruzzi is locationally and economically transitional with the central region. Sicily and Sardinia, as islands, are very much

Figure 1.1: Italy: Regional Boundaries and Main Towns

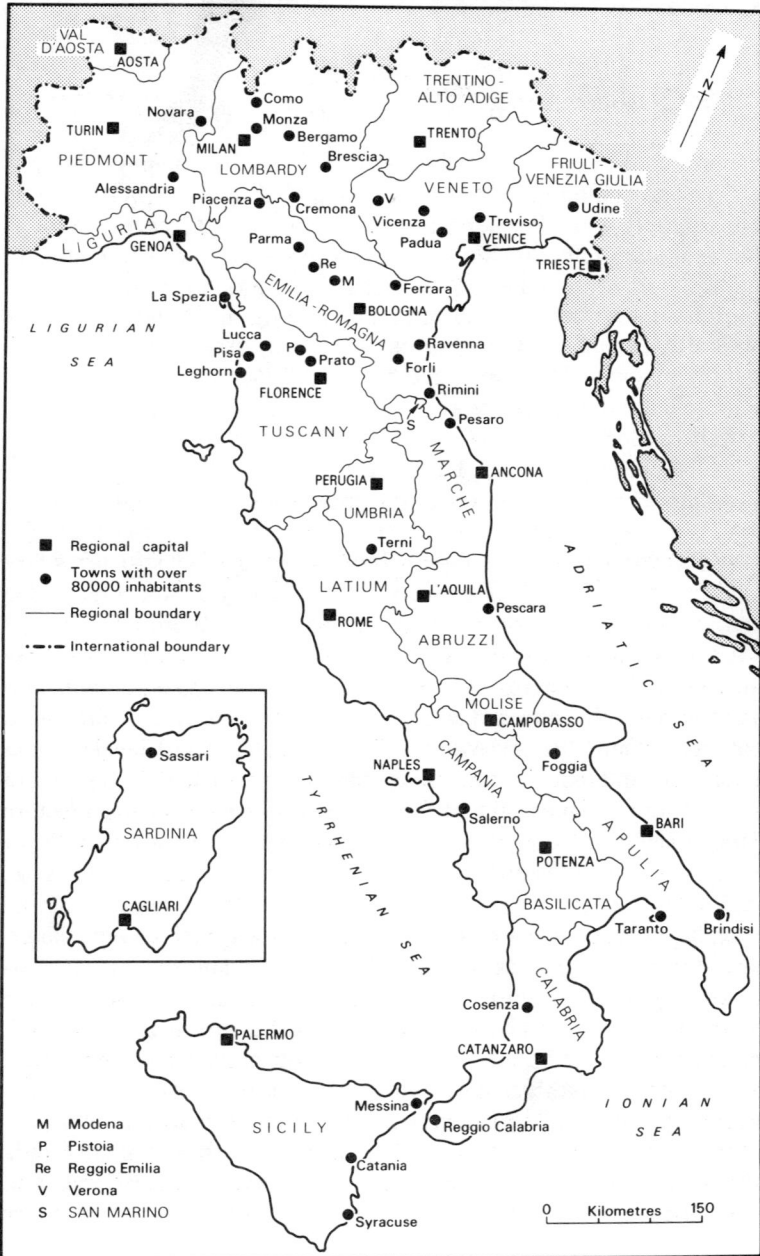

separate regional entities, having as little in common with each other as they do with the mainland.

Natural Resource Framework

According to ISTAT the Italian territory is 38.7 per cent mountains, 39.7 per cent hills and only 21.6 per cent plains, figures which compare unfavourably with all other EEC countries except Greece. Although this mountain-hill-plain division is morphological rather than altitudinal — there are, for example, areas of 'low mountain' in south-west Sardinia and zones of 'high hills' in Tuscany and central Sicily — generally speaking the mountain category comprises land over 1,000 m and the plains include most land below 300 m. Figure 1.2 shows the main relief and drainage features.

Italy to a large extent owes its present form to the mountain-building of the Miocene period which led to the shaping of the Alps and Apennines more or less as they are today, modified subsequently by glaciation. With the Alps dominating the northern borderlands and providing the cavea for the theatre of the Po Plain, the main relief structure of the peninsula is the Apennines which wind uniformly south, conditioning climate, agriculture, communications and historical events.

Crystalline rocks dominate the Western Alps and the higher parts of the Central and Eastern Alps. Small glaciers survive in places and there are considerable snow-fields. Jagged, frost-shattered pinnacles stand out, as at Monte Viso and Monte Bianco (Mont Blanc). Flat-bottomed, U-shaped valleys seam the Alpine massif; minor valleys 'hang'. Limestone is the dominant rock in the southern part of the Alps east of the Ticino River. In the Dolomites tower-like blocks of limestone with flat tops give silhouettes rather different from those of the pointed crystalline Alps.

Many of the higher parts of the Apennines are also composed of limestones; in the Apuanian Alps of Tuscany and in the Gran Sasso of Abruzzi alpine landforms result through glaciation. Sandstone is widespread in the northern Apennines where the topography is somewhat more rounded. Particularly on the eastern flanks, the Apennines are bordered by a belt of clays and marls. The clays are much subject to gulleying and areas of badlands called *calanchi* exist, particularly in Basilicata. Where clays are overlain or interleaved with sandstone or limestone, landslips are frequent occurrences. The limestone-sandstone-clay sequence reappears in Sicily. In Sardinia and Calabria, by

Figure 1.2: Main Relief and Drainage Features

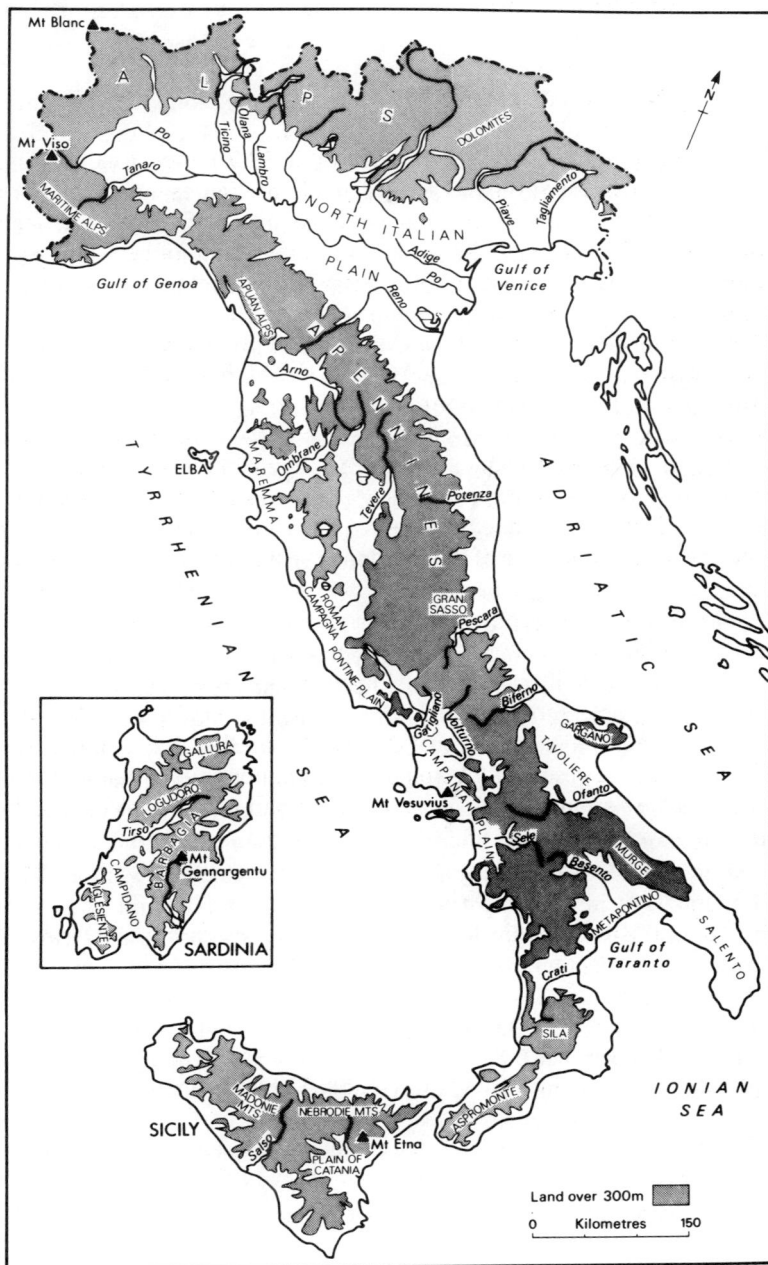

contrast, crystalline landscapes recur but, unaffected by glaciation, the relief is lower and more rounded than in the Alps. Volcanic landscapes naturally call to mind celebrated Etna and Vesuvius, but also exist elsewhere, in Latium and Sardinia.

Most plains in Italy are alluvial. A partial exception is the Po Plain whose morainic hills and pebbly gravels owe much to the work of glaciation. In the Apulian Tavoliere the alluvial veneer is a rather thin covering for the Quaternary sea-bed. A distinction can be drawn between the great triangular Po Plain of the North and the smaller coastal plains of the peninsula and islands. In the Po Plain man's mastery of hydraulic technology, key to the development of the Italian plains, explains a rapid and early economic development culminating in considerable nineteenth century industrial growth. In the peninsula, particularly towards the South, and in the islands, the coastal flatlands, with their violent silt-laden floods, their malaria and their emptiness, have proved a difficult environment to exploit. Areas like the Sele and Garigliano Plains in Campania, the Metapontino of Basilicata, the pocket-plains of Calabria, the Plain of Catania and the Sardinian Campidano have been forsaken since the close of the classical era, yielding only recently, in the 1930s or the 1950s, to new techniques of reclamation, drainage and irrigation.

The main climatic influences are Italy's latitudinal position, the strong maritime influences of the Mediterranean Sea (no part of the peninsula is more then 80 km from the sea), and the presence of mountain areas, particularly their relation to air mass movements. Yet the classic Mediterranean climate, with its long, hot droughty summer and its mild, rainy winter, does not occur widely in Italy, being confined to the islands and the lower third of the peninsula. Hardly any rain falls in the summer in the South, but north of Rome summer rainfall increases and in the Po Plain summer precipitation exceeds winter. The mountain-girt interior location of the North Italian Plain gives it a quasi-continental climate. Milanese summers are as hot as at Bari in the South, but winter temperatures equate to those of Alsace far to the north. Temperature inversions in the Po Valley give Turin and Milan short severe winters with January means of 0°C and 1°C respectively. Milan can experience 60 days of frost per year and as many days of fog. With increasing industrial pollution of the atmosphere the city's smogs are becoming notorious.

Mean annual rainfall decreases southwards, but altitude is a powerful local control. Alpine regions may receive 3,000 mm and high Apennine locations over 2,000 mm. The driest places are the southern coasts of Apulia, Sicily and Sardinia where only 300-400 mm are recorded, making dry-farming a hazardous undertaking. The more even seasonal distribution of precipitation in the North permits the growth of a wide variety of crops, supports natural meadows and generally sustains a healthy agricultural regime which has acted as a solid plank for industrial development since at least the early nineteenth century. By contrast the South's chronic lack of moisture during the growing season limits crop variety and poses a continual threat to yields. The impetus to industrial development through a prosperous agriculture has therefore been missing in this part of Italy.

Whilst it is true that it is possible to find within Italy virtually every European land use existing from Scotland to Turkey, the legend of Italy as the garden of Europe is largely mythical. The fertile, garden-like areas — around Florence and Naples, behind Palermo and on the lower slopes of Etna for example — are in truth the result of centuries of painstaking modification of the natural environment: laborious cutting of terraces, meticulous control of water, expert management of soil and crops. Only one-quarter of the land deemed suited to farming is level or gently sloping; the rest is hill or mountain.

The industrial significance of these geological and precipitation features lies primarily in river regimes. The most striking feature is the contrast between the rivers originating in the Alps which have a considerable perennial flow often based on impermeable geological structures, and those originating south of the Po which have irregular flows developed on porous rocks. Many rivers in the peninsula and the islands dry up completely for a part of the year; their economic potential, for irrigation, navigation and power generation, is extremely limited.

But we should be careful in ascribing neo-deterministically the agricultural and industrial backwardness of the South solely to physical factors. No one can deny that the South is short of level land or that the severity of the summer drought generally increases as one proceeds down the peninsula. But this is not the whole story. There have been historical periods — under the Greeks and the Arabs, for instance — when the South made use of its environmental resources so successfully that an advanced civilisation and economy flourished. Capua and Pompeii, for example, were leading centres of commerce and industry in their day. At other times, man has abused the environment. And this is the key. It is not that development possibilities have been mechanistically held down by physical factors; rather the parameters should be stated in reverse. Much of the problem of the South results from the long-term inefficient use of environmental resources. The erosive phenomena, the poor soils, the scrubby vegetation, the malaria and the desertion have been exacerbated by persistent environmental mismanagement, often carried out under the uninterested hegemony of a colonial regime. The processes may be essentially physical but their intensity and frequency of occurrence and their damaging effects are conditioned by human intervention.[2]

Mineral Resources

Italy has been niggardly treated in the provision of the natural resources which might have played an important role in the early development of industry. The geological youth of the country prescribes only a limited range of mineral deposits (Table 1.2). The two main metalliferous areas of the country are the oldest geologically: south-west Sardinia, and Elba and adjacent parts of Tuscany (Figure 1.3). In the Alps, minerals are generally widely dispersed and small-scale in occurrence; the one important area — Cogne in Val d'Aosta — is 2,000 m above sea level.

Table 1.2: Output of Major Mineral and Fuel Products, 1980

	'000 tons
Metallic minerals:	
Iron	184,624
Aluminium (bauxite)	23,260
Lead	26,941
Zinc	129,164
Mercury (1978)	139,973
Non-metallic minerals:	
Sulphur	100,852
Pyrites	858,992
Potassic salts	1,301,649
Marine salt (1978)	973,507
Felspar	344,301
Fluorspar	151,965
Fuel deposits:	
Coal (lignite)	1,932,571
Crude oil	1,800,130
Methane (million cubic metres)	12,531

Source: *Annuario Statistico Italiano 1981,* Rome: ISTAT (1982), p.131.

Note to Figure 1.3: The existence of deposits on the map does not necessarily imply their current exploitation.

Figure 1.3: Major Fuel and Mineral Deposits

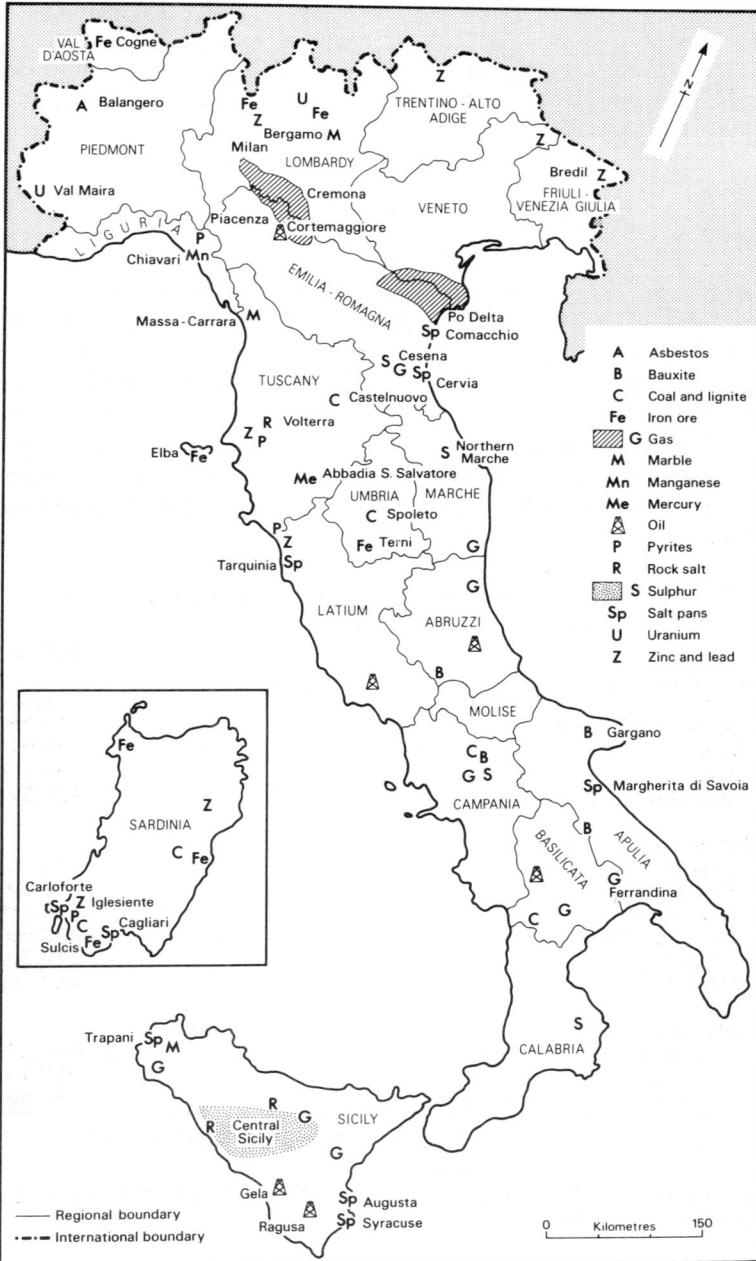

A	Asbestos
B	Bauxite
C	Coal and lignite
Fe	Iron ore
G	Gas
M	Marble
Mn	Manganese
Me	Mercury
	Oil
P	Pyrites
R	Rock salt
S	Sulphur
Sp	Salt pans
U	Uranium
Z	Zinc and lead

——— Regional boundary
·—·—· International boundary

0   Kilometres   150

Iron ore is poorly represented. Elba supplies half the total output and the rest comes from Cogne, Lake Como, Terni (Umbria) and Iglesiente (south-west Sardinia). Of the important minerals, only in the output of mercury does Italy rank among leading world producers, coming third after the USSR and Spain. The entire Italian output originates from the Monte Amiata area in southern Tuscany. Italy is also the fourth-ranked producer of pyrites (from the Tuscan Maremma region), fifth of asbestos (from the Balangero mines near Turin), sixth of fluorspar (from Sardinia and parts of Northern Italy) and eighth of salt.[3] Half the salt is mined as rock-salt in central Sicily and around Volterra (Tuscany); the rest comes from marine evaporation, the largest pans being at Cagliari, accounting for half the sea-salt, Trapani (Sicily) and Margherita di Savoia (Apulia). In addition, Italy is self-sufficient in aluminium (from the bauxite deposits of the Gargano), sulphur (from Sicily) and lead and zinc (mostly from the Sardinian Iglesiente); production of all these is, however, falling. In fact, output from all extractive industries dropped 3.1 per cent during 1970-80, the only major branch of industry to register a fall. Italy is also famous for certain stones, the most distinguished being the Massa-Carrara marbles quarried in northern Tuscany.

The development of energy resources will be examined in more detail in Chapter 5. Here it is sufficient to note the location of the major occurrences, aided by Figure 1.3.

The small amounts of coal which exist in Sardinia and Tuscany are of poor quality and production has fallen off rapidly since the 1950s. The Sulcis mines in south-west Sardinia closed down completely in 1972. In the 1930s small quantities of oil and natural gas were being produced in the North Italian Plain, as well as pitch for asphalt at Ragusa in southern Sicily. Further small discoveries of oil were made in the Abruzzi. Richer fields struck by Gulf Italia in 1954 at Ragusa and by ENI (the Italian energy authority) two years later at nearby Gela brought hopes of an oil bonanza but the early promise was not fulfilled. The Sicilian oilfields proved to be of limited size and produced heavy, bituminous, sulphurous oil of poor quality.

Italy's most important known natural resource is undoubtedly natural gas, located mainly in the Lombardian and Emilian sections of the Po Plain, with further occurrences in Apulia, Basilicata and Sicily. These supplies were, however, not discovered until after the First World War and played no important role in Italy's industrial development until 1944. There are, moreover, considerable areas in Italy with geological conditions favourable for hydrocarbon accumulation, notably in a belt extending from the Po Plain down the Adriatic coast and into Basilicata. Recent offshore exploration in the Adriatic has yielded promising results.

Hydro-electric power generation is favoured in the Alps which have the advantage of great vertical drops, hanging valleys and heavy and evenly spread precipitation. One drawback is winter freezing. Many of the more important stations are located at the mouths of tributary Alpine valleys. Over 70 per cent of all Italian hydro-electricity is generated in the Alps, and here 17 of the 21 major stations are to be found. Other main producing regions are the high Apennine parts of Umbria, Latium, Abruzzi and Calabria. In many localities it has been necessary to build reservoirs to increase and regulate the flow of water to the generators. Hydro-electric power accounted for over half of Italy's electric power just after the war, but has since fallen back to less than a third. This proportion is likely to fall further since it is reckoned that over 80 per cent of hydro-electric potential has already been harnessed. Finally, it is worth noting the underground steam resources which are tapped at Lardarello in Tuscany for electricity production.

Human Resources: Population Evolution and Settlement

As with most modern industrial economies, the greatest and most enduring Italian resource has been the skill and industriousness of the population. Although modern industrial growth has come only relatively recently, these important human qualities were evident much earlier in Italian economic history.

Early figures on population evolution are necessarily imprecise. At the beginning of the Christian era it is reckoned that Italy had a population of around 7 million rising to 10 million by the fourteenth century. Epidemics ensured the long-term stability of the population over the next 300 years; in the two terrible plagues of 1630 and 1657 2 million people died. After 1700 demographic growth speeded up somewhat, although it was still below that of the rest of Europe. The population reached 18.1 million in 1800 and 26.1 million in 1861.[4]

Traditional Italy has been described as a country agricultural in occupation but urban in its mode of life. Like the pyramids of Egypt, Italian cities are so venerable that they seem to have been in existence for all time. No other country can boast such a magnificent urban heritage, whose origins go back two and a half millennia. The Etruscans and the Greeks first brought urbanism to Italy, though much has still to be discovered concerning the character of Etruscan towns, and Greek urban influence was limited to Sicily and the South. The Romans greatly developed the urban character of Italy, founding 70 new colonies and up-grading many more native settlements into urban centres.

Whereas elsewhere in Western Europe urban life did not survive the Dark Ages, in Italy towns preserved their continuity as agricultural and trade centres. Urban population started to grow after the tenth century, aided by towns' juridical, ecclesiastical and educational functions. Notable here is the early founding of universities at Bolgona, Padua, Pisa and Naples. From the twelfth century on, republican city-states flourished in Central and Northern Italy; by the early thirteenth century some 200-300 self-governing urban polities stretched from the Alps to the borders of the Kingdom of Naples. Most were small or medium sized towns; the chief exception was Venice, ruler of a great maritime empire. South of Rome powerful monarchic dynasties discouraged city-republic development.

As the Commercial Revolution of the later Middle Ages gathered pace, the republican city-states were eventually succeeded by the more despotic rule of the *signori* whereby a few dominant city-states were controlled by wealthy families such as the Florentine Medici. The map of late medieval Italy revealed an economic landscape of powerful city-states, each dominant over a wide area. Nowhere else in Europe was the metropolitian city so large, dwarfing other types of town. Venice remained pre-eminent, but there were also Genoa, Milan and Florence, doubling their populations in a century or less. Rome, too, had a special status as the papal seat. Further south, the fortunes of Naples and Palermo were too closely tied to the stagnant Spanish empire.

From the early sixteenth century on, and in contrast to the pattern in England, France and Holland, Italy embarked upon a long era of economic decline during which levels of living progressively deteriorated. Infant mortality increased in this period, and from 1660 the annual rate of population growth was no higher than 3 per thousand moving up to 6 per thousand after 1820. After 1870 a new phase started, characterised, especially in the North, by those trends associated with the 'demographic transition.' Death rate fell from 30 per thousand per year in 1875 to 15 per thousand in 1930. This change, telescoped into 55 years in Italy, took 125 years in England and 150 in France and Sweden.[5]

It is important to stress that the demographic transition did not occur at the same time or at the same rate in all parts of the country. The South lagged behind the North, although this simple regional picture is complicated by different rates of outmigration and other fertility differentials such as those based on urban-rural contrasts and on socio-economic class. Already in 1871 urban fertility in the North was lower than rural, a clear indication of family limitation influences resulting from an emerging industrial society. In the South, by contrast, urban and rural rates were similar at this time. It is also evident from the unique 1931 Census data on fertility and husband's occupation that smaller families were characteristic of higher status groups, especially in the North. Higher birth rates continue to be focused on the South, a reflection of the still predominantly rural milieu and of the stronger influence there of the pro-natalist Catholic Church.

Since 1861 a pattern of more or less regular decennial censuses enables population to be charted more precisely. As Table 1.3 shows, the Italian population more than doubled from 1861-1981. Average annual growth rates, already established at 6 per thousand in the early nineteenth century, have remained remarkably stable since, with the exception of a sharp temporary drop associated with the First World War. Some tendency to an increasing rate of demographic growth in the post Second World War period is noticeable: mean annual rates of increase were 6.4 per thousand during the 1950s, 6.7 per thousand during the 1960s and 7.7 per thousand during the 1970s. By 1985 the Italian population probably exceeds 57 million.

Table 1.3: Population Census Figures, 1861-1981

Census date	Population within: contemporary boundary ('000)	present-day boundary ('000)	Average annual rate of increase (‰ based on present-day boundary)
31.12.1861	22,122	26,328	--
31.12.1871	27,303	28,151	6.7
31.12.1881	28,953	29,791	5.7
10. 2.1901	32,965	33,778	6.6
10. 6.1911	35,845	36,921	8.6
1.12.1921	38,449	37,856	2.4
21. 4.1931	41,652	41,043	8.6
21. 4.1936	42,994	42,399	6.5
4.11.1951	47,516	47,516	7.4
15.10.1961	50,624	50,624	6.4
24.10.1971	54,137	54,137	6.7
25.10.1981	56,244	56,244	3.8

Source: Earlier censuses from *Annuario Statistico Italiano 1977*, Rome: ISTAT (1977), p.8.

There has been considerable spatial variation in this population growth. During the late nineteenth century the Sicilian and Apulian littorals were among the areas of greatest increase, whereas much of Basilicata and Calabria witnessed large-scale emigration and consequent population decline. Mountain depopulation has been severe in all parts of Italy, impelled by the combination of mounting population pressure and an inhospitable habitat. Physiographic divisions contained in the censuses reveal the basic changes. In 1871 23.5 per cent of the Italian population lived in the mountain zone; in 1971 only 12.8 per cent. The hill zone decreased its proportion less dramatically from 47.5 per cent to 38.8 per cent, whilst the plains increased from 27 per cent to 48.4 per cent.

There have also been regional contrasts of a non-physiographic nature. These have been especially marked since the last war. Between 1951 and 1971 Italy's population grew by 13.6 per cent, but rates of growth varied from only 6.2 per cent for the South to 17.7 per cent for the North and 18.9 per cent for the Centre, dominated by urban growth in the capital. That these rates ran counter to the pattern of natural increase, which was far higher in the South (29 per cent over 1951-71) than the North (10.3 per cent), is explained by net migration figures — a loss of over 4 million in the South over the 20 year period and a gain of 1.9 million in the North and Centre.

The key to Italian population change over the past hundred years is emigration. Since unification over 25 million Italians have left their country, mostly for work reasons. About half emigrated overseas, chiefly to the Americas around the turn of the century and to Australia more recently. Most post-war emigration has been to Europe, particularly France, Germany and Switzerland. Because of the dubious nature of return migration statistics, it is difficult to be precise about the proportions of emigrants who stayed abroad permanently. One estimate puts the net migratory loss for 1861-1971 at about 8 million.[6] By the mid 1970s, however, a century of Italian emigration had come to an end; the outflow had shrunk to a trickle outweighed by incoming migrants returning from abroad and by immigrants from other countries, chiefly Yugoslavia, seeking work in Italy.[7]

The internal migration system, which has progressively overtaken external migration in importance during the post-war period, is made up of three overlapping flows: highland to lowland, rural to urban and South to North. The leading centres of in-migration are the city-regions surrounding Milan, Turin and Rome; also important are Genoa, Bologna and Florence. During 1951-81 every southern province experienced a net migratory loss, the outflow being heaviest in the highland spine from Abruzzi to Calabria. Other areas of high out-migration are central and western Sicily, and Veneto and Friuli-Venezia Giulia in North-east Italy.

Internal flows of population are closely related to increasing socio-economic disparity between Italian regions, the main archetypes being the depressed rural uplands of the South and the industrially booming cities of the North. Severe social problems have accompanied these massive rural-urban, South-North population shifts. In Milan, Turin and their industrial satellite towns there has been great strain on public services, especially housing, schools and hospitals. Inevitable tensions have resulted, especially when southerners experience difficulty in finding lodgings because of local landlords' prejudice against them. However, the claim by many northerners that all southern migrants are poor, uneducated peasants with no preparation for city life and work has been confounded by sociological enquiries which show that many migrants had already rejected their rural way of life and, largely through the effects of television and the media, had embraced urban values before they left their native villages.[8] This 'anticipatory socialisation' explains southerners' fairly rapid acceptance of urban industrial society with its different patterns of kinship, friendship and inter-marriage.

It is, of course, internal migration, developing largely in response to industrial development, that generates Italy's pattern of recent urban growth. Discounting the classical and medieval periods, Italian urbanisation initially lagged behind that of other European countries, a situation related to the late emergence of Italy as a state, its industrial backwardness until recently, and the economic and cultural divide between North and South. The urban pattern at the time of unification was made up of a network of relatively minor centres which were the old capitals of traditional city-states. This partly explains the shifting of the Italian capital from Turin to Florence in 1865 and thence to Rome in 1871, movements which were due to the political exigences of the moment rather than rational economic choice. Urbanisation has, however, progressed particularly rapidly since 1945 in parallel with the country's industrial development. In 1808 there were only five cities of over 100,000 inhabitants (Milan, Venice, Rome, Naples and Palermo); by 1861 the number had risen to eleven, and a century later it was 32 (16 in the North, 6 in the Centre and 10 in the South). In the North these cities are distributed along two axes (Turin-Trieste and Milan-Bologna), defining the framework of a coherent urban system. In the

South, on the other hand, the fewer major cities are isolated and there is no continuity in the urban network.

The 32 officially designated metropolitan areas increased their collective population by 49.5 per cent during 1951-71, a rate of increase approximately three and a half times the national. Their share of total population increased from 33 per cent in 1951 to 43 per cent in 1971. The most notable increases were in Milan, Turin and Rome, but a number of medium sized southern towns, such as Bari, Taranto and Cagliari, also grew quickly in response to government-fostered industrialisation. Since 1971, however, some big northern cities have been losing population.

The four Italian 'million cities' differ widely. Milan is the major industrial city and the commercial heart of the North. Turin is the centre of the automobile industry. Rome has relatively little industry apart from construction, being largely an administrative and tourist city. Naples is essentially the decaying former capital of a truncated empire, now with some of the worse housing conditions and poverty in the whole of Europe. To an increasing extent the 'dual capitals' of Rome and Milan overshadow other Italian cities. Of the 50 largest Italian industrial corporations, 17 have their headquarters in Milan, 8 in Rome, 7 in Genoa and 6 in Turin.[9]

Post-war urban growth has been mostly chaotic and unplanned. Along with the problems associated with assimilating large numbers of migrants, the big cities have indulged in an orgy of housing speculation resulting in disorderly suburbs of densely-packed apartment blocks with minimal public recreation space. In one sense Italy may be said to be 'over-urbanised' because rural-urban migration has progressively outstripped urban-industrial employment opportunities. The manifest need to restrict mushrooming metropolitan development because of the diseconomies of urban concentration — overcrowding, noise, pollution, traffic congestion, rising crime and unemployment — goes unheeded when politicians have too many vested business interests at stake.

Spatial movements of population have been associated with marked occupational shifts. Table 1.4 charts these over the period 1861-1981. Agriculture's share of the working population has dropped markedly, the pace of decline accelerating since the Second World War. Until 1971 industry and the tertiary sector increased their proportions more or less in parallel to balance the outmovement from farming. In reflection of these occupational changes, salaries and pay have risen more quickly in industry than in agriculture. More recently wages have risen fastest in

Table 1.4: Employment by Sector at Census Dates, 1861-1981

Census	Active population as % of total	% active population in:			
		Agriculture	Industry (including construction)	Other	Seeking first job
1861	59.5	69.1	18.0	12.1	0.8
1871	57.2	66.8	18.9	13.3	1.0
1881	54.6	64.6	20.0	14.3	1.1
1901	50.1	60.9	21.9	15.8	1.4
1911	48.2	57.5	23.2	17.6	1.7
1921	47.0	54.7	24.3	19.1	1.9
1931	45.3	50.8	25.8	21.4	2.0
1936	44.9	48.1	26.7	22.7	2.5
1951	43.5	40.0	30.3	24.4	5.3
1961	38.7	28.9	40.1	29.5	1.5
1971	34.7	17.2	43.5	37.0	2.3
1981	39.8	10.1	35.7	44.0	10.2

Source: Earlier census figures from *A Century of Economic and Social Development in Italy 1861-1961*, Rome: ISTAT (1965), p.54.

the tertiary sector which has, in fact, expanded its employment rather faster than industry in recent years as Italy moves to the 'post-industrial' phase of development. The growth of the tertiary sector is due to two factors: the expansion of the tourist industry which in a space of a few years has changed the landscape and life-style of entire regions, especially along the coasts; and the pathological spread of state bureaucracy throughout Italian society.

Table 1.4 also reveals a steady long-term drop in the active population as a percentage of total population, at least until 1971. This decline is not entirely real, being due in part to new ways of classifying jobs. In the past, when the majority of the population was rural, farmers' wives were recorded as actively employed because they helped with the farm work; in the city wives are not regarded as employed unless a formal outside job is taken. The low figure for the actively employed of 34.7 per cent in 1971, is also connected with regional and structural imbalance, being much higher in northern industrial areas (Piedmont 40.8 per cent, Lombardy 40.7 per cent) than in rural southern regions (Basilicata 29.8 per cent, Calabria 30 per cent).

In spite of the overall high levels of industrial skill and adaptiveness of the Italian working population, there are certain negative elements in Italian demography. Probably the most notorious is that Italy has a higher rate of infant mortality than any other country of a comparable level of development (in Western Europe only Portugal has a significantly higher level). The explanation for this, as for so many apparent paradoxes in Italian economic and social life, lies in the North-South contrast, the highest infant mortality figures being recorded in the South.

Another qualitative shortcoming is education, which is generally out of phase with needs of the country.[10] Free education is available to all children but the curricula are redolent of a period when education was mainly for the elite. Students leave school and college equipped with an out-of-date culture ill-suited to the industrial society in which most have to earn their living. The educational system is also dualistic. In 1950 Italy had an illiteracy rate of nearly 30 per cent and at the same time one of the highest percentages of population as university students of any country in the world. This situation has not changed greatly. Illiteracy has fallen steadily since 1950, but pockets of cultural poverty persist; in Calabria illiteracy is still 15 per cent. Many Italians are in fact 'semi-literate'; 70 per cent of the workforce have only a primary school certificate which effectively means they can do little more than read or write a limited vocabulary.[11] In universities most students still plump for arts or humanities degrees which given them an education of little vocational relevance to the needs of industry or the economic opportunities potentially open to graduates.[12] The inflated bureaucracy is the traditional outlet for many of these graduates, but competition for white-collar jobs is now so fierce that graduate unemployment has become a severe problem.

Current Population Distribution

The present population of Italy is distributed at a mean density of 188 persons per square kilometre (Table 1.1). Although the density varies greatly from one district to another (Figure 1.4), there is no one limited part of the country with a large share of the population. Areas of high density are numerous and occur in many parts of the country, unlike the pattern in some European countries, like Sweden, Holland and Greece, where a major population concentration occurs.[13]

Areas of high density are mostly those which have high agricultural productivity and/or industrial-urban clusters. The largest continuous region of high density is the Po Plain within which some differentiation of densities may be described. In the west, Turin (1,181,000) dominates a series of population clusters in lower Piedmont; here the key reason

Figure 1.4: Population Distribution, 1981

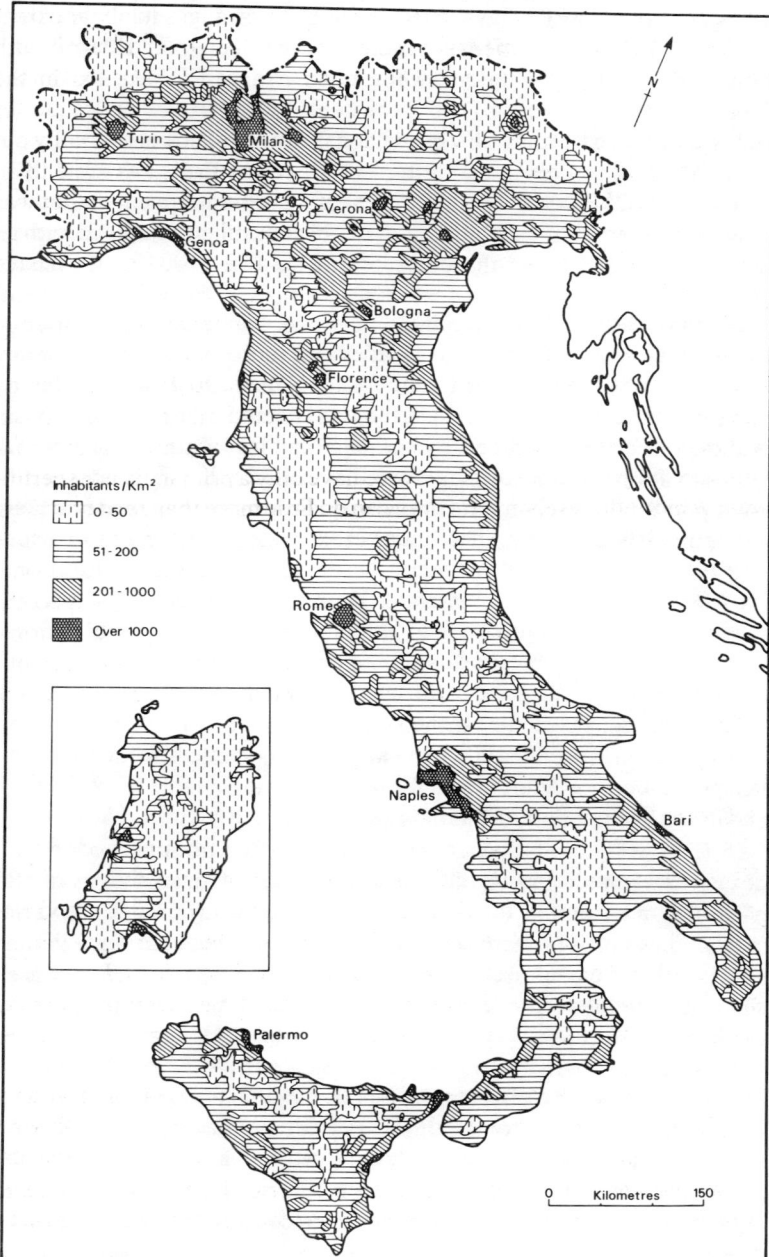

for urban growth has been the expansion of the Fiat works and its linked industrial plants, which have acted as magnets for migrant labour from the South. Further east there is a more extensive belt of high density in Lombardy, focusing on the sprawling city of Milan (1,724,000). Rural densities are high here too, and these densely settled rich agricultural zones extend eastwards to Veneto and Emilia. The most important manufacturing centres in the eastern Po Plain are Bologna (490,000) and Padua (232,000). Densities generally diminish east of Padua towards the amphibian landscapes of the coastal lagoons, the only major exceptions being the cities of Venice (364,000) and Trieste (270,000).

South of the Po Valley topographical constraints confine the main clusters of dense population to smaller and more scattered localities. On the Adriatic coast a belt runs from Ravenna to Pescara; recent demographic growth here is linked to tourism and maritime functions. Although more constrained by the encroaching Maritime Alps, the Ligurian littoral is more densely settled, with 812,000 inhabitants in the great port city of Genoa. Horticulture and tourism are also important along this Riviera coast. The linear urban system of Liguria extends into the Arno Valley of northern Tuscany, dominated by Florence (462,000) where high value-added manufacturing employs a large share of the population. The main population centre in Central Italy is Rome (2,800,000) but the capital is surrounded by relatively low rural densities.

The high density zones of the south are typically lowland areas of high agricultural productivity focusing on a major city. The most important population concentration in the Mezzogiorno is Naples (1,233,000) and its fertile hinterland of the Campanian plains. On the Adriatic coast Bari (357,000) is also surrounded by intensive farming and hence dense rural population. A third belt of high density stretches between Messina and Catania in eastern Sicily. Palermo (651,000) and its surrounding citrus orchards is a more isolated node of high density. It is worth noting the contrast between Sicily and Sardinia, islands of equal size, but with the former containing over three times the population of the latter.

Low density areas, with less than 50 persons per square kilometre, are characterised by physical handicaps such as high altitude, rough terrain, poor soils, low and variable rainfall and past association with malaria. The most continuous low density zones coincide with the mountain ranges: the Alpine fringe along the northern frontier, and the Apennine spine. In the Alps the higher parts are devoid of human settlement; most of the population is found along the valley floors, particularly at points where the valleys open out on to the North Italian Plain. The mountain core of the peninsula is generally thinly-peopled but contains several densely populated basins and valleys, particularly in Tuscany and Umbria. Between Leghorn and Civitavecchia stretches the Maremma, a formerly malarial marsh juxtaposed with rough, stony terrain inland. Some of the lowest densities of all are found in Sardinia, an isolated region of shepherds and granite mountains.

Notes and References

1. Walker (1967), pp.95-7. Walker is the standard regional text on Italy in English, but see also Cole (1968) which, although briefer, is more imaginatively presented, as well as the recent translation of Bethemont and Pelletier (1983).

2. These points are further explored in an interesting essay by Poncet (1969).

3. These rankings are from Vedovato (1973), p.233.

4. Figures from Cipolla (1965) who puts the error of pre-1800 population estimates at plus or minus 15 per cent.

5. Ibid., pp.579-80.

6. Del Panta (1979), p.208.

7. See King (1976) for a more detailed account of Italian migration trends.

8. Alberoni and Baglioni (1965), pp.104-32.

9. Zariski (1972), p.44.

10. Acquaviva and Santuccio (1976), pp.150-7, 169-70.

11. Sylos-Labini (1972).

12. Moreover, the contribution of universities to industrial research is minimal. Whereas other comparable countries have research organisations that are a real force for development, Italy does not. Research activity is stagnant and ignored by politicans. The following figures on research personnel per 10,000 inhabitants are illuminiating: USA 36, Great Britain 29, Holland 26, USSR 22, Japan 19, France and Germany 18, Belgium 17, Italy 6. Source: Avveduto (1968), p.153.

13. This section on population distribution is based largely on Cole (1968), pp.61-3 and Rodgers (1978), pp.84-8.

2 THE BUILD-UP OF INDUSTRY IN THE NORTH

It has been pointed out by more authors than one cares to remember that Italy is a cross between a developed and an underdeveloped country. This does not mean that Italy as a whole is a semi-developed economy. It means that different parts of Italy are at different levels of development. Most treatment of Italian regional inequality tends to focus on the reasons for the South's backwardness. This chapter approaches the familiar North-South dichotomy from the other side, by documenting the build-up of industrial prosperity in Northern Italy. This in turn basically involves an examination of factors favouring industrial polarisation in the Po Plain. The time span covered is up to 1914.

Early Historical Perspectives

Although this book is primarily concerned with modern industrial development which, in the case of Italy, 'took off' in the last years of the nineteenth century, early patterns of industrial production should also be noted, for some of these have been remarkably continuous over several centuries.

In ancient times the Italian peninsula was the transfer point of Greek culture and merchandise to Western Europe. The peaceful centuries of the early Roman Empire were a period of widespread prosperity and witnessed great achievements in engineering, architecture and public administration. By the second century AD the Empire formed a single market, united by a far-reaching network of highways, many of which still exist today, and supported by a newly-built system of ports, aqueducts and canals. In fact the Roman legacy in the present-day geography of Italy is still quite strong. Apart from road alignments, the major Alpine passes — Brenner, San Bernard, Simplon and Mont Cenis — were all used by the Romans to connect the peninsula to the north. Most Italian cities are Roman or pre-Roman foundations: those which are not such as Venice, Novara and Bergamo, are the exception rather than the rule. Although primarily military and commercial in character, many Roman towns also had industrial functions. Milan, for example, was a major centre of metal-working and textile manufacture in Roman times. Other metal industries were based on the iron, copper and tin deposits of Elba and Etruria. Lead, for Roman plumbing, was also plentiful and often yielded silver as a smelting by-product. One of the main outlets for the Roman metal industry was the military, but, as legions dispersed to the frontiers of the empire, weapon manufacture became more provincial in location.[1]

Structural changes in the later Roman Empire weakened this economic buoyancy.[2] The drying up of the flow of war captives, the main source of slaves, cut the supply of cheap labour to industry and construction. Industry was faced with growing competition from the provinces which had copied production techniques pioneered in Rome. Population declined and by Nero's reign towns were deserted, industries had contracted and fields were abandoned for want of hands to till them.

But the decline was not uniform. Certain towns, such as Milan, Padua and Ravenna, continued to grow into the fifth century. Milan, which replaced Rome as the seat of fading imperial government, still supported flourishing textile and metal industries. In the north-east corner of the Po Plain Aquileia, which has no modern successor, was another centre of manufacturing and transalpine trade. Ravenna became the final capital of the Western Roman Empire in the fifth century and was for a further 200 years the headquarters of Byzantine Italy.

The Roman era is significant in one other respect. In regional development terms it marks a historic watershed. Before Rome, the South was pre-eminent; the cities of Magna Graecia had no parallels in the North. After the North was colonised by the Romans, however, it drew level with the southern peninsula in terms of agriculture, industry, towns and communications. And as the dim mists of the Dark Ages began to disperse, it was clear that the North had already stolen a march on the South and taken the first step on the road to eventual industrial superiority.

The decline of the Empire was hastened by barbarian incursions from the north. In 568 the Lombard invasion took place, crossing the Julian Alps and overrunning Venetia and the Po Plain as far west as Milan. The Lombard capital was established at Pavia. The formation of small duchies eventually carried the Lombard incursion down the Apennines through Tuscany and Umbria to Benevento and Basilicata. By 650 the Lombards held the Po Valley and the highland spine as far south as Benevento; their kingdom reached the sea only at Pisa and Genoa. The remnant Byzantine area embraced the coastal regions, including the entire Adriatic seaboard, in close contact with Constantinople and the eastern Mediterranean.

By the eighth century there is evidence of a return to an exchange economy under the later Lombard kings.[3] Trade along the Po axis revived, salt from the Venetian lagoons being exchanged for grain from the western plain. Towns like Verona, Pavia and Piacenza, which had escaped the worst deprivations of war, started to flourish again. Byzantine Italy's economic prosperity was linked more to external trade with the eastern Mediterranean. As in the days of Magna Graecia, Apulia, Calabria and Sicily exported their wines, olive oil, wool and grain. Linen manufacture, using local flax, flourished at Naples and there was silk-weaving at Messina and Syracuse, where the mulberry tree had been inherited from the Ancient Greeks. At least until the Arab threat developed in the ninth century, the Byzantine cities of Ravenna, Bari, Amalfi and Naples enjoyed a prosperous commercial existence. One part of Byzantine Italy predestined for particular industrial and commercial importance was Venice, isolated by geography and politics from the Lombard territory inland. By the ninth century Venice had established commercial relations with Sicily, Greece and Egypt and was beginning to profit from its intermediate location between the Byzantine trade area on the one hand and the Lombard and Frankish domains on the other. Rome, by contrast, languished. From a population of perhaps 2 million in the Augustan period, it shrunk to around 40,000 by the seventh century.

The Saracen occupation reached its apogee in Sicily. Whereas the southern mainland was plundered from the Arabs' insecure bases at Bari and Taranto, Moorish Palermo achieved a level of cultural brilliance unequalled since the Hellenic period. Intensive irrigated agriculture revitalised Sicilian rural life and in the coastal towns shipbuilding and the manufacture of silk, linen, leather and metal goods developed. Palermo became the most prosperous port of the Tyrrhenian seaboard, a position it retained for a time under the succeeding rule of the Normans.

The Rise of the City-Republics and the 'First Industrial Revolution'

The eleventh and twelfth centuries marked a period of sharp economic change which transformed the northern half of Italy from a sparsely peopled region dominated by ecclesiastical estates and vast areas of forest and marsh into the urbane, economically active Italy of the

Renaissance. The doubling of population between the tenth and fourteenth centuries was accompanied by large-scale rural-urban migration. Marshy land in the Po Valley was reclaimed for farming and forested hillsides in the Apennines cleared and terraced. Marketing systems became more elaborate and in the larger towns banking and credit institutions evolved. Long-distance trade, not an innovation in the Po Plain, gathered momentum. An eleventh century document reveals Pavia's merchants trading with regions beyond the Alps including England, and there is no reason to believe Pavia was unique; other North Italian towns involved in long-distance commerce were Milan, Cremona, Verona, Vercelli and Asti.[4] The French trade route stimulated the development of Piacenza at the Po crossing and Lucca beyond the Apennine gateway. Venice continued to prosper, and was soon joined by the maritime emporia of Genoa and Pisa on the opposite coast. Judging by the repeated expansion of city walls, many towns grew quickly between 1100 and 1250. The twelfth century was the period when large numbers of towns in North and Central Italy achieved autonomy: these were the communes or city-republics, each with a central town surrounded by its *contado* of food-supplying countryside which typically stretched out about 15-20 kilometres round the city.

The emergence of the urban communes in the twelfth century was accompanied by important socio-economic changes. The rise of the urban bourgeoisie represented the triumph of business and industrial capital over landed wealth, and of artisan and commercial enterprise over peasant farming.[5] Another indicator of economic evolution was the appearance of urban craft guilds from the second half of the twelfth century; examples are millers, tanners, clothiers, builders, vintners and various smiths. Venice had 142 such guilds but most other cities had less than 50.[6] It was the custom for all tradesmen practising the same craft to locate their businesses in the same street, a fact preserved in the present-day street names in the central areas of old-established Italian towns.[7]

A close study of the economic history of the period shows that different towns and industries rose to prominence at different times. After about 1000 Milan took over from Pavia as the major inland industrial centre of the Po Plain. Milanese economic strength was based on early work on drainage and canal-building, to which lower Lombardy has owed much of its prosperity ever since. In the late twelfth century a woollen industry developed in the city, soon producing abundant cloth for export. The most celebrated Milanese industry was arms manufacture, stimulated by increases in the demand for weapons and facilitated by raw material supplies from nearby Alpine valleys. Production, mostly in workshops specialising in armour, swords, etc., reached its peak in the fourteenth century.

From Lombardy, the revival of town life spread south into Tuscany and Central Italy. The first town in Tuscany to attain more than local importance was Lucca, which was also the first place outside of Southern Italy to specialise in silk manufacture. Roughly contemporary with the rise of Lucca was Siena, where mining was important. Florence was a later-comer. As late as the mid thirteenth century this city was still closely encircled by independent urban communes and powerful feudal lords. By 1300, however, its population had reached 100,000. Florentine wealth was derived from a mixture of commerce and textile-processing, the finished products of which were exported to the Levant via Pisa, Venice and Fano. By the early fourteenth century the Florentine clothmakers' guild was perhaps the largest industrial corporation in Italy.[8]

The growth of Pisa and Genoa at this time was due more directly to trade than to industrial production *in situ,* though Pisa did have a sizeable woollen industry. Pisan wealth was nourished by imports of salt, grain, iron and silver from territories under Pisan rule and by the entrepôt functions performed for Lucca, Florence and other Tuscan towns. Genoa's commercial hinterland was larger, consisting of Lombardy, Piedmont, western Emilia and even adjacent parts of France and Switzerland. Genoa ousted Pisa in the Battle of Meloria in 1284 but Genoa was finally eclipsed by all-powerful Venice in the War of Chioggia, 1378-81.

Apart from mining and metal-smelting, all industries of medieval Italy were located in cities. Two basic types of industries existed at this time. Artisan industries serving a small clientele of regular customers provided for the daily needs of the local town and country population. Larger, more specialised industries produced goods for wider regional and foreign markets. The leading industry here was textiles, especially woollens. Profits from wool provided the financial means of converting Florence into one of the foremost architectural treasures of all time. The woollen industry also made strides in Lombardian and Venetian communes. Padua's woollen industry was the major factor in the town's rapid growth from 15,000 inhabitants in 1275 to 30,000 in 1320. The North Italian cotton industry grew alongside the woollen and in some places, such as Bologna, overshadowed it. A high degree of economic interdependence and of product specialisation was characteristic of the

medieval Italian cotton manufacturers.[9]
Industry made great advances in the communal age. In a sense this could be regarded as Italy's first industrial revolution. In one judgement, the rate of economic expansion during the pre-Renaissance was so rapid that it remained unequalled until the 1950s.[10] Certainly Italy enjoyed indisputable supremacy in the economy of the medieval world. No other comparably-sized area of Europe was so heavily populated with large towns. By 1400 Venice had nearly 200,000 inhabitants, and Milan was not far behind. Four other cities — Genoa, Florence, Naples and Palermo — just exceeded or approached 100,000 and the Lombard Plain supported a further dozen towns of between 20,000 and 50,000 inhabitants.[11] Italian trading activities traversed the entire known world, indeed expanded it. Merchants cultivated markets from the Baltic to West Africa, from London to Peking. Italy of the Renaissance (the fourteenth and fifteenth centuries) appeared as a land of abounding wealth and cultural exuberance. Men like Christopher Columbus, Amerigo Vespucci, Galileo Galilei and Leonardo da Vinci put Italy at the forefront in the fields of exploration, engineering and physics; in painting, sculpture and literature this was the era of masterpieces never again to be equalled.

But impending difficultues clouded the economic horizon. By the fifteenth century Italy's commercial monopoly was threatened by English and French trading power. The woollen industry faced competition from Flanders. Maritime trade was perforce shared with the mercantile marines of Provence and Catalonia. Regional economic differentiation within Italy became sharper, not only between North and South, but within the North also. One malaise was the growing disequilibrium between town and country, and in particular the increasing fiscal burden imposed on the *contado* by the town, thereby reducing the countryside's capacity to absorb the manufactured goods of the city. The rise of the despotic states in the later Middle Ages enlarged fields of territorial economic dominance; some of the smaller towns lost their independence. After Venice had conquered the eastern plain, towns like Padua and Verona suffered economic decline and lost population. Milan and Florence had a similar dominating effect in Lombardy and Tuscany respectively. Southern Italy, after the precocious growth of Bari and Amalfi in the eleventh century, saw increasing socio-economic concentration at Naples and Palermo.[12]

Medieval Industry in Venice

Among all the medieval city-states of Italy Venice — *La Serenissima* — reigned supreme, pre-dating and outliving all rivals. Venice's economic glory derived fom her unique role as intermediary between east and west. The Byzantine connection provided a ready-made entrée into eastern trade. Navigable rivers in the lower Po region gave easy access inland. The Brenner Pass led to Central Europe. Venice enjoyed the best of both worlds; she was in Italy but not of it, remaining aloof for 500 years from the entanglements of the mainland. By 1400, when the population approached 200,000, the city owned 330 large sea-going vessels manned by 36,000 sailors. The Venetian shipbuilding industry was the largest and most technologically advanced in the world, employing 16,000 workers.

By the fifteenth century Venice was the wealthiest city in Italy, possibly in Europe. 'In this land where nothing grows,' wrote the Venetian chronicler Marin Sanudo, 'you will find an abundance of everything, for all manner of things from every country and corner of the earth which has stuff to send are brought to this place, and there are plenty to buy, since everyone has money,'[13] Oriental goods — spices, drugs, fruit, wine, cotton, jewels — flowed one way; European metals and manufactures moved in the other direction.

As the city's commercial monopoly faded in the later Middle Ages, economic policy encouraged the development of local industry to nourish an export trade threatened by failing supplies of manufactured goods from outside.[14] One of these local industries was textiles. The manufacture of fine quality woollen cloth had been in existence since the late thirteenth century, but production expanded by more than ten times in the sixteenth century. Other branches of the Venetian textile industry were silk, linen, cotton and canvas. A second key industry was glassmaking, established in the thirteenth century on the island of Murano. The unique colours achieved by the glass-masters of Murano and a tradition for high quality gave Venice the foremost reputation for glassware in the whole of Europe. The third, and most important of Venice's medieval industries was shipbuilding, although in later years it was subject to fluctuating military and commercial fortunes and suffered from shortage of timber supplies. In addition to these three basic Venetian industries there existed a whole constellation of other activities of a specialised, often luxury nature. Examples were chemicals, soap, dyes, paints, sugar-refining, leather, wood and jewellery. During the sixteenth century Venice also became a leading centre of printing and bookbinding.

Economic Decline in the Seventeenth Century

The post-Renaissance industrial decline of Italy was broadly due to the collective difficulty of producers in facing competition from the expanding Atlantic community. The great change came about mainly between 1600 and 1670; in these 'seven black decades' the industrial structure collapsed.[15] The industries of Venice, too dependent upon their ability to sell a large proportion of their output abroad, faced new competitors selling similar, often blatantly imitative goods at lower prices. Textiles were particularly affected. Similar fates befell Florence, Milan and Genoa, the other members of the 'medieval industrial quadrilateral'. In Florence in the last decades of the sixteenth century there were 120 woollen firms producing about 14,000 cloths annually. By 1627 there were only 62 firms and annual output was 8,000 measures. Although there are no precise figures for later years, decline continued and by the end of the seventeenth century there was much unemployment. Genoese silk followed a similar path. At the end of the sixteenth century some 18,000 looms were at work in the territory of the Genoese Republic (the city and the 'Two Rivieras'). In 1675 looms numbered only 2,564. In Milan at the start of the sixteenth century 60-70 woollen firms produced 15,000 cloths annually. In 1709 only one firm remained, producing less than 100 cloths. The Milanese building and metal industries suffered similar, if less drastic, declines. The story in other major towns of the North differed little. The excessive powers of the obsolete guilds compelled Italian industry to continue with antiquated business and production methods. Cost of labour was higher than elsewhere. The plagues of 1630 and 1657 culled about one-third of the inhabitants of larger cities; this sudden population fall provoked further wage increases just at the time when Italian industry needed to bring its production costs into line with those of its competitors.

This severe loss in Italy's economic momentum saw the country industrially overtaken by England, France and the Netherlands after the late sixteenth century. New trade routes to the Americas favoured Europe's Atlantic ports, and the Portuguese, English and Dutch dominated the Indian Ocean. By the eighteenth century Italy had become an economic backwater: industrial production had reverted to the handicraft stage, trade was at a low level, entrepreneurial activity was minimal, and 80 per cent of the active population was engaged in agriculture. Only in the North-west did a spark of dynamism penetrate traditional conservatism with the first stirrings of industrial revival in Lombardy.

The South, meantime, had followed a very different economic path. After the Normans had ousted the Arabs from Sicily and the Byzantine forces from the southern mainland in the eleventh century, the kingdom of Two Sicilies was established. Under a centralised autocracy, urban and industrial development was stifled. The South remained deeply rural and feudal, languishing particularly under Spanish rule after 1500.

From the early sixteenth century, however, Rome recovered some of its ancient magnificence and regained its place amongst the great cosmopolitan cities of Europe. Its population, only 30,000 at the end of the fifteenth century, rose to 140,000 at the end of the sixteenth. In the next 200 years Rome became the city of the popes, and of numerous churches, palaces, squares and fountains. Naples, another 'capital city', followed a similar demographic and economic path, growing so rapidly in the first half of the sixteenth century that at the 1547 city census its population of 212,105 had overtaken that of Venice and Milan and was probably the second largest in Europe after Paris.[16] Yet Naples, like Rome, was not destined for industrial greatness. Artisan crafts, the building trade and some luxury industries like silk absorbed a lot of labour, but the pre-conditions for the development of heavy industry were absent and most manufactured goods had to be imported. A mid eighteenth century description of Naples by the traveller John Moore shows how overcrowded and economically insecure the city, whose population then stood at 350,000, had become:

> There is not a city in the world, with the same number of inhabitants, in which so few contribute to the wealth of the community by useful or productive labour as at Naples; but the number of priests, monks, fiddlers, lawyers, nobility, footmen and beggars is to surpass all reasonable proportion, the last alone are computed at thirty or forty thousand.[17]

Economic Background of the Risorgimento

The flourishing city-states of Northern Italy, for all their prosperity, had a countervailing effect in that they served to strengthen the centrifugal forces which prevented the formation of a united Italy.[18] They failed to adapt to long-term political change. While less developed countries like Spain and France had established themselves as unified nation-states to reap the economic benefits of physical size, larger markets and a wider resource base, Italy remained deeply fragmented.

It took a foreigner to alter all that. Italy's nationalist movement of the nineteenth century — the Risorgimento — took its cue from the French Revolution and the Napoleonic occupation. The sweeping innovations introduced by the French, the boundary reshuffles and the widening of horizons had a profound influence on Italian life. A sense of national pride was born at last, and Italian writers began to link Italy's political future with projected economic greatness. Unification was advocated to provide a larger market for industrial enterprise. The emergence of this liberal, nationalist, technological philosophy spawned a new entrepreneur class which, around the middle of the nineteenth century, broke out of the vicious circle of familism, traditionally-accepted feudal values and subsistence economics.

The beginnings of industrial change occurred in the early nineteenth century. Liberated from the monopolistic guilds — abolished in Tuscany in 1770, in Lombardy in 1787, in Sicily in 1786, in Naples in 1821 and in Piedmont in 1844 — entrepreneurs were free to enter the major trades and to enlarge markets beyond the local scale. The progressive development of agriculture along more capitalist lines also provided some stimulus to industry. New life appeared in the textile industry. Woollen manufacture took a firm hold at Biella in Piedmont, at Schio in Venetia and at Prato in Tuscany — locations which are still important today. The silk industry showed signs of growth around Como and in Piedmont, where production doubled between 1750 and 1850. The cotton industry took root along the Olona and Lambro river valleys near Milan, where some factories had up to 500 workers. The machine-building industry developed in response. In 1860 it employed 9,000, producing equipment such as spinning jennies, mechanical looms, water wheels and railway carriages. Arms manufacture extended from Milan to Turin, Genoa and Naples. Shipbuilding also expanded, the main yards being Orlando at Genoa, Westermann at Sestri Ponente, the state enterprise at Castellammare di Stabia and the Austrian-controlled yards at Trieste. The Sicilian sulphur mines were exploited to the point where they accounted for 90 per cent of world output. Other expanding industries of the mid nineteenth century were glass, metal-working and sugar-refining. Cheap glass lengthened the working day and enabled workers to have light in cold and inclement weather. Iron and tool-making developed at Brescia and along the Tuscan coast. As reading, writing and book-keeping became more common the paper industry had a boom, particularly at Fabriano in Marche and at Bologna.[19]

No single development equalled that of railway building. 'Railways', stated the Piedmontese writer Massimo d'Azeglio, 'would sew up the Italian boot'. This was also the view of Cavour. The first line to be built was actually in the South — 7 kilometres of track around the Bay of Naples, opened in 1839. The line was sponsored by Ferdinand II who refused to travel on the inaugural run for fear of an accident! Other lines followed in the North: Milan-Monza (13 km) in 1840, Padua-Mestre (33 km) in 1842, the Venetian causeway (80,000 wooden piles sunk in the lagoon) in 1846 and Turin-Moncalieri (8 km) in 1848. Starting later than in England, France and Germany, Italian railway building also progressed more slowly, owing to lack of political unification, general economic backwardness and the high costs of construction in a mountainous terrrain.[20]

The pace of industrial growth prior to 1861 should not be exaggerated. Basically, progress was slow except in a few northern localities. Italy remained bitterly divided into the eight territorial units created by the Vienna settlement of 1814-15 (Figure 2.1). In the north-west the Kingdom of Sardinia embraced Piedmont, Savoy, Nice, Liguria and of course Sardinia itself. The Lombard-Venetian Kingdom, under Austrian rule, occupied the north and north-east. Four small principalities — the duchies of Tuscany, Lucca, Parma and Modena — were survivals from the Middle Ages. The Papal States stretched in a broad belt across the peninsula north-east from Rome, isolating the Bourbon-ruled Kingdom of the Two Sicilies to the south.

Levels of economic development were as diverse as this political map. Piedmont, Lombardy, Venetia and Tuscany had already entered the industrial age. The Papal States contained much remote hill country dedicated exclusively to farming. Some embryonic industrial growth had been fostered by the Bourbon kings at Naples, but the greater part of the Kingdom of the Two Sicilies remained poor and backward, with an economy and way of life unchanged for centuries.

Unification and Its Effects on the Pattern of Industrialisation

This is not the place for a detailed investigation into the events behind Italian unification. There is an extensive literature on this crucial formative period of Italian history. Here, apart from a brief indication of the main political events, we will concentrate on the impact of unification on the emerging pattern of industrial development.[21]

Early moves towards unification met with little success. Between 1817 and 1848 secret societies such as the *Carbonari* and Mazzini's

Figure 2.1: Italy in 1859, Just Before Unification

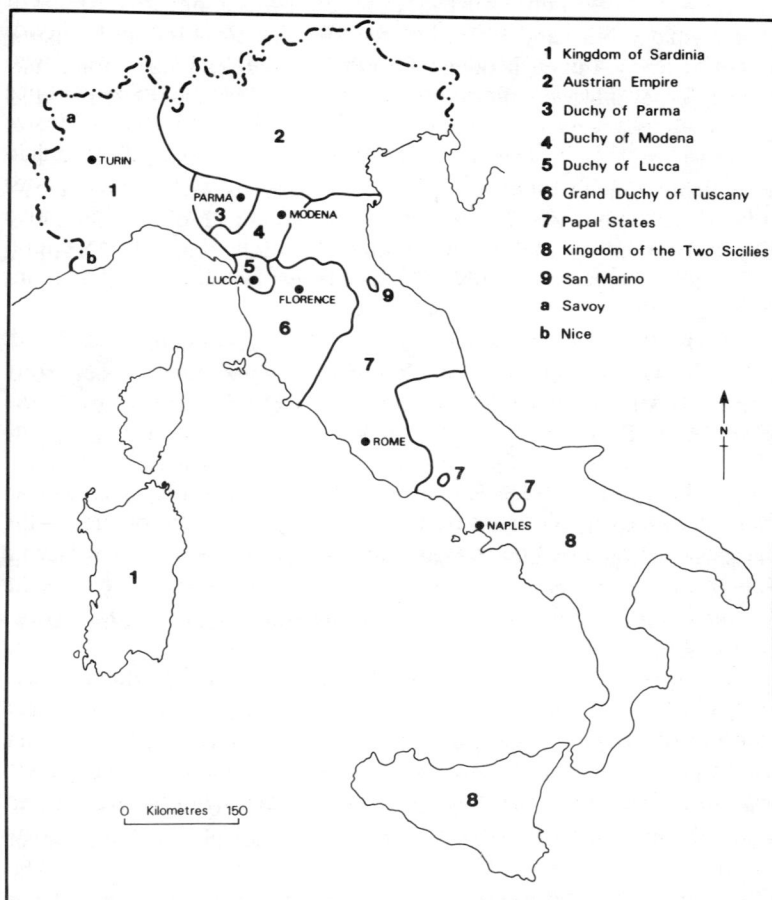

Legend:
1 Kingdom of Sardinia
2 Austrian Empire
3 Duchy of Parma
4 Duchy of Modena
5 Duchy of Lucca
6 Grand Duchy of Tuscany
7 Papal States
8 Kingdom of the Two Sicilies
9 San Marino
a Savoy
b Nice

Giovane Italia ('Young Italy') organised conspiracies and uprisings, all of which were put down. Riots intensified in 1848, coinciding with revolutionary upheavals elsewhere in Europe. A popular revolt in Milan forced the Austrian garrison to flee the city but by 1849 the Austrians had rallied and crushed the Piedmontese and the Venetian Republic.

This was, however, only a temporary setback. In the 1850s the Kingdom of Sardinia, with its energetic prime minister Camillo Benso di Cavour, strengthened its economy and defence. France joined Sardinia in 1859 to oust Austria. Lombardy was annexed to Sardinia which yielded Nice and Savoy in turn to France. Revolutions breaking out in Tuscany, Lucca, Modena, Parma and the Romagna region of the Papal States allowed these regions to join Sardinia: Austria was powerless to intervene.

A year later, in 1860, Giuseppe Garibaldi and his famous thousand republican volunteers made dramatic and unexpected progress in advancing the cause of unification in the South. Garibaldi occupied Sicily, crossed to the mainland and eventually captured Naples, obliterating the Kingdom of the Two Sicilies. Garibaldi then ceded his conquests to the Piedmontese who had moved south to annex most of the Papal States. Only Rome and its environs remained.

On 17 March 1861 a newly elected Italian parliament proclaimed the establishment of the Kingdom of Italy. The first king was Victor Emmanuel II, formerly King of Sardinia. In only two years the fragmented political map of Italy had been almost completely consolidated. In 1870 the Franco-Prussian war and withdrawal of the French garrison from Rome enabled Italy to seize the Eternal City and its surrounding province. Trento and Trieste remained in Austrian hands, not to be incorporated into Italy for another 50 years.

Italian unity, it has been said, was the reward of clever diplomacy, good timing, and luck.[22] Motives of general geographical propinquity prevailed over any grand design of economic planning. What unification achieved was the bringing together of two distinct societies — the capitalising, industrialising North and the feudal South — into a single political unit under the leadership of the North. This *blocco storico* — the historic alliance between northern capital and southern land — subsequently conditioned the entire economic and political development of the country. The northern leadership was essentially elitist. The Risorgimento lacked widespread peasant support, for no real effort had been made to mobilise the masses who, especially in the South, had been dragooned into the new nation with contempt rather than fraternal enthusiasm. The so-called 'southern brigandage' of 1860-5 was really a primitive, pre-political form of peasant uprising against the Piedmontese, a protest which cost more lives than all the wars of the Risorgimento combined. The Piedmontese were amazed at the conditions they found in the South. When Farini arrived in Naples as governor after the city's liberation by Garibaldi, he wrote to Cavour: 'This is not Italy! This is Africa . . . the bedouins are the flower of civic virtue beside these country bumpkins . . . '[23]

With this social context in mind, we can begin to understand early post-unification economic philosophy. From 1861 to 1878 Italy was ruled by a patriarchal oligarchy, most of whose members came from a professional or landowning background, knowing little about the nature of the industrial society emerging in northern Europe or America. The only Italian industy with some members in governmental power was textile manufacturing, still very much geared to the cottage structure. Heavy industry, trade unions and mass politics were feared rather than desired or even understood by Italy's new ruling class. There were good reasons for this uncertainty. Industrialisation would disrupt the rulers' tacit partnership with the more senior states of Europe. It would also tear up the structure of paternalistic relations in the textile industry in which home-weaving and putting-out systems meshed so well with the peasant society. The new government feared what it saw abroad: the emergence of an industrial proletariat with no sense of obligation or restraint towards the traditional ruling class.[24]

The Piedmontese bureaucracy subscribed to the classical liberal economic doctrine of free trade. They thought that by removing obstacles to the free movement of goods, capital and people between countries and between the different Italian regions, beneficial effects would accrue to all concerned. As Allum points out,[25] no liberal economist believes this today. In fact, the post-unification experience of Italy bears out perfectly the contention of cumulative contrast between favoured and unfavoured regions.

Unification consummated the industrial dominance of the North over the South. Prior to 1861, Naples was an important industrial centre, and cotton manufacturing was prominent in the belt of small towns stretching between Caserta and Salerno. As soon as unification occurred, the tariffs which had protected southern industries were removed. A common customs union and free trade within united Italy exposed the southern economy to the blast of competition from the more efficient northern producers. Handicraft industries, in particular, were dealt a mortal blow. The North's geographical proximity to other European countries which had industrialised earlier favoured this regions' industrial growth at the expense of the remoter South. Fiscal policies also favoured the polarisation of industrial wealth in the North. The Piedmontese tax system was extended to the rest of the country, doubling the land tax rates in the South within five years, to the obvious detriment of the southern peasantry, so dependent on the land for their livelihood. Monetary unification saw the Piedmontese lira established as the new currency, and the Sardinian National Bank of Turin, being the biggest and strongest of the Italian banks, became the *de facto* central bank, merging eventually with the Tuscan Bank to form the Bank of Italy in 1893. Piedmont's large internal debt was transferred to the whole country, which, given the lack of pre-existing southern public debt, meant that a large proportion of the new national debt was met by southern taxpayers. The tariff war with France meant that the most productive and dynamic southern farmers, the vine, fruit and vegetable growers, were deprived of their major export outlet. George Hildebrand, an economic historian of the classical liberal school, concluded his review of the economic effects of unification by stating that the South 'was doomed economically from the start, incapable of maintaining, let alone closing, the enormous gap that separated it from its northern partners'.[26] Ill-equipped to defend itself against the concentration of economic and political power in the North, industry in the South collapsed and the region became an agriculturally backward area from which manual labour could be drawn to support the continuing industrialisation of the North. While in the North an industrial bourgeoisie was established and a working class was emerging within the liberal private enterprise climate, the South maintained a closed value-system, its social structure dominated by landlords, rentiers and farmhands.[27]

Several figures reinforce the socio-economic contrast.[28] Illiterates accounted for 53.7 per cent of the population over six years of age in Lombardy and 54.2 per cent in Liguria and Piedmont (1861); the figure for mainland Southern Italy was 86.3 per cent, for Sicily 88.6 per cent, and for Sardinia, highest of all, 89.7 per cent. Symptomatic of the North's technological superiority was the founding of the polytechnics in Turin (1859) and Milan (1863). In 1864 employment in the crucial group of metal-using industries was already strongly weighted towards the North (63 per cent of the workers) as opposed to the Centre (15 per cent) and South (22 per cent). Total production of iron (29,000 tons in 1864) was nearly all from Lombardy (40 per cent), Tuscany (30 per cent) and Val d'Aosta (25 per cent). The metal concerns of Naples, the only centre of any consequence in the South, were mostly controlled by foreign entrepreneurs — English, French, German and Swiss — who had been aided by court-conferred privileges. In the field of shipbuilding the South accounted for only 18 per cent of the ships built by tonnage (though 60 per cent by number) in 1867, when 60 per cent of total tonnage was built in Genoa alone.

One piece of evidence contradicts the picture of post-unification concentration of industry in the North. This is the employment situation as revealed in the 1861 and 1881 censuses which show the South to have a larger share of its active population working in industry than the North (30.7 per cent as against 26.6 per cent in 1881). Two reasons probably account for this. One is the general unreliability of nineteenth century census reporting methods. The 1881 census, in particular, appears to be a 'rogue' census, whose results seem frequently at variance with reliably established long-term trends. The second reason concerns the definition of 'industrial employees' which in the early Italian censuses clearly included all kinds of building and handicraft workers in rural as well as urban environments. Women working in southern domestic trades like textiles and foodstuffs also inflated the figures. The drastic decline of women in 'industrial' employment in the South from 1,078,000 in 1881 to 216,000 in 1936 is an indication of the exaggerated industrial reporting in the earlier year.

The temporal pattern of Italian industrial development in the early years after unification can be outlined more briefly. Progress towards industrialisation was generally slow. The proportion of GNP derived from industry did not increase at all during the first 40 years of Italian unity, remaining at around 20 per cent until the turn of the century. In the 1860s world industrial techniques leapt forward, but to carry these out required huge, irreversible investments. Italy had iron ore, chemicals and abundant labour: industries could rise on such foundations, but an appropriate economic orthodoxy geared to massive industrial growth was lacking. The governments of the day were not committed to major industrial expansion. Military spending weighed heavily on the exchequer as politicians moved in pursuit of misdirected colonial objectives in North and East Africa. At home, banks favoured Roman real estate to sound industry building. Power was another weak link. The principal cheap energy source was water power in the Alpine valleys, so entrepreneurs had to locate their mills at an inconvenient distance from the main markets until the advent of hydro-electric power 30 years later.

The years of 1861-80 were a period of industrial foundation-laying, not a period of industrial growth. The exact nature of industrial change is difficult to assess for the evidence is patchy, but steady progress was certainly achieved in the well-documented textile industry. Spurred by a crisis in the domestic supply of raw material (due to silkworm disease), the silk industry began to import raw silk and moved to the final phase of the spinning process, throwing. Cotton-spinning became the dynamic industry of Piedmont, moving later to Lombardy. The number of cotton spindles increased from about 450,000 in 1861 to 745,000 in 1876 (England, however, already had 33 million spindles by 1860!). The main nucleus of wool production was at Biella in Piedmont. Other industries also began at this time. Sugar manufacturing started in 1873 and in 1875 Francesco Cirio founded the food preserves industry that was to become world-famous. In 1872, in Milan, Pirelli established the first nucleus of the rubber industry. Iron production increased threefold during 1860-80 but suffered from problems of poor quality and the steel component, which at this time was becoming the dominant element of West European metallurgical industry, was still completely absent.[29]

Other changes took place. In 1870-4 the first industrial enquiry was implemented, followed in 1876 by the first factory statistics. In 1878 the onset of social tensions in industry provoked the first major strikes. The depression which began in 1874 led to an 8 per cent drop in industrial output by 1880 and paved the way for the transfer of political power from the Destra or Right, dominated by large landowners, merchants and bankers favouring the *status quo,* to the Sinistra or Left which, composed of new industrialists and small businessmen, stood for active stimulation of the economy.

Stifled Industrial Development in the 1880s

Things began to change after 1880. An agrarian crisis developed in the late 1870s, provoked specifically by the increased imports of North American cereals and generally by the world economic recession of the late 1870s and early 1880s. The total value of agricultural production fell by 21 per cent during 1880-7. This rural slump discouraged investment in land and farming, diverting it to industry which expanded rapidly with an annual growth rate of 4.6 per cent over the period 1881-7.[30] The switching of investment from agriculture to industry on the part of many landowners also involved a South-to-North transfer of capital.

Protectionist customs tariffs were introduced in 1878 and 1887 and, although they ultimately provoked a commercial war with France, initially they provided a protective umbrella for Italian industrial growth. The Sinistra's swing from *laissez-faire* liberalism continued with direct government support and patronage of heavy industry. The Baccarini law of 1882 gave quotas to Italian machinery for railway development, direct assistance was given in 1885 to the shipyards, concentrated in Genoa, Leghorn and Naples, and a full-cycle iron and steel works was fostered in 1886 at Terni in the hills of Umbria to supply the merchant marine. The rekindling of industrial growth in the 1880s saw particular progress made in four sectors: metallurgy, mechanical industries, chemicals and textiles.

Meagre raw materials remained a fundamental constraining problem, but the lack of coal was mitigated by two changes. One was the drop in freight charges which caused the price of imported coal to halve in ten years: imports of coal thereby increased threefold between 1878 and 1888.[31] The second fillip to energy production was the founding of the Edison Company in Milan in 1884 and the development of electricity as a source of industrial power, a process in which Italy actually had a pioneering role — the first plant in Europe for lights was opened in Milan in 1883 to supply the Scala Theatre and the Biffi restaurant. The Milan region was industrially the most active part of the country at this time, with several other Italian firms born there in the 1880s. Examples are Franco Tosi (mechanical trades), Ernesto Breda (railway and engineering equipment), Ercole Marelli (electrical goods) and Carlo Erba (chemicals). Southern industry, on the other hand, languished.

The founding of industries on a factory scale, the creation of railways and new port facilities, and the general expansion of population, especially in urban localities, gave a tremendous impetus to the building trades. The production of building stone, marble, bricks, tiles, cement and glass all boomed in the last two decades of the nineteenth century. An important technical development was the production of Portland cement after 1873. Cement factories were established in most regions, given the wide distribution of limestone and clay in Italy, but particular concentrations developed in the provinces of Bergamo and Como, and at Casale Monferrato in Piedmont.[32]

Industrial growth in the 1880s was eventually stifled by the world depression which made the years 1889-96 the 'blackest in the economic history of the new kingdom'.[33] The banking system virtually collapsed in 1893-4 leading to the dismissal of prime minister Giolitti for alleged involvement in irregularities in the Banca Romana. Promising developments in virtually all major sectors of industry were suddenly checked; the annual industrial growth rate slumped to 0.3 per cent during 1888-96.[34] Only the textile industry continued to grow, because of its access to sources of capital independent of the central banking system and because of its enterprise in exploring foreign markets.[35]

The 1888-98 tariff war with France ruined established patterns of trade. Falling prices and falling trade affected rural and industrial workers alike. In Sicily impoverished workers formed unions called *fasci* and took part in strikes and other protests, many of which were brutally put down in 1893 and 1894. Amongst the industrial unions of the North ideas of Marxism, anarchism and revolutionary syndicalism took root. As the economy collapsed, so effective population pressure became more acute, leading to the mass emigration of the last decades of the nineteenth century. Although by the turn of the century Italian industrial growth spurted again, the rate of employment creation was insufficient to absorb the demographic surplus and the notion of the desirability, indeed inevitability, of emigration was widely established amongst the population, particularly in the South.

Early Railway Growth

Transport was a particularly vital need of the new Italian state, especially given Italy's rugged terrain and elongated shape. In 1861 Italy had 1,623 kilometres of railways built and a further 1,442 kilometres under construction. Piedmont and Lombardy had over 90 per cent of the completed track; the rest of Italy, especially the South, was poorly supplied (Figure 2.2).

A frenzy of railway-building activity followed unification. Railway length tripled over the period 1860-70. From an annual average of 176 kilometres of new track laid during the decade before 1861, the rate jumped to 376 kilometres per year during 1861-76, and remained at about 300 kilometres per year through to 1905. After the opening of the Frejus or Mont Cenis tunnel (13.6 km) in 1871 — the first tunnel to be driven using pneumatic drills — Piedmont was connected to France and thence, via Calais, to England. In 1882, the St Gotthard was finished (14.9 km), linking Northern Italy, especially Milan, with Switzerland and Germany. The Simplon was finished in 1906, the longest tunnel in Europe, 19.7 km.

Plans for a complete national network envisaged two basic coastal axes, one leading from the heart of the Po Plain down the Adriatic, following the line Turin-Milan-Piacenza-Bologna-Brindisi, the other following the Tyrrhenian coast from Genoa via Rome to Reggio Calabria. Gradually these lines came into being. Between 1861 and 1877 railway construction costs absorbed 20 per cent of the national budget. State aid was lavish and great efforts were made to connect remote parts of the country, which meant particular changes in the South. In 1861 the South had only 6 per cent of national rail length, by 1875 the propor-

Figure 2.2: Railway Development in the Nineteenth Century

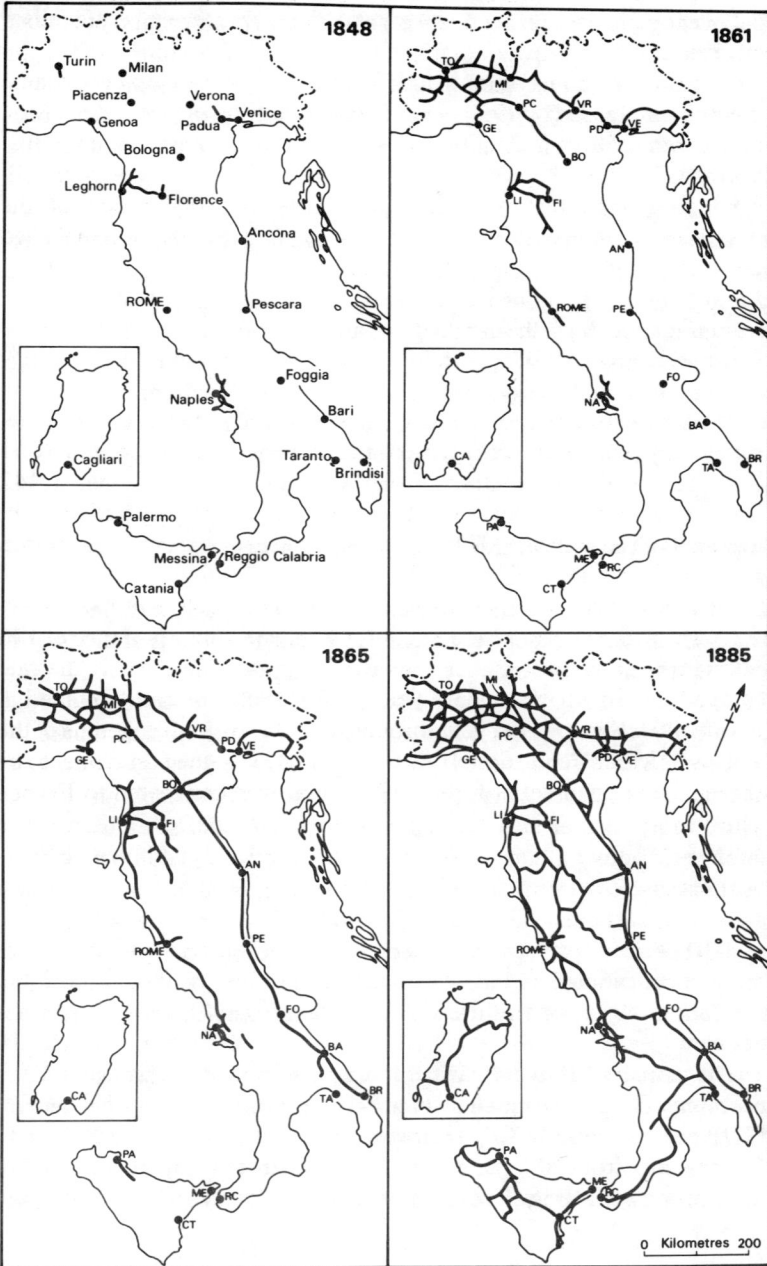

tion had risen to 32 per cent and by the turn of the century it was almost equivalent to the South's share of population and area (just under and just over 40 per cent respectively). Yet the rapid proliferation of the rail network in the South|was not matched by its use. The volume of freight carried on the railways — a useful indicator of regional economic growth — increased by 175 per cent in the South during 1872-85, compared with 250 per cent in the Centre and 230 per cent in the North.[36]

Yet although railway building was important in binding the country together in its formative years, and although no other industrial undertaking matched it in magnitude, the Italian 'railway boom' was not the driving stimulus to industrial development that it was elsewhere. As in pre-unification days, the demand for rails, engines, carriages and trucks continued to be supplied, with few exceptions, from abroad. Only the sleepers were home-produced, leading to extensive deforestation and erosion, particularly in the South. The process of railway building was not closely related to the progress of industry in time or space.

Industrial Take-off at the Turn of the Century

In the very last years of the nineteenth century the pace of Italian industrial expansion quickened appreciably. Whilst the origins of this 'spurt' can be traced to the ending of the world depression in 1896, Italian industrial output figures start to rise only in 1898, with continued rapid growth through to 1908, when the rate of expansion was markedly reduced. ISTAT figures show an average annual industrial growth rate of around 4 per cent for the period 1897-1914.[37] Gerschenkron puts the figure rather higher at 5.4 per cent per annum, and stresses the difference in industrial growth rates between the 1896-1908 period (6.7 per cent) and the 1908-14 period (2.4 per cent).[38] Particular spurts are associated with the years 1899-1902 and 1905-8 when rates of growth of 8-10 per cent per year occurred. The proportion of gross domestic product contributed by industry rose from 19.6 per cent in 1895 to 25 per cent in 1914, agriculture's share falling from 49.4 per cent to 43 per cent.

The effects of Italy's industrial 'big push' were felt throughout the economy. Gross investment, which had averaged less than 9 per cent of GDP over the period 1861-95, rose to 14.5 per cent during 1896-1913. Exports rose from 10.7 per cent to 14.3 per cent of GDP over the same time periods. GDP itself rose 45 per cent between 1896 and 1913, an increase over twice as great as that recorded in the much longer 1861-95 period.[39] Table 2.1 shows that fixed investments in public works, housing and industrial plant grew especially rapidly in the decade after 1896. For the first time since 1861 the Italian population enjoyed a significant rise in real *per capita* income.

Italian industrial take-off took place within the framework of the European industrial revolution's 'second wind', the main technological features of which were the large-scale use of new materials like steel and certain chemicals, the use of new sources of energy, and the remarkable development of the machine industry. Perhaps most important of all was the expansion of the assembly industries, and specifically the birth of automobile manufacture on a large scale. Although handicapped by lack or shortage of basic minerals, raw materials and capital, Italy was able to participate fully in this 'second wind'. Three factors account for this. First, food production expanded, in spite of a falling agricultural workforce, and the prices of basic foodstuffs (bread, pasta, rice, wine, sugar and fruit) remained stable. Secondly, many industries were export-orientated (such as textiles) and thus preserved a balanced foreign account. Thirdly, emigrant remittances contributed a peculiarly Italian form of private industrial finance through bank savings. In the decade 1901-10 an average of 600,000 emigrants left the country each year, mostly bound for overseas. These emigrants sent back portions of their earnings to their kinsfolk and brought back savings when they returned. Calculations for the 1901-13 period show that against a commercial trade deficit of 10,230 million lire, invisible items showed a

Table 2.1: Level of Fixed Capital Investment, 1861-1911

	million lire
1961	654
1866	747
1871	718
1876	911
1881	1,170
1886	1,369
1891	1,036
1896	1,011
1901	1,412
1906	2,278
1911	3,096

Source: *Indagine Statistica sullo Sviluppo del Reddito Nazionale dell' Italia dal 1861 al 1956*, Rome: ISTAT (1957), pp.264-5.

credit of 12,291 million lire, over half of which came from emigrants' remittances.[40]

International comparisons of industrial growth at this time have to be made and interpreted with caution. Italian industrial growth during 1898-1908 was double the rate in the United Kingdom, but the latter had of course already experienced 'take-off' some time before. France, which had only a slightly inferior growth rate to Italy, also industrialised earlier. When the comparison is made with countries at similar stages of industrial development, such as Sweden (average annual industrial growth of 12 per cent during 1888-96), Japan (8.5 per cent during 1907-13) or Russia (8 per cent during 1890-1900), then Italy emerges as a rather slow developer.[41]

It is not entirely clear why Italy's industrial take-off should have been so weak, but three factors help to provide a partial explanation.[42] First is a shortcoming we have already briefly noted: the lack of synchronisation between industrial development and railway building. Railway construction was virtually complete before industrial take-off. In many countries nineteenth century industrialisation coincided with railway fever, the former acting as the vital stimulus to, and yet benefiting from, the latter. During the great years of Russian industrialisation — 1888-1900 — railway length increased by 70 per cent. Italian rail length grew by only 10 per cent during 1896-1908. Secondly, government involvement with industrial development was not well-planned. Public assistance generally involved tariff protection for basic sectors like iron and steel. Thirdly, the political and labour situations were unstable. The political climate during 1896-1908 was not conducive to steady economic development. A disastrous harvest in 1897, coupled with governmental hesitation over wheat duties, led to the *anno terribile* of 1898 in which strikes and disorders spread to many regions, culminating in the Milan insurrection. Under Giolitti's neutral policy, strikes reached unprecedented proportions, causing in some years a loss of nearly 4 million man-days. Such strike action led to some improvement in the economic position of workers and in general conditions of labour.[43] But this points to a crucial historical difference. In most other European countries rapid industrial growth in the nineteenth century was *followed,* at some distance, by a period of upward adjustment in the standard of living. This enabled, for a time, labour to be more ruthlessly squeezed to fuel industrial investment and expansion. In Italy the two processes, growth and improved conditions, tended to coincide.

One further comment may be added. Initial industrial development in many other European countries appeared to be often guided or inspired by an overriding economic ideology: economic liberalism in England, nationalism in Germany, Marxism in Russia for example. The observer of Italian industrialisation at this stage cannot help but notice the lack of a comparable orthodoxy. Cavour's liberalism belonged to an earlier age, the euphoric era of unification. Protectionism was often ineptly applied and hardly constituted a strong intellectual movement. The lack of 'ideological grease in the wheels of Italian industrialisation' probably made them turn more slowly.[44]

Nevertheless, the conundrum in which Italian industrialisation found itself must be stressed. Scarcity of private and foreign industrial capital made the role of banks as industrial investors more important than in other European countries. The void created by the failure of Italian banks in 1893 was filled by the German bankers' initiative of promoting two new credit banks, the Banca Commerciale and the Credito Italiano. These institutes followed the German model of deposit and investment banks, becoming heavily involved in industrial finance. Grasping the great potential in the hydro-electrical industry and profiting from the conditions created by protectionism, these banks did not confine themselves to direct financing of industrial expansion but participated in shareholding ventures, industrial organisation and technical assistance. This industrial commitment of the banks, together with protectionism and other forms of state intervention such as the supporting of strategic industries like iron and steel and shipbuilding, led some observers to condemn Italian industrial development as pathologically misshapen. The point is, however, that given Italy's unavoidable handicaps of a late start and shortage of basic raw materials including capital, this path was probably the *only* way that the country could force rapid industrial progress to materialise. The severe side-effects of this model — the sacrificing of southern agriculture and industry, the pandering to large financial interests, the illicit collusion between banks and industrialists — are therefore seen as unfortunate rather than avoidable.[45]

The turn of the century witnessed particular expansion in Italian heavy industry. The birth of the hydro-electric industry was critical here. A large part of the capital set free by the nationalisation of the railways in 1905 was directed towards this branch of investment, which was also supported by the big commercial banks. Capital invested in electricity generation soared from 37 million lire in 1897 to 559 million lire in 1914. The development of hydro-electric power had a tremendous psychological effect, giving a sense of release from the industrial impotence to which many thought Italy was doomed because of her lack of energy resources.[46]

Protected and encouraged by the state, the iron and steel industry developed strongly. Terni was further expanded and modernised, and new plants were founded at Piombino in 1903 and Bagnoli in 1905. Pig-iron output increased from an average of 8,000 tons per year in 1895-7 to 427,000 tons in 1913. Steel output also increased, from 60,000 to 933,000 tons over the same time span. These production figures should, however, be put in perspective internationally. Annual pig-iron production, 1912-14, was 4.6 million tons in France, 11 million tons in Great Britain and 14.7 million tons in Germany. The steel figures were 3.5 million tons in France, 6.5 million tons in Great Britain and 14 million tons in Germany.[47]

In the mechanical engineering sector, vehicles were the main stimulus to expansion. Fiat was founded in Turin in 1899 and the number of automobile firms rose from 7 in 1904 to 70 in 1907, after which a process of concentration began. The car industry nurtured a whole series of ancillary trades such as aluminium, tyres and carriage-building. Bicycle manufacture also developed strongly as a precursor to vehicles. In 1913 there were 1,225,000 bicycles, 17,000 motorcycles and 20,000 vehicles in circulation. Another promising mechanical initiative was the production of typewriters, started by Olivetti at Ivrea in 1911.

Overall, the heavy extractive-manufacturing industries increased their share of total industrial output by value from 19.8 per cent in 1891-5 to 30.6 per cent in 1911-15. The agriculture-based industries (food, drink, tobacco, hides, skins and textiles) dropped their share from 74.2 per cent to 59.2 per cent over the same period. The progress of the textile industry at this time, although patchy, should not be under-valued. That its rate of increase appears low in comparison to the 'new' industries like automobiles is primarily due to the higher point of departure. In fact textile progress at this time was considerable: conquest of the domestic market; accentuation of its character as an export industry; and mechanisation and electrification of both spinning and weaving. In the years immediately preceding the First World War textiles accounted for 20 per cent of the total product of manufacturing industries, 30 per cent of all workers engaged in manufacturing, 40 per cent of exports by value and 60 per cent of non-food exports. Cotton production was the most buoyant textile branch, increasing from less than 1 per cent of world output to 3.5 per cent by 1914. Imports of raw cotton doubled between 1895 and 1914. In 1913 the Italian cotton industry employed 116,000 workers, two-thirds of them female. Nine-tenths of this labour force was in Lombardy, Piedmont and Veneto, 65 per cent in Lombardy alone. Silk production, on the other hand, declined, although Italy remained Europe's main silk producer. Wool tended to remain linked to family-sized operations and grew only moderately at its major centres of Biella, Schio and Prato. In 1914 the 15 largest wool companies accounted for only 10 per cent of the capital invested in this industry. Employees in wool numbered less than half those in cotton.[48]

The industrial revolution was brusquely interrupted by a sudden economic downturn in 1907. Industrial output remained stationary for four years. Fiat shares dropped from 445 to 17 lire each between January and September 1907. Other industries were also affected. It was a worldwide crisis, but particularly severe in Italy where its effects lasted in some ways until the First World War.

A basic reason for the 1907 crisis was the limitation of the Italian domestic market. Italy's large number of low-income peasant families constrained demand for manufactured products. In some sectors a crisis of over-production brought plummeting prices and a trend towards cartels. Examples were Ilva (steel), Unione Zuccheri (sugar), Istituto Cotoniero Italiano (cotton) and Consorzio di Filatori di Lana e Pettine (wool).

After 1907, the Italian economy was slow to break out of the vicious cycle which checked further growth. Industrial output, wages, purchasing power and hence domestic demand all stagnated. Industrial enterprises had to exist by bank loans, constantly renewed, instead of by long-term bond issues, which the public would not buy. The banks, in turn, were caught by the need to keep their capital potentially liquid to meet demand from their depositors. Both bankers and industrialists were trapped. In this situation the Italian state was forced to become the arbiter. With one hand the government drained the money market of available capital, but with the other hand it favoured certain industries, mostly connected with arms or public transport, by special orders and salvage operations.[49]

Nevertheless, by the outbreak of the First World War, Northern Italy's centres of industry produced a wide range of manufactured goods with modern organisation and techniques. In some branches, such as vehicles and chemicals, Italian factories were as technologically advanced as any in the world. Italy had, during the period from 1898 to 1914, emerged from the more backward Mediterranean realm to join the European fold of industrialising capitalist countries.

Fifty Years of Unity

The 1911 Industrial Census came at a propitious time, enabling a balance to be made of fifty years of Italian unity.[50] The Italian population had reached 36 million, an increase of 38 per cent over 1861. Although a majority of the population still lived in the countryside, 2.3 million persons earned their living from industry, 23.2 per cent of the working population. The historic, long-term shift away from farming had started.

But the 1911 Census also revealed more precisely than ever before the major national problem of all time — the division of Italy into two halves. The major industrial developments — electric power generation, mechanical industries, rubber, chemicals, etc. — were more than ever concentrated in the North. In 1911 64.1 per cent of industrial employees were in the North, 14.9 per cent in the Centre and 21 per cent in the South. Workers in the vital metal-mechanical branch of industry were distributed 68.7 per cent, 12.9 per cent and 18.4 per cent in the North, Centre and South respectively. The number of total industrial firms was spread somewhat more evenly — 49.2 per cent, 18.4 per cent and 32.4 per cent — reflecting the larger size of industrial operations in the North. Half the industrial firms with motor power were concentrated in the three regions of Lombardy, Piedmont and Liguria which covered 20.7 per cent of the national area and contained in 1911 27.4 per cent of the national population. Table 2.2 shows that industrial polarisation in the North was increasing. In 1901 Lombardy, Piedmont and Liguria had 35.2 per cent of total industrial workers; by 1911 their share was 38.7 per cent.

Table 2.2: Industrial Employment in Selected Regions, 1901 and 1911

Region	% of Italy's total industrial workers	
	1901	1911
Lombardy	20.1	21.8
Piedmont	11.3	12.4
Liguria	3.8	4.5
Veneto	8.5	8.3
Tuscany	8.0	9.4
Campania	9.8	8.8
Sicily	9.3	7.8

Source: Romeo (1963), p.105.

To a certain extent, the process of industrialisation in North-western Italy was conducted like that of an autonomous small country. Lombardy and to a lesser extent Turin, Genoa and Venice had coteries of industrial intellectuals who followed closely the French and English technical and economic literature and who were keen to introduce new production methods into their territories. Italy's political unification was still a comparatively recent fact which had done little to impinge on economic and social patterns indelibly forged in the past. The two Italies continued to follow their earlier, separate paths; political unification had not led to economic unification. Fifty years of nationhood had not reduced the ever-widening gap between North and South; at best it may have reduced the rate of widening.[51]

Notes and References

1. Walker (1967), p.15.
2. Luzzatto (1961a), pp.1-6.
3. Ibid., pp.26-7.
4. Waley (1978), pp.3-4.
5. Luzzatto (1961a), p.66.
6. Waley (1978), p.14.
7. Examples are Via dei Fabbri (Smith Street), Via dei Pistori (Baker Street) and Via dei Tessitori (Weaver Street), Luzzatto (1961a), p.83.
8. Luzzatto (1961a), pp.96-7.
9. Mazzaoui (1972), p.263.
10. Molho (1969), p.2.
11. Walker (1967), p.30.
12. In his investigation into North-South relations during the city-republic period (the Norman period in the South), Abulafia (1977) shows that Sicily and the South made an important contribution, by supplying essential food and raw materials, to the development of the northern communes. The failure of the South to develop free communes and urban industry at this time was not entirely due to Norman central control; there is more than a suggestion that northern merchants saw it in their interests to stifle industrial development in the South by saturating southern markets with the textiles used to pay for local raw goods.
13. Quoted in Luzzatto (1961a), p.151.
14. Rapp (1976), pp.6-10.
15. Cipolla (1952).
16. Luzzatto (1961a), p.163.
17. Quoted in Walker (1967), p.37.
18. Albrecht-Carrié (1960), pp.7-9.
19. Clough (1964), pp.15-21.
20. Ibid., pp.23, 26.
21. A detailed note on sources on nineteenth century Italian industrial development is in order here. Among English-language accounts the best is Cafagna (1971); also useful is Clough (1964). There are several histories of Italian industry which concentrate on the nineteenth century. The first, and still useful, is Morandi (1966, but originally published in 1931). The most thorough study, especially useful for the pre-unification period, is

Caizzi (1965). Other studies include Barbagallo (1951), De Rosa (1973), Luzzatto (1968), Romeo (1963), Tremelloni (1947), the anthology edited by Caracciolo (1969), and the bibliographic compilations by Corna Pellegrini (1973), Della Valle (1964) and Mori (1959).

22. Kish (1969), pp.8-9.
23. Quoted in Allum (1973a), pp.8-9.
24. Webster (1975), p.8.
25. Allum (1973a), p.22.
26. Hildebrand (1965), p.281.
27. Acquaviva and Santuccio (1976), p.7.
28. See Eckaus (1961), pp.288-99.
29. Cafagna (1971), pp.289-91.
30. This figure is the estimate of Gerschenkron (1955).
31. Ibid., p.273.
32. Clough (1964), pp.94-5.
33. Luzzatto (1961b).
34. Gerschenkron (1955), pp.363-4.
35. Cafagna (1971), p.294.
36. Eckaus (1961), p.308.
37. Fuà (1965), p.14.
38. Gerschenkron (1955), pp.363-4.
39. Allen and Stevenson (1974), p.3.
40. Cafagna (1971), pp.300-3.
41. Gerschenkron (1962), p.78.
42. Gerschenkron (1955), pp.366-73.
43. An inspection of certain factories in 1900 showed that one in six of the workforce was under 12 years of age. A law in 1901 prohibited employment of children under 12 (under 14 in mining) and stated that no youth under 15 should work more than 11 hours per day. The female workday was set at 12 hours. By 1914 demands for an 8-hour day were being felt. See Clough (1964), pp.161-2.
44. Gerschenkron (1955), p.373.
45. Romeo (1963), pp.110-11.
46. Cafagna (1971), p.311.
47. Romeo (1963), pp.78, 112.
48. Cafagna (1971), p.305; Romeo (1963), pp.90-4.
49. Bonelli (1969).
50. *Censimento degli Opifici ed Imprese Industriali 1911,* the results of which are effectively described in Caizzi (1965), pp.406-10.
51. Eckaus (1961), p.301.

3 INDUSTRIAL IMPERIALISM, WAR AND FASCISM

The Italian industrial development spurt which ended in 1908 bequeathed to Italian industry a number of fundamental structural problems which conditioned the entire subsequent political and economic development of the country through to the Second World War. After 1908 it became clear that Italy's new industries were over-expanded, producing far beyond the absorptive capacities of the domestic market. The key to survival thus became the quest for foreign outlets in an attempt to enlarge Italy's 'economic space'. There was a need not only to export industrial goods, but also to find outlets for Italy's entire industrial system — skills, technology, labour and all. This explains Italy's audacious imperialist policies in search of colonial space that might absorb and sustain both industrial products and the surplus manpower that was not fully absorbed in industrial growth at home.[1] Between 1909 and 1913 an annual average of nearly 680,000 Italians emigrated, a yearly outflow of almost 2 per cent of the Italian population. In 1913 the figure touched an all-time high: 872,598, of whom 559,566, 64 per cent, went overseas. What was significant, though, was that this emigration took place at a time when industrial production was increasing, yet obviously not absorbing the bulk of excess rural manpower. Italy simultaneously sent forth from her ports industrial exports like automobiles, machines and rubber tyres (from the North), and a mass of illiterate rural labourers (from the South).

Industrial Imperialism and Competition

Italian economists of the time foresaw possibilities for the creation of the Italian 'economic hinterland' in several areas: the Balkans, the East African uplands, Libya and Asia Minor. In reality, most of these areas offered little of lasting benefit to the Italian economy; indeed some colonial ventures proved financially disastrous. Many benefits were short term and restricted to certain sectors of industry. The shipping companies, for example, found the transport of Italian troops to Eritrea highly profitable, and Pirelli's insulated cable factory enjoyed lucrative Red Sea contracts.

On the eve of the First World War, eastward expansion seemed more promising, with imperialist designs on the Balkans and Asia

Minor capable of yielding more tangible results than the leap-in-the-dark African strategies. In 1905 the Italian Geographical Society sent a 'mission of commercial geography' through the Asiatic provinces of Turkey to report on Italian business prospects there. Particularly high hopes were entertained in the Balkans, which offered a fertile field for electrification, transport lines, harbour construction and land reclamation. All these activities would provide employment for Italy's growing corps of engineers and technicians, and outlets for Italian machinery products. In return the Balkan region could furnish cotton, wool, hides, lumber and olives, the basic materials for a wide range of textile and food processing enterprises to operate under Italian control, with the 'mother country' supplying industrial planning, supervision and skilled labour. Such, at least, was the theory of it all.

Italy's undertakings in the Balkans — particularly her projects in Montenegro which was one bridgehead that the Italians could develop easily — were also part of a wider objective. Montenegro itself offered little, but it linked with the richer mineral and hydro-electric potential of the Adriatic coast, and with the trans-Balkan rail scheme. In an era of giant railway achievements, this was Italy's golden opportunity to match the Berlin-Baghdad, Cape-Cario, or trans-Siberian lines. A rail route cutting through the Balkans linking the Danube, Romania, Southern Russia and Serbia with the Adriatic would provide Italian industry with outlets, profit and prestige. Trade and traffic would increase at Venice and Bari.

Austrian and French competition thwarted the rail ambition, however, and the project dissolved in the Italo-Turkish and ensuing Balkan wars of 1911-12. The Danube-Adriatic rail scheme of 1908 showed how little Italian power counted on a wider European scale. Only in primitive, unmapped Albania was some lasting Italian impact made. With 100,000 South Italians of Albanian speech and descent, Italy had a unique entrée here, and the Straits of Otranto separating the two countries are only 80 kilometres wide. Colonial penetration took the form of private initiative, followed by large quasi-governmental industrial, public works and cultural operations, which continued into the 1930s. However, here as elsewhere, speculative planning tended to run far ahead of disposable capital.

At the same time as the Italian industrial system attempted to expand abroad, Italy was herself invaded by industrial competition from outside. The main threat came from Germany. Especially after 1894, German industry and industrial finance identified Italy as a promising area for the export of industrial products and systems. By 1906 the German economic presence was arousing hostility. Germany took less of Italy's manufactured exports than did Austria, France or Britain, but sold Italy more manufactured products than any other two countries combined. Particularly in the field of electrical and power station engineering, Germany made Italy an economic colony, supplying before 1913 88 per cent of Italy's installed machinery in these fields. Cheaper Italian manpower and the existence of tariff barriers encouraged big German firms like Siemens, AEG Berlin and Halske to manufacture parts in Italy. The German aims were apparently to keep Italy tied to German methods and machinery and to forestall the rise of independent industries in Italy. Whilst the Germans were able to control certain key points in Italian industry, there was never any chance of complete control over the whole Italian industrial economy. The dangers of German industrial penetration were probably exaggerated at the time. Indeed some link was probably beneficial, for it is difficult to envisage great Italian achievements in fields like electrification and machine manufacture without some initial dependence on Germany.

Structural Changes: Interlocking and Militarism

Before the First World War, Italy was still struggling to find her feet industrially and compete in world markets. Foreign rivalry not only made her export position insecure but also dominated many domestic industrial markets. Perched precariously on the outer rim of industrial Europe, Italy tried to compensate for industrial weakness by political adventure which became especially audacious after 1911. As Webster makes clear, [2] Italy's *via dolorosa* from the Libyan enterprise of 1911 to the First World War and the imperialistic interventions of Salandra and Sonnino make sense only in the light of the country's industrial pattern. An unbalanced, top-heavy industrial structure, economically dominated by the big credit and investment banks, acted as a perpetual spur to expansion abroad. Centralised industrial groupings, bound together by interlocking directorships and dependent upon state subsidies, preferential treatment and protection, constituted a powerful political pressure group campaigning for ambitious foreign development schemes.

All the worst features of Italian industrial imperialism with its speculative militaristic involvements, are shown clearly in the iron and steel industry. Although not an economic absurdity in Italy, the production of iron and steel had to operate with great technical efficiency to be viable. Cost minimisation meant complete cycle production with the metal kept hot from blast furnace to rolling and final moulding. It also required, then as now, long-term planning and continual replacement of obsolete equipment: a policy of reinvestment at the expense of immediate profit. But the Italian iron and steel industry arose as a fragmented and highly speculative financial enterprise, very dependent upon an artificial cushion of governmental support.

One of the early iron and steel firms was the Società Veneta per Costruzioni ed Imprese Pubbliche, whose president was the engineer-politican Stefano Breda. In the late nineteenth century it was heavily involved in public works but it gradually moved from aqueducts, bridges and railways into more overtly militaristic production. Ernesto Breda, cousin of Stefano, received artillery ammunition contracts of such a size that he was able to diversify away from his locomotive shops and set up special plants for arms manufacture. The Terni steel mill was given big orders for armour plate by Admiral Brin at the naval ministry. The prices paid were very high and accompanied by generous interest-free advances. Terni's inland site had the advantage of military security but prospects for non-military production were poor.

The Steel Trust — the nexus of political, banking, military and indus-trial interests that was formed in the expansionist years prior to the First World War — also had links in other directions. In 1881 the government sponsored the formation of the Navigazione Generale as a merger of Rubattino and Florio, the two subsidised steamship lines, in order to concentrate capital and governmental control in this militarily impor-tant sector. Shipping and shipbuilding interests were heavily involved in colonial adventures during the East African campaigns of 1887 and 1896. Thereafter Italy's shipping magnates became the most out-spoken partisans of the country's new imperialism, since they had so much to gain from colonial and war situations.

The Steel Trust had one great competitior, the fiercely independent Ansaldo concern of Genoa. Like its rival Ansaldo was nationalistic, autarchic and expansionist. Yet it aimed even higher. Ansaldo's goal, explict by 1914, was to create a vertical industrial combine starting with ore and fuel and ending with delivery of finished products any-where in the world. Although this ambition came into being only for one brief period at the end of the war, the foundations for it were laid by 1914.

The early fortunes of Ansaldo were with the Bombrini family, a dynasty of political capitalists who favoured the firm with credits and investments. The multifarious activities of the Bombrinis are an excellent example of the 'political capitalism' of the time. Specialists in aqueducts, they financed Apulian land improvement and built the rail network in the Salento (the heel of Italy). They also had mineral interests in Albania.

Ansaldo's decision to expand from steel, locomotives and electrical goods into artillery, ammunition and armour plate brought the firm's rivalry with the Steel Trust to a head. Vertical expansion was a life-or-death matter for Ansaldo and an independent steel plant a necessity. Thus was begun in 1914 the great steelworks at Cornigliano Ligure outside Genoa.

The Italian motor industry, which had emerged as the most outstanding example of individual industrial talent in Italy, was also attracted by the state's warmongering postures. Substantial use had been made of Fiat trucks in the Libyan desert during the 1911-12 war, and Fiat found in the Italian state its best customer for naval engines. The North Italian engine manufacturing concern of Franco Tosi showed a similar pattern of development. Starting in Legnano as a repair shop for cotton mill machinery, Tosi graduated to the manufacture of boilers and steam engines. After 1900 new lines of production — turbines and generators — developed in response to Italy's torpedo-boat programme. In 1914 a further stage of integration with the state came when Tosi opened a shipyard in Taranto, a venture supported by the promise of naval contracts and by the state releasing much cheap waterfront land.

On the eve of war the web of interlocking relations joined the management of the Steel Trust, so dependent on the Banca Commerciale, to the rubber magnate, Pirelli, who was also on the board of the Credito Italiano (the second big industrial bank), to Agnelli of Fiat and even to the more independent Ansaldo group. Industrial interests had thus coalesced on an institutional and personal basis into a giant interlinked combine supported by, and at the service of, the state. The nation's entire industrial establishment was involved in imperialism in one way or another. Italy's new industrial ambitions meant colonial expansion in the East, alliance with the Entente and divorce from, and eventual war with, the Central Powers.

Italian Industry and the First World War

The First World War inflicted great long-term costs on Italian industry. Resources that should have been devoted to economic growth were channelled instead into the war effort. State expenditures, 15 per cent of national income in 1910, rose to 55 per cent by 1918. By the time Italy joined the Entente powers, modern warfare was big business. Those industries most profoundly affected, in a positive sense, were munitions, military equipment, machines, mining, shipbuilding and clothing, all concentrated in the North. From 1913 to 1917 the steel and mechanical sectors increased their share of total Italian manufacturing output from 5.2 per cent to 10.8 per cent and from 21.6 per cent to 31.8 per cent respectively. Many war-linked firms enjoyed profit rates of up to 30 per cent during the bonanza of the early war years. In a seller's market the motto was 'produce and never mind the cost'.

Italian steel output was forced up by one-third in spite of a drop in imports of ore and scrap. Iron ore output was raised from 334,000 tons per year during 1909-13 to 999,000 tons in 1917. But lack of coal was a great hardship. Imports fell from 10 million tons annually before 1914 to 5 million tons in 1917. Domestic lignite production was expanded three and a half times during the war but this was an insufficient response: the sulphur content was too high for smelting and even ruined the locomotives when used on the railways. Hydro-electric power production was more effective in offsetting domestic dearth of fossil fuels but was of course locationally restricted to the Alpine forelands.

Inflated profits and high demand also encouraged technical innovation and economies of scale. A number of new industrial sectors, such as chemicals (for explosives) and aviation, grew rapidly. Fiat's development was especially dramatic; vehicle production increased from 3,300 in 1914 to 25,000 in 1918, including a shift to valuable heavy vehicles for war. Ansaldo also enjoyed phenomenal growth, increasing its capital during the war years from 30 million lire to 500 million lire and its labour force from 4,000 to 56,000. It took over the Cogne iron mines, ore from which was smelted with coal from nearby La Thuile to supply steel to Cornigliano. It also expanded its shipbuilding yards along the Ligurian coast, exploited water power sites for hydro-electricity, manufactured vehicles, airplanes and telephones, and had a dynamite factory at Avigliana near Turin.[3]

Although the war stimulated the artificial expansion of certain industries, the long-term economic effect was debilitating. Industries producing for civilian markets contracted. The cessation of commerce with enemy countries disrupted trade and starved industries dependent upon imported raw materials. Much wartime industrial growth was unplanned and, in the long term, unviable. The period following the war was marked by constant difficulties and failures of producers who had become temporary giants during the war and found conversion to peacetime products hard. Steel output fell by 45 per cent between 1917 and 1921, and Fiat's automobile output was reduced by a similar proportion. As the post-war depression deepened, many businesses folded, especially in 1921. Some of the bigger failures were Ilva (steel), Ansaldo (bankrupting the Banca di Sconto) and the Lloyd Mediterraneo shipping line. Italy's participation in the war, with 600,000 lives lost and over one million soldiers wounded, had yielded few economic benefits. A widespread sense of disillusionment prevailed.

Labour problems were also thrown up. Demobilisation reduced the army from 3 million in 1918 to 500,000 in 1920. Unemployment statistics are unreliable but indicate 2 million out of work at the end of 1919. Desperate workers began to occupy factories and seize land in an attempt to improve their lot. Strikes cost a loss of 906,471 man-days of work in 1918, jumping to 18,887,917 in 1919. Railways, textiles and the metallurgical trades were worst hit. In 1920 a month-long factory occupation occurred, involving 600,000 workers in different parts of the country, but concentrated especially in Milan where 280 factories, including the Alfa Romeo plant, were taken over.[4]

This swelling tide of workers' demands was embodied in the rising power of socialist organisations. In Piedmont a group of young men led by the Sardinian Antonio Gramsci began to preach social revolution; the capitalist system was to be overthrown and replaced by factory-based workers' councils. Although Gramsci's ideas were fundamental to the development of international communist thought, the movement did not achieve its long-term goal in Italy. Instead, out of the disillusionment and disorder of the immediate post-war period another movement emerged which' was to dominate Italy for the next 20 years.

Fascism and Industry

The sudden rise of Italian Fascism after 1920 had important industrial causes and ramifications. To a large extent it developed out of, and as a panicky reaction to, the failure of workers to take over the factories permanently in 1920. The 'reaction theory' is not, however, the whole story. In Italy Fascism and socialism arose more or less simultaneously as efforts to cope with problems of chronic industrial imbalance. They were parallel rather than diametrically opposed solutions. Indeed Mussolini and many other prominent Fascists were originally socialists but parted company with the Socialist Party over the question of imperialism — in Mussolini's case his insistence on Italy going into the

First World War. It has also been pointed out that the Axis and Tripartite pacts of the 1930s and 1940s were between nations — Italy, Germany and Japan — with a common industrial experience and in which ideologies of Fascism and imperialism evolved in much the same way out of structural industrial problems.[5]

An anti-communist, anti-labour stance united Fascism with the industrial leaders. Fascism's rise to power created the authoritarian climate that the industrialists needed without having to worry about interference or opposition from workers. Industrialists were one of the groups who gained most and yielded least under Fascism. A study of the two most influential industrialists' groups — Confindustria and ASIA — shows how they worked together (Confindustria playing the dominant role) to prosper as a powerful pressure group enjoying the privileges of a public agency under the Fascist regime.[6] The relationship found symbolic expression in the centre of Rome where, in Piazza Venezia, Mussolini's headquarters in the Palazzo Venezia faced directly across the square to Confindustria's office in a modern facsimile of the same Renaissance palace. In the early years, when the more misguided facets of Fascist economic doctrine had not yet become apparent, politically pragmatic industrialists had no reason to fear Fascism any more than any other political ideology.

By the time the Fascists came to power in late 1922 the economy had recovered its pre-war levels and was, in fact, quite buoyant. Fast growth and rising prosperity naturally consolidated the Fascists' power. In the 1924 elections, the last democratic elections to be held in inter-war Italy, the Fascists polled 65 per cent of the votes. The appointment of Alberto De Stefani to the Treasury in 1922 ushered in Fascism as a liberal and relatively non-interventionist economic doctrine. Early Fascist industrial policy was 'productivist'; the route to military power and socio-economic stability was to be through expanded production rather than by revolutionary programmes of wealth redistribution. One of De Stefani's specific acts was to encourage foreign capital for industrial investment. From 1922 to 1925 and, less so, to 1927, considerable economic improvement took place. Unemployment dropped to less than one-quarter of its former level, and national and *per capita* incomes rose at about 4 per cent per year. Industry finally adjusted to peacetime demand, increasing its output by 41 per cent during 1920-5. In the mechanical sector 200 new firms were founded between 1922 and 1925. By 1927 workers in mechanical industries numbered 478,900, 14.5 per cent of total industrial workers, compared to 257,700, 11.2 per cent, in 1911 (Table 3.1). Dramatic transport

Table 3.1: Industrial Employment by Sector, 1911, 1927 and 1938

Sector of industry	'000 employees			%		
	1911	1927	1938	1911	1927	1938
Food and drink	305.3	343.1	529.7	13.2	10.4	12.7
Extractive	286.6	270.7	434.2	12.4	8.2	8.3
Metallurgical	141.7	122.5	103.6	6.2	3.7	2.5
Mechanical	257.7	478.9	823.0	11.2	14.5	19.8
Chemicals	50.6	99.5	127.9	2.2	3.0	3.1
Textiles	495.2	642.9	628.6	21.5	19.4	15.1
Clothing and skins	285.5	521.7	524.2	12.5	15.8	12.6
Building	122.0	332.6	558.5	5.3	10.1	13.4
Wood industries	209.7	286.1	283.6	9.1	8.7	6.8
Other	150.2	204.4	239.2	6.4	6.4	5.7
Total	2,304.5	3,302.4	4.162.5	100.0	100.0	100.0

Source: Romeo (1963), pp.155, 184.

improvements were made, especially the railways which were made to run on time by Fascist militiamen. By the mid 1920s, the railways were paying substantial profits into the Treasury.

Mussolini's ignorance of economic matters was revealed in his stubborn insistence on unrealistically up-valuing the lira to the 'quota 90' (about 90 lire to the pound sterling) in 1927. Deflation ensued, soon to be accelerated by the world depression starting in 1929. Unemployment rose until 1935, when publication of employment data ceased. The 1931 census indicated an overall rate of unemployment of 5 per cent, but it was probably nearly 20 per cent in the industrial sector.[7] Balance of payments deficits became serious. Gold reserves fell by 74 per cent during 1927-39 and the 1936 balance of trade deficit was greater than total visible exports.[8] As unemployment rose and an economically desirable devaluation of the lira was held off until 1936, industrial output, wages, imports and exports all fell. Wages were slashed by 30 per cent during 1926-36, but because the cost of living fell also, industrial wages' real value was diminished by a lesser amount, 12 per cent.[9] Industrial production slumped by 33 per cent during 1929-32, imports fell 29 per cent and exports 25 per cent. As Table 3.2 shows, the depths of the industrial depression were reached in 1932. The natural response of industry to shrinking markets at home and abroad was oligopolistic concentration, a process particularly marked after 1927. Fascist policy tended to encourage this industrial restructuring, which resulted in certain industrial sectors being further dominated by one concern: Fiat in cars, Edison in electrical concerns, Montecatini in chemicals, Snia Viscosa in artificial fibres and Italcementi in construction materials are examples. Industrial workers became restive from the middle of the 1920s. A general strike called by Lombardy's metal workers in 1925 spread to Turin and Trieste. Faced with a resurgence of strike activity Fascism abandoned liberal attitudes and increasingly adopted policies of state intervention in economic matters, leading eventually to the grandiose and unrealistic programme of economic self-sufficiency, or autarchy, of the 1930s.

Strikes were anathema to the Fascist system which in response gradually extended its control over labour. Strikes were declared 'acts of war'. Under a plan of 'integral syndicalism' nurtured by Edmondo Rossoni, the leader of the Fascist labour policy, employers, technicians and workers were organised into Fascist unions, termed corporations. Special representatives of these corporations met at national level to determine wage and other labour matters, but the state set itself up as the eventual arbiter of these discussions. Restrictions on internal migration were introduced to try to tie rural workers to the land and prevent them from swelling the restive ranks of urban unemployed. All this took place in a bitter climate of wage reductions. The Rocco Law on Corporations (April 1926) and Rossoni's Labour Charter (April 1927) were the legal bases of Fascist economic dogma whereby the state effectively had direct control over both capital and labour.

This spelt doom for the non-Fascist unions. Workers found that they could not get jobs unless they co-operated with the Fascist system. The Catholic unions were dissolved in 1926 and the Socialist General Confederation of Labour moved its organisation abroad in 1927.

Table 3.2: Industrial Production during the Depression

	All industry	Textiles	Industrial output index Metallurgy	Mechanical	Construction
1929	100.0	100.0	100.0	100.0	100.0
1930	91.8	89.9	84.0	91.3	93.7
1931	77.6	80.5	70.8	79.6	62.8
1932	66.8	66.3	65.3	67.8	56.5
1933	73.7	75.0	79.1	68.8	66.9
1934	79.9	72.4	82.5	72.6	97.4
1935	89.0	64.7	108.4	93.8	130.4

Source: Caizzi (1965), p.469.

In the 1930s autarchic ambitions were more explicit. The 'Battle for Grain' increased wheat production from 4.8 million tons per year before the war to an annual average of 7.6 million tons during 1935-9, an amount sufficient to meet internal demand. An ambitious programme of land reclamation, drainage control and malaria eradication provided additional agricultural land, much of which was settled by war veterans. New crops like cotton were introduced.

In the field of industry, hit harder by the deflation following the artificial stabilisation of the lira and by the deep depression of the 1930s, the Corporate State's task was more difficult. The Istituto Mobilare Italiano (IMI) was created in November 1931 to make loans to tottering private businesses, but many concerns were beyond economic reprieve. A new body, the Istituto per la Ricostruzione Industriale (IRI) was founded in January 1933. Although in the long run IRI was to change the whole character of the Italian industrial economy, its original task was only to help the main banks (Banca Commerciale, Credito Italiano and Banco di Roma) which had lost their liquidity positions with the sudden decline in value of industrial securities. But IRI found that it had to assume direct control of businesses that it was originally designed only to help via the banks. The number of such businesses became so large that IRI began to group similar concerns under subsidiaries. The first of these was Società Finanziaria Telefonica (telephones), created in late 1933. Others were Finmare (shipping), formed in 1936, and Finsider (iron and steel), formed in 1937. By the late 1930s the Italian state had a larger share of industry than any other European state outside Russia.

Special efforts were made to expand those branches of industry which could produce goods for which Italy was highly dependent upon imports. The state-owned Azienda Generale Italiana Petroli (AGIP) built refineries to handle Iraqi oil. AGIP also carried out an intensive search for oil and gas in the North Italian Plain and started to exploit Albanian oil through a subsidiary company. Another subsidiary, Azienda Nazionale Idrogenazione Combustibili (ANIC), was established for hydrocarbons and an effort was made to increase domestic coal output by pushing mining activity at the Bacu Abis and Sulcis mines in Sardinia. Bauxite was discovered in the Gargano.

These autarchic and monopolistic interventions might conceivably have had some benefit if carried out in a time of peace, but they occurred partly as a necessary correlative to Mussolini's increasing imperialist ambitions. The re-taking of Libya dragged on till 1930, but much more important was the war in Ethiopia (1935-6), a country which, as a member of the League of Nations, had a strong claim on the world's conscience. Mussolini wanted to enlarge the small East African empire by adding Ethiopia to Eritrea and Italian Somaliland, still clinging to the old idea that through acquisition of colonial territory Italy could enhance its own economic well-being. The effect, however, was the reverse. With autarchy as the naïve guiding principle, the economy was subjected to war demands. 'Obligatory' targets were set for agricultural production, industries were taxed heavily and attention was diverted away from the feasibility of economic development within Italy itself. In fact, the economy did improve temporarily after the Ethiopian campaigns, but Mussolini's imperialism and international events conspired against long-term peaceful development. The late 1930s were the prelude to an economic and political holocaust: the Second World War, the demise of Fascism and the collapse of the Italian economy.

Some of Fascism's achievements were beneficial, although there is diversity of opinion as to how beneficial.[10] Social security was introduced. Family allowances, first provided to help the Biella wool-workers on short-time in 1933, were applied to all industrial workers in 1934. Free medical care was supplied to low-income urban groups. The 'Christmas bonus', a feature of Italian wages today, was introduced in 1938. As Table 3.1 shows, big employment increases were made in the mechanical, chemical and building sectors. Particular growth points included motorcycles, domestic and office appliances such as cookers and typewriters, artificial fibres and public buildings. Substantial advances were made in the fields of land reclamation and rural settlement planning. Perhaps the most widely-known achievements of Fascism were the disappearance of beggars from the streets and the punctuality of trains.

But whatever limited gains were made by Fascism, the loss of personal liberty and, later, participation in war more than offset them. Structural problems remained acute. The problem of the South received little attention; autarchic industrial policies generally favoured manufacturing expansion in established northern centres. The only exceptions were the investments by IRI in metallurgical industries in Naples and the expansion of mining in Sardinia and Sicily. By 1938 the South, with 37 per cent of Italy's population, had only 18 per cent of manufacturing employment. Table 3.3 gives percentage data for industrial variables in eight regions (this should also be compared with Table 2.2 to pick out trends since 1901). Other disequilibria concerned wage rates. Hourly pay was nearly twice as high in the chemical and metallurgical trades as in the textile and clothing industries.[11] Partly this was explained by the sex of the workers, females dominating textile employment. Women's wages were kept exceptionally low — less than half the male rates — as an act of Fascist policy to discourage female employment in order to boost the birth rate.

Table 3.3: Industrial Indicators for Selected Regions in the Late 1930s

Region	% population 1936	% active population 1936	% industrial employees 1937-9	% installed power 1937-9	% industrial share capital 1937-9
Lombardy	13.5	14.9	30.0	27.9	40.0
Piedmont	8.2	10.1	14.8	17.2	13.0
Liguria	3.4	3.6	4.8	8.4	11.5
Veneto	9.9	9.9	8.5	7.2	5.6
Tuscany	6.9	7.1	7.4	7.9	4.0
Campania	8.6	7.5	4.9	5.4	4.9
Calabria	4.0	7.2	3.1	2.6	0.8
Sicily	9.2	7.2	3.1	2.6	0.8

Source: Romeo (1963), p.188.

War Again

In spite of Mussolini's belligerent philosophy and desire for military glory, the Italian economy was woefully unprepared for war.[12] Industrial output was a fraction of that of the countries Italy had to fight. Steel production was about one-third of the French and British outputs. Italian car production was 52,000 in 1938, compared to 300,000 in both France and Britain. Italy had only one-tenth of the locomotives of Great Britain. The stockpiling of essential war materials was difficult because autarchy had broken down Italy's trade links. After entering the war, Italy was immediately blockaded by Britain on the seas. This had a devastating effect because 60 per cent of Italian imports were essential foodstuffs, 80 per cent of which came via the Straits of Gibraltar or the Suez Canal. Only trade with Germany increased.

Had Italy chosen to remain neutral, substantial economic and industrial benefits would probably have accrued. In the period between the Anglo-French declaration of war on Germany in September 1939 and Italy's entry into the conflict in June 1940, the belligerents rushed to Italy with industrial orders, and Germany envisaged using Italy as a gap in the economic blockade imposed on her. Yet in spite of these manifest economic advantages of neutrality, Mussolini remained convinced that not to join Germany would be a sign of weakness and would bring down the wrath of Hitler whom he both feared and admired. In spite of the Duce's claims that Italy could mobilise 8 million bayonets and that her airplanes 'were so numerous they could blot out the sun', Italy's armed forces were rather pitiful — by June 1940 only 1,630,000 men could be mobilised.

Italy suffered enormous economic losses owing to the war. Air raids and destruction during the fighting inflicted vast-scale damage on buildings, roads, railways, ports and electricity installations. Disrupted internal communications aggravated local shortages of food and other essential goods. Cut off from northern suppliers, the South was deprived of most industrial produce. The seven weeks that intervened between Mussolini's fall in July 1943 and the signing of the armistice with the Allies in September allowed Germany to shift troops into Northern Italy, thereby splitting the country in two. The Germans were solidly entrenched in the North and Centre; the Allies occupied the South, including Sicily and Sardinia. Bitter fighting ensued for over a year and a half, wreaking much havoc on the country's landscape and economic life. In areas like the Florence-Bologna and Rome-Naples axes where prolonged fighting took place marked depopulation of devastated country areas occurred.[13]

Quantitative estimates of war damage seem to differ. The following selection of data, drawn from various sources,[14] should be taken as broadly indicative rather than precisely accurate. The industrial output index, having climbed appreciably before the war (1936 = 86, 1938 = 100, 1940 = 110), fell dramatically as soon as Italy entered the fray. By 1945 it stood at 29, the lowest since 1884. Steel output, one illustration, dropped from 2,322,856 tons in 1938 to 394,756 tons in 1945. In 1945 real *per capita* income was 49 per cent of the 1938 level and below that at unification. About one-third of the national wealth had been destroyed. Official deaths from war causes were 444,523, of whom 291,376 were military personnel. The colonies were lost, except for Somaliland over which Italy was to hold trusteeship for another ten years. Unemployment soared to 2 million, as it had done after the previous war. Average daily energy intake was 1,737 calories per head in 1945, compared to 2,652 before the war. Many Italians were on the verge of starvation. Agricultural production was down by 40 per cent; a severe drought in 1945 hardly helped. Inflation was rampant; the retail price index (1938 = 100) was 273 in 1943 and 2,392 in 1945.

Official destruction statistics showed especially heavy losses in housing and transport. Of the 33.6 million rooms existing in 1941, 1.8 million were completely destroyed, 1 million partially wrecked and 3.3 million damaged. On the railways, the war destroyed 25 per cent of track, 60 per cent of the locomotives and 50 per cent of the freight wagons. There were losses of 50 per cent of automobiles, 30 per cent of buses, 60 per cent of trams and 90 per cent of trucks. Over 8,000 bridges and 90 per cent of port buildings were destroyed or damaged.

Although industrial output in 1945 was only a quarter of the 1940 level, productive capacity only dropped by about 20 per cent. The damage to industrial plant was not as serious as originally expected. Much of the damage was concentrated in the South, where heavy fighting and bombardment had wiped out whole complexes and entire sections of the road and railway networks. IRI's patrimony lost 25-30 per cent of its capital value, with Finmare's fleet reduced to one-seventh of its pre-war tonnage. Alfa Romeo's aeronautics factory at Pomigliano d'Arco, Ansaldo's works at Pozzuoli and other industries in the Naples region were very heavily damaged. Ansaldo's workforce at Pozzuoli dropped from 6,000 during the war to only 300 in 1946. In Central Italy severe losses were incurred at Terni and Leghorn. Northern Italy's large industrial concerns were generally less damaged. Reduction of capacity in North Italian steelworks was estimated at 15 per cent whilst the textile industry and giants like Ansaldo of Genoa, Dalmine of Bergamo and Alfa Romeo and Motomeccanica of Milan emerged from the war practically unscathed. The preservation of electricity capacity in the North helped that region's recovery greatly, whilst in the Centre and the South power production was down by 32.5 per cent and 58.3 per cent respectively compared to the 1941 figures.

Notes and References

1. This argument is developed in detail by Webster (1975), on whom much of the early part of this chapter is based.
2. Ibid., pp.41-2.
3. These details of wartime industrial production are from Clough (1964), pp.178-85, 190, 204-5 and Romeo (1963), pp.113-21.
4. Clough (1964), pp.207-9.
5. Webster (1975), p.168.
6. Sarti (1971).
7. Hildebrand (1965), p.155.
8. Allen and Stevenson (1974), p.6.
9. Hildebrand (1965), p.350.

10. Gualemi, for example, maintains that much condemnation of Fascist economic policy is misplaced. Leaving the ethics of autarchy to one side, he argues that the Mussolini government, in common with other countries in the international capitalist system, pursued policies which generally developed Italian industry in an efficient and integrated way. See Gualemi (1976), p.115.

11. For detailed figures see *Annuario Confederazione Fascista degli Industriali* (1937), *15*, pp. 800-1.

12. See Clough (1964), pp.260-77.

13. See the map, based on 1936-47 comparison, described by Gambi (1949).

14. Allen and Stevenson (1974), pp.7-8; Caizzi (1965), p.519; Grindrod (1955), p.39; Repaci (1960); and *Annali della Congiuntura Economica Italiana 1938-47*, pp.1-2.

4 THE FRAMEWORK FOR POST-WAR DEVELOPMENT

The Rebirth of the Italian Economy

At the conclusion of hostilities in 1945, the Italian economy had reached its nadir. Internal commerce had broken down for want of transport and of goods to sell. Foreign commerce had been destroyed by autarchy, blockades and reliance on now-ruined Germany. Inflation was rampant — 9.4 per cent per month between July 1946 and September 1947. Foreign exchange and gold reserves were non-existent. Many Italian industrial workers were still held prisoners of war, or were stuck in deportation centres in Germany. The glamour of the Fascist regime had evaporated, along with ideas of national superiority. Prospects for recovery seemed hopeless; most experts thought that it would take at least a decade to regain pre-war levels of industrial production.

Yet, astoundingly, the country rose like a phoenix from the ashes of war. Industrial recuperation was particularly rapid. In 1948 the index of industrial production (1938 = 100) was at 102 and it continued to climb steadily, reaching 164 by 1953. How did this economic fairy story come about? Like many cases of rapid economic growth from initially unpromising positions, the recovery resulted from a fortuituous concatenation of circumstances which combined economic factors (to be dealt with shortly) with the emergence of an exceptionally talented and dedicated group of men such as Alcide De Gasperi, Luigi Einaudi and Amintore Fanfani.[1]

Within little more than a year of the cessation of hostilities a new constitution was drafted and the machinery of the new state was functioning well. A referendum disposed of the monarchy and Alcide De Gasperi took over as the principal political leader of the reconstruction period. In the peace settlement, signed at Paris on 10 February 1947, Italy was treated with considerable leniency from the economic point of view. The colonies were lost (except Somaliland which Italy retained until 1960), but this was probably a blessing in disguise since Italy's overseas territories had been an economic liability. Britain and the USA asked for no reparations and pressed other powers to reduce their claims. Out of the shattered morale of military defeat and the political collapse of Fascism emerged, amazingly, a strong desire for economic progress. New industrial techniques — the backlog of unexploited technology — were introduced. Natural gas began to be intensively exploited. Foreign trade also developed. Faced by huge unemployment, which reached 2.4 million in 1948, labour was generally co-operative in achieving greater production; indeed the new constitution declared Italy to be a republic founded on labour.

Two factors were particularly decisive in the recovery period of the late 1940s: American aid and Luigi Einaudi's monetary policy. American aid came in two phases. In the first phase, 1945-7, the prime needs were to feed the population, free the country from economic paralysis and alleviate the trade and payments deficit (£256 million in 1946). About £295 million was provided by the United Nations Relief and Rehabilitation Administration programme, the US Foreign Economic Administration and other gifts and remittances. In 1947 this *ad hoc* response was replaced by a more concerted effort to realise certain economic goals, made more attainable by the quelling of inflation. Thus came into being the European Recovery Program (ERP), also known as the Marshall Plan, which covered the period 1948-52 and provided aid, mostly gifts, to West European nations recovering from war. Italy received £757 million, 12 per cent of total ERP aid. Without it, Italian industrial recovery would have been much slower, for 70 per cent of the sum received went on industry, railways and public works.

The second factor was the solving of the inflation problem by Luigi Einaudi's classical economic policy of hard money and selective credit. Before he became Budget Minister and Vice Prime Minister in 1947 Einaudi had, as Governor of the Banca d'Italia, made a survey of Italian industries, categorising them on the basis of their productive and competitive potential. Within his 1947 policy of tight money to combat inflation, Einaudi made credit available only to those firms with good competitive possibilities. Other firms were left to fend for themselves, with the result that many sold out or went bankrupt. Italian industry was thus rationalised on a more competitive basis but there were side effects.

One was the greater concentration of capital in the North, to the obvious detriment of southern industrial development. Politically the 'Einaudi Line' was made possible by the restructuring of De Gasperi's government in 1947 (excluding the Communists who at that time were dedicated to precipitating crises as a prelude to revolution) and the splitting of the trade union movement in 1948. If Einaudi's policy reeked of century-old Piedmontese economic liberalism and if it was criticised by Keynesians and by the American aid experts, no matter: 'Einaudi's masterpiece' had the final answer — it worked. Prices stabilised, industry grew, and unemployment started to come down.[2]

The census year 1951 marked the first year after the war that could be regarded as relatively normal in economic terms. By then the average Italian had recovered his pre-war level of prosperity. Italy was placed exactly in the middle of the 55 nations supplying *per capita* income figures to the United Nations Statistical Office. It could, therefore, rightly be described as semi-developed. The real develoment problem, however, still lay in the South which at that time comprised 42 per cent of the land, 38 per cent of the population and only 20 per cent of the national income. Whilst *per capita* income levels in the main industrial centres of the Po Valley were not far below those of northern Europe, southern incomes and living conditions were more akin to those of the Third World. Southern provinces such as Agrigento, Avellino and Potenza had average incomes of less than 20 per cent of the figure for Milan. Even the richest southern provinces — Naples, Bari, Cagliari — only attained 40 per cent of the Milanese level.

Regional contrasts were especially marked in the industrial field. Only 21.3 per cent of the southern labour force was employed in industry, as against 36.2 per cent in the North. The South, with over one-third of the national labour force, counted only 22.5 per cent of national industrial labour and 19.5 per cent of the manufacturing industry labour. Unemployment and underemployment were higher in the South, and activity rates lower (37.1 per cent as against 48.9 per cent in 1951). Industrial capital per worker in the North was ten times the figure for the South where most industrial units were small, artisan concerns.

The Economic Miracle

From 1950 to 1962 Italy enjoyed an unprecedented period of economic and industrial growth. The world 'miracle' is often applied to this period, signifying the unexpected and spectacular way in which the country, modestly endowed by nature, ill-used by Fascism and ruined by war, burst forth economically. More prosaically, this period is sometimes referred to as 'the long boom'. Italy's rate of growth at this time was more rapid than that of any other West European country. Only West Germany was on a par. It was especially fast between 1959 and 1962, coinciding with Italy's accession to the Common Market in 1958 and the phenomenal growth of exports that trade liberalisation produced. Hildebrand, who has studied the boom in detail, calculated the following compound annual rates of increase for the period 1950-61:

total real product 5.9 per cent, industrial output 8.8 per cent, real consumption 4.7 per cent, real investment 9 per cent and real exports 13.5 per cent.[3] The boom was led by the massive expansion of export-oriented northern industry. Firms contributing significantly to the expansion were automobiles, chemicals, oil products, electrical goods, furniture, plastics and artificial fibres. Domestically-oriented industries such as food and textiles expanded much more slowly, although housing and general construction became big business with the need to reconstruct war damage and provide infrastructures.

Economic progress during the 'miracle' was without parallel in the country's history. The rate of growth was about twice that of the industrial growth spurt at the turn of the century. Unemployment, still 8.7 per cent in 1956, fell to 2.4 per cent by 1963. Fluctuations of expansion and contraction were diminished to such as extent that one could justifiably speak of the end of the economic cycle.

There are a number of explanations and interpretations of the 'economic miracle'.[4] American aid was one factor, or course, facilitating industrial investment and the bulk purchase of industrial raw materials. In an economy being rebuilt after war damage, profit margins were high and there was a seemingly endless array of investment opportunities for Italian entrepreneurs. The continued expansion of world trade and the favourable terms of trade with raw-material-supplying countries enabled Italy to be quickly inserted into the American-led world capitalist trading system, participating in such institutions as GATT, OECD, IMF and the World Bank. In February 1953 Italy entered into the European Coal and Steel Community, which encouraged free trade in coal and ferrous metals amongst the six co-operating members. It was also a founder member of the Common Market, created by the Treaty of Rome which came into effect on 1 January 1958. Joining the EEC and the decision to adopt a free trade policy towards foreign countries furnished Italian industry with a competitive prod which produced an expansion-oriented inventiveness amongst industrialists. They also enjoyed a strong bargaining position over a divided labour movement. Governmental influence was decisive. The classical flavour of the 1947 monetary policy continued in the 1950s when it was blended with some of the newer doctrines of state encouragement of economic development. The bold policies of ENI, the state hydrocarbons agency created in 1953, resulted in the exploitation of natural gas in the Po Valley as a steady supply of cheap fuel for northern industrial development. The Sinigaglia Plan rationalised IRI's steel plants so that for the first time Italy had a steel industry operating more or less at world market prices. Even more far-reaching was the change in the automobile industry to a mass instead of a luxury market, symbolised by Fiat's decision to manufacture the '600' in 1953. By 1960 industry contributed 46.6 per cent of national income, compared to 34.2 per cent during 1936-40.

Although industrial growth continued beyond the 'long boom', economic downswing interrupted the pattern in 1963-4 and 1969-70. The twenty-year intercensal period 1951-71, during which total industrial output roughtly quintupled, breaks down into three distinct phases of moderate, rapid and slow growth, as shown by the indices in Table 4.1. Nevertheless, it is a measure of the magnitude of post-war economic growth that real *per capita* income increased more during 1951-71 than in the entire period 1861-1951.

Table 4.1: Indices of Growth, 1951-71

| | Annual % changes | | |
	1951-57	1958-63	1964-71
GNP	5.3	6.6	4.7
Manufacturing output	6.8	11.7	5.4
Productivity	4.8	7.2	5.0
Gross fixed investments	9.8	10.2	1.6

Source: Ciocca *et al.* (1975), p.314.

The highly encouraging aggregate statistics for industrial growth almost entirely conceal the continuing problem of the South. In relative terms, the boom had a detrimental impact on the South, widening the income gap between the Mezzogiorno and the rest of the nation. The fastest growing region during the boom (Latium) grew at twice the rate of the slowest (Sardinia).[5] In 1951 the South's mean *per capita* income was 48.2 per cent of the level of the rest of the nation; in 1960 this had become 42.3 per cent.

It was in the boom period that the government initiated its cautious plans to alleviate poverty in the South. The year 1950 saw two important pieces of legislation: the land reform, which expropriated large areas of inefficiently-farmed southern latifundia; and the setting up of a special fund for developing the South, the Cassa per il Mezzogiorno. The widening income gap during the 1950s does not necessarily entail utter condemnation of southern invervention, for the South's income did rise in absolute terms, and it is perhaps not surprising that it could not keep up with the booming industrial economy of the North. Nevertheless, it has been claimed that it was the North that was, in the early years, the main beneficiary of the Cassa funds since this region was the supplier of heavy equipment for improving southern infrastructures. Only in the late 1950s did the Cassa begin to try to promote industrial expansion directly in the South. A more detailed evaluation of southern industrial policy and the role of the Cassa is reserved for Chapter 11.

Comparison of figures from the 1951 and 1961 Industrial Censuses reveals the extent to which the industrial boom was spatially polarised. Three-quarters of new industrial jobs created were in the North, which gained 1,025,518 industrial employees, an increase of 35.9 per cent over 1951. The South gained 117,556, an increase of only 16 per cent. The relative share of the South in total industrial employment fell from 17.3 per cent in 1951 to 15.1 per cent in 1961. Moreover, much of the 'industry' which existed or developed in the South during the 'miracle' was artisan activity, small scale and economically precarious. In 1961 the average southern manufacturing establishment contained 3.4 persons, compared to 10.3 persons in northern manufacturing units. Some interesting survey work done at this time by Sylos-Labini showed that southern industrial employment was far more precarious than that in the North (i.e. there was a greater concentration in insecure jobs like construction), and that the proportion of 'precarious' industrial jobs was increasing in the South and decreasing in the North. For instance, Piedmont had 16 per cent industrial employment classified as precarious in 1951, dropping to 10 per cent in 1961. Lombardy's figures were 20 per cent (1951) and 10 per cent (1961). The southern region of Calabria had 58 per cent of its industrial jobs classed as precarious in 1951, rising to 61 per cent in 1961. Sicily's figures were 51 per cent (1951) and 57 per cent (1961), Campania's 53 per cent (1951) and 55 per cent (1961).[6]

Economic Planning and the Structure of the Industrial Economy

The long boom obviated the need for economic planning. The northern industrial economy seemed to be in such a healthily expanding state that there was little pressure to tamper with it. It is true that as early as 1954 the Vanoni Ten-Year Plan had come into being, but this was not so much a plan as a loosely connected set of proposals.[7] With the end of the boom in the mid and late 1960s, realisation of the need for economic planning emerged, but a coherent set of easy-to-grasp goals and policies has proved difficult to identify. A national economic plan of sorts came into being in 1965, but basic disagreements occurred over the form it should take. Within government and allied circles three schools of thought are identifiable.[8] Liberal economists like Ugo Papi favour 'indicative planning' along French lines, with the government using techniques of encouragement and persuasion, such as tax and credit incentives, to influence the workings of the market economy, and with the 'plan' being a set of economic projections rather than a list of firm commitments. A second group of economists, including Pasquale Saraceno, believed that government is bound, to a certain extent, by the goals set forth in its plans and must therefore be prepared to intervene directly to help make the forecasts come true. This is 'normative planning'. Thirdly, there are more radical economists such as Paolo Sylos-Labini who insist that planning must embody changes in the socio-economic system, including profound structural changes in the public sector and severe checks on the activities of big business. The centrist Christian Democrats, in power in various forms and coalitions since the war, tend to belong to the liberal school of thought and regard normative economic planning as an undesirable first step on the road to collectivism. Politicians in the post-war period have skirted round rather than squarely confronted planning issues. Economic planning is regarded as a ritualistic shibboleth rather than a definite policy based on careful analysis of ends and means. Planning language is often vague and esoteric; projections are broad rather than specific; much room is purposely left for ambiguity. Such tendencies towards generic approximation are termed in Italian *pressapochismo* or 'just-about-ism'. Ambiguity and compromise are usually essential as a means of keeping the shaky coalition governments of post-war Italy together.[9]

There also seems to be a cultural bias against planning in Italy, a lack of rapport between industrial and administrative elites. To a certain extent this reflects their different regional origins — industrialists from the North, administrators from the South. Figures quoted by Acquaviva and Santuccio reveal that the South, with 36 per cent of Italy's population, supplies 65 per cent of the administrative class, 77 per cent of judges and 76 per cent of prefects; the North, with 45 per cent of the population, supplies 14, 7 and 6 per cent, respectively.[10] Although competition for secure clerical jobs in government is intense, the bureaucracy as an institution is ridiculed and reviled. It is overmanned, inefficient and corrupt. Numbers employed in public administration have increased more rapidly than those working in any other sector. While the total population increased by 74 per cent between 1881 and 1961, administrative personnel multiplied fourteen times. The trend continues: administrative personnel in the private sector increased by 12 per cent during 1961-71, those in the public sector increased by 34 per cent. Public service personnel now account for 30 per cent of tertiary sector employment in Italy, compared to 13 per cent in France, 14 per cent in Belgium and 19 per cent in West Germany.[11]

Lack of co-ordination is another serious problem. Feuds between various ministries; the existence of separate and sometimes contradictory plans for the South; the relative independence enjoyed by quasi-state bodies like IRI and ENI; the tendency to cope with each new problem by creating a new agency or passing as 'special law' specific to that industry, city or region — all are manifestations of a lack of common purpose in economic planning which reflects the overwhelming necessity of political compromise. Administrative criteria for the allocation of public funds are so archaic that money often goes unspent or is used for other purposes. No public money can be spent in Italy without going through at least five administrative stages; the average delay between the granting of funds and the decision on how to spend them is reckoned to be 900 days.[12]

The success of post-war industrial growth — at least until the late 1960s — has therefore been largely through market forces and private initiative. The extent of the change as it affected employment between 1951 and 1971 is shown in Table 4.2, the most conspicuous feature of which is the enormous fall in numbers employed in agriculture — a drop of almost 5 million. The magnitude of this reduction can be appreciated by considering the fact that 2.6 million left agriculture during the whole of the previous 90 years (1861-1951). The outflow from agriculture was greater in the 1961-71 decade (43 per cent reduction in numbers of farm workers) than in the 1951-61 period (31 per cent drop), although the rate of decline has slowed during 1971-81 (Table 1.4). The proportion of the population engaged in agriculture declined from 40 per cent in 1951 to 10.1 per cent in 1981.

Table 4.2 shows that the 5 million loss from the primary sector is compensated by gains in all other sectors — manufacturing, construction, public administration and the various tertiary activities. In spite of the industrial boom, manufacturing employment has not increased spectacularly; the 1.5 million increase in jobs during 1951-71 accounts for only a part of the outflow from agriculture. Rather more dramatic has been the increase in numbers of people working in construction and

Table 4.2: Employment by Sector 1951-71

Sector	1951 '000	%	1961 '000	%	1971 '000	%
Agriculture and extractive	8,785	44.6	6,357	31.1	3,768	19.5
Manufacturing	4,456	22.6	5,485	26.9	6,011	31.0
Construction	1,109	5.6	1,896	9.3	1,874	9.7
Trade and allied services	1,874	9.5	2,492	12.2	2,745	14.2
Various services	1,627	8.2	1,808	8.9	1,991	10.3
Electricity, gas, water, communications	704	3.6	975	4.8	1,202	6.2
Public administration	1,138	5.8	1,415	6.9	1,805	9.3
Totals (may not tally due to rounding)	19,623	100.0	20,430	100.0	19,395	100.0

Source: Allen and Stevenson (1974), p.105.

public administration. Many females left the labour force altogether. Total employment fell between 1951 and 1971 even though the total population increased from 47.5 million to 54.1 million. Inevitably, the activity rate fell concomitantly, from 43.5 per cent in 1951 to 34.7 per cent in 1971, but then rising to 39.8 per cent by 1981 (see Table 1.4). Even so, Italian activity rates are amongst the lowest in the world; within Europe only Portugal has a lower figure. The continuing rapid decline in agricultural employment, the stabilisation and now slow decline of industrial employment and the growth of the service sector are characteristics of the 'post-industrial' nature of the contemporary Italian economy.

Although all major fields of industry except textiles increased their employment during 1951-71, 78 per cent of the growth in manufacturing jobs came from four branches; engineering (44 per cent alone), chemicals, clothing and metal-working. Nevertheless, it must be stressed that the notable expansion of high technology northern industry during the 'miracle' was the result of large injections of capital rather than reliance on massive inputs of labour. This tended to emphasise further the 'dual' structure of Italian industry, meaning a polarisation between a few giants and a myriad of tiny workshops. In 1971 88.8 per cent of manufacturing establishments had a workforce of less than 10 persons, and 23.3 per cent of the workforce was in such tiny units. Table 4.3 shows that these figures are not changing dramatically. In 1981 the respective percentages were 84.7 and 21.5. The fall in the construction industry figure between 1961 and 1981 is due to the very marked

Table 4.3: Mean Number of Workers per Firm by Industrial Sector, 1951-81

Sector	1951	1961	1971	1981
Extractive	14.3	14.2	12.2	15.8
Manufacturing	5.5	7.4	8.4	8.3
Construction	12.3	13.3	6.2	3.7
Gas, water and electricity	11.8	13.3	17.5	22.5

Sources: Allen and Stevenson (1974), p.32; *6° Censimento Generale dell' Industria e del Commercio, 1981, vol. I Primi Risultati sulle Imprese e sulle Unità Locali, Tomo I Dati Nazionali, Regionali e Provinciali,* Rome, ISTAT (1983), p.5.

growth in the number of establishments, from 67,500 in 1961 to 326,000 in 1981.

Although the small, family-run businesses are in a sense still the roots of Italian industry, there has been an increasing power cluster around the 'big four' of Fiat, ENI, IRI and Montedison which dominate the Italian economy (such firms as Pirelli, Olivetti and Assicurazioni Generali are closely allied to this quadrumvirate). The eight Italian firms appearing in the Fortune list of the 200 leading non-American firms are listed in Table 4.4; note that for the purposes of this ranking the government-controlled IRI complex does not count as a single enterprise.

The big corporations have responded to the economic problems of the post-boom period by searching for higher levels of productivity and by reducing labour requirements. This had led to mergers and associa-

Table 4.4: Italy's Largest Industrial Companies

Company	Sector	Annual sales £m	Assets £m	Employees no.	Rank outside USA
Montedison	chemicals	1,158	2,281	142,326	8
Fiat	cars	1,068	814	158,445	13
ENI	oil	722	2,013	59,960	28
Pirelli	tyres	475	497	69,285	54
Italsider (IRI)	steel	443	1,325	37,427	64
Olivetti	typewriters	296	166	60,681	101
Snia Viscosa	artificial fibres	221	216	29,500	135
Alfa Romeo (IRI)	cars	158	143	17,858	185

Source: Willis (1971), p.190.

tions with large foreign companies, thus giving Italian big industry a multinational character. The industrial leaders form a co-ordinated group because of their common northern origins and their growing interchangeability in terms of personal connections and joint board memberships. It has been claimed that the 'big four' can put together almost any deal necessary and in recent years there has been increasing co-operation between them to plug the gaps in Italy's industrial capacity.[13] Italy has, incidentally, almost no restrictive practices or monopolies policy, a fact not unrelated to the financial ties between big business and the Christian Democrat and Liberal parties.

The small firms that have survived have done so by decentralising the productive process by returning to the 'putting out' or 'cottage' system — the reverse strategy to that of the larger companies. In this way, they employ marginal, low-wage labour exploited by meagre piece-rates. They lower labour costs, by-pass trade unions and avoid insurance and social security payments. Such a system has always been common in the clothing, footwear and leather trades, but it is now being extended to hosiery, light engineering and manufacturing. Statistics on cottage industry workers are not available, but they probably number about 2 million, mostly women. This backward structural development has been forced by the length of the recession as the only way to maintain competitiveness. The result, however, is a growing structural duality in Italian industry which partly coincides with, and therefore reinforces, the North-South geographical dualism. The existence of a large area of hidden employment in the putting-out system also deprives the government of tax revenue and an adequate map of the economic reality on which it ought to operate. Entepreneurial effort in many firms is directed towards finding formulas which evade the norms of wage standards. This is a system of hidden wage dualism.[14]

Finally, in this section, we need to say something about the spatial structure of Italian industry as revealed in recent censuses. Figure 4.1, compiled on a provincial basis, shows the continued concentration of manufacturing employment in the northern heartland of the Po Plain. Table 4.5 gives more detailed data for 1961 and 1971 but at the cruder scale of the regions. Again Lombardy and Piedmont emerge as the manufacturing employment leaders. Calabria actually lost manufacturing employment over the 1961-71 period — the only region to do so. Calabria and Basilicata are the least industrialised regions of the country; each has less than one-tenth of their working population engaged in industrial occupations (excluding construction), and each has less than 1 per cent of the nation's total industrial employment.

Table 4.5: Employment in Industry (Manufacturing and Extractive) by Region, 1961 and 1971

	Industrial workers as % active pop'n		% change 1961-71	Industrial workers as % national total, 1971	Active pop'n as % national total, 1971	Ratio
	1961	1971				
Piedmont-Val d'Aosta	40.0	45.3	+13.2	15.0	9.5	1.58
Liguria	24.0	24.8	+ 3.3	2.9	3.4	0.85
Lombardy	45.8	48.0	+ 4.8	29.9	17.8	1.68
Trentino-Alto Adige	17.5	22.3	+27.4	1.3	1.6	0.81
Veneto	23.8	33.9	+42.4	9.3	7.9	1.18
Friuli-Venezia Giulia	22.5	31.2	+38.7	2.6	2.3	1.13
Emilia-Romagna	23.3	29.8	+27.9	8.6	8.2	1.05
Tuscany	28.9	34.6	+19.7	8.2	6.8	1.21
Umbria	16.5	25.7	+55.7	1.3	1.4	0.93
Marche	15.4	25.8	+67.5	2.5	2.7	0.93
Latium	13.2	16.4	+24.2	4.7	8.2	0.57
Abruzzi-Molise	9.5	12.0	+26.3	1.4	2.7	0.52
Campania	13.2	16.5	+25.0	4.4	7.7	0.57
Apulia	9.1	14.2	+56.0	3.1	6.2	0.50
Basilicata	5.7	9.1	+59.6	0.3	1.1	0.27
Calabria	7.0	6.7	− 4.3	0.7	3.2	0.24
Sicily	10.0	11.3	+13.0	2.8	7.0	0.40
Sardinia	11.3	13.1	+16.0	1.0	2.3	0.43
Italy	23.4	28.5	+22.0	100.0	100.0	1.00

Source: Sica (1973), pp.19,22.

Figure 4.1: Index of Manufacturing Employment, 1981

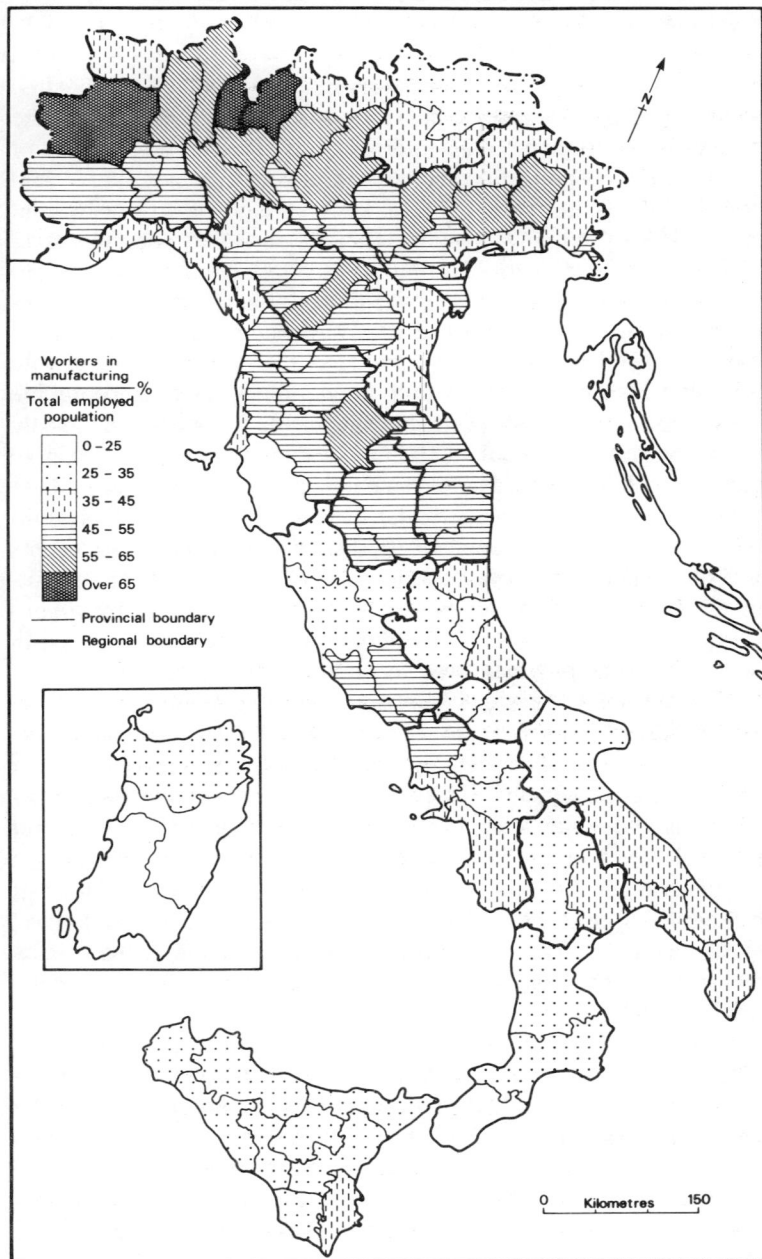

Workers in
manufacturing
——————— %
Total employed
population

0 – 25
25 – 35
35 – 45
45 – 55
55 – 65
Over 65

——— Provincial boundary
——— Regional boundary

0 Kilometres 150

Source: *6° Censimento Generale dell'Industria e del Commercio, 1981, Vol. I Primi Risultati sulle Imprese e sulle Unità, Locali, Tomo I Dati Nazionali, Regionali e Provinciali,* Rome: ISTAT (1983).

The State Holding Section and Its Role in Italian Industrial Development

Mixing public funds with private is very much part of the Italian industrial system. IRI — the Istituto per la Ricostruzione Industriale — is the prime example. Italian public enterprise has attracted a great deal of attention from economists and industrial planners outside Italy,[15] and has been used as a model for state intervention agencies in Britain, France, West Germany, Sweden, Canada and Australia. The state holding sector made vital contributions to Italian industrial development during the post-war reconstruction and boom periods, and continued to expand in the 1960s and 1970s. Although the state sector was originally established primarily because of the need to rescue private concerns which had fallen on hard times, its role is now to provide services and intermediate products that private firms could not easily produce because of the scale or risk involved, and whose foreign supply could be too heavy a burden for the balance of trade. At present there are approximately 350 firms in which there is a total or partial state participation; they employ around 700,000 people. State industry accounts for about 45 per cent of total fixed investment, 11 per cent of gross output, and 8 per cent of employment in industry (excluding construction) in Italy. Between 1951 and 1971 about 40 per cent of the increase in manufacturing employment was accounted for by state firms.

The state holding sector comprises four integrated iron and steel works producing 98 per cent of the cast iron and 66 per cent of the steel produced in Italy, 40 per cent of the national oil requirement, 80 per cent of chemicals and pharmaceuticals, 80 per cent of banking, 45 per cent of the motorway network and the management of all air transport and much of maritime transport.[16] The state is also gaining ground in such fields as cars, textiles, urban infrastructure, electronic and nuclear engineering, foodstuffs and supermarkets. Some concentrations of state firms are massive, forming the main economic framework of whole towns in the cases of Genoa, Trieste, Piombino, Terni, Taranto and Gela.

State-controlled firms have it within their power to set up groups of plants simultaneously to create those external economies of scale which might, especially in the industrially barren South, be otherwise lacking. Such opportunities are often unavailable in the private sector. There is also the effect of stimulating private competition. IRI's decision to set up the Alfa Sud car plant at Pomigliano d'Arco near Naples has forced a private firm like Fiat to establish competitive facilities in the South in order to preserve a share of the southern market. Yet, quantitatively, the state sector has never come to terms with the scale of the problem of the South, supplying, between 1961 and 1971, an annual average of 5,300 new industrial jobs, as against an annual outmigration from the region of 230,000. Its action has inevitably always been set within the ideological limits that allow for manoeuvring of fiscal and financial incentives and provision of infrastructures in the 'hope' that the underdevelopment problem will be solved. Nor has the state sector been free of the corruption which plagues Italian political life; in December 1979, for example, the president of ENI, the state hydrocarbon agency, was suspended for alleged irregularites in dealings over supplies of Saudi Arabian oil.

Until about 1963 the state industries worked hand-in-glove with private enterprise. Latterly, however, the government has tacitly allowed state enterprises to sever some of their links with private industry. This change coincided with the end of the 1950-62 boom and with the shift in the Christian Democrat coalition structure known as the 'opening to the Left'. Now it seems to be official policy to build up state control in many large-scale and key industries, sometimes to the detriment of the private sector. The increase in state industrial activity has been especially marked at times when private industrial growth is weak, and vice versa. In this way the state sector tends to equalise overall industrial growth rates.

IRI and ENI, the two main holding companies, have also acted politically, drumming up support for their demands in parliament, seeking to acquire positions of power within the major government parties and trying to influence public opinion. This role has been played with particular aggressiveness by ENI, especially when it was under the dynamic leadership of Enrico Mattei in the years before 1962 (when Mattei was killed in an air crash). Both IRI and ENI are said to have financed the efforts of Amintore Fanfani to restructure the Christian Democrat Party and lead it to a *rapprochement* with the socialists in the late 1950s and early 1960s.[17] Like many big private corporations in Italy, ENI also finances a mass-circulation newspaper, *Il Giorno* of Milan

The structure of state participation in Italian economic life is rather complex. Only the bare outlines will be sketched here. Basically the system is hierarchical. At the top level are the governmental institutions (the Ministry of State Holdings, responsible in turn to CIPE, the Interministerial Committee for Economic Planning); at the middle level are the *enti di gestione* or public entrepreneurial organisations; and at the

base are the operating companies which have the juridical form of joint-
stock companies with their share capital wholly or partly owned by an
ente di gestione. The linchpins of the state holding system are the *enti*,
which are five in number. These are IRI (industrial reconstruction),
ENI (hydrocarbons), EFIM (manufacturing industry), EAGAT
(spas) and the Cinema agency. A sixth, EAGAM (metallurgy and mining), was wound up in 1977, its shareholdings passing to IRI and ENI.
The turnover, investment and employment characteristics of these *enti*
are given in Table 4.6, from which it can be seen that IRI and ENI between them account for 93 per cent of the turnover and investment and
89 per cent of the employees in the state holding sector.

Table 4.6: State Shareholding Enterprises: Turnover, Investment
and Employment, 1974

	Turnover billion lire	%	Gross fixed investment billion lire	%	Employment '000 persons	%
IRI	8,180.2	65.5	1,852.0	63.9	514.7	75.2
ENI	4,674.0	27.1	847.8	29.2	92.4	13.5
EFIM	662.3	3.8	124.1	4.3	40.6	5.9
EGAM	667.0	3.4	67.0	2.3	34.0	5.0
Others	25.1	0.2	5.8	0.3	3.2	0.4
Total	14,208.6	100.0	2,896.7	100.0	684.6	100.0

Source: Keyser and Windle (1978), p.77.

The three-tier structure described above has several elaborations.
IRI has a number of *finanziarie* or financial holding companies which
are interposed between it and the operating companies. Each *finanziaria* is responsible for a group of companies operating in a particular
industrial or service sector, such as shipbuilding or telephones. Some
IRI *finanziarie* were created before the war, as was mentioned in the
last chapter. These were STET (telephones), Finmare (shipping) and
Finsider (iron and steel). Further holding companies were formed after
the war: Finmeccanica (1947), Finelettrica (1952 but dissolved in
1962 when electricity was nationalised) and Fincantieri (1959). The
most recent is Italstat (1973) which co-ordinates the public works
activities of the group. Under each *finanziaria* a series of companies
producing in the same sector operates. Thus, for example, Finmare
embraces the Italia, Lloyd Triestino, Adriatica, and Tirrenia shipping
lines; Fincantieri includes Italcantieri, Ansaldo and other shipyards;

Finsider includes Italsider (the largest individual IRI operating company), Dalmine, Terni and 25 other iron and steel concerns. Where there are very few operating companies in a sector, IRI control is direct. This is the case, for example, with the three big banks (Banca Commerciale, Credito Italiano and Banco di Roma), the national airline Alitalia, the radio and television network RAI-TV and the Autostrade motorway sector. The spatial structure of IRI's operations, classified by sectoral employment, is portrayed in Figure 4.2, which shows predominant clustering of activities in Milan, Genoa, Trieste, Piombino, Terni, Naples and Taranto. All told, IRI controls some 150 firms.

In ENI the equivalent of IRI's *finanziarie,* called *capogruppi,* are involved more directly in production. Created out of AGIP in 1953, ENI now controls 160 companies, mainly concerned with the exploitation, production, refining and distribution of natural gas and oil. It has also spread into nuclear energy, chemicals, textiles, plant engineering and construction. Half of ENI's plants are abroad. The main *capogruppi* are AGIP (the key organisation, involved in exploration, exploitation and marketing of oil and gas products), AGIP Nucleare (nuclear energy), ANIC (refining and petrochemicals) and SNAM (pipeline and tanker transport). SNAM Progetti and Saipem are construction groups building refineries, pipelines and other energy-related projects.

From the financial point of view, the *enti* are wholly government-controlled, their equity capital being provided by a special endowment fund. The layers below the *enti* can seek equity capital from the public, although the *enti* retain the controlling interest. Given the fragmented nature of private shareholding, such control can be achieved with as little as 15 per cent of the equity capital. This participation of private capital distinguishes the state holding sector from the truly nationalised industries (such as railways and electricity) which are virtually entirely government-financed. The state holding sector also has much greater freedom of operation.

Table 4.7 shows the economic distribution of state holding enterprises. Investments in the manufacturing sector accounted for about half the total state holding investment in 1967 and 1976, but rose well above this proportion between these two dates, due largely to the expansion in investment in iron and steel. The main sectors are iron and steel, hydrocarbons, telephones and motorways, together making up about three-quarters of total state sector investment.

Few can deny that the state holding sector has played a major role in Italian post-war economic life. Posner and Woolf [18] claim that the

Figure 4.2: IRI Industrial Plants

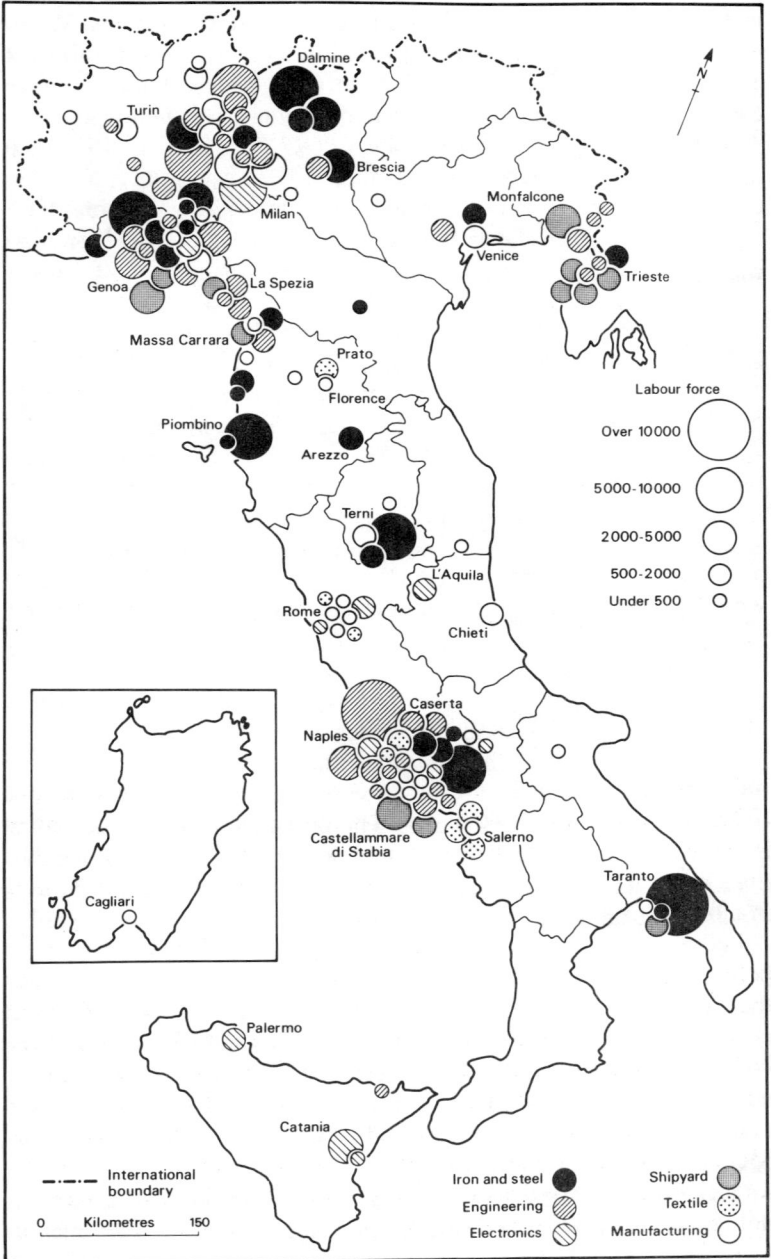

Source: Borlenghi *et al.* (1976).

Table 4.7: State Shareholding Enterprises: Investment by Sector, 1967-76 (per cent)

	1967	1970	1973	1976
Iron and steel	19.62	21.61	26.01	16.50
Cement	0.23	1.25	0.90	0.29
Engineering	4.85	12.45	7.48	7.08
Shipbuilding	1.56	0.65	1.63	1.39
Hydrocarbons	16.94	16.20	10.24	17.70
Chemicals	2.02	9.24	6.73	4.02
Textiles	1.30	0.57	0.58	0.56
Others	3.05	2.36	3.15	1.65
Total, Manufacturing	49.57	64.33	56.72	49.29
Telephones	22.32	17.67	27.47	34.00
Radio	2.69	0.63	0.25	0.23
Shipping	0.66	0.65	0.81	6.78
Airlines	6.75	4.48	2.91	2.19
Highways	16.81	10.37	11.02	6.13
Others	1.20	1.87	0.80	1.38
Total, Services	50.43	35.67	43.24	50.71
Grand Total	100.00	100.00	100.00	100.00

Note: The percentage figures hide a progressive increase in total investment through time: a roughly five-fold increase between 1967 and 1976. The 'grand total' figures for the four years given in the table are (in billion lire) 684.1, 1,325.2, 2,401.8 and 3,476.2.

Source: Keyser and Windle (1978), p.75.

Italian economic miracle owed as much to the activities and methods of IRI and ENI as it did to other developments such as the EEC, foreign investment and the rise in domestic consumption. The sector's operations in key areas like steel, oil and chemicals have made for lower costs in other industries dependent on these products.

Perhaps more important, however, is the state holding sector's *social* policy implications. In the early post-war years IRI held on to labour that, on sheer economic criteria, should have been laid off. Plant closures have been averted and delayed. Both IRI and ENI have taken on board 'lame ducks' and have occasionally turned them into profitable concerns: examples are ENI's intervention with Lanerossi (artificial fibres) and IRI's with ATES (electronics) and Costruzioni Metalliche Finsider (steel structures). During the 1960s this 'hospital for sick firms' role diminished. Currently there are too many patients, not enough bed spaces and too little financial 'medicine' available. In any case a new agency, GEPI, was set up in 1971 with the specific aim of rescuing small and medium firms in 'transitory difficulties'.[19]

The second, and more important 'social' role of the state holding sector has been its contribution to the post-war development effort in the South. A law of 1971 stipulated that at least 80 per cent of investments in new plant by state-held industries and 60 per cent of total investments by the state holding sector must be located in the South (proportions of 60 per cent and 40 per cent respectively had operated since a law of 1957). The 1971 law also establishes that companies with a state participation must make at least 30 per cent of the total value of their purchases from companies in the South. This regulation, apart from being impractical because of the absence of appropriate supply industries located in the South, is also illegal in terms of the Treaty of Rome which forbids such preferential buying.

The state holding sector has made serious attempts to comply with the 1957 and 1971 laws, although in locating its various enterprises in the South it has had the full support of the Cassa package of industrial incentives which was originally designed to attract private industries. Virtually all the sector's investment in new industrial plant has been in the South and between 1958 and 1971 49 per cent of its manufacturing investments and 40 per cent of its total investments have been there.

These geographical changes in the sector's investments inevitably coincide with similar though less dramatic changes in respect of employment (less dramatic because many of the major investments — iron and steel, oil refining, petrochemicals — were in capital intensive plants). In 1957 19 per cent of the state sector's manufacturing employment was in the South, in 1971 28 per cent. Over 1958-70 the sector's industrial investments accounted for over one-third of total southern industrial investment. The sector's manufacturing activities employed 6 per cent of southern manufacturing employees in 1958, 10 per cent in 1970.[20] Beyond manufacturing, the state sector has made other contributions to southern development, notably the motorway programme, heavily involving IRI and pushed ahead with remarkable speed.

Outside of the directives given to the state holding sector to locate a certain proportion of its activities in the South, there has been little overall guidance given to state industry by higher authorities. Since the failure of economic planning in the 1960s and the absence of any form of proper economic plan since 1971, CIPE has had to carry out its overseeing role in an economic vacuum. The state holding system now operates without the advantages of either the capitalist or the socialist worlds: government has impeded market forces thus preventing necessary rationalisation, and yet has not provided the potential advantages of centralised planning. Increasing political interference by the Christian Democrats and the falling standards of management have tarnished the previous image of the Italian state holding sector as an enlightened method of applying modern management techniques to achieve government strategies. In contrast to the dynamism of the 1950s and 1960s the state industrial sector can now be characterised as a machine without a driver, a lumbering giant bereft of effective ministry control. Huge losses have been made in recent years. An analysis by the reputable Milan newspaper *Corriere della Sera* estimated the net losses of IRI, ENI, and EFIM in 1977 and 1978 as £700 million; total indebtedness had reached £14.7 billion, a sum very nearly equivalent to total annual turnover, or to 12 per cent of GNP. Losses have been made even in fields where private firms remain profitable. Thus the IRI food and confectionary firms Motta and Alemagna have poor records in comparison to private companies like Ferrero and Buitoni-Perugina. And Alfa Romeo's losses, exacerbated by the ill-managed Alfa Sud venture, contrast with the continuing, though now declining, profits of Fiat.

Some of the current economic problems of the state industrial sector can be explained by the fact the IRI and ENI operate in fields like oil, petrochemicals, textiles, steel and shipbuilding which have been in a state of international crisis over the past few years. Like other Western industrial companies, IRI faces the prospect of losses in Iran where several projects were under way, such as the Bandar Abbas steel and port complex. Some of the stronger units under the IRI/ENI umbrella have been the banks, STET, SNAM Progetti and Saipem.

Industrial Labour

Labour has been a crucial element conditioning the path of post-war industrial development: in some respects, given the paucity of industrial raw materials, *the* overriding factor. Continuing high unemployment in the 1950s, averaging at 7-8 per cent over the decade, and a weak and divided set of labour unions enabled wages to be kept fairly low during the period of the 'miracle'; indeed, sub-marginal wage increments were one of the driving-forces of the boom itself. During 1953-60 wages were rising by 4.6 per cent per year, compared to an annual industrial growth rate of 8.3 per cent.[21] Widening industrial profit margins enabled the boom to be sustained by further industrial investment but the capital-intensive nature of this industrial expansion limited its employment-creating potential. Only for a brief period in the early 1960s did the official unemployment rate drop below 3 per cent, and falling activity rates and high emigration have been constant features of post-war Italy. Hildebrand gives a structural explanation for high unemployment during the post-war industrial boom: a rapid shedding of labour from agriculture, coupled with statutory restraint on internal migration until 1961 and an inability of southern industry to expand to absorb former agricultural workers. He saw the problem as economic rather than demographic, long-term rather than cyclical.[21]

Low wages during the 1950s and early 1960s certainly helped to keep the prices of Italian industrial products down and made them highly competitive in the international market. A comparison of labour costs in EEC countries for a sample of 17 major manufacturing industries in 1960 showed Italian labour costs as lowest in 13 industries and second lowest in three; only rubber was exceptional.[22] The Italy-EEC wage gap then narrowed appreciably during the 1960s. The years 1969-70, when wages in Italy increased by an average of 32 per cent, were the period when Italian labour achieved more or less 'European' wage rates. In 1970 Italian rates were only 12 per cent below the EEC average. During the 1970s this tendency was reversed. In 1976 Italian wages were 27 per cent below the EEC mean (a figure which probably conceals an even greater relative drop because of the entry in 1973 of two low-wage countries, Britain and Ireland). However, an important paradox needs to be noted here. Although in *absolute* terms Italian labour costs are the lowest in the Community, in *relative* terms — i.e. in relation to productivity — they are amongst the highest, 42 per cent above the EEC average.[23] Between 1970 and 1976 the unit cost of labour fell in every Western country except Italy. And as profit margins have fallen in the light of higher wages, so the proportion of gross fixed industrial investment derived from undistributed profits and amortisations falls — from 57 per cent in 1968 to 31 per cent in 1975.[24] This progressive destruction of the 'capitalist surplus' increases firms' dependence on external sources of capital, but at the same time banking houses are becoming much more cautious in providing industrial credit.

The turning-point in Italy's post-war industrial labour relations came in the so-called 'hot autumn' of 1969. Up till then the economic system benefited from a trade union policy which was concerned primarily with defending jobs rather than pressing for improved wages and conditions. But entrepreneurial decisions geared primarily to expansion meant that social investments were deficient. The major sufferers were the southern industrial migrants in northern cities, who became increasingly alienated by a poor or non-existent infrastructure of schools, shops and other services. To have a good factory wage meant little to the newly urbanised industrial worker if much of it went on inhospitable, crowded accommodation, on transport and on expensive medical bills. This led to an accumulation of unsatisfied aspirations which finally exploded in a wave of strikes and demonstrations in late 1969.

Trends in labour relations are partly explained by changes in the organisation of labour. The labour confederations and unions organise only a majority of workers. They claim a membership of 9 million out of a total labour force of 19.5 million, but this is an exaggeration—the real figure is probably between 6 million and 7 million and probably only a fifth of these form an industrial proletariat in the true sense (i.e. work in factories of over 100 employees).[25] The organising efforts of Italian unions have been seriously hampered by regional, sectoral and political differences. Close ties between unions and political parties have diverted energies away from labour improvement into party wrangles. In many instances political parties have exploited unions for their own ends.

The largest union is the Communist dominated Confederazione Generale Italiana del Lavoro (CGIL) which has its strength in the mechanical and engineering industries where relatively high wages are paid. The second largest, the Confederazione Italiana Sindacati Lavoratori (CISL), is allied to the Christian Democrat party and the Church. Third comes the Social Democratic Unione Italiana del Lavoro (UIL). Finally there is the neo-Fascist Confederazione Sindacati Nazionali Lavoratori (CISNAL), which has few members and is of little industrial importance.[26] Pluralism in the labour movement has prevented the presentation of a united front, to the obvious advantage of industrial employers, most of whom are allied to their own organisation, Confindustria.[27] Generally, unions are weak, have chronic difficulties in collecting members' dues, are unable to achieve co-operative relations with employers, many of whom are paternalistic and authoritarian, and lack the means to embark on prolonged strikes. Plant-level bargaining is the exception rather than the rule, contracts being hammered out at a national level for each industrial sector. This has both advantages and disadvantages. On the one hand industry-wide agreements have helped to strengthen the overall position of labour where its organisations were weak; on the other hand the collective contract has been greatly criticised because of extreme regional differences in labour supply, cost of living and employment opportunities, which are not recognised in national wage levels. A single wage level from Piedmont to Sicily provides egalitarian satisfaction but at the same time removes a major incentive to the industrial development of the labour-rich South. In practice, however, northern firms usually pay somewhat higher wages than southern ones. Several conditions bring this about. First, there is a greater presence there of large firms which follow contract rates more closely. Second, northern firms tend to pay higher productivity bonuses. Third, skill levels are higher in the North. Fourth, more overtime is worked in the North. One partial exception is that highly skilled positions in southern industry may carry higher salaries than equivalent jobs in the North because of the difficulty of attracting suitable applications to the Mezzogiorno.

The events of 1969's 'hot autumn' had a unifying effect on the trade union movement. Once mortal enemies, the three main labour confederations (CGIL, CISL, UIL) came to rely on each other for mutual support, shaking themselves free of party political allegiances and acting more independently in their members' interests. In 1978 unions were adopting a more conciliatory approach to industrial management, but by 1980, the year in which Fiat announced 14,000 redundancies, they were once again split.

Nevertheless the unionised sector represents only one side of the dual labour market. The other side is made up of workers in small firms and workshops, often with low skill levels and a rural background. Workers in self-employed and family labour categories are covered only to a limited extent by social security laws, union regulations, family allowances and other organised benefits. This condition allows many small establishments to extend the labour factor to compensate lower per-unit capital investment and thus compete successfully on the fringe of big industry. Organised labour and the government have been trying to reduce the dual character of the labour force. There has been a broadening of regulations to encompass the small-scale sector or 'grey employment zone'. This extension of control has been more an effort to prevent big industry from securing parts and sub-assemblies from small-scale labour where lower wages and piece rates operate. Companion efforts have been made to induce large firms to spread employment. One of these devices has been to impose tax penalties on overtime.

The dual labour market had distinct spatial, sectoral and sexual manifestations. The unionised sector predominates amongst male employment in large, high-wage, high-productivity industry in northern towns. Any shift away from this characterisation — to rural localities, to small industries, to the South and to female labour — increases the importance of the non-unionised sector. Some indication of this dualism can be obtained by looking at average rates of pay by size of manufacturing establishment. If the mean wage of firms employing 200-500 persons is 100, the figure for firms below 50 employees if 65, and that for firms with over 1,000 employees, 127.[28] Table 4.8, which compares data on prevous job fields of industrial workers in Turin and Syracuse, shows very little difference in occupational background of the workers themselves but marked differences in the father's background. However, the job categories are not homogeneous. A Turin industrial background involves a well-established pattern of small and medium industries, as well as Fiat. In Syracuse, on the other hand, manufacturing in scarce, and those workers from an industrial background come mostly from construction and mining activities which are seasonal and precarious in nature. Moreover, in the South, where the stock of industrially experienced workers is low, there has been a tendency to hire workers with lower qualifications than the jobs require. A skilled job, for example, has often been given to a semi-skilled worker.[29]

Many non-unionised industrial workers can be characterised as 'peasant workers'.[30] Rather like migrants, peasant workers see their industrial work as temporary or part-time. They retain their land as a cushion against redundancy in the industrial sector. The peasant worker is a prominent character in accounts of the early history of industrial societies, and in underdeveloped countries. In Italy he is still common,

Table 4.8: Backgrounds of Industrial Workers in Turin and Syracuse (per cent)

| | Turin | | Syracuse | |
	Worker's background	Father's background	Worker's background	Father's background
Agriculture	17.3	33.0	19.9	44.9
Craft and services	33.1	40.5	31.0	38.7
Industry	49.6	23.5	49.1	16.4
No information	--	3.0	--	--
Number in sample	306	306	336	336

Source: Ammassari (1969), p.8.

and a critical component of the post-war dual labour market structure. Peasant men have been a source of labour for small enterprises attempting to evade union restrictions imposed on the large industries. Rural women have been an essential element in the revival of the putting-out system.

The final aspect of Italy's dual labour market is the male-female difference. In 1940 women's wages were 50 per cent of men's, but by 1960 they had reached 80 per cent and are now approaching parity for most equivalent jobs, especially those with a high skill or status component. The problem, however, is that many women are locked by the cottage system into low pay jobs which evade official records. There are still considerable obstacles to women working in industry in Italy.[31] The low figure for Italian female employment (27 per cent of the labour force is female, compared to 37 per cent in West Germany, for example) is explained by lack of job opportunities in a perpetually high unemployment economy and by social custom. The social mores against women working are particularly well established in Sicily and the South. In Palermo province only 9 per cent of women work, compared to 28 per cent in Turin and 30 per cent in Milan. The employment of women outside the home has been strongly deprecated by official Catholic thought, as expressed by Pope Leo XIII's *Rerum Novarum* of 1891: 'a woman is by nature fitted for home work and it is that which is best adapted at once to preserve her modesty, and to promote the good bringing-up of children and the well-being of the family'. Such a traditional attitude is still remarkably widespread in the South, although alternative female lifestyles have developed in northern cities, along with strong women's movements.

Labour continues to pour out of agriculture as it has done for more than a century, but it now appears that this outflow is not entirely related to the presence of industrial job opportunities, which have slumped. The results are continuing emigration (though now on a reduced scale compared to the 1950s and 1960s) and falling activity rates, especially in the South. The characteristic mechanism of falling Italian activity rates has been described as follows.[32] A family leaves agriculture because one of its members finds a better paid industrial or service sector job. The other members, mostly old people, juveniles and housewives, who until then had carried out some kind of agricultural activity, lose employment when the move takes place. Hence the family's participation rate declines, but its income rises. However, the decline in the participation rate is often only apparent since, even after the transfer, the 'peripheral' labour may find marginal work. But, while the marginal activities within the framework of the agricultural family were reported in the labour statistics, those performed after the move escape registration since they are frequently concealed in order to circumvent the collective contract, tax or welfare regulations.

All of which serves to question severely the official activity rates of Italian labour. The general rate — 39.8 per cent in 1981 — is the product of two components, one of which is relatively stable over time (the male rate), and the other unstable (the female rate); therefore it is largely determined by the latter. But the female rate depends to a large extent on how the facts are recorded. It is quite probable that most of the 2 million or more 'clandestine workers' who should be added to the 22.2 million officially recorded labour force are female. Female activity rates *are* low in Italy, but maybe not as low as official figures suggest.

The male rate also bears further scrutiny. Between the ages of 25 and 54 it is close to 100 per cent and similar to that of other industrial countries. At the extremes, Italian male rates are extraordinarily low, and fast declining. The 15-24 cohort is 49 per cent active in Italy, compared to 56 per cent in France, 73 per cent in Spain and 76 per cent for Britain. The upper age bracket (over 60 years) is only 26 per cent active in Italy, compared to 43 per cent in France, 48 per cent in Spain and 53 per cent in England. The reasons for the contrast lie respectively in the Italian trend to continue higher education well into the 20s age band, and in Italian pension rights which start at 60 as opposed to 65 in some other comparable countries.

The Italian Economy in the Seventies: A Decade of Uncertainty

At the end of the 1960s the crisis of the international monetary system, which made further violent lurches in 1973-4 and 1979-80, put one of the main pillars of Italian industrial development — the growth of world trade — in jeopardy. The 1970s and early 1980s have been an unremitting succession of alternating phases of inflation leading to balance of payments deficits, then recession accompanied by falling growth rates — 1-2 per cent per year compared to an average of 5-6 per cent during the 1950s and 1960s. Inflation was running at just under 20 per cent during 1979-80, falling somewhat in the early 1980s. Labour costs have risen at an annual average of 15 per cent since 1973 — faster than any other advanced industrial country.

The feasibility of long-term economic planning in Italy has been undermined by the breakdown of the Centre-Left coalition and continuing political instability: a change of government every 10 months, on average, since the war. The National Economic Plan for 1965-9 (the Pieraccini Plan) was delayed in its implementation until 1967 and its provisions were only loosely adhered to. Another National Economic Plan, for 1971-5, never materialised, although the support document — the 'Progetto 80' — became well-known. A further plan for the period 1973-7 was abandoned. The timing and nature of post-war events in Italy have produced the classic planning conundrum: when planning is possible it does not take place; when planning is needed and tried, it is impossible.[33] Stuart Holland has shown how the stubbornness of regional probems and economic stagnation in mature capitalist countries like Italy have increasingly challenged the orthodoxy of combined neo-classicial and Keynesian theory.[34] The credit policies which have been applied in the 1970s have been more vigorous and based on a more thoroughly developed basis of theory and statistics than in the 1950s and 1960s. Yet the experience of the last decade indicates that, in a situation which is for other reasons hostile to industrial growth and economic stability, credit control is by itself unlikely to be a solution to economic ills. Increasing indebtedness of industrial firms to the banks had been a buffer against disaster, not a real solution to the problem of decreasing competitiveness.

Another facet of the Italian reliance on the free market economic growth model is the growing contradiction between private profit and social welfare. This conflict is particularly unfortunate considering the poor state of Italian civic and social amenities such as education, health, public housing and recreational facilities. The public administration is so committed to painfully complex legalistic procedures that action on truly social or economic criteria rarely seems to materialise. Delays and bottlenecks obstruct any speedy decision. Parliament produces thousands of minor, inconsequential statutes, but bills that might lead to fundamental change or involve controversy are shipwrecked in a labyrinth of tricky procedural channels. It was the archaic public administration system that effectively disarmed the Pieraccini Plan, preventing the achievement of virtually all of its social investment targets. Allen and Stevenson[35] make the point that the post-war industrialisation of Italy is a case of growth without development. Italy is still in the midst of a dangerously transitional phase during which democratic attitudes and processes have yet to take root firmly and during which political mechanisms of a bygone age appear increasingly inadequate to cope with the problems of the late twentieth century.

On the planning front, there was some hope that things might improve with the creation of the regional governments in 1970-2. A 1977 law granted regional governments power in four fields: administrative organisation, social services, economic development and town and country planning. Although some commentators have recognised a new dynamism in these new regional administrations, especially in the more industrialised regions where economic planning has become more streamlined and with greater local feedback, cynics maintain that the creation of the regions does not really alter the basically centralised character of the system. It has been pointed out that central government retains all the important levers of economic power, exporting to the regions problem issues like crime and drugs control. [36]

The Italian bureaucracy still awaits renovation after 40 years of post-war progress. But, as it is a refuge for so many white-collar unemployed, this is unlikely to take place in the near future. The unemployment situation is full of paradoxes. Although the 2 million mark was passed in 1980, at the same time there are reckoned to be 2 million job vacancies. But the jobs available and the aspirations of the job-seekers do not match up. Half the unemployed are graduates. There is a strange relationship between educational attainment and unemployment among the young: the higher the qualification, the greater is the chance of being unemployed. Rates of unemployment are roughly twice as high in the South as in the North. They are also especially high in younger age groups: the national figures are 33 per cent for 14-19-year-olds and 21 per cent amongst 20-4-year-olds. The 1981 census recorded a national unemployment rate of 14.8 per cent with 10.2 per cent of the working population still seeking their first job.

Table 4.9 shows that manufacturing industry in the 1970s has been growing at less than 3 per cent per year. Textiles, mechanical trades, oil and coal derivatives and the working of non-metallic minerals have had the lowest rates of expansion. Outside manufacturing, the extractive industries have contracted. Industrial investment has generally been feeble since the end of the boom in 1963. Theoretically, a recovery in capital accumulation can come from two sources: squeezing real wages to levels comparable to those of the 1950s, or attacking upper and middle class incomes by higher taxation. The first brings the government on to a collision course with the unions, the second stimulates right-wing backlashes of a particularly unpleasant kind. So far the strength of the unions has blocked a recovery in capital accumulation at the workers' expense, while the parasitic strata have used their strength in government circles to paralyse attempts to erode their wealth and power. As the natural

Table 4.9: Indices of Industrial Output, 1970-81

	1970	1971	1972	1973	1974	1975	1976	1977	1978	1979	1980	1981
All manufacturing industry	100	100	104	114	119	108	121	123	125	133	141	138
Food industries	100	104	108	120	123	116	127	123	131	142	147	147
Textiles	100	98	106	115	113	104	123	120	114	129	136	132
Metallurgical	100	98	106	119	132	117	131	131	135	138	147	143
Mechanical	100	97	96	104	115	101	109	113	115	121	134	132
Transport equipment	100	100	103	111	113	102	110	114	121	124	141	144
Working of non-metallic minerals	100	99	102	113	121	107	117	120	119	127	140	136
Chemicals	100	101	110	125	131	126	143	145	158	169	176	171
Oil and coal derivatives	100	101	104	110	106	89	96	95	100	100	85	83
Electricity and gas	100	106	114	123	125	126	141	143	149	155	158	155
Extractive industries	100	95	97	100	102	95	99	94	94	101	97	93

Source: *Annuario di Statistiche Industriali 1981*, Rome, ISTAT (1982), p.3.

way round this impasse, Italy's black economy, estimated to add around 10-20 per cent, perhaps even 30 per cent, to GNP, enjoys widespread support amongst small firms and in many respects is the most flourishing sector of Italian industry. In the long term, however, a vigorous economic system cannot be built upon the basis of evasion of taxes and social security contributions. Hence the crisis — *la crisi* — which has become so permanent as to negate the very meaning of the term. Kidnapping and urban terrorism are amongst the most unpalatable aspects of Italian society in the 1970s and 1980s, but they are of course only the surface manifestations of a more fundamental malaise.[37] The kidnapping and then murder of former prime minister Aldo Moro by the Red Brigades in 1978 was the event which hit the international headlines, but it was symptomatic of the re-emergence since the mid 1970s of the class antagonisms which had been damped down by rising standards of living in the 1950s and 1960s.

Reading back over some of the studies made on Italian economic development in the past reveals some prophetic words. Twenty years ago Shepard Clough wrote that it did not seem logical or historically feasible that the great growth of post-war Italy could continue indefinitely. Flippantly, he said that if it did there would soon be such a surfeit of motor scooters and small cars that life would be unbearable! More seriously, he pointed out that Italy hardly had the resources for unlimited industrial growth and might be hard-pressed to acquire those raw materials it needed as others bid more earnestly for them.[38] More than ten years ago Raphael Zariski wrote that we should exercise due caution in our expectations for the future of Italy's burgeoning industrial society: prosperity is not assured for all time. He asked whether industry could continue to grow in a country with such an inadequate school system, insufficient provision for low-cost housing, and over-burdened medical services; might not industrialisation, with its accompanying pollutants, impose too heavy an ecological burden on a land that has already been violated many times over by the hands of man?[39] The tragedy of July 1976 at Seveso near Milan when a poisonous cloud of dioxin rose from the Swiss-owned Icmesa chemicals plant sterilising land, killing animals and maiming human life is a stark answer to this question.[40]

Notes and References

1. Clough (1964), p.290 Also on this early post-war period see De Cecco (1972); Grindrod (1955), pp.21-46; Saraceno (1959); Wiskemann (1971), pp.1-24.
2. For a detailed analysis of the Einaudi policy see Hildebrand (1965), pp.15-43.
3. Ibid, pp.47-8. The Italian annual rate of growth of exports 1950-62 (13.5 per cent) was more than double the world rate (5.8 per cent) and much higher than the rates for Western Europe (7.4 per cent) and the EEC (9.3 per cent).
4. Not surprisingly, such a unique period in Italian economic development has been studied by a large number of scholars, including many leading economic development theorists. Space prevents a full listing of sources but the following are some useful English language analyses: Allen and Stevenson (1974); Ciocca *et al* (1975); Clough (1964); Hildebrand (1965); Kindleberger (1967); Lutz (1962); Scimone (1964); Stern (1967); Tosco (1964). The Italian sources are naturally even more numerous: especially noteworthy are the books edited by Graziani (1969, 1972, 1975); also D'Antonio (1973), Fuà (1969) and Prodi (1973).
5. Compilation of detailed regional income statistics in Italy is largely the work of one man, Gugliemo Tagliacarne, who, in a series of papers spanning 20 years, has elucidated regional contracts on the basis of a host of indicators such as wages, car ownership, diet, energy consumption, etc. Most of his work was published in Italian in a long series of articles in the journal *Moneta e Credito* in the 1950s and early 1960s; good English summaries can be found, however; see Tagliacarne (1955 and 1973).
6. Sylos-Labini (1964).
7. The goals of Vanoni's scheme were to reduce unemployment to frictional levels (achieved by 1963), to increase exports in order to create a balance in trade and payments (also achieved), and to reduce the economic differential between North and South to 'approximate parity' — i.e. raising the South's mean *per capita* income from about one-half to at least three-quarters of the level of the North (not achieved). Vanoni proposed closer trade ties with Western Europe and a freeing of trade, capital and labour movements. The 'plan' envisaged a 5 per cent annual increase in national income (this was exceeded), amounting to an increase of 63 per cent in the ten-year period, but in order to promote a high rate of saving from industrial development, it proposed an increase in consumption of only 30 per cent in the ten years. Although the scheme served as a set of guidelines for politicians and economic administrators, it was criticised from many sides: by liberals for being too inflexible, by communists because it had no means of enforcing its recommendations, and by labour because the required savings were too burdensome.
8. Di Fenizio (1965), pp.333-5.
9. For more details see LaPalombara (1966) and Zariski (1972).
10. Acquaviva and Santuccio (1976), p.157.
11. Ibid., pp.137-9.
12. Allum (1973a), pp.25-6.
13. Allum (1973b), p.341. Powerful as the industrial 'ruling class' is, its power is not total, nor immune from internal disagreement. Thus, for example, Fiat was defeated by an alliance between IRI and southern politicians over the location of the Alfa Sud plant near Naples. It was, nevertheless, significant that the conflict ended in a series of Fiat-IRI agreements covering components and marketing. On the background to the Alfa Sud project see Barbato (1968).
14. Fuà (1978).
15. See, for example, Allen and Stevenson (1974), pp.217-66; Dechert (1963); Holland (1972); Keyser and Windle (1978); Posner and Woolf (1967); Saraceno (1975). Useful fold-out charts of the organisational structure are available for IRI at the back of Holland's (1972) book and for ENI in Dechert (1963), pp.12-13.
16. Borlenghi *et al* (1975), p.255.
17. Zariski (1972), p.216.

18. Posner and Woolf (1967), pp.58-70.

19. GEPI (*Società di Gestione e Partecipazioni Industriali*) operates under CIPE and has funds supplied by IMI (*Istituto Mobiliare Italiano*, a special credit institute providing medium and long-term industrial credit, orginally founded in 1931), IRI, ENI and EFIM. Since it started, GEPI has acquired shareholdings in 97 companies, one-third of them in textiles and one-quarter in mechanical engineering. Some of the larger GEPI interests are in SAVI (lifts), Seimart (electronic consumer goods), San Remo (suits) and IAC (shirts). For further details see Keyser and Windle (1978), pp.128-9.

20. Figures mostly from Allen and Stevenson (1974), pp.259-60.

21. Hildebrand (1965), pp.61-2. The calculations were based on data from seven major sectors of industry.

22. Vannutelli (1962), p.371.

23. Cavallari and Faustini (1978), pp.252-5.

24. Carli (1977), pp.13-14.

25. Allum (1973a), pp.40, 96.

26. There have been several specialist studies of Italian labour organisation. See Lloyd (1925) and Surace (1966) for the early history of the labour movement, and Gualtieri (1946), Horowitz (1963), LaPalombara (1957) and Neufeld (1961) for later coverage.

27. Confindustria is the central organisation that claims to represent all Italian businessmen. It is analogous to the British CBI but more powerful. Although LaPalombara (1964) indicates that it only accounts for 80,000 of Italy's estimated 680,000 firms, it does comprise most of the larger enterprises, employing over 20 workers. Confindustria also embraced all the para-state enterprises until they were forced to withdraw by the government in 1957, when they formed their own association, Intersind.

28. Fuà (1978), p.127.

29. Ammassari (1969), p.19.

30. Paci (1973), pp.192-201.

31. Archibugi (1960).

32. Fuà (1977), pp.222-3.

33. Archibugi (1978), p.50. For an outline of economic and industrial planning mechanisms in Italy see Fraenkel (1975) and Pasquino and Pecchini (1975).

34. Holland (1976).

35. Allen and Stevenson (1974), p.42.

36. For a brief review of the regional devolution question see Scattoni and Williams (1978).

37. See Marcelloni (1979) for a review of the development of urban struggles in the post-boom period.

38. Clough (1964), p.366.

39. Zariski (1972), pp.35, 336.

40. For a moving account of the Seveso incident see Fuller (1977). Confindustria surveys indicate that industry spends about 5-8 per cent of its research budgets on pollution control and environmental improvement (Gucciardi, 1973, pp.307-8). Generally, however, it appears that standards of neutralising industrial effluent in Italy are lax.

PART TWO

THE MAIN SECTORS OF ITALIAN INDUSTRY

5 FUEL, POWER AND INFRASTRUCTURES

This chapter is basically concerned with transport and power, two basic infrastructural pillars of modern industrial development. In most developed countries responsibility for these 'foundation industries' rests with government; Italy is no exception, although this has not always been the case, and even today certain elements remain in private hands. Particular stress should be laid on the fact that the construction of a complete network of roads, railways, shipping, airlines and telecommunications has been the means by which the fragile and fragmented Italian state has been consolidated. Transport networks were instrumental in both political and economic unification, although the latter was not pushed very hard, nor is it yet completely achieved today with parts of the Mezzogiorno remaining peripheral and isolated.

Throughout almost the entire country, relief poses great obstacles for the development of internal transport. Land travel was extremely difficult before the coming of the railways. There are hardly any long distance country-spanning road routes that are not cut at least once by mountains. Only one river, the Po, is navigable for small vessels and canal construction has not proved possible outside the Po Plain. Coastal sea transport does, of course, provide some compensation, but some of the main natural ports, such as Venice, Trieste and Genoa, are not optimally placed on the major present-day trade routes of the Mediterranean, and intra-Italy sea journeys are often long — 800 km between Genoa and Palermo, for instance.

Water has been important to Italian industrial development in other senses too. Fast-flowing perennial alpine streams, fed by glaciers and a vast system of lakes, attracted cotton and woollen textile industries to the northern valley towns. The South, on the other hand, has few rivers of commercial importance; many watercourses are completely dry in summer. The shortage and unreliability of water supplies for industrial processes continues to be a problem in the South where some large coastal industrial complexes have been forced to build their own desalination plants. The situation is not helped by the fact that the kinds of industry which have developed recently in the South — petrochemicals, steel, vehicle manufacturing — are extraordinarily heavy demanders of water. Shortage of water forces Bari industrialists to pay prices for industrial water almost equivalent to those for domestic users.[1] The use of water for power generation is considered later in this chapter.

Railways

The early development of the Italian railways was briefly outlined in Chapter 2 and summed up in Figure 2.2. The main framework of the present-day system had already been achieved by the end of the nineteenth century, with 16,000 km in existence by 1896. The maximum extent of the network was reached in 1941 (23,277 km), since when there has been a slow but steady contraction. Today the network stretches to just under 20,000 km, of which 16,000 km are controlled by the state.

Italian railway development was especially rapid in the years immediately following Unification: in 1860-1 railways absorbed about one-fifth of the new state's budget. By 1865 this financial burden stimulated the government to sell the railways to private companies. Four companies were formed: the Compagnia delle Ferrovie Alta Italia, with holdings in the Po Valley; the Compagnia delle Strade Ferrate Romane, with lines along the Tyrrhenian coast from Rome to the French border; the Società Italiana delle Ferrovie Meridionali, which had the Adriatic network from Emilia to Apulia and a cross-line to Naples; and the Società Anonima Vittorio Emanuele, with holdings in Calabria and Sicily. In the post-1873 economic crisis the government took many railways back again; a new plan followed in 1884 which attempted to reduce expenditure and rationalise the construction of secondary lines. The plan redistributed the railways into four regional networks — the Mediterranean, the Adriatic, the Sicilian and the Sardinian. Both mainland networks fed into Rome, Milan and Naples but northwards the Mediterranean line linked to France whilst the Adriatic line was oriented towards Austria. Each of the networks was leased to and controlled by a semi-public agency: the Mediterranean by the Società Italiana delle Strade Ferrate del Mediterraneo, backed by the Banks of Rome and Turin; the Adriatic by the Società delle Ferrovie Adriatiche, backed by Credito Mobiliare; the Sicilian by the Società delle Strade Ferrate della Sicilia; and the Sardinian by the Ferrovie Sarde. In all cases, the state owned the trackbeds, lines and stations, the companies the rolling stock. This scheme, too, did not function well and at the first lease renewal date, 1905, the arrangement was mutually terminated, most of the railways passing back to full state control under the Ferrovie dello Stato, usually abbreviated FS.[2]

The process of railway construction naturally acted as a stimulus to allied industries. At first most of the locomotives and specialised equipment were imported, mainly from England and France, whilst only the simpler equipment like carriages and lines were made in Italy, at the Pietrarsa works in Naples and at Ansaldo's in Genoa. Soon, however, the Italian machine industry began to acquire the necessary techniques to manufacture the more complex equipment. Ansaldo produced its first locomotive as early as 1854 and by 1903 70 per cent of Italy's railway equipment was supplied domestically.[3] Railway buildings also led to the pioneering of construction techniques for tunnels and bridges, needed in such large numbers in Italy's mountainous topography. The line between Pisa and the French border, which runs along Liguria's precipitous coast, has 140 tunnels and at its time of building was one of the most elaborate feats of railway construction in the world. Almagià has estimated that the Italian rail network would have been one-third shorter if it had been constructed on flat land![4]

Re-nationalisation in 1905 was followed by a decade of rapid modernisation and electrification, especially of the northern and Alpine lines, which to some extent made up for the weak influence that Italian railway development had exerted on domestic industrialisation in the early Unification years. Based on cheap sources of hydro power, Italy was one of the first countries to develop electric traction. Electrification was especially important because of the lack of Italian coal reserves and the difficulty of using steam with so many long tunnels which created problems of ventilation and hampered signalling.[5] Italian railway electrication had effects beyond the electric power industry itself, stimulating a range of subsidiary and allied industries, many of which were destined to have great importance. During the 'electrification decade' Mannesmann and Falck were called in for the steel girders and pylons that upheld the new power lines, Pirelli supplied insulated cables and wires, Olivetti provided electric gauges and meters and the Milan firm Marelli was the chief supplier of motors and other electrical apparatus.[6]

Figure 5.1 shows that the present network is densest in the North Italian Plain, whilst there are empty spaces in highland regions like the Alps, northern Apennines and Basilicata. Italian railways constitute 15 per cent of the EEC network; they carry 21 per cent of total EEC passenger traffic but only 9 per cent of total rail freight traffic (calculated in terms of passenger-kilometres and ton-kilometres respectively). Railway 'density' is relatively modest: 290 metres of line per 1,000 inhabitants and 53.6 km per 1,000 sq. km of territory. Although there appears to be overall spatial balance in the network (the South, for

Figure 5.1: The Current Rail Network

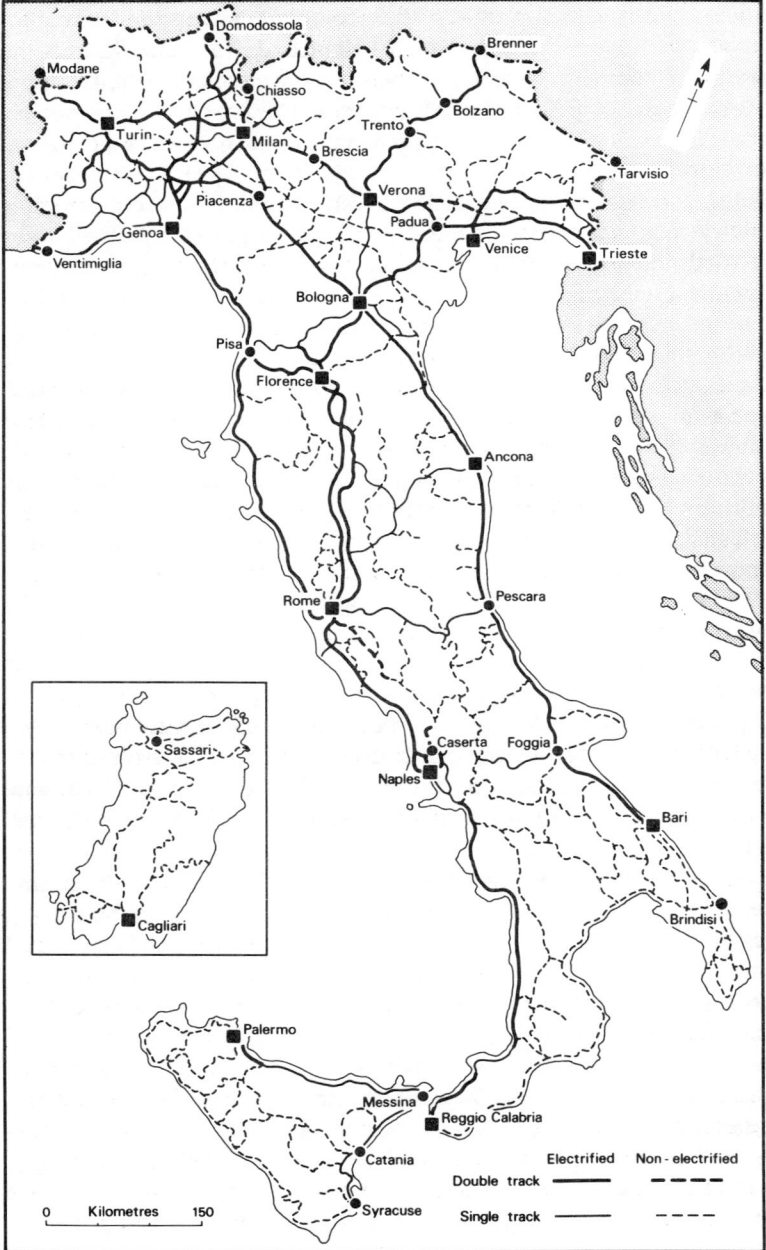

example, has 38 per cent of the rail length, roughly equivalent to its share of national population), there are considerable qualitative differences between rail services in the North and the South.[7] The South has only 15 per cent of its lines double-tracked and 26 per cent electrified, compared to figures of 35 per cent and 60 per cent respectively for the North. Southern rail usage, especially freight usage, is far below northern levels and is growing at a slower rate. Over 44 per cent of southern rail length is under concessionary management to private railway companies, compared to only 15 per cent for the North. These 'private' railways contain a lot of narrow gauge track, they provide infrequent passenger services and often carry no freight. Even on FS routes, southern services are in general slower, less frequent and more subject to delays. The fastest services are Milan-Bologna-Florence-Rome and Turin-Milan-Venice, on which trains maintain average speeds in excess of 150 km per hour. Bologna is the key centre of the whole system, linking the peninsula services to the northern lowland network. The heaviest long-distance passenger and freight traffic is naturally between major urban centres like Milan, Turin, Genoa, Bologna, Venice, Rome and Naples. Apart from the Tyrrhenian line to Reggio Calabria, freight traffic is much less in the South (Figure 5.2), a reflection of its weaker regional manufacturing economy. National rail passenger movements over recent decades have remained remarkably stable in terms of numbers (approximately 160-90 million tickets sold per year) but have increased in terms of passenger-kilometres by over 70 per cent between 1951 and 1976, owing to the increase in average trip length. Freight movements by rail have fluctuated in terms of crude weight (58 m tons in 1951, 69 m tons in 1963, 50 m tons in 1976) but have increased by 40 per cent in terms of ton-kilometres over the 1951-76 period.

Like most European railways, the FS is well provided with sidings feeding industrial complexes and warehouses. The container concept was first viewed with suspicion as it was feared that it would interfere with this established traffic. The adoption of sea-containers has broken down this attitude and in 1967 Milan Rogoredo station became the terminal for the Rotterdam-Milan container service. Since then container terminals have been built in other major cities, and 1970 saw the introduction of an internal container service between Milan and Naples using trains of 100 specially built wagons. The FS also operates train and car ferries from the mainland to Sicily (Villa San Giovanni-Messina, started in 1899) and to Sardinia (Civitavecchia-Golfo degli Aranci, started in 1961). It is second only to the Japanese railways in its

Figure 5.2: Freight Traffic on the Main Rail Axes

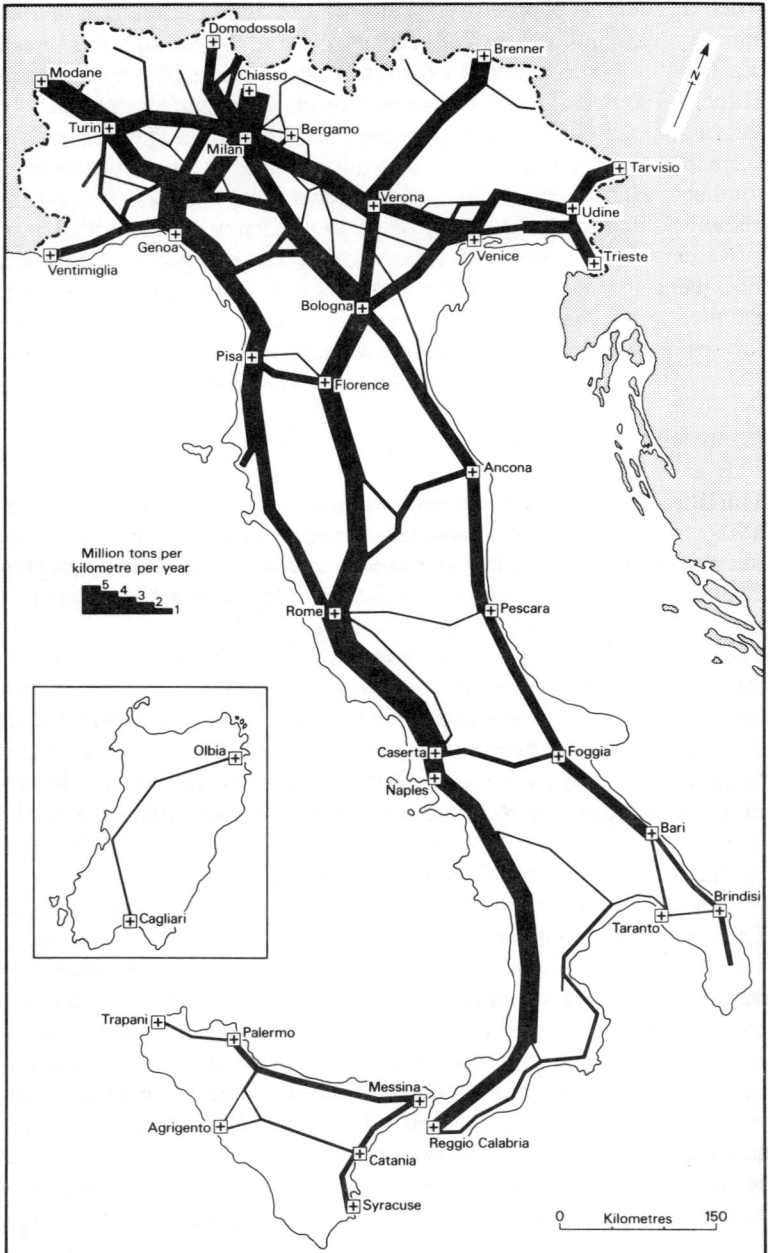

Source: Celant (1976), p.1078.

computerisation of train bookings and freight control systems. But whereas in other countries rail traffic capacity is increased by improved signalling, the Italian FS still finds it necessary to lay extra track, doubling the main interregional arteries such as Milan-Florence-Rome-Naples-Reggio Calabria, which carries 30 per cent of the total Italian rail traffic, and Bologna-Brindisi. In 1969 it was decided to quadruple-track Florence-Rome; this was largely achieved by a complete re-routing of the new double line which straightens the curves, shortens the distance and allows speeds of 200-50 km per hour.[8]

Italian railways are run on semi-military lines — a hangover from the Fascist era — and, with over 200,000 employees, are vastly over-manned. Fares are extremely low and the network is therefore subsidised to a greater extent than any other European rail service.

Roads and Motorways

The Roman road system is the foundation of the modern road network. Many modern roads follow Roman routes, modern engineers being unable to improve on the alignments chosen by Roman engineers. Examples are the Via Appia from Rome to Brindisi, the Via Flaminia from Rome to Rimini and the Via Emilia from Rome to the Po Plain. The Roman network centred more exclusively than the present system on Rome itself but there were then, as now, other important centres, especially in Campania and the Northern Plain. Well-known for their straightness in flat or open country, Roman roads did adapt to relief features where necessary. In spite of the Roman network's greater density in lowland areas, the Romans constructed several routes across the central and southern Apennines and a corniche road around the Riviera. They were also familiar with sixteen Alpine passes.

There was little development of roads after the decline of the Roman Empire until the nineteenth century. The long series of wars and invasions and consequent political and administrative fragmentation militated against any extension of the Roman system, which continued to be more than adequate. Some roads, such as the Ligurian Coast route, fell into disrepair during the Middle Ages whilst others, such as the trans-Apennine links between Florence and the Po Plain, became more important with the rise of city-states in North-Central Italy. Since the medieval period the most important changes have probably been the building of carriage roads in the Alps, given great impetus by Napoleon during the first decade of the nineteenth century. In the latter part of that century attention was switched from the building of roads to railways. This meant that when the motor age did come to Italy, the road system had become quite inadequate.

In fact, the road network remained rather primitive right up to the 1950s, particularly in the South where many villages were only served by narrow tracks. Many upland roads in the South are still poorly surfaced, twisting and frequently impassable during and after heavy rain. Landslips and mudflows are a special problem in the zone of clay hills which fringes the Apennines in Molise, Basilicata and Calabria, reappearing in central Sicily. The Cassa per il Mezzogiorno has done much good work in improving and surfacing country roads in the South, and now most settlements are served by bituminised roads.

By 1980 Italy had 295,000 km of roads (not counting town and suburban streets), a 72 per cent increase over 1951. Apart from motorways, to be considered shortly, the road network is classified into state, provincial and communal roads, 44,000 km, 103,000 km and 148,000 km respectively. State roads, *strade statali,* are numbered, with an 'SS' prefix, and provide interurban and, where there are no motorways, interregional links. These roads are mainly of excellent quality now, with some dual carriageway. They are under the control of the Azienda Nazionale Strade Statali (ANAS), whose distinctive red highway stations are a well-known feature of the main road scene. Provincial roads link smaller towns and are under the control of the provincial administrations. Commune roads are locally administered and mostly serve villages and hamlets.

Italy has pioneered the development of motorways, *autostrade*. [9] The first was built from Milan to the lakes in 1925. The most famous is the 'Autostrada del Sole', running from Milan to Reggio di Calabria. The first stretch of this 'highway to the sun', Milan to Florence, was opened in 1962, a beautiful road cut scenically through wooded Apennine valleys. Today the 6,000 km of Italian *autostrade* vie with the West German *autobahnen* as the most extensive motorway network in Europe.

Italian motorways are marvels of style and engineering. In upland areas they sweep across the topography in harmonious curves, regardless of cost (in fact Bologna-Florence cost four times as much, per kilometre, as Milan-Bologna). Those passing along precipitous coasts, such as the Riviera motorway and the Sicilian stretch between Messina and Taormina, spend most of their time either in tunnels or on viaducts. The cross-Sicily motorway has long stretches carried on great single pillars, because of the instability of the clay subsoil. The most impressive project for the future is the bridge over the Straits of Messina which will connect the Autostrada del Sole to the Sicilian network. Italy's first motorways were built during the decade 1925-35. Many of these were for tourist movements (Milan-Lakes, Rome-Ostia, Naples-Pompeii, Florence-Viareggio), but some also catered for urban-industrial traffic (Milan-Bergamo, Bergamo-Brescia, Turin-Milan, Padua-Mestre). The period of most rapid progress, however, was 1955-75, when the majority of the present network was built. The means by which Italy was able to create such an extensive motorway network so quickly involved entrusting the construction and running of the motorways to concessionary companies. Toll income is an integral part of this system.[10] This formula freed the construction and management of motorways from the shackles of the state budget and the delays of state bureaucracy. The key company is Austrade Spa, an IRI subsidiary formed in 1956 to build the Autostrada del Sole. Now this company is responsible for 43 per cent of the motorway network. Another 22 concessionary companies account for 41 per cent of motorway length, leaving 16 per cent entirely in state hands. This last portion, administered by ANAS, includes many southern motorways (Salerno-Reggio, Palermo-Catania, Palermo-Trapani-Mazara) where the expected traffic could not be enough to generate much toll income; these so-called 'promotional motorways' are therefore free.

The motorway network is built on three main axes (Figure 5.3). The first runs east-west through the Po Plain connecting many of the major industrial centres of the region — Turin, Milan, Brescia, Vicenza, Padua, Mestre and Trieste. This main transverse axis has many northward offshoots — to Chiasso and the Tunnels of Mont Blanc, Great St Bernard and Brenner — which link to other European networks. The other two main axes run down the peninsula. One starts at Milan and proceeds, via Piacenza, Parma and Modena, to Bologna where it strikes southwards across the Apennines to Florence, thence down to Rome, Naples and Reggio Calabria. This is the Autostrada del Sole. The other continues from Bologna down the Adriatic coast connecting Ancona, Pescara, Foggia, Bari and Taranto. The Tyrrhenian and Adriatic coast motorways are linked by two cross-Apennine routes, Rome-Pescara and Naples-Canosa.

The motorway network has had a strong influence on Italian spatial organisation, lowering travel time and thresholds of accessibility quite dramatically. In the north the large-scale industrial developments around S. Donato Milanese near Milan and the much-needed growth of industry around Bologna are directly attributable to the existence of the

Figure 5.3: Italian Motorways

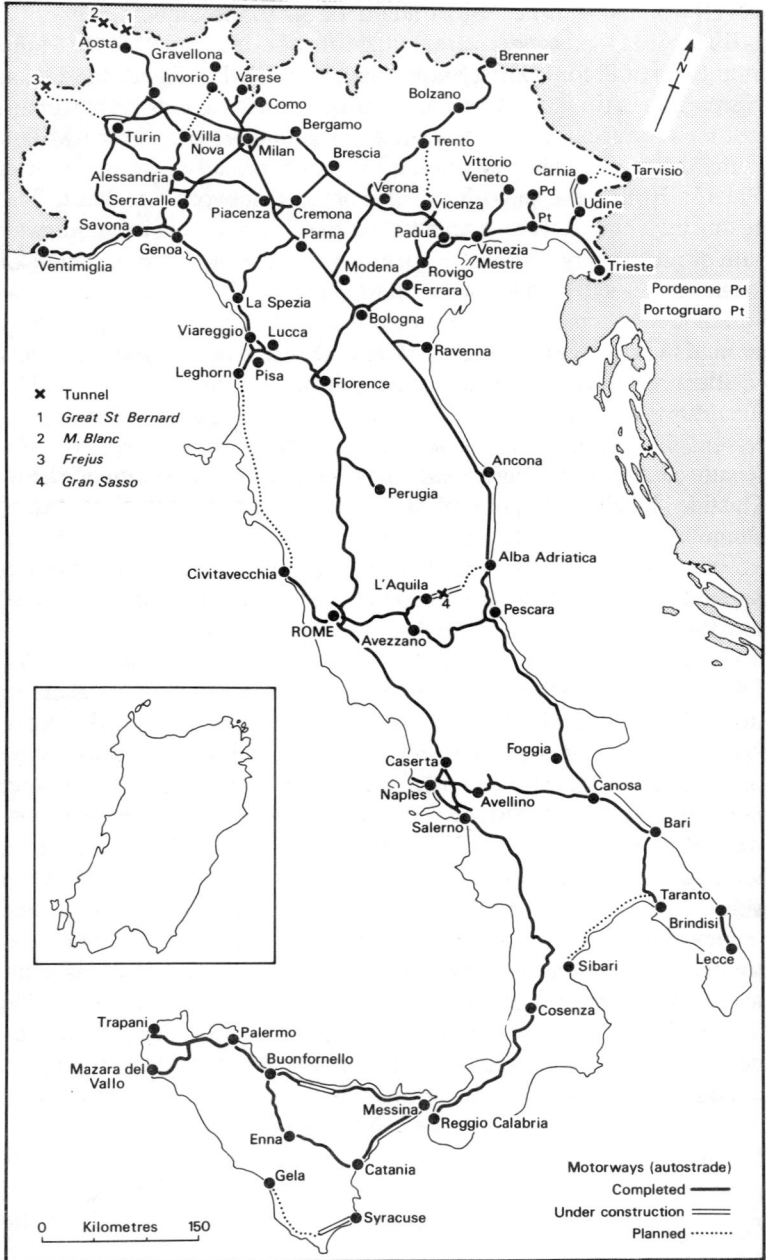

network. The most dramatic example of the motorway-induced development occurs on the Rome-Naples stretch where, in the province of Frosinone, it crosses the Cassa per il Mezzogiorno's boundary for aids to southern industry. Since 1968 more than 600 new industrial plants have arisen in this locality.[11] In addition to their main interurban and interregional function, motorways also open up previously isolated areas through which they pass; examples are the Bologna-Florence, Salerno-Reggio and cross-Sicily motorways. On the other hand, shortening the peninsula has also exposed the South to the easier penetration of northern-produced goods, both agricultural and industrial.

Another notable feature of the Italian motorway system is the way in which new forms of embryonic urban settlement are springing up around the service stations. Although these new settlements carry low resident populations, they are interesting functionally for they provide, in addition to restaurants, motels, fuel and garage services, a range of leisure and cultural activities such as parks, churches, swimming pools, leisure centres, shopping arcades, sports facilities and conference halls. Outside Naples the hub of the first 'motorway town' is taking shape.[12]

Italian geographers and planners have not been slow to point out the network's defects, however.[13] The proliferation of locally-based concessionary companies has allowed the network to grow incrementally and haphazardly, lacking an effective overall plan. Abruzzi and Sicily, for example, probably have motorways far beyond their current or likely future needs. Little attention has been given to relieving congestion around towns like Milan and Rome by building urban motorways or motorways spurs. Inter-mode transport planning (e.g. between railways and motorways) is non-existent; indeed the motorway network almost exactly corresponds to the map of the main rail arteries; for long stretches railway, motorway and state highway run side by side.

New motorway construction will probably slacken off in the future as the network reaches maturity, as motorway construction costs escalate and as the rising cost of motor fuels checks the growth of road traffic. The 1976-80 medium-term economic plan placed a moratorium on new motorway routes, so the present network is static, save for projects already identified and under construction.

Table 5.1: Changing Transport Mix, 1955-75

Percentage shares of passenger traffic:

Year	Rail	Air	Motorcycle	Car	Bus	Coastal and other
1955	28.8	0.01	20.3	21.7	17.4	11.8
1975	9.9	0.5	6.9	70.8	10.7	1.2

Percentage shares of freight traffic:

Year	Rail	Coastal	Air	Road	Pipeline	Inland waterway and other
1955	26.9	9.5	---	62.7	0.7	0.2
1975	13.3	20.3	0.01	55.8	10.2	0.4

Source: Vallega (1980), p.353.

New Transport Trends

Table 5.1 indicates the extent to which the Italian transport mix, both of passenger and freight movement, has changed in the post-war period — a change which has been little short of revolutionary. Various factors account for this.[14] Some are purely economic, such as the general increase in personal incomes and the projection of economic processes such as industrialisation and urbanisation on to the human landscape. Others, such as the importance given to mobility as one of the values of free time and the possession of a vehicle as a status symbol, are of a social nature. The result is that the pattern of personal transport by car has increased to a greater extent than in almost all other Western countries, where the growth of income has taken place against a stronger and more balanced economic background.

In the 1950s personal transport was fairly evenly distributed amongst, in order of importance, railways, cars, motorcycles and buses. Twenty years later all modes except the car had decreased, some, like the railways, quite dramatically. Personal car-based mobility is terribly important for the new Italian way of life. This trend has been aided by the cheapness of buying and running cars in Italy, due to the mass-production of low-cost, small-engined cars, the epitome of which are the Fiat 500 and Panda.

Freight movements over the 20-year period covered by Table 5.1 also show enormous changes. The share of the railways has dropped by one-half, to be compensated largely by pipeline and coastal movements. Again this can be related to Italy's particular model of rapid industrialisation based on mass transport of imported raw materials, notably oil. Road traffic remains important, with a lot of agricultural produce and manufactured goods shifting from the railways to the motorways.

The rapid fall-off in rail usage is due, at least in part, to the failure of the rail services to adapt themselves to the changing needs of a rapidly industrialising and urbanising society. Passenger services quickly lost out to private motoring, and also to internal air transport for longer trips such as Milan-Naples, Rome-Bari, etc. The freight services offered by the railways have proved so inadequate that a lot of goods which should, by their nature, be carried by rail, have been lost to heavy lorries plying the motorways. Some of these trends have been arrested in the last few years, however. The sharply rising cost of personal motoring in Italy has shifted some passenger traffic back to the railways. The attempt by the FS to improve commuter services into main cities and the increasing train speeds on key inter-city routes like Florence-Rome are important here. For medium-length inter-town travel, such as between provincial capitals, the railways cannot, however, compete with the locally organised express bus networks.

Seaports and Airports

With 7,400 km of coastline, including the long North-South haul, and with so many usable ports, sea transport has played an important role throughout Italy's economic history.[15] The Italian peninsula has for centuries been one of the great trading areas of the world. Today more then 90 per cent of Italian imports and over 65 per cent of exports pass through the ports. Many ports have been in use at least since Roman times. Shipping was important, if not crucial, to the development of the new nation in the late nineteenth century, providing, for a time, the industrial shot-in-the-arm that the foreign-dominated railways had failed to yield. With Italian industry's need to import so much in the way of raw materials and with the sale abroad of finished goods to pay for imports, Italy quickly developed a powerful mercantile marine. The first steamship in the Mediterranean was built and launched at Naples in 1818. In 1862 the Italian merchant fleet was the third largest in Europe after those of England and France, and it was given a further fillip by the opening of the Suez Canal in 1869. Unlike most other Italian industries, the shipping network had a balanced regional distribution; the main ports were Genoa, Venice, Naples and Palermo. The two important nineteenth century shipping companies were Florio of Palermo and Rubattino of Genoa; they merged in 1881 to form the Navigazione Generale. The turn of the century, however, saw a downturn in the fortunes of Italian ports and shipping which corresponded to the shift from wood and sail to iron and steam. Italy was short of iron and steel and had to import coal for the new ships. Capital for the necessary port enlargements was scarce. Coastwise traffic suffered from competition from the emerging railway network. Economic crises and tariff wars cut foreign trade by 12 per cent during 1874-8 and by a further 20 per cent during 1888-93. Shipping subsidy plans tempered only slightly the rate of decline. Italian ships carried 45 per cent of the merchandise in and out of Italian ports in 1871 but only 21 per cent in 1894. By 1914 Italy's fleet had fallen to sixth in Europe, a position it has held ever since.

Post-war reconstitution of the Italian merchant marine has been guided by Finmare, the IRI financing company for shipping, in collaboration with ENI, Italsider and some private companies. Coastwise shipping, almost exclusively carried out by Italian vessels, doubled over the period 1938-60, largely because of the growth and interdependence of steel plants, the massive development of port-located petrochemicals plants and the expansion of other coastal industries based on natural gas. The most important shipping lines, all part of Finmare, are the Italia line operating to the Americas, the Lloyd Triestino to East, West and South Africa, and the Tirrenia to the Western Mediterranean, North Africa and Western Europe.

Italy's many ports have been studied in great detail by Italian geographers.[16] Although over 200 ports are recognised and classified by the Italian authorities, mostly along the Tyrrhenian coast and in the islands, the really important ports fall into four main groups. These are the northern Tyrrhenian group (Genoa, Savona, La Spezia, Leghorn), the northern Adriatic group (Venice and Trieste), the southern Tyrrhenian group (Naples, Salerno) and the southern Adriatic and Ionian Sea group (Bari, Brindisi, Taranto). Sicilian and Sardinian ports obviously form the fifth and sixth groups, but they are less important than the four mainland clusters. Figure 5.4 shows Italy's main ports and their import/export balances.

Genoa is unquestionably the principal port of Italy although Naples has more ships docking (around 20,000 annually) and more passenger movements (about 1.2 million arrivals per year). Naples is well down on freight handling, however — a reflection of the traditional industrial

Figure 5.4: Major Port and Airport Traffic, 1979

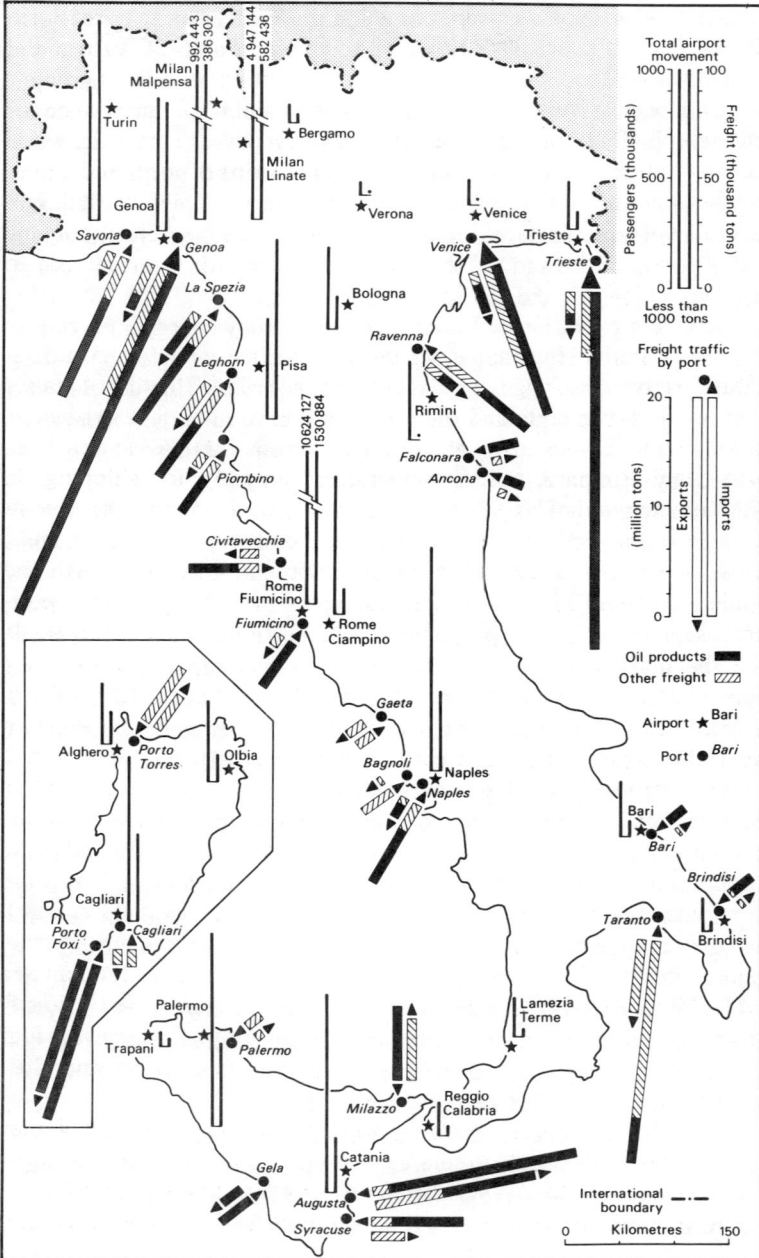

Source: Bethemont and Pelletier (1983), p.79.

weakness of the South; the second port of Italy for cargo handling is Trieste. Like Genoa's entrepôt function for Switzerland, Trieste also directs much of its freight on to the foreign hinterlands of Austria and Yugoslavia. Genoa's primacy rests on its multi-functional character, being the biggest freight handler as well as retaining an importance for internal (chiefly to Sardinia) and international passenger traffic.[17] It is the only Italian port to rank alongside the great ports of northern Europe like Rotterdam, Antwerp and Hamburg. Genoa's chief drawback is lack of level land for development. This has led to the seaward extension of port facilities and has stimulated the growth of two nearby ports, Savona to the west and La Spezia to the east.[18]

The recent evolution of Italian port traffic shows interesting trends with regard both to the changing cargo mix and to the regional location of different types of freight movement. Other variables include the ratio of in to out movements and the proportion of total cargo made up of international movements. Table 5.2 shows some of these features for ports handling over 2 million tons of freight in 1979.

Annual cargo movements in Italian ports averaged over 380 m tons during 1972-9. Prior to this the growth of freight handled by Italian ports had increased parallel to the development of the economy as a whole. Between 1952 and 1972 total cargo grew 7.7 times, the biggest increase, 13.7 times, being registered by 'liquid bulk' items, of which oil was the major entry. Liquid bulk's share of total cargo therefore increased from 40.4 per cent in 1952 to 54.4 per cent in 1962 and 71.9 per cent in 1972, then falling back to around 67 per cent by the end of the 1970s. Containerisation is a growing trend. By the mid 1970s Italian ports were handling over 3 m tons of container traffic per year, two-thirds of it international. Container facilities are present in all the major ports. Attempts are being made, without much success, to set up a container sorting terminal serving the whole Mediterranean. Leghorn, where there is plenty of space, seems the best option but efforts are also being made at Cagliari where a huge new 'canal-port' is being built.[19]

The freight pattern has been overturned in the last two decades by the growth of specialist, one-product ports. Examples are the steel ports of Bagnoli (near Naples) and Taranto, and the oil ports of Milazzo, Augusta and Gela (all in Sicily) and Porto Foxi and Porto Torres (both in Sardinia). Ports like Augusta and Port Foxi, which hardly figured at all before the early 1960s, now rival — in tonnage — traditional commercial ports like Genoa and Trieste. Indeed Augusta is now the third port in Italy by the weight criterion, but ordinary commercial traffic

Table 5.2: Cargo Traffic in Italian Ports, 1979

Port	International ('000 tons)		Coastal ('000 tons)		Total ('000 tons)
	In	Out	In	Out	In and Out
Genoa	40,929	1,924	5,349	2,478	50,680
Savona	11,422	1,102	2,355	114	14,993
La Spezia	10,147	1,624	787	2,778	15,336
Leghorn	7,124	2,340	2,207	1,205	12,876
Piombino	3,179	250	2,160	962	6,551
Civitavecchia	1,121	315	5,036	1,096	7,568
Fiumicino	4,309	184	264	987	5,744
Gaeta	1,503	517	41	1,071	3,132
Venice	15,677	2,289	8,334	1,450	27,750
Trieste	38,375	1,359	426	1,540	41,700
Ravenna	8,008	2,116	2,142	825	13,091
Ancona	1,736	644	1	3	2,384
Falconara	2,381	2	182	818	3,383
Bari	402	106	1,643	38	2,189
Brindisi	688	221	1,747	194	2,850
Taranto	19,319	1,888	711	4,310	26,228
Naples	6,385	1,014	1,644	943	9,986
Bagnoli	2,656	38	260	365	3,319
Palermo	343	253	1,414	562	2,572
Milazzo	5,992	2,728	543	2,654	11,917
Augusta	16,253	4,665	1,763	9,347	32,028
Gela	1,006	282	2,426	1,778	5,492
Cagliari	203	233	1,304	1,068	2,808
Porto Foxi	14,020	6,368	655	6,261	27,304
Porto Torres	4,889	2,197	636	1,429	9,081
Italy (all ports)	238,405	46,549	54,925	56,754	396,633

Source: *Annuario Statistico Italiano 1981*, Rome: ISTAT (1982), pp.163-4.

accounts for less than 2 per cent of total freight. Yet although many old-established ports have been eclipsed by the new industrial ports, it is still possible to identify, on the basis of the value and diversity of trade, the front-rank ports, all of which are also major towns or cities — Genoa, Savona, La Spezia, Trieste, Venice, Leghorn and Naples.

Overall the ratio of imports to exports is about 3:1. This has remained fairly stable over the past 30 years. Coastal (i.e. internal) traffic remains steadier than international flows. Crude oil and refined products account for about two-thirds of imports by weight and an even greater proportion of exports. Coal makes up one-sixth of imports; much of this commodity comes in to Savona. The oil and steel ports are the main reason why the Mezzogiorno deals with a greater proportion of sea freight — 45 per cent — than its share of industry or of national population. The new product-specific ports of the Mezzogiorno were developed solely to service industries planted there by the South's development programme; they have no real hinterlands other than their immediate industrial complexes which in turn are linked not to their respective regional economies but to the immediate export of processed products such as steel or petrochemicals.[20] In Table 5.2 such ports (Taranto, Augusta, Gela, Porto Foxi) exhibit a common pattern: massive import of raw material from abroad; export of processed products both abroad and to other Italian ports. Oil ports like Porto Foxi, on the south coast of Sardinia, consist of jetty-mounted pipelines or 'floating buoy' terminals which feed straight into the oil refineries they serve. The lack of port-hinterland links in the South is also exemplified by the case of the Fiat factory at Surbo, near Lecce, which makes agricultural and earth-moving machinery; this industry cannot export through nearby Brindisi (35 km away via an excellent main road) because of the lack of appropriate handling facilities for such heavy items, so it has to sustain the extra costs of a long overland haul to Naples.

The port sector is undoubtedly the most unsatisfactory in the entire Italian transport system. In spite of its importance to the country's economic and trading performance, it has been totally neglected by national economic policy. Ambitious ideas are floated about South Italian ports forming a bridgehead between Europe and North Africa and linking with the Third World beyond the Suez Canal, but there are conflicting views as to how this might come about.[21] Bari's annual trade fair — the Fiera del Levante — is the main expression of this southern and eastern link.

Italian port policy has many flaws, the major one being that there is hardly any policy at all![22] The classification of Italian ports rests on a scheme devised in 1885! The limited sums available for port development have always been too widely dispersed over too many ports; no port has ever received what it really needs and vital strategic improvements can never be fully financed. Responsibility for port development has traditionally been divided between the Ministry of Public Works and the Ministry of the Mercantile Marine; in the South the Cassa per il Mezzogiorno also enters the picture, and in recent years the regional governments have played a role. The result has been bureacratic confusion leading to little action — a common story in Italy. Another problem has been the obstructive stance frequently taken by heavily unionised port labour.

Recently some more specific guidelines have emerged. Some of the major ports are administered by their own consortia; this permits more effective development planning. The leader here is Genoa whose *consorzio* was set up as long ago as 1902. The need for selective expansion of certain key ports has led to a new fourfold classification; ports of *national* interest such as Genoa, Trieste and Leghorn (these also, of course, have a major international orientation); ports of *regional* interest like Pescara on the Adriatic or Olbia in Sardinia; ports of *local* interest (harbours used by smaller craft and by fishermen); and finally the specialised industrial ports. Transfer of most of the responsibility for port planning to one body — the Ministry of the Mercantile Marine — will hopefully allow more realistic concentration on necessary key projects in the major ports.

The movement of industrial goods by air is small so only a brief note on airports is needed.[23] Since 1957 air services have been reconstituted under Alitalia, a largely state-owned company with subsidiaries (Ati, Itavia, Alisarda) responsible for internal flights. Most intercontinental flights come in to Rome and Milan. These two are also the major destinations for European flights and are the principal nodes in the internal network. In summer when tourist and migrant traffic are at their peaks there are also European flights into a range of other airports such as Turin, Genoa, Verona, Bologna, Venice, Rimini, Pisa, Naples, Brindisi, Palermo, Catania and Cagliari. Over 80 per cent of all air freight focuses on Milan and Rome, although Turin and Pisa are also quite important for goods traffic. Between 1960 and 1970, the main period of Italian air transport's expansion, air freight increased 10 times, passenger traffic 7 times and skilled airline workers grew from 4,800 to over 16,000. Already by the end of 1970, however, the sector was showing strains, with the first financial deficit declared since 1958. The oil crisis deepened the depression in air transport, which reached its nadir in 1975 during which the effects of spiralling fuel costs, inflation and falling demand were exacerbated by the worst wildcat strikes in Italian civil aviation history: more than 13,000 flights were cancelled in that year. Some restructuring followed this débâcle. Ati eliminated flights into little-used airports like Florence, Forlì, Foggia, Lecce, Taranto and Comiso, reduced frequency on lines making heavy losses, and sold off many of its older craft. In the South a number of air links were discontinued when new motorways took away much of their traffic: this was the case for Palermo-Catania, Naples-Bari and Naples-Reggio Calabria. Alitalia retrenched on its North Atlantic routes where international competition is fierce and concentrated instead on European traffic, where demand has remained buoyant. In 1979 Alitalia once again moved into profit. Interestingly, whilst the share of passenger traffic into Italian airports carried by Italian airlines fell slightly between 1971 and 1979 (41.3 per cent to 40.4 per cent), the Italian-carried share of total freight increased quite strongly from 42.2 per cent in 1971 to 49.9 per cent in 1979.

Italian airports suffer many of the same problems noted for the ports: excessive number (90 civil airports for a country like Italy is far too many), inefficient administration, lack of modernisation, frequency of strike action. The main problem is the organisational obstacles to getting investment to improve the important airports. In recent years the regional authorities in Lombardy and Latium have made efforts to upgrade their major airports and Milan (Linate and Malpensa) and Rome (Ciampino and Fiumicino) have now achieved a reasonable working efficiency. Much still needs to be done to modernise certain key regional airports like Turin, Genoa, Pisa, Venice, Naples, Palermo, Catania and Cagliari. The integration of airports with their respective regional transport systems of road, rail and bus services also needs to be developed.

The Changing Pattern of Power Sources

The supply of energy has always played a determinant role in mankind's journey through the various stages of development. It is particularly crucial in the evolution of industry. Considering its level of industrial development, Italy is one of the poorest countries in domestic energy resources in the Western world, being forced to import over 80 per cent of energy requirements. About three-quarters of Italy's energy requirement comes from imported oil, a level of dependence that makes the country extremely vulnerable to the oil price effects of Middle Eastern geopolitical events such as the Yom Kippur war of 1973 and the Iranian revolution of 1979. Although Italy was able to cope with the energy problems of the mid 1970s by *ad hoc* measures, the latest crisis is having major repercussions and the spectre looms of large-scale blackouts before the end of the century.

National coal deposits are largely accounted for by low quality brown lignite from the Sulcis field in Sardinia, discovered in 1871 but now no longer worked. Small quantities of anthracite have been mined at La Thuile in Val d'Aosta and Seui in the Sardinian Barbagia. Istrian coal from Arsa was lost to Yugoslavia after the Second World War. Mussolini's autarchy drive expanded production of the Sulcis mines to 1.3m tons in 1940 and a new town, unimaginatively called Carbonia, was built. After a drop in output caused by the war, a number of new mines were opened at Serrucci and Cortoghiana and annual output rose to average around 1 million tons during 1947-57, since when competition from foreign coal, the introduction of fuel oil and exhaustion of the mines have caused a steady drop in production. Unemployment has been a serious problem and in the late 1950s many Sardinian miners emigrated to work in the coal mines of Belgium and France.

Shortage of coal reserves encouraged Italy to pioneer the field of electrical power. The birth of the Italian electricity industry can be traced to the founding of the Società Edison by Giuseppe Colombo, professor of engineering at the Milan Polytechnic, in 1882. By 1938 electricity production accounted for 30 per cent of the national power requirement. The Alps and parts of the Apennines enabled widespread development of hydro-electric power but already by the early 1950s most of the economically feasible sources of water power had been tapped. Emphasis then switched to thermal power stations and by 1954 these accounted for 20 per cent of all Italian electricity. Large thermal generating plants were built in each of the major industrial centres and have been used particularly in the autumn and winter seasons when water power is short. The changing pattern of electricity generation can be illustrated by a few figures. In 1960 hydro-electric stations produced 46,106 million KWh of electricity and thermo-electric stations 10,134 million. In 1978 hydo power was little changed — 47,138 million KWh — but thermal electricity, including coal, gas, oil, geothermal and nuclear sources, had jumped twelve-fold to 120,276 million KWh (Figure 5.5).

Before 1962 electricity production was fragmented. The state

Figure 5.5: Regional Pattern of Electricity Production, 1979

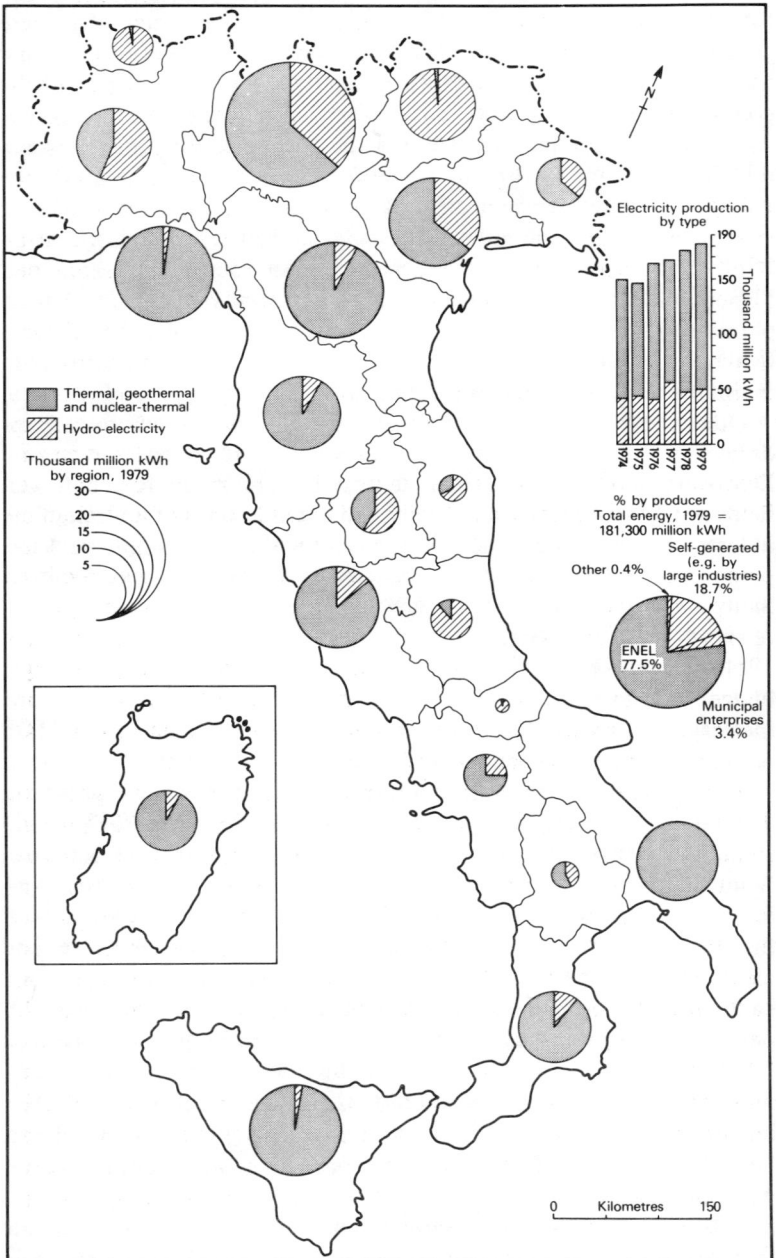

Note: For regional names, *see* Figure 1.1.
Source: *Annuario Statistico Italiano,* Rome: ISTAT (1981), p.88a.

railways produced 7 per cent, municipalities 6 per cent, and IRI, through its subsidiary Finelettrica, 26 per cent. Consumers who produced their own power, such as big private industries like Fiat and Montecatini, accounted for another 16 per cent and private electricity companies, of which Edison was the largest, produced the rest, about 45 per cent. Each company had a virtual monopoly position in its region, a situation leading to high prices, poor services and varying voltages.[24] For these reasons, and because electricity was regarded as a vital public utility, agitation for nationalisation was intense, and in 1962 parliament voted to establish ENEL (Ente Nazionale per l'Energia Elettrica), combining 1,200 private companies into a single public body. ENEL now possesses a wide range of power-producing facilities, including hydro-electricity, thermal electric plants, geothermal energy and nuclear power stations.

Other sources of energy were also developed in the 1950s. At Lardarello in Tuscany a plant was built to operate on natural steam. Discovery of oil, first in a small deposit in Abruzzi and then in larger fields at Gela and Ragusa in Sicily, led to wild hopes of an Italian oil industry based on indigenous reserves, but the oil yields have been paltry. Compared to the gushing oil wells of nearby Libya, those of Sicily are but a dripping tap. The only really significant domestic source of energy to be developed in recent decades is natural gas. Already by 1960 natural gas contributed 11.6 per cent of the country's energy budget, and annual output now runs at around 12,500 million cubic metres, although an equivalent amount is imported, from Holland (46 per cent), Russia (40 per cent) and Libya (16 per cent).

The trend in energy consumption, by sources, is shown in Figure 5.6. Total energy consumption quintupled in the 25 years 1955-79. Oil consumption expanded fastest, at least until 1973, followed by natural gas. Solid fuels, hydro-electricity and geothermal energy remained stationary in output but a falling percentage of the expanding total. Nearly all of the 'hydro-geo-nuclear' band on Figure 5.6 is made up of hydro-electricity (7.2 per cent in 1979), with small contributions, 0.4 per cent each, from geothermal and nuclear power. Hydrocarbons supplied 23 per cent of energy needs in 1949, 55 per cent in 1964 and 84 per cent in 1979. Table 5.3 shows the trends in energy dependence, which are mostly increasing. Recent indications, partly deriving from the 1979-80 oil price increases, are that Italy's economic vulnerability to the energy factor has worsened. To some, the 'nuclear option' seems attractive as a way out. However, opposition from environmental groups in the Senate, and the usual Italian syndrome of delays in big projects, mean that the nuclear programme is running many years behind schedule.

Figure 5.6: Energy Consumption of Primary Sources, 1955-79

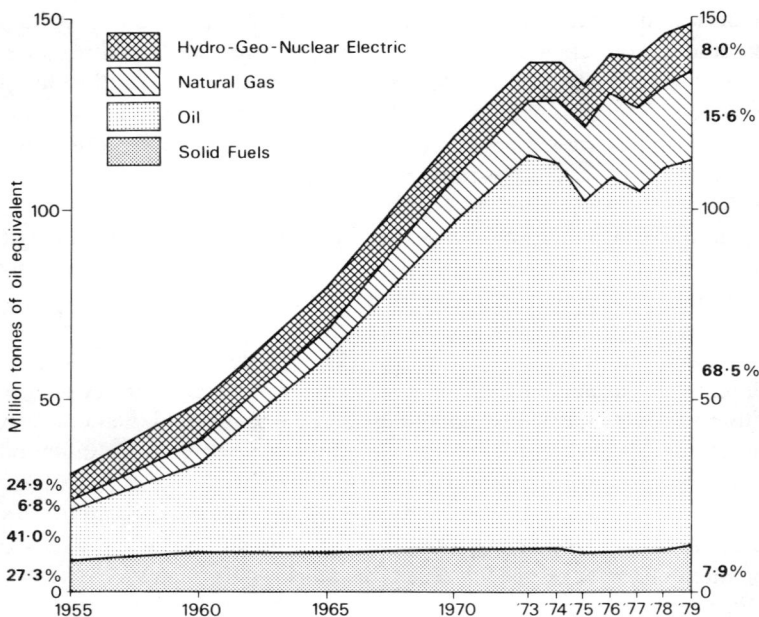

Source: Colombo (1980), p.19.

Table 5.3: Trend in Energy Dependence: Percentage Consumption Due to Imports

	1965	1973	1979
Oil	92.5	98.9	98.7
Natural gas	--	11.3	51.6
Solid fuels	79.1	81.8	91.2
Electric power	--	1.9	8.8
Total	72.0	81.8	82.7

Source: Colombo (1980), p.21.

Hydro-electric power

Italy pioneered this form of energy, opening one of the first generating plants using water at Tivoli in 1885 and being one of the first countries to transmit electricity from water sources to an urban centre — the Tivoli-Rome 5,000 volt line constructed in 1892. Blanchard, writing in 1928, called hydro-electric power the 'silver lining' of the otherwise bleak Italian power situation.[25] Its rapid development in Northern Italy had important repercussions for the whole regional pattern of industrialisation, giving the North a big advantage over the South, an advantage that was reinforced by the well-known tendency for established industries to draw satellite trades around them. Hydro-electric power provided an ideal and flexible source of energy for small industrial establishments that could not afford steam engines. Electricity was used in the textile industry from 1899. It also provided a substitute for coke in the iron industry, after the adoption of the electric furnace; the first Moissan electric arc furnace was installed in Turin in 1903. Electricity was introduced into the tramway system in 1890 and the first railway line to be electrified was the 58 km Milan-Varese in 1901. The number of communes with electricity grew from 410 in 1898 to 4,000 in 1914.[26]

About three-quarters of Italy's hydro-electricity is generated in the Alps. Although some of the basins are small and isolated, the physical setting is, in general, well suited to the development of hydro-electric power. The height of the Alps is responsible for a heavy and evenly-distributed precipitation and for sufficiently low temperatures to maintain extensive snowfields and glaciers. Vertiginous drops furnish a high head for the streams. Many moraine-dammed lakes constitute natural reservoirs which serve to equalise the stream flow. A drawback is winter freezing but this, like summer drought in the South, only reduces the quantity of electricity generated since many schemes involved the construction of dams to create reservoirs to regulate flow. Almost all the larger hydro-electric stations in Italy use a high vertical fall of water but a relatively small volume. Many important stations stand at the lower ends of secondary Alpine valleys. Water is collected from tributary streams into a series of tunnels which, following the contours, converge at a suitable point where the water can be fed down the penstock to the generators on the valley floor.[27] The fact that many secondary valleys are 'hanging' as a result of glaciation is an obvious asset.

In some areas hydro-electricity development has quite radically altered the landscape of the Alps through the addition of dams, artificial lakes, power and transformer stations, power lines, pipes and new hamlets. New roads and employment opportunities have helped to arrest the decline of the mountain economy.[28] Whilst the Po itself is too gentle in profile for effective hydro-electric utilisation, the Oglio, Adda, Ticino and Dora Baltea have been greatly modified by hydro-electric generation, containing between them 19 schemes which exploit a head higher than 750 metres. The Adda upstream of Como has a large constellation of power plants which has been crucial for the industrial development of the Milan district. The northern Apennine slopes which lie on the opposite flank of the Po Plain are much less suited to hydro-electric power. The slopes are gentler, the rocks more porous and the precipitation lower and more seasonal; here there are only 7 reservoirs for hydro-electric purposes, compared to 108 on the Alpine side.[29]

In general the flow of hydro-electric power is from the Alps, the highest areas of the central Apennines and the Calabrian Sila to densely-populated areas of lowland nearby, but long distance transmission is increasing. Naturally, production and consumption by region do not coincide. Nearly two-thirds of hydro-electric power is produced in four regions: Lombardy, Trentino, Piedmont and Veneto. Trentino is the largest net exporter of water power, whilst Lombardy, although being the largest producer, needs to take energy from adjacent regions. With the exception of Calabria, most southern regions have electricity deficits. Figure 5.5 shows the regional pattern of electricity production.

Electricity and Industry

In a recent paper Giancarlo Lizzeri, Chairman of ENEL, has drawn attention to the many interesting insights that electricity consumption statistics can throw on the changing character and regional distribution of Italian industry, which currently absorbs 60 per cent of ENEL's output.[30] The ENEL data start in 1963 and Lizzeri makes comparisons between this base year and 1977 or 1978. One of the most remarkable features is the rapid growth of electricity consumption in the South, which increased its share of total national consumption from 15 per cent in 1963 to 26 per cent in 1977. One of the main factors behind this increase was the development in the South of certain types of industries with very high energy requirements. Southern industry accounted for 12.4 per cent of national industrial power in 1963, and 25.6 per cent in 1977. For certain types of industry the increase was more marked: steel 9 to 26.9 per cent, non-ferrous metals 0.6 to 31.7 per cent, petrochemicals 18.7 to 41.6 per cent and synthetic fibres 7.9 to 34.4 per cent. By 1973 these sectors accounted for 75 per cent of the total power consumption of manufacturing industry in the South; this proportion has declined slightly since then. Measured in terms of *per capita* power consumption (domestic and industrial), the South's value was 41 per cent of the national figure in 1963, rising rapidly to 73 per cent in 1978. Mean annual growth of *per capita* power consumption 1963-78 was 11 per cent for the South and 7.4 per cent for the Centre-North.

There are fairly specific reasons for these high rates of southern increase: the non-availability of alternative power sources like natural gas over wide areas of the South; the self-generation of electricity by many large industrial plants such as chemicals, steel and aluminium-refining; the general increased level of well-being of the population in terms of housing and living conditions; and of course the lower base-levels against which the rates for the South are measured in the first place.

Secondly, ENEL data on numbers of medium-voltage consumers — which are almost exclusively small to medium sized industries — provide an interesting indication of the growth of this scale of enterprise. During 1970-8 the number of these consumers increased 105 per cent in the South, 88 per cent in the Centre and 52 per cent in the North. Certain regions stand out as particularly affected by the rapid growth in these newly-formed small and medium firms: Sicily, Apulia, Calabria, Latium, Abruzzi, Tuscany, Umbria, Veneto and Trentino — in other words, the Deep South, Central and North-eastern Italy. It appears, particularly in the South, that the crisis of the industrial giants is being replaced by a new, smaller-scale industrial take-off, although Lizzeri warns that this expansion may soon be stifled by shortage of electricity in this power-deficient region.

Oil and Gas

This section is best begun with a note on the institutional background to hydrocarbon exploitation in Italy.[31] AGIP was created by the state in 1926 and given the task of searching for, extracting and refining oil. Until the creation of ENI in 1953, AGIP was the fulcrum of a range of state companies in the oil and gas industries. These included the formerly Dutch-owned Romsa (Raffineria Oli Minerali) which operated a refinery at Fiume (now Rijeka in Yugoslavia), ANIC (created by AGIP, Montecatini and the state railways in 1936 to process hydrocarbons), and SNAM (Società Nazionale Metanodotti), set up in 1941 to build and manage methane pipelines. AGIP also played a dominant role in post-war reconstruction of the heavily-damaged oil and gas industries, and continued its widespread exploration activities. In the scramble for prospecting and production rights, however, conflict emerged between the role of the state and the large, foreign-owned private companies. The arrival on the scene of the energetic and unscrupulous Enrico Mattei[32] tipped the balance firmly in favour of the state. Appointed originally to wind up AGIP, he gained it a reprieve on the strength of Po Valley discoveries and subsequently built the ENI oil-gas empire, with AGIP preserved as one of its main subsidiaries. Under Mattei, ENI was granted the monopoly of oil and gas prospecting, production and distribution for the entire Po Valley. With its headquarters at the appropriately-named Metanopoli, near Milan, ENI now ranks as one of Europe's great industrial combines, employing 88,000 workers and controlling 160 companies. Its most dramatic period of expansion was from 1954 until Mattei's untimely death in 1962; during this period fixed investments increased eight-fold, sales grew by 170 per cent and employment by 250 per cent. Most of this expansion was financed by the Po Valley gas finds. After Mattei's death, ENI went through a difficult period. Partly this was a direct consequence of the loss of a powerful leader for whom there was no ready substitute, but partly it was due to the overstretching involved in the large oil and petrochemicals investments at Gela in Sicily in the early 1960s. Steadier growth resumed in the late 1960s, with investment growing by 280 per cent, sales by 130 per cent and employment by 45 per cent over the period 1966-72. Since the 1973 energy crisis ENI has once again been in trouble, compounded in the last few years by allegations of corruption.

Oil and gas are often found in association but in Italy only the latter has yielded a significant contribution to domestic energy resources. Although Italy has long entertained hopes of major oil discoveries, the Eldorado has never materialised. Until 1949 only small amounts of oil had been found, mainly in the Cortemaggiore area near Piacenza. Richer fields were then found in Sicily: at Ragusa, discovered by Gulf Italia in 1954, and at Gela, struck by ENI two years later.[33] Unfortunately, the Sicilian oil is heavy and sulphurous. The only other notable fields are at Vallecupo (ENI) and Alanno (Petrosud) in the Abruzzi and the recently located Malossa source near Milan (ENI). Today domestically-produced oil accounts for only a little over 1 per cent of the oil used in Italy. For 30 years ENI has been involved in developing and securing oil supplies abroad, a policy severely curtailed by the take-over of foreign companies operating in OPEC's Middle Eastern empire. ENI's 'import drive' was deflected elsewhere — to Rumania, Russia and, most recently, Venezuela. The decision to import crude from the USSR was controversial but it opened the way for major Soviet orders not only from the Italian energy and petrochemicals industries but also from other industrial sectors not related to energy. Even so, most oil continues to come to Italy from the Middle East, especially Saudi Arabia (30 per cent), Kuwait (9 per cent), Iraq (20 per cent) and Libya (14 per cent).

Methane had been found in Northern Italy in the 1920s but serious exploitation of Italy's natural gas deposits began in 1944 with the discovery of large gasfields at Caviaga, 40 km from Milan and ideally situated for industrial use. During the ensuing ten years a programme of exploration by AGIP and by private companies yielded several other finds — at Vallecupo and San Salvo (Abruzzi), Ferrandina and Pisticci (Basilicata) and Gagliano Castelferrato (Sicily). The largest finds, however, continued to be located in the Po Valley, particularly in the south-eastern delta region near Ravenna: Ravenna Mare-Sud (1960), Casenatico (1961) and Porto Corsini Est (1963). Natural gas pipelines were laid from the Abruzzi to Rome and Naples, from Ferrandina to Bari and from the various sources to the main industrial centres in the Po Plain. Today the main focus of attention has shifted to offshore exploration.[34] In the South the main offshore source is the Luna A field lying off Crotone in Calabria, supplying 1,470 m cubic metres annually. Much greater quantities — about 10,000 m cubic metres, or 70 per cent of annual domestic gas production — come from the Romagna offshore fields, developed by AGIP. Some 18 gasfields are currently under exploitation in the shallow waters off Ravenna and Rimini. Exploration proceeds apace and discoveries will be critical for solving Italy's tight energy budget. In 1978 more workable oil and gas deposits were discovered off Ragusa and further out in the Sicilian Channel, as well as in the Adriatic and Ionian Seas. Currently ENI's biggest project in the hydrocarbons field is the 2,500 km 'Transmed' pipeline to carry natural gas from Hassi R'Mel in Algeria via Tunisia and Sicily to Minerbio near Bologna. Technical and political problems have delayed the project's progress but from 1985 Italy will receive from Algeria 12,300 million cubic metres of gas annually for 25 years.

Italy and the Energy Crisis

One of Italy's major economic problems is how to sustain an industrial boom built on cheap oil now that this fuel has become so expensive.[35] In 1973 the false wisdom of ENEL's all-oil policy was exposed. Now some oil-fired power stations are being switched to coal but this hardly constitutes a viable long-term solution, for coal is also expensive. Hydro-electric power has not expanded much since 1960, though some experts reckon another 20 per cent increase could be achieved.

Energy planning is difficult in Italy, where any kind of planning is difficult to carry through, and the population as a whole is not well informed about the energy problem. Although the oil price increases appear to have had little effect on private mobility — traffic chaos in cities like Naples and Rome is still as appalling as it was ten years ago — in other respects Italians have had to adjust to a new kind of normality which includes government regulations on office and home heating. Energy awareness has also been growing rapidly as a factor in industrial decision-making.

For a time nuclear energy appeared to be the only valid alternative to imported oil as the driving force for the future expansion of Italian industry. Some still hold to this view, particularly since the oil price leaps of 1973-4 and 1979-80.[36] There is certainly an *economic* rationale for nuclear expansion, for despite the fact that the initial outlay is twice as much as for a thermal plant of the same power output, the nuclear plant has much lower running costs. In the early 1960s Italy was in the vanguard of nuclear power development. At this time three small nuclear stations were built, at Latina (153 MW), Garigliano (150 MW) and Trino Vercellese (247 MW). A fourth, bigger plant was added in 1973 at Caorso on the Po (840 MW).[37] The more cautious attitude toward nuclear plant proliferation now prevalent in Italy, and in other European countries, has slowed down this sector of the domestic and industrial energy field. Of the 'new wave' of four nuclear power complexes to be built by 1985, on only one, the twin plants (1,000 MW each) at Montalto di Castro in Latium, has construction started, and that will not be ready by 1985. Of the other three, in Molise, Lombardy and Piedmont, the first has been blocked by the regional government whilst the other two founder on disputed choices of sites.[38]

The future outlook for Italy's energy situation is in some respects quite alarming. ENEL forecasts for 1990 predict increasing shortfalls in production when compared to demand. These imbalances will be especially serious in southern regions where any ambitious schemes for further industrialisation may well be constrained by the energy factor.[39] Of the southern regions, only Calabria will continue to have a small energy surplus. On the other hand, because of the general economic recession, electricity demand grew much less during the 1970s than was predicted by ENEL on the basis of the rapid growth of the 1960s. In 1971 ENEL forecast a doubling of electricity demand by 1980; in fact only half this increase materialised. It is now clear that, had the predicted increase occurred, installed capacity would have failed to cope. Massive black-outs would have occurred because of the failure to press ahead with new plants. Both the thermal and nuclear programmes have ground to a halt because of local opposition over the siting of plants and the wider environmental and safety debates. What one commentator has called 'the sad history of ENEL' — opting for oil only, failure to build new plants when needed, shelving the nuclear programme, ignoring other forms of energy research — is only now being realised.[40]

Since 1973 there has been a great deal of discussion on energy in Italy but very little concrete action. The so-called Energy Plan of 1975 was criticised and then abandoned. The major political parties cannot decide their energy options whilst some smaller parties adopt rhetorical and dogmatic positions. The 1976 'revised plan' replaced the 1975 plan's emphasis on nuclear power with greater reliance on coal. Most recently, the Ministry of Industry's Draft Energy Plan, drawn up in 1980, forecasts energy demand for 1990 and attempts to apportion this demand amongst the changing fortunes of the various supply sources. A projected increase in demand of 35 per cent reflects strong energy-saving policies and an annual rate of growth of energy demand of 2.8 per cent. Of the sources, hydro-electric and geothermal power will remain roughly constant in output but contribute a declining proportion of the total — 7.6 per cent in 1979 to 5.8 per cent in 1990. Nuclear will increase from 0.4 per cent to 5 per cent and natural gas from 15.6 per cent to 18.5 per cent. The major changes anticipated (or hoped for?) are a marked increase in coal — 7.9 per cent to 18 per cent — and a drop in oil requirements from 68.5 per cent in 1979 to 51.7 per cent in 1990 (though effectively this involves maintaining the *quantity* of oil imported constant at 1979 levels). 'Other' sources, primarily solar, could account for 1 per cent by 1990; their real impact will not be felt until well into the twenty-first century.[41]

Notes and References

1. Viterbo (1975), p.222.
2. This paragraph is based on Clough (1964), pp.68-71.
3. Clough (1964), p.27; Webster (1975), p.65.
4. Almagià (1959), p.864.
5. For the history of the electrification of the railways, see Molino (1972).
6. Webster (1975), p.93.
7. These are analysed in the SVIMEZ monographs by Cagliozzi (1975a and 1975b).
8. See Kalla-Bishop (1971), pp.170-6 and Molino (1976).
9. This account of Italian motorways is based on Apicella (1978), Beretta (1968), Murralli (1980), Nice (1976) and Pacione (1974a).
10. Because tolls have to be collected at access points and toll-stations are expensive to build, Italian motorways have relatively few entry/exit points. This greatly reduces the potential for short-trip use.
11. Cataudella (1968); Mori (1965); Pacione (1974a).
12. Pacione (1974a), pp.39-40.
13. Apicella (1978); Nice (1976); Secchi (1973); Tarulli (1973).
14. Vallega (1980).
15. Clough (1964), pp.71-81, 324-6.
16. The most noteworthy series of studies are the twelve volumes on various ports and groups of ports published between 1936 and 1959 under the auspices of the Centro di Studi Geografia Economica of Naples University. Space does not permit a full listing of these volumes but reference may by made to the concluding summary volume by Barbieri (1959) which also gives full bibliographic details of the preceeding eleven.
17. For interesting, though now dated, studies of the port of Genoa, see the various works of Rodgers (1957, 1958 and 1960).
18. Brusa (1964); Vallega (1977).
19. Innocenti (1970).
20. See Celant (1976), Landini (1975) and Ruggiero (1973) for expositions of this general viewpoint.
21. Cagliozzi (1970); Fuga (1976).
22. See Flore (1972) and Panunzio (1978).
23. Based on Ruggiero (1980).
24. Dalmasso (1964).
25. Blanchard (1928), p.264.
26. Clough (1964), p.96; Dalmasso (1964), p.451.
27. For instructive maps of this see Cole (1968), pp.135, 139.
28. For an example of this see Albertini (1959).
29. Bevilacqua and Mattana (1976), p.183.
30. Lizzeri (1979).
31. Allen and Stevenson (1974), pp.231-6; Keyser and Windle (1978), pp.106-14.
32. Mattei's charisma and his buccaneering approach to industrial management and politics are described in two English-language biographies: Frankel (1966) and Votaw (1964).
33. Rochefort (1960).
34. Pacione (1979).
35. Pacione (1976).
36. See, for example, the paper by Fogagnolo (1975) who is the managing director of AGIP Nucleare.
37. See Migliorini (1975) for the location factors behind Italian nuclear power stations.
38. Gasparini (1979).

39. Spinelli (1970).

40. Ippolito (1980), p.25.

41. In the short term there is much that could be done to use solar panels for domestic heating, particularly in the sunnier South of Italy; such use is already widespread in some other Mediterranean countries like Israel and Cyprus. A solar power station is currently being built on the slopes of Mount Etna above Bronte.

6 TEXTILES, CLOTHING AND FOOTWEAR

In Italy, as in many other European countries, the chief pioneer industry, in terms of the modernisation of industrial production and its centralisation in factories, was textiles. Indeed, this is a branch of manufacturing in which Italy has enjoyed a high reputation for centuries, as the earlier account of medieval and Renaissance industry showed. In the later Middle Ages Lombardy and Tuscany were leading world centres of woollen and silk manufacturing. However, it was not until the Napoleonic Wars that the first signs of modern industrialisation could be noted. At this stage factory machinery, capital and technicians were largely foreign. The greatest early nineteenth century progress was made in the Milan district where the cotton industry, using first water power and then imported coal for small steam mills, is generally considered to be the first evidence of modern factory industry in the country.

The textile industry's progressive industrialisation had a most dramatic effect on regional patterns of textile employment, as Table 6.1 shows. Initially, in 1881, textile activities were common throughout the country, with very high figures in some southern regions like Calabria and Apulia —high figures based almost exclusively on artisan enterprise. As the textile trade became factory based in Lombardy and Piedmont so it collapsed in other regions. The sharp fall in textile workers in southern regions is spelt out in Table 6.1 which also shows, in the bottom row, the long-term national trend in textile employment. In the post-war period the regional growth pattern has changed again, decline in northern regions being partially offset by some growth in virtually all regions south of Tuscany and Emilia. Provisional results of the 1981 Industrial Census confirm the trend of continued growth in the Centre but not in the South.

Nevertheless, the textile industry's modern distribution very much reflects its early patterns of development. More than any other major branch of manufacturing, textiles remain concentrated in the Northwest, with 61.5 per cent of employees in Lombardy and Piedmont alone. The lower Alpine valleys and the fringes of the Alpine chain, from Turin right across into Veneto, were the home of the silk industry; Como was, and still is, the leading centre. Wool and flax were produced in this same geographical region, and cotton clung to this distribution too. A long tradition of woollen manufacturing also exists at Florence

136

Table 6.1: Rates of Employment in Textile Industries, by Region, 1881-1971 (per 1,000 Population)

Regions	1881	1901	1911	1921	1931	1951	1961	1971
Piedmont-Val d'Aosta	23.1	26.1	33.6	33.6	42.1	44.2	34.7	23.0
Lombardy	60.7	58.0	56.7	55.3	60.7	51.7	36.6	25.1
Liguria	22.3	13.3	14.7	8.6	9.7	7.9	3.7	2.8
Trentino-Alto Adige	—	—	—	3.0	5.3	5.7	4.8	5.0
Veneto	15.3	12.4	15.0	10.6	19.5	19.4	16.8	15.0
Friuli-Venezia Giulia	10.4	21.5	22.0	10.8	16.2	16.5	13.0	10.8
Emilia-Romagna	26.2	8.2	7.3	5.0	5.2	4.9	11.6	11.4
Tuscany	20.5	13.4	12.0	9.8	13.1	16.8	21.0	21.9
Umbria	9.8	6.6	10.0	4.5	4.7	5.2	6.4	9.3
Marche	36.8	14.2	11.9	7.8	8.8	5.3	5.3	6.9
Latium	17.4	5.0	4.8	1.8	1.7	1.5	1.9	2.8
Abruzzi-Molise	63.5	20.7	6.8	3.8	2.2	1.5	2.4	3.9
Campania	62.4	21.7	12.4	6.4	6.2	4.4	2.9	4.3
Apulia	84.0	19.4	8.2	3.5	2.3	1.1	2.2	4.9
Basilicata	70.6	15.0	4.8	3.9	1.2	0.8	2.0	4.3
Calabria	176.7	81.0	36.0	15.9	4.5	1.0	1.9	5.0
Sicily	66.4	12.1	4.6	2.4	1.0	0.5	0.7	3.3
Sardinia	11.2	2.6	2.7	1.8	1.6	0.5	1.5	5.5
All Italy	47.8	23.6	19.5	15.5	17.3	15.4	13.3	11.8

Source: Golini and Gèseno (1981), p.78.

and Prato in Tuscany. Certain small towns, otherwise relatively unknown, have become indelibly associated with the textile industry: the best examples are Biella and Prato for wool and Legnano and Busto Arsizio for cotton.

The importance of the textiles sector in the Italian industrial economy has shrunk over the years. From over a third of total manufacturing employment in 1951, textiles' share dropped to below a quarter by 1981, although the total number of textile workers held firm during this period (1,363,000 in 1951, 1,405,300 in 1980); the relative drop was due to an increasing total manufacturing workforce. The share of exports plummeted rather more sharply, from 42.3 per cent of total manufacturing exports in 1951 to 17.4 per cent in 1981. Fierce competition from abroad, both in home and foreign markets, has been a major cause of this decline; at home, difficult trade union relations have not helped. Nevertheless, the textile sector retains second place to the mechanical in terms of both manufacturing employment and exports. The Italian reputation for textile design and fashion leadership still holds, with Rome and Milan two of Europe's leading centres of *haute couture*.

Structure of the Industry

The main structural characteristic of the textile industry is its large number of very small firms. In 1981 84.4 per cent of firms had less than 10 employees; these enterprises accounted for 22.9 per cent of textile workers. There is, however, some organisational variety between branches. Large units are the rule in rayon and synthetics; some large enterprises exist in the cotton branch; whilst wool, knitting and hosiery concerns are predominantly small. In the natural fibre sphere there are only four firms of any size — Marzotto, Lanerossi, Lanificio e Canapificio Nazionale and Beniberg. In artificial fibres the giants are Snia Viscosa and Châtillon.

Tables 6.2 and 6.3 provide fuller details of the structural and geographical characteristics of the Italian textile industry. The dominance of the regions of Lombardy, Piedmont, Veneto and Tuscany is striking; together they contain more than four-fifths of both factories and employment. The region of Lombardy has 65 per cent of all cotton factories, 91 per cent of silk factories and 29 per cent of hosiery and knitting factories, whilst Piedmont has 46 per cent of all woollen factories, 18 per cent of cotton factories and 10 per cent of hosiery and knitting factories.

Table 6.2: Number of Factories and Employment in the Textile Industry, 1976

Textile branch	Number of factories classified by number of employees						Total	
	10-49	50-99	100-199	200-499	500-999	over 1,000	No.	%
Wool	611	146	92	73	14	6	942	23.4
Cotton	329	156	109	108	27	7	736	18.3
Silk	199	93	62	12	3	—	369	9.2
Hard natural fibres	45	20	14	12	3	—	94	2.3
Hosiery and knitting	919	263	116	61	15	2	1,376	34.2
Man-made fibres	54	29	17	17	4	—	121	3.0
Miscellaneous textiles	251	64	46	22	4	—	387	9.6
Total No.	2,408	771	456	305	70	15	4,025	100.0
%	59.8	19.2	11.3	7.6	1.7	0.4	100	
	Number of employees							
Wool	14,796	10,045	12,445	21,265	10,069	9,040	77,660	23.0
Cotton	8,404	11,072	15,468	33,716	9,326	11,570	99,556	29.5
Silk	5,576	6,744	8,557	3,386	1,857	—	26,120	7.7
Hard natural fibres	1,098	1,375	1,903	3,536	1,718	—	9,630	2.9
Hosiery and knitting	21,479	18,315	16,078	17,761	9,349	2,617	85,599	25.3
Man-made fibres	1,412	2,076	2,385	5,049	2,497	—	13,419	4.0
Miscellaneous textiles	6,032	4,756	6,269	6,316	2,422	—	25,795	7.6
Total No.	58,797	54,383	63,105	91,029	47,238	23,227	337,779	100.0
%	17.4	16.1	18.7	26.9	14.0	6.9	100	

Note: Only units employing at least 10 workers are included.

Source: Picarelli (1977), p.47.

Table 6.3: Textiles: Number of Factories and Employment by Region, 1976

Regions	Wool	Cotton	Silk	Hard natural fibres	Hosiery and knitting	Man-made fibres	Miscellaneous textiles	Total	No. of Employees	%
Piedmont-Val d'Aosta	431	133	7	15	136	28	67	817	68,489	20.3
Lombardy	55	480	335	30	405	52	177	1,534	138,963	41.2
Liguria	1	6	—	4	9	—	4	24	2,580	0.8
Trentino-Alto Adige	5	7	3	2	9	3	4	32	3,090	0.9
Veneto	51	39	12	4	214	14	49	383	39,880	11.8
Friuli-Venezia Giulia	2	20	2	2	25	4	3	58	11,192	3.3
Emilia-Romagna	14	4	1	4	248	3	10	284	15,582	4.6
Tuscany	337	14	—	9	80	2	37	479	24,866	7.4
Umbria	4	3	—	1	35	1	3	47	4,858	1.4
Marche	2	3	1	3	53	1	4	67	3,157	0.9
Latium	16	4	1	2	29	5	5	62	6,733	2.0
Abruzzi-Molise	9	2	—	1	13	1	3	29	1,355	0.4
Campania	8	13	7	16	14	1	4	63	6,815	2.0
Apulia	—	4	—	1	92	2	10	109	5,844	1.7
Basilicata	—	—	—	—	1	1	2	4	370	0.1
Calabria	1	—	—	—	4	1	—	6	564	0.2
Sicily	2	3	—	—	5	1	4	15	1,455	0.4
Sardinia	4	1	—	—	4	1	2	12	1,986	0.6
Total	942	736	369	94	1,376	121	387	4,025	337,779	100.0

Note: Only units employing at least 10 workers are included.
Source: Picarelli (1977), p.48.

The textile industry, like most traditional branches of manufacturing, has been severely hit by the economic crisis of the last few years. The vulnerability of some sections of the industry has prompted a series of self-imposed rationalisations aimed at streamlining production and curbing cost inflation.[1] The strong development of mechanical and electrical engineering industries in the 1960s in those regions important for textiles also forced up the price of skilled labour, to the detriment of the textile employer. One reaction was for the structure of the textile industry to 'disintegrate' by breaking into smaller and more flexible units: this has especially been the case in Tuscany. Data to prove the existence of this trend are rather sketchy, however. Some indications are given by comparison of figures reported in the 1971 Industrial Census and other figures given by Picarelli and by Militerno and Tondini for the late 1970s.[2] This comparison shows that whilst total workers engaged in textiles held steady, those in factories with at least 10 employees fell by 13 per cent. Only the man-made fibre branch expanded strongly, by 10.5 per cent in terms of numbers of factories employing at least 10 workers and by 7.9 per cent in terms of numbers of workers employed in such factories. There was a particularly drastic loss of employees from the cotton sector (34.2 per cent between 1971 and 1981), continuing a long-term trend established since the 1950s. The textile crisis is also a specifically northern phenomenon, with half the job losses occurring in Lombardy alone, and another 46 per cent occurring in Piedmont, Veneto and Emilia. Tuscany, the South and parts of the North-east are proving more resilient, with some new enterprises being created in these regions in recent years.[3]

Another structural feature worthy of mention is the scant participation of public enterprise in the textile industry. With its predominant structure of small and medium factories, the textiles industry represents the antithesis of typical public sector involvement in big projects. Overall, public enterprise accounts for only 3.5 per cent of total textile employment — a modest stake indeed compared to other industrial branches (metallurgy's 35.6 per cent for instance). Nevertheless, state holdings represent some of the biggest enterprises in the textile sector. ENI controls, through its subsidiary Tescon, several large firms: Lanerossi and Il Fabbricone in wool; MCM, Filatura di Sondrio and Tessitura di Sondrio in cotton; and Rosabel in knitting and hosiery.

In spite of the continuing crisis of textiles in Italy, the industry's total production has held steady or increased slightly over the last decade, fluctuating initially downwards but then irregularly upwards from a base of 100 in 1970 (1971 97.7, 1973 114.6, 1975 104.2, 1976 127.2,

1978 113.9, 1980 135.8) — a pattern which matches the overall index of Italian industrial output remarkably closely. Within textiles, hosiery and knitted goods have increased most strongly in recent years. The buoyant export of these lines of textile products keeps the overall export position of textiles relatively healthy. However, the fact that the import of fabrics and yarns is increasing faster than exports constitutes a warning for the future. Fifteen years ago exports accounted for half of total textiles sales by value; now the proportion has dropped to one-third.

Finally, before we examine individual branches of the textile industry, a note on labour productivity. Official figures indicate a tripling of sales per employee over the period 1970-80. One possible explanation for this might be the amount of new investment together with an increase in sales and the simultaneous contraction of the labour force and of labour's proportion of value added. If this were indeed the case, it would be possible to paint a highly favourable picture of the general state of the textile industry. The fact is, however, that labour efficiency has declined — this is confirmed by all the pertinent trade union reports — and absenteeism levels have reached 17 per cent. The apparent contradiction is explained by the trend of the textile industry to make heavy use of outwork which is unregistered and underpaid. This progressive structuring of the textile industry into small businesses with a small number of essential workers and a large number of domestic outworkers not only reduces firms' costs but also gives them an operating flexibility which makes them less vulnerable to economic trends — although at the expense of sweated female labour.[4]

Silk

Silk is an industry of the past. It flourished in medieval times and in the nineteenth and early twentieth centuries, but today it is a residual industry only.

Sericulture was introduced into Sicily by the Moors as early as the ninth century. Palermo became the first centre of the industry. Very soon after, mulberries were cultivated and silkworms reared by monks at Catanzaro in Calabria. Venice also developed an early silk industry, in the twelfth century, based on trading contacts with the East. The art of silkworm culture and weaving soon spread to other parts of Northern and Central Italy, encouraged by the great Italian dukes and princes. Milan, Florence and Genoa all became important, especially for the production of rich silks. Weaving and sericulture then developed on a larger scale at Lucca and at Bologna where a water-driven machine for twisting and spinning silk was developed. The fourteenth and fifteenth centuries, the Renaissance, were the golden age of Italian silk, consumed in large quantities in dresses, curtains and hangings in the brilliant courts of the realm. Catania, Palermo, Catanzaro, Siena and Genoa became famous throughout Europe for their silk cloths and velvets. Mulberries and silk cocoons began to be widely cultivated in the northern plain, where Verona and Vicenza became important centres of the industry. Later, during the late sixteenth century, smaller places emerged as 'silk towns' — Mantua, Ferrara, Reggio nell'Emilia and, eventually, Como. In Rome the manufacture of silk was encouraged by the popes.

The seventeenth and eighteenth centuries saw the industry in decline. Political events, wars and then, in the early nineteenth century, silkworm diseases, were the main factors behind this. Como was the only silk manufacturing centre to progress during the eighteenth century.

The nineteenth century revival of silk was much more geographically concentrated than the pattern of the medieval industry. Northern Italy — Piedmont, Lombardy and Veneto — became the silk heartland, with the town of Como pre-eminent for production and Milan for commerce. By the mid nineteenth century there were, in Lombardy and Piedmont, about 750 silk mills, mostly dependent on water power. At that time silk reeling (the process of getting the filament of raw silk yarn from the cocoon) and throwing (the preparation of the filament silk for weaving) gave employment to 150,000 people, mainly peasants working seasonally in small mills scattered over the countryside of Northern Italy.

Luciano Cafagna[5] stresses that it was these mills that gave the Italian workforce its first training in industrial labour. The sale of silk was the first non-agricultural economic activity to interest capital-owning landlords and merchant bankers on a large scale. Trade interests resulted in an influx of Swiss and German businessmen who were later to play an important part in turning Italy's embryonic industrial energies in other directions. Therefore, the development of the silk industry contributed in several ways towards forming the external economies for further industrial development. It was a kind of 'pioneering sector' in nineteenth century industrialisation. For some hundred years, from the Restoration to the First World War, silk products led the field in Italian exports, contributing a more of less constant one-third of their total value.

Nevertheless, considerable change took place within the industry during this period. Silk spinning underwent a minor revolution. Spurred on by a crisis in domestic supplies of the raw material (due to silkworm disease in the 1860s), the industry started to import some raw silk from abroad and moved more weight into throwing, the final phase of the spinning process. The highest levels of production and export were reached in the 1900s. In 1906, the peak year, 10,400 tonnes of silk were exported, mainly to France. In 1907, however, the value of silk exports began to fall. Far Eastern competition began to be felt and the rayon industry, offering a substitute product, appeared. There was talk of a crisis in the silk industry, but this was exaggerated. The value of silk exports held fairly steady until 1914, continuing to represent between one-third and one-quarter of total exports. The quality of the silks exported improved considerably.

The silk industry has been shrinking for almost the whole of the twentieth century, although the serious decline started after 1930. The present distribution of silk production and manufacture is likewise a contraction from the patterns of the past. The industry is now confined to an arc of towns to the north of Milan from Varese through Como to Treviglio. Como remains the headquarters of silk manufacture. The only significant producing areas are in Veneto (especially the Euganean Hills) and scattered parts of Lombardy, Fruili and Marche. Regular lines of mulberry trees are still a familiar element in the agricultural landscape of the northern part of the Po Plain, but they are gradually being sacrificed to the demands of mechanisation as raw silk declines with rising living standards. The structure of the industry, what remains of it, is still highly fragmented, with the various separate and subsidiary operations (spinning, throwing, dyeing, printing, etc.) carried out by small individual concerns. By 1976 silk production was running at 1,180 tonnes per year; at the 1971 census employment was only 18,950; the 1981 census did not identify silk as a separate employment category. Nevertheless the industry survives on a modest scale, quality is high and the luxury market, chiefly in the USA, relatively assured.

Cotton

Like silk, the historical geography of the cotton industry has both a medieval and a nineteenth century phase. The chronology of the medieval period has been fixed by Mazzaoui: a rapid growth of the industry in the twelfth and thirteenth centuries, levelling off in the fourteenth, followed by uneven decline in the fifteenth.[6] The introduction of cotton was related to the expansion of Italian overseas commerce in the period of the Crusades. Already widely used in the Islamic Mediterranean, it rapidly penetrated the port markets of Venice, Pisa and Genoa, whilst in the south the Arabs introduced its cultivation into Sicily, Calabria and Apulia, regions where there is still some cultivation today. The main region for the medieval cotton industry was the North Italian Plain. The main centres were Pavia, Piacenza, Bologna and Milan but its presence in the early thirteenth century was noted in virtually every town of significance, and in many more besides. Guilds of cotton producers are reported for Verona in 1214, Padua in 1236 and Parma in 1253 and many cities made arrangements for the organised immigration of specialised cotton artisans. Several cotton centres also sprang up in Tuscany — Florence, Arezzo, Poggibonsi, Pontremoli and, further south, Todi. Especially critical in the spatial structure of the medieval cotton industry was the transport network. The system of waterways (the Po, Adige, Mincio and Ticino rivers and the Naviglio canal between Bologna and Ferrara) provided a cheap means of transport for a bulky commodity like cotton whilst landwards the Alpine passes gave access to northern Europe, notably the Frejus between Piedmont and France and the Brenner between Veneto and the Germanic realm.

The medieval cotton industry had many features characteristic of an industrial structure of the modern era. Rapid expansion of markets, organised movements of skilled workmen, product standardisation and technological innovation in the various production processes are all characteristic of powerful entrepreneurial interests, not of the limited vision of the traditional artisan. Many of the specialised processes of the industry required pools of skilled yet cheap labour which were housed in the newly-built suburbs of the cities. In addition to urban workers, cotton entrepreneurs also drew on reserves of rural female labour for spinning and bleaching.

Clear signs of economic crisis appeared in the industry during the fourteenth and fifteenth centuries. Among the causes of this decline can be listed the following: general economic dislocation, including international monetary instability and shifting commercial routes; the demographic losses of the Black Death which eroded the pool of cheap labour; and the virtually total dependence of the cotton industry, unlike silk and wool, on foreign supplies of raw material. The advent of a regionally fragmented economy in the fifteenth century marked the end of the North Italian production zone. Only the main centres such as Milan and Venice continued to thrive; elsewhere the cotton industry stagnated or declined.

The nineteenth century growth of the cotton industry was initially rather slow. However, after about 1830 cotton emerged as the most attractive commodity, after silk, for traders and the landed nobility to invest in. Machines were brought in by foreign industrialists. The Muller brothers introduced the first mechanical spinning jenny in Italy in 1808 at Intra, Piedmont. Steam power was first applied to spinning in 1816 and the first spinning mule was established in 1823 at Solbiate near Como. A Swiss consortium founded the South's main centre of the cotton industry at Salerno.

By the middle of the nineteenth century there were about 60 cotton-spinning mills in Piedmont and Lombardy, together working 200,000 spindles. There were, at that time, about 3,500 spindles per factory and 30 spindles per worker. Nevertheless, industrial concentration in the manufacture of cotton in Italy was beginning to take place, transforming certain towns and districts in Piedmont and along the northern margins of the Po Plain. Later, a spatial shift in cotton manufacture from Piedmont to Lombardy took place, so that by 1900 Lombardy had 44 per cent of cotton spindles and 55 per cent of looms in Italy, compared to figures for Piedmont of 28 per cent and 25 per cent respectively.

Unlike other branches of the textile industry, cotton enjoyed uninterrupted development, remaining relatively unaffected by the crisis around 1890. It drew great benefit from the tariff measures of 1878 and 1887 which guaranteed the expanding home market.[7] Exports developed fast, especially to Latin America where there were large Italian emigrant colonies. The rate of expansion of the cotton industry was most impressive between 1900 and 1914: the number of mechanical looms nearly doubled from 70,600 to 120,000 and spindle numbers grew from 1.9 million to 4.6 million. Aside from expanding markets both home and overseas, the new use of hydro-electric power gave a further boost. Unlike the silk industry which flourished as a supplier of semi-finished goods to the industry of the industrialised countries of Europe, the cotton industry supplied the consumer markets of non-industrial or semi-industrial countries with finished products.[8]

Production figures for the inter-war period indicate stable levels of output of cotton, declining somewhat during the late 1930s and then slashed by the war. The post-war trends in annual production for cotton yarn and cloth are shown in Figure 6.1. Maximum figures were reached in the early and mid 1960s, with uneven decline since 1968 followed by renewed growth in the late 1970s. Employment, however, has declined continuously and comprehensively since the 1950s.

Currently, clothing accounts for half the output of the cotton indus-

Figure 6.1: Cotton Production, 1946-80

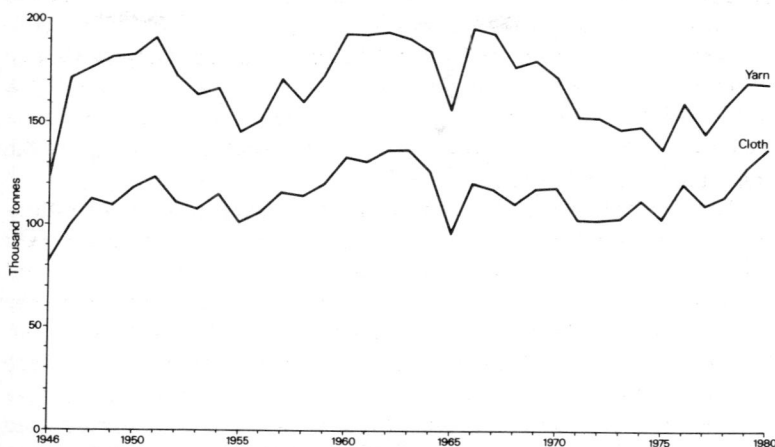

Sources: *Sommario di Statistiche Storiche dell'Italia 1861-1975,* Rome: ISTAT (1976), p.94; *Annuario di Statistiche Industriali 1981,* Rome: ISTAT (1982), p.61.

try, followed by household uses (linen and furnishing fabrics) which account for 40 per cent of the output, and industrial and miscellaneous uses (industrial bindings, tents, lint, cotton wool, etc.) which absorb the remaining 10 per cent. These are approximate estimates; the proportion going for clothing is diminishing.

The drop in equipment and production over the last 20 years has been more marked for spinning than for weaving. This difference is explained by the development of the hosiery and knitwear industry which now absorbs, by weight, about 35 per cent of cotton yarns produced, compared to 60 per cent taken for weaving and 5 per cent for the production of sewing threads and other purposes.

The third main sector of the cotton industry deals with 'finishing', e.g. dyeing and printing. The discovery of the colouring properties of certain lichens in Florence around 1 300 gave birth to important activities in the realm of yarn and fabric dyeing. Indeed, perhaps the best known feature of Italian textiles is their colour and design — an ability to bring fabrics to life that somehow seems to elude the textile industries of other parts of Europe. No statistics are available on the quantity and value of this sector's production, but it has absorbed one-quarter of the cotton industry's investment in recent years and appears to be on the increase.[9]

Figure 6.2: Employment in the Cotton Industry, by Province, 1981

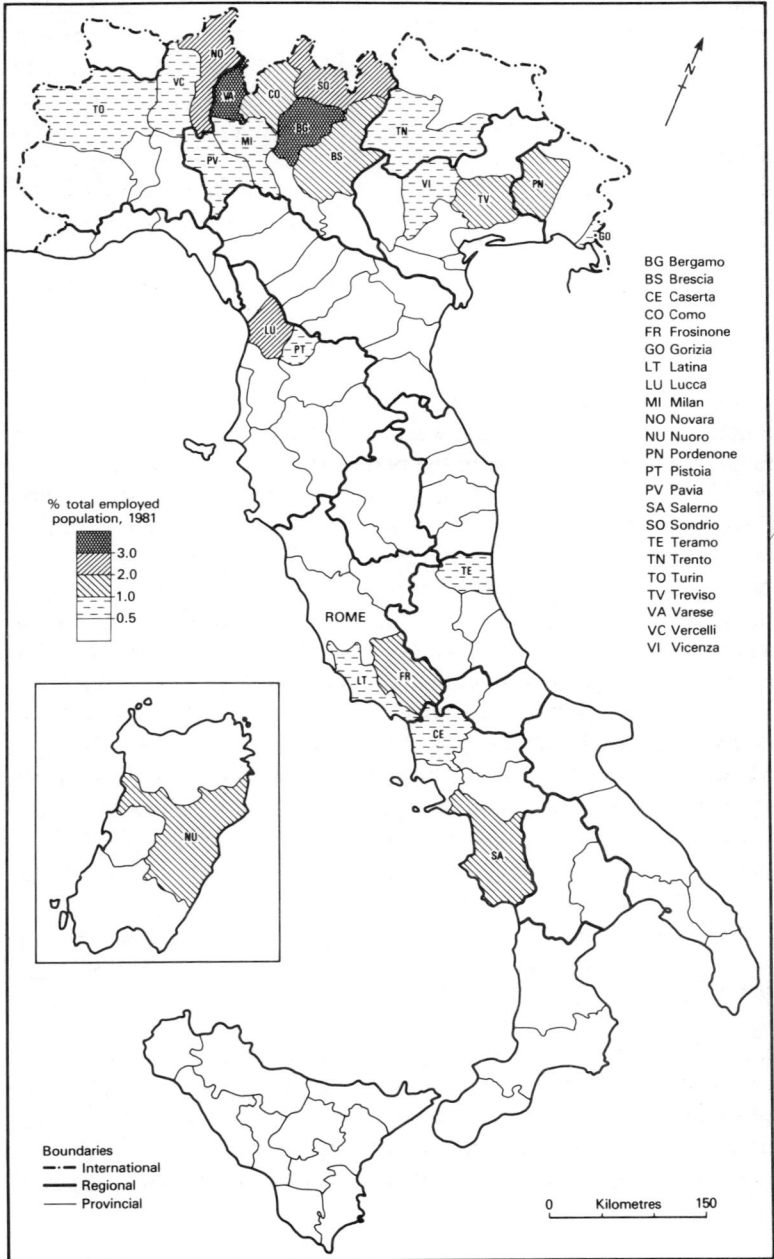

BG Bergamo
BS Brescia
CE Caserta
CO Como
FR Frosinone
GO Gorizia
LT Latina
LU Lucca
MI Milan
NO Novara
NU Nuoro
PN Pordenone
PT Pistoia
PV Pavia
SA Salerno
SO Sondrio
TE Teramo
TN Trento
TO Turin
TV Treviso
VA Varese
VC Vercelli
VI Vicenza

% total employed
population, 1981

3.0
2.0
1.0
0.5

ROME

Boundaries
—·—· International
—— Regional
—— Provincial

0   Kilometres   150

Source: As Figure 4.1

Figure 6.2 shows the pattern of employment in the cotton industry by province, based on provisional data from the 1981 Industrial Census. The main feature of the distribution is the continuous belt across northern Italy coinciding with the lower Alpine valleys and the high Po Plain. The density of cotton employment is particularly high in the provinces of eastern Piedmont (Novara and Varese) and western and northern Lombardy (Como, Bergamo, Brescia, Sondrio). In this 'core' are to be found the famous 'cotton towns' of Busto Arsizio and Gallarate (Varese province) and Legnano (Milan province), each containing dozens of mills. Another major concentration of traditional cotton production lies in the Val Seriana, north-east of Bergamo. Other provinces with significant employment in cotton include Treviso and Pordenone in North-east Italy, Lucca in Tuscany, Frosinone near Rome, Salerno and the Sardinian province of Nuoro.

The Val Seriana can be taken as a brief case study of a declining cotton region.[10] Cotton developed as the main industry in the valley in the nineteenth century. The first warning of the dangers of such occupational specialisation came in the period 1929-32 when 70 per cent of the 10,000 workforce in the textile industry in the valley lost their jobs. Early post-war development was rapid, however, and by the 1950s the textile industry (mostly cotton) employed 15,000 workers, 87 per cent of the Val Seriana's manufacturing workforce. Mill closures again became serious during the 1960s and 1970s, so that the textile labour force fell by one-third to 10,125 in 1971. Economic collapse provoked a demographic loss of 7.4 per cent of the area's population during 1961-71. In the lower part of the valley the population held stable since ex-mill workers could commute to other jobs in Bergamo or even to the Milan industrial zone. Communes in the upper part of the valley lost 20-40 per cent of their populations, however. Industrial reconversion in these areas, if it takes place at all, is a slow process, whilst modernisation of the cotton industry itself almost inevitably leads to lower labour requirements.

Wool

Like silk and cotton, the wool industry too has medieval origins. It was important in Tuscany in the twelfth century when Lucca was the chief centre. Later it spread to Florence but declined after the Renaissance. The other main centre of medieval wool production was Venice where a remarkable expansion of high quality cloth production, largely geared to export markets, took place in the sixteenth century.[11] On the face of it, Venice had few reasons to attract a wool industry. There was a chronic shortage of land, a wide range of other industries competed for labour, and there were no streams to operate mills (Venetian cloth had to be sent to mills at Treviso for fulling). The answer lay in the particular economic and political circumstances of the time. The sudden diversion of the rich spice trade to the Atlantic sea route as a result of Portuguese voyages around Africa left Venetian merchants high and dry and seeking an alternative business to develop. At the same time the textile industries of mainland towns like Milan, Brescia and Pavia were in disarray through wars and foreign occupation. Venice's opportunism expanded cloth production from 2,000 pieces per year in 1517 to a peak of 29,000 in 1602. Thereafter, and with striking symmetry, the trend was reversed, and production was back again at 2,000 pieces per year in the early eighteenth century. Failure to innovate and reduce prices in the face of new competition from England, Holland and the rejuvenated mainland towns of Northern Italy, and contraction of demand for high quality cloth in Levantine markets were the main reason for the collapse.

The history of the Italian wool industry in the nineteenth century has many features which are similar to that of the cotton industry. Wool manufacture too tended to be concentrated in the North, in Alpine valleys and on infertile but well-watered high terraces above the Po Plain. Originally rough hill land nearby was important for grazing but as the industry developed more wool was imported. Alpine streams supplied the soft water required for scouring, and provided the driving force for machinery, first directly and later through hydro-electricity. However, compared to cotton, progress in the wool industry was slower. Achieving a better quality product required greater technical efficiency than in the other textile branches; mechanisation was less extensive and woollen goods did not develop a strong export position. The number of wool industry workers increased only slowly from 25,000 in 1867 to 50,000 in 1914. At the beginning of the twentieth century nearly half the woollen looms and one-third of the spindles were still hand-operated, but power-driven machines took over after 1914, by which time industrial concentration was occurring. Successful companies had also emerged, such as Lanerossi at Biella (the North's main woollen town) and Kosslër Mayer of Prato in Tuscany (where a speciality was made of coarser and regenerated 'shoddy' products). Aided by tariff protection, the main technical effort at this time consisted in promoting the manufacture of finer and more costly combing wools in preference to the traditional coarse carding wools. These advances were not insignificant, but Italy was obviously some way behind the leader, England, which had 2.8 million spindles in wool in 1914, compared to Italy's 883,000.[12]

After the First World War the wool industry expanded steadily and generated a surplus for export. This upward trend was checked by the world slump starting in 1929, and by the Second World War, but then revived in the post-war period. Woollen spinning grew explosively in the early 1970s, the number of spindles leaping from 900,000 in 1970 to 1.6 million in 1974. This latter year, however, was a year of falling production and much redundant plant. Since then production has stabilised at 509,170 tons of yarn per year and 195,675 tons of cloth (mean annual output figures for 1976-80). The wool industry has been somewhat less affected by recent economic pressures than cotton. Employment in wool fell by 17 per cent during 1971-81 (cf. 34 per cent for cotton). The vast majority of raw wool used now is imported; the fibre obtained from Italy's own flocks is unsuitable for the finer fabrics now in demand and is largely used for mattresses, felts and upholstery.

The current distribution of employment in the wool industry (Figure 6.3) shows a more concentrated pattern than that for cotton. There are fewer provinces with significant employment in woollen manufacture, bearing in mind that similar numbers are employed in the two industries. Three main areas stand out. The first is Vercelli province in Piedmont; in this province 19.5 per cent of the employed population are engaged in the wool industry. Vercelli province contains the Biellese (the area around Biella) which accounts for half of Italy's wool employment. Here spinning is more important than weaving. The industry is structured in a large number of small or medium sized mills located in narrow but densely settled valleys such as the Elvo, Cervo and Strona. However, Val Sesia, 20 km east of Biella, has only big mills, mostly owned by firms in the Consorzio Filatori di Lane e Pettine, a cartel formed in 1905. The second district centres on Prato near Florence, with adjacent Pistoia province also important. Prato specialises in shoddy with a large number of small concerns in the town and in adjacent valleys and basins of the Arno-Serchio river system. The wool industry in this part of Tuscany retains a certain dynamism and flexibility, achieved by the myriad of small enterprises corresponding to specialised stages of production. The third area is Vicenza province in Veneto. At Schio and Valdagno are large weaving mills belonging to two of Italy's leading manufacturers, Lanerossi and Marzotto.

Figure 6.3: Employment in the Wool Industry, by Province, 1981

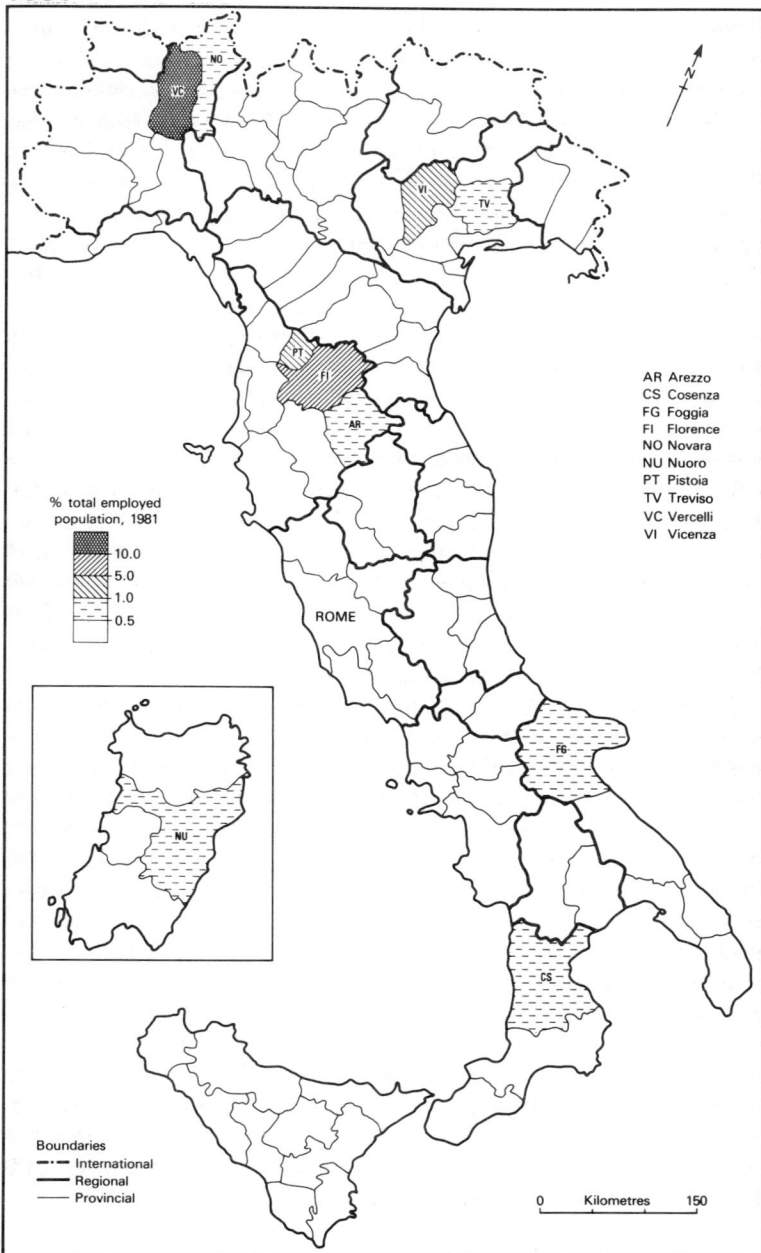

% total employed
population, 1981

- 10.0
- 5.0
- 1.0
- 0.5

AR Arezzo
CS Cosenza
FG Foggia
FI Florence
NO Novara
NU Nuoro
PT Pistoia
TV Treviso
VC Vercelli
VI Vicenza

ROME

Boundaries
- International
- Regional
- Provincial

0   Kilometres   150

Source: As Figure 4.1.

Artificial and Synthetic Fibres

Other textiles manufactured in Italy include hemp, jute and linen. None of these accounts for much employment. Far more spectacular has been the rise during the last 50 years of 'man-made' fibres which can be divided into two distinct groups — artificial fibres, made from cellulose, and synthetics, made from hydrocarbons. Many Italian textile firms use several different fibres in their manufacturing and there has been a tendency for existing silk, cotton and woollen weaving factories to change partly or entirely from natural to artificial or synthetic fibres.

The first factory in Italy for the production of rayon from cellulose was opened in 1908 and Italy emerged as a major producer of rayon between the wars. Much of the necessary raw material — from cane, poplar and eucalyptus — is home-grown. Historically there was a preference on the part of rayon manufacturers to be near water sources (for power and for cleaning), other textile industries (for labour familiar with textile processes) and chemical industries (for certain essential chemicals). As a result most rayon mills have been located in the area north of Milan and Turin. Rayon manufacture is highly capital intensive and production is therefore concentrated in the hands of a small number of firms operating a few large plants. Torviscosa, 30 km south of Udine, can be considered a company town owned by Snia Viscosa, the main concern in the rayon industry.

Since the war Italy has shared in, and in some respects pioneered, the 'second generation' of man-made fibres, the synthetics. The phenomenal expansion of synthetic fibres up to 1973 edged the rayons out of certain sectors of the market with the result that artificial fibre production stagnated at a plateau of around 180,000-200,000 tons annually for the period 1961-71, then declined rapidly to an output of only 65,000 tons in 1980 (Figure 6.4). Expansion of synthetic fibres came to an abrupt halt in 1974-5, since when production has levelled off at around 400,000 tons per year.

Synthetic yarns are really part of the oil and chemical industries, but they pass into textiles when woven. Five types of fibres are produced: polyamide (nylon), polyvinyl, polyester, acrylic and polypropylene. Polyamide was the first synthetic fibre to be produced (in 1938), but its importance has gradually been overtaken by the more recent development and expansion of polyester and acrylic fibres, much used in clothing manufacture. By 1980 these two fibres accounted for more than 60 per cent of synthetics output (Table 6.4)

Figure 6.4: Output of Man-made Fibres, 1946-80

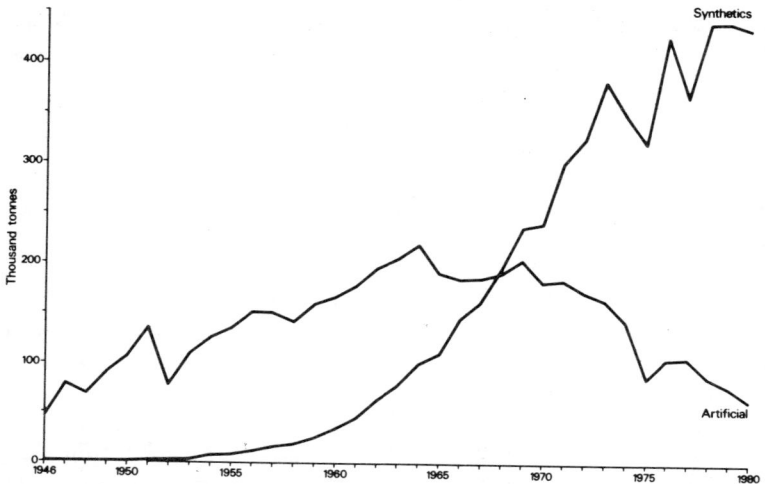

Source: *Annuario di Statistiche Industriali 1981,* Rome: ISTAT (1982), p.254.

As with rayon, production of synthetic fibres is in large, heavily capitalised units controlled by big firms such as Snia Viscosa, Montefibre (the fibres subsidiary of Montedison) and the state-controlled ANIC. These three concerns account for 70 per cent of production. Much of the earlier production capacity in synthetic fibres was set up as an offshoot of the northern chemical industry, but in the last 15 years much new plant has been established in the South, lured there by the generous grants and incentives offered by the Cassa per il Mezzogiorno. Snia Viscosa switched strongly from artificial to synthetic fibres in the early 1970s, doubling capacity at its acrylic staple plant at Villacidro in Sardinia, and opening a new polyester plant at Naples and a new polyamide line at Castellaccio south of Rome. ANIC's main plants in Southern Italy were the acrylic fibre complex near Pisticci in Basilicata and a joint venture with Montedison at Ottana in central Sardinia. Sardinia was also the locus of fibre initiatives by SIR (Società Italiana Resine), until its recent demise Italy's third-biggest chemical company and fourth-largest synthetic fibre concern. Under the flamboyant leadership of Nino Rovelli SIR established polyester facilities at Porto Torres and acrylic production at Ottana.

Table 6.4: Production of Synthetic Fibres, 1960-80

Year	Polyamide tons	%	Polyvinyl tons	%	Polyester tons	%	Acrylic tons	%	Polypropylene tons	%
1960	25,381	81.6	1,726	5.5	3,243	10.4	775	2.5	—	—
1965	61,916	58.1	2,641	2.5	12,183	11.4	21,435	20.1	8,387	7.9
1970	102,533	42.4	6,614	2.7	38,319	15.8	72,829	30.1	21,675	9.0
1975	96,667	30.2	1,242	0.4	75,345	23.5	112,792	35.2	34,332	10.7
1980	114,672	27.6	—	—	81,850	19.7	170,660	41.0	48,450	11.7

Source: Balella (1972), p.116; *Annuario di Statistiche Industriali 1981*, Rome: ISTAT (1982), p.80.

One of the curious features of the Italian synthetic fibres industry is the strange mixture of co-operation and rivalry that it contains. Montedison is the largest shareholder in Snia Viscosa, with a 34 per cent stake, and the two firms collaborate a good deal on research and plant design. Yet, at the same time, they remain distinct entities and compete as rivals in the same markets. Montefibre's relations with ANIC are even more ambiguous. They participated equally in the setting up of a fibre complex in central Sardinia, but clash over plans for future developments.

By the early 1970s the Italian chemical fibres industry faced a daunting array of problems: rising costs of labour and of raw materials; an influx of cheap fibres from Eastern Europe and the Far East; excess production on European and world markets leading to a slump in prices; and a weakening of domestic demand. Undeterred, Italian producers pushed ahead with their ambitious expansion plans, contributing two-thirds of Western Europe's 37 per cent increase in synthetic fibre capacity over the period 1975-80. Italy is now second only to West Germany as Europe's main man-made fibre producer.

The period 1975-80 was one of high production but staggering financial losses. It was also a period of radical restructuring, drastic cuts in proportion of capacity utilised, revised production schedules, new backing consortia, heavy write-offs and injections of billions of lire in fresh capital. In contrast to the 1960s and early 1970s when the demand for chemical fibres seemed insatiable, the emphasis has now changed to one of market-seeking. Montefibre, the biggest producer, is concentrating on traditional textile clients in clothing and fabrics, while Snia Viscosa is showing greater interest in industrial outlets such as the car, engineering and construction, shipbuilding and pipe-making industries. While Snia Viscosa still struggles with its financial backers and with overmanning, Montefibre has cut much of its excess labour and rationalised its production into fewer centres. This has included hiving off its share in the uneconomic Ottana polyester complex to the state so that ANIC now controls the entire 'white elephant' of fibres in central Sardinia, as well as the Pisticci plant which badly needs modernisation. Montefibre is now consolidating production at its new plant at Acerra north-east of Naples. This new development boasts the highest productivity and, when fully operational, will account for the whole of Montefibre's polyester manufacture and half its total fibres output.

Clothing

Along with footwear, to be considered in the next and final section of this chapter, clothing can be considered as the best expression of the processes of small-scale dynamic industrialisation which over the past 25 years have revolutionised the economic structure of the 'third' Italy — that part of the country which is interposed between the industrial North-west and the rural South. The regions most deeply involved in this latest 'industrial revolution' are Emilia-Romagna, Marche, Tuscany and Umbria; also affected are Veneto, Friuli-Venezia Giulia and Abruzzi.

The industrial censuses and the various other ISTAT publications make it difficult to isolate data on the clothing industries.[13] Only restricted statistical information can be picked out, and production data are lacking. The general indications are that the clothing industry (not including knitwear and hosiery) has stagnated over the past decade. Output in 1975 and 1978 was 15 per cent and 9 per cent respectively below the level of 1970. Hosiery and knitwear, on the other hand, survived the crises of the 1970s to provide much of the net surplus in Italy's textile trade balance during the decade. Much of the rapid growth in hosiery and knitwear between the late 1950s and the late 1970s (reaching an annual rate of increase of 19 per cent between 1968 and 1972) was sustained by penetration of the European market, especially within the ambit of the Common Market. More than half of total output is exported to, in order of importance, West Germany, France, USA, the Netherlands, Belgium and Switzerland. Indeed Italy has become Europe's major exporter of hosiery and knitwear, the main products exported being woollen outerwear and ladies' stockings and tights. Prospects darkened in the early 1980s, however, with a 42 per cent drop in foreign orders between 1980 and 1981.

Although knitting frames were known to be in operation in Turin in 1850 the real growth of the knitwear and hosiery trades took place after 1920. Most factories were set up in the north: for knitwear in and around Turin, Milan, Biella and Bologna; and for hosiery in Piedmont, Veneto and the Lombardian provinces of Brescia and Varese. This pattern has, however, been greatly modified by developments in the last 25 years. Table 6.5 shows that whilst hosiery and knitwear employment has stagnated over the period 1961-81 in some of the northern regions where the industry was first established (notably Lombardy and Piedmont), there has been quite phenomenal growth in the number of hosiery and knitwear employees in Veneto and in central regions such

Figure 6.5: Employment in Hosiery and Knitwear, by Province, 1981

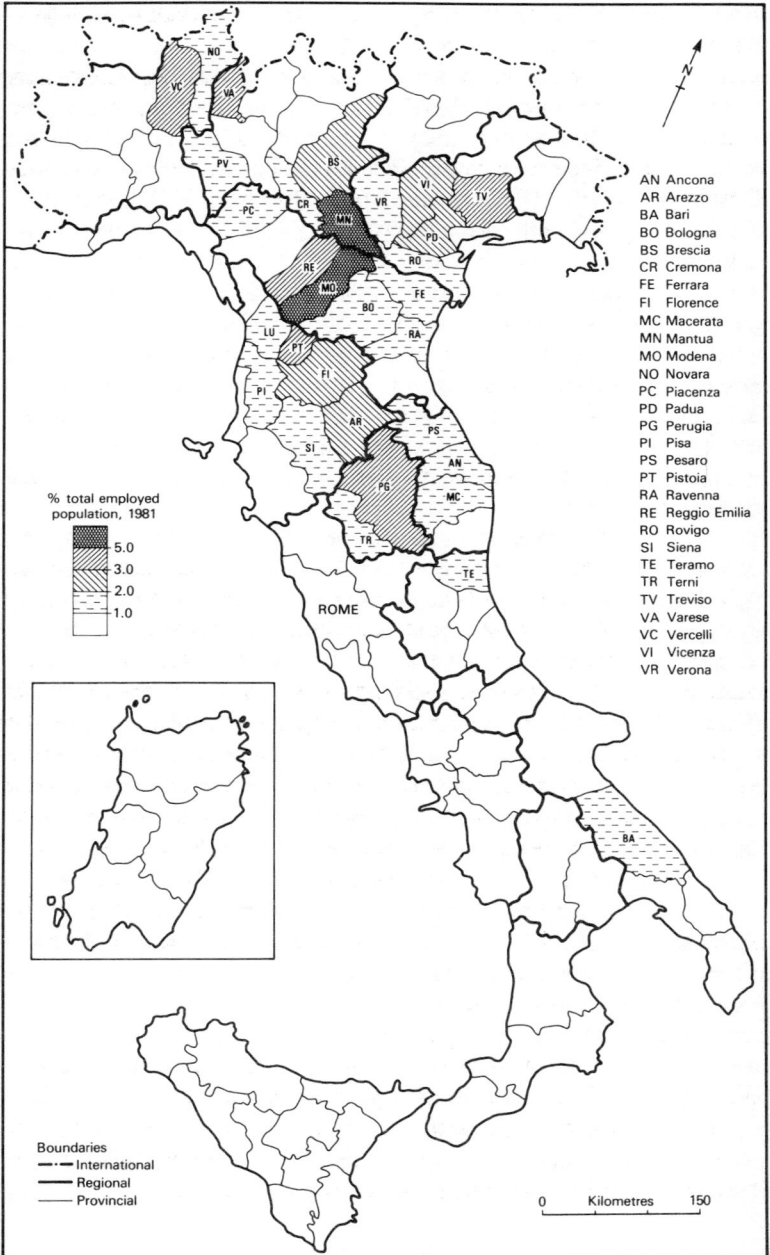

AN Ancona
AR Arezzo
BA Bari
BO Bologna
BS Brescia
CR Cremona
FE Ferrara
FI Florence
MC Macerata
MN Mantua
MO Modena
NO Novara
PC Piacenza
PD Padua
PG Perugia
PI Pisa
PS Pesaro
PT Pistoia
RA Ravenna
RE Reggio Emilia
RO Rovigo
SI Siena
TE Teramo
TR Terni
TV Treviso
VA Varese
VC Vercelli
VI Vicenza
VR Verona

% total employed
population, 1981

5.0
3.0
2.0
1.0

ROME

Boundaries
—·—·— International
—— Regional
—— Provincial

0   Kilometres   150

Source: As Figure 4.1.

Table 6.5: Employees in Hosiery and Knitwear by Region, 1961-81

Region	Number of employees 1961	1971	1981	1961-71	% change 1971-81	1961-81
Piedmont-Val d'Aosta	14,878	13,031	12,874	− 12.4	− 1.2	− 13.5
Lombardy	46,827	48,583	49,767	+ 3.7	+ 2.4	+ 6.3
Trentino-Alto Adige	587	1,173	798	+ 99.8	−32.7	+ 35.9
Veneto	12,014	24,134	27,038	+100.9	+12.0	+125.1
Friuli-Venezia Giulia	1,798	2,773	1,838	+ 54.2	−33.7	+ 2.2
Liguria	1,545	1,734	1,046	+ 12.2	−39.7	− 32.3
Emilia-Romagna	20,807	28,596	33,451	+ 37.4	+17.0	+60.8
Tuscany	8,698	13,029	20,459	+ 49.8	+57.0	+135.2
Umbria	2,303	4,854	7,309	+110.8	+50.6	+217.4
Marche	2,279	4,840	5,875	+112.4	+21.4	+157.8
Latium	2,982	3,306	2,493	+ 14.3	+24.6	− 16.4
Abruzzi-Molise	1,503	1,850	2,375	+ 23.1	+28.4	+ 58.0
Campania	1,273	1,443	2,040	+ 13.4	+41.4	+ 60.2
Apulia	3,570	7,487	7,956	+109.7	+ 6.3	+122.9
Basilicata	291	448	529	+ 54.0	+18.1	+ 81.8
Calabria	970	893	510	− 7.9	−42.9	− 47.4
Sicily	1,532	1,905	1,479	+ 24.3	−22.4	− 3.5
Sardinia	733	838	497	+ 14.3	−40.7	− 32.2
Italy	124,590	160,917	178,334	+ 29.2	+10.8	+ 43.1

Sources: Zinno (1974), pp.797-9; *6° Censimento Generale dell' Industria e del Commercio, 1981, Vol. I Primi Risultati sulle Imprese e sulle Unità Locali, Tomo I Dati Nazionali, Regionali e Provinciali,* Rome: ISTAT (1983), Table 5.

as Tuscany, Umbria and Marche. In Umbria the number of employees more than tripled, and this excludes unrecorded domestic workers. Also interesting is the strong growth of this textile branch in some southern regions such as Apulia and Basilicata, juxtaposed with regions of sharp decline in Calabria and Sardinia. The provincial pattern (Figure 6.5) shows two main areas of concentration of employment: in the north, in provinces like Vercelli, Varese, Mantua, Treviso and Modena; and in the centre, in provinces including Florence, Pistoia, Perugia and Arezzo. The central provinces are those of the most dynamic growth, which affects knitwear much more than hosiery. The latter, accounting for 6.4 per cent of hosiery and knitwear firms and 17.8 per cent of employees, remains rooted in the North, with 62 per cent of both firms and employees in Lombardy alone.

Table 6.5 shows that employment in hosiery and knitwear grew particularly rapidly during 1961-71, the rate of growth in 1971-81 being only about one-third of the rate of the previous decade. By 1981 hosiery and knitwear firms contained nearly 180,000 workers, about one-third of total textiles employment excluding clothing and linen. To this number should be added another estimated 100,000 (possibly more) domestic workers who participate in knitwear manufacture. The mean number of employees per firm, as recorded by successive industrial censuses, was 5.6 in 1961, rising to 7.4 in 1971 but then dropping back to 5.8 in 1981. Mean number of employees is significantly higher in northern regions (Lombardy 14.9, Veneto 11.7) than in central or southern regions (Tuscany 5.2, Marche 4.3, Apulia 4.4). Northern firms are more mechanised and the hosiery firms, concentrated in the north, are on average three times as large as the knitwear concerns.

These data indicate a progressive repatterning of the knitwear industry into smaller units in the central regions of the country. Entry into the industry is easy, requiring only small amounts of capital and a minimum of technical knowledge. Another relevant factor is 'the spirit of independence, improvisation and creativity' which is said to be characteristic of the solid peasantry of the northern Apennines.[14]

Studies of Carpi, near Modena, give interesting details of the organisation of production in and around the town now known as the 'world knitwear capital'.[15] In the space of 20 years, between 1951 and 1971, Carpi grew from a small agricultural centre of 15,000 to a manufacturing town of 50,000. Knitwear originated as a part-time activity of female agricultural labourers who could only find farm work for about 75 days per year. From 3,000 declared knitwear employees in Carpi in 1961, the number grew to 7,500 by 1981, but there is an undeclared army of up to 50,000 outworkers in surrounding districts. Three main types of knitwear workers can be identified: homeworkers, artisans and those employed on the production lines of larger firms.[16] Wages are fixed by union legislation in the larger firms; in the smaller enterprises wages are lower and jobs less secure, although the more skilled workers are well remunerated. Younger, single women tend to work in larger factories, whilst older women and those with family responsibilities are trapped into homework and are therefore excluded from the mobility chains to the better jobs, most of which are in Carpi itself. Males are to found mainly in the artisan group, where they make up just over the half the workers. The more disadvantaged groups in the knitwear trade are those in the low value-added production jobs with lower skill content which lie along decentralisation routes from Carpi into adjacent provinces. These homeworker circles and small subcontracting artisans are subject to the monopsonistic power of the commissioner/buyer. This individual is the key element in the productive structure of the outwork system, the intermediary between his band of maybe 200 outworkers and the market. He supplies raw materials and a portfolio of designs,and then collects the finished products and consigns them to market, usually a large wholesaler in West Germany.

Whilst the small scale and flexible structure of knitwear production enable it to respond easily to the changing conditions of fashion and the market, there are several problems associated with such productive fragmentation. Compared with larger industrial units, small knitwear concerns have difficulties securing credit and cheap supplies of raw material. Marketing is another problem and the small producers are often at the mercy of big regional and national merchants. This stranglehold can only be broken by more direct collaboration between producers' and retailers' organisations. The necessity for producer co-operative action is even greater when dealing with foreign markets, especially if the intention is to open up new market areas, like those in the Eastern bloc, which have yet to be properly exploited. In short there is a need to redirect the considerable horizontal expansion of the knitwear industry in recent decades into a vertical dimension as well.

The rest of the clothing industry (i.e. exluding knitwear and hosiery) has a broadly similar regional distribution to that for hosiery and knitwear, although often different individual provinces are involved as the main producers (Figure 6.6). The most remarkable concentrations in relative terms (i.e. as a proportion of the total employed population of the province) are the central provinces of Arezzo (14.3 per cent) and Teramo (9.6 per cent). Perugia (6.7 per cent) is also important, as is a

Figure 6.6: Employment in the Clothing Industry, by Province, 1981

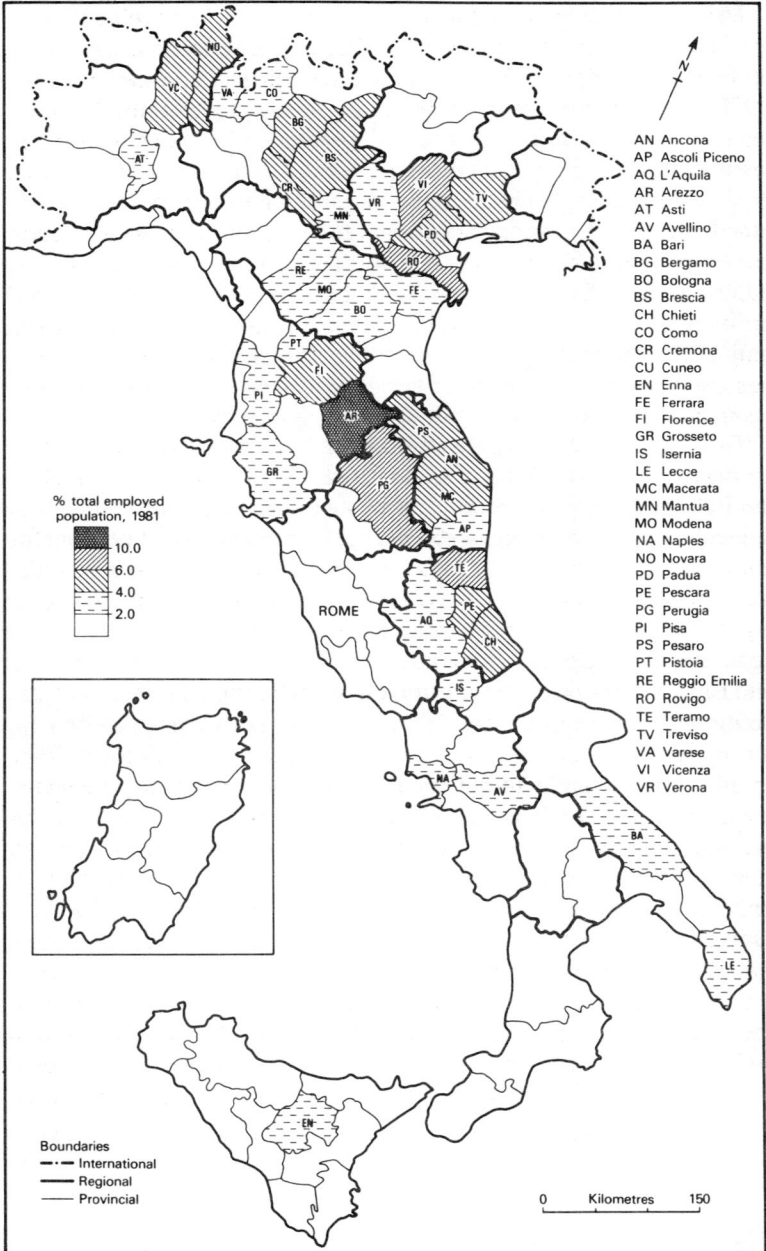

% total employed
population, 1981

10.0
6.0
4.0
2.0

ROME

AN Ancona
AP Ascoli Piceno
AQ L'Aquila
AR Arezzo
AT Asti
AV Avellino
BA Bari
BG Bergamo
BO Bologna
BS Brescia
CH Chieti
CO Como
CR Cremona
CU Cuneo
EN Enna
FE Ferrara
FI Florence
GR Grosseto
IS Isernia
LE Lecce
MC Macerata
MN Mantua
MO Modena
NA Naples
NO Novara
PD Padua
PE Pescara
PG Perugia
PI Pisa
PS Pesaro
PT Pistoia
RE Reggio Emilia
RO Rovigo
TE Teramo
TV Treviso
VA Varese
VI Vicenza
VR Verona

Boundaries
—·— International
——— Regional
——— Provincial

0   Kilometres   150

Source: As Figure 4.1.

range of northern provinces like Rovigo (8.5 per cent), Vicenza (6.4 per cent), Bergamo (4.9 per cent), Novara (4.6 per cent), etc.

Mass production of clothing in Italy only really developed after the Second World War, although small nuclei of specialisation, such as underwear in Milan and hats at Pavia and Voghera, had emerged by the 1920s. Dependent on chain stores for high-turnover retailing, the clothing industry's development has been constrained by the slow development of big department stores in Italy. There is still a lingering preference, especially in the South, for the small retailer, often combined with the small dressmaker and tailor. Italians tend to demand higher standards of finishing and fitting with their clothes than most other European nations, so that the percentage of costly hand-finishing on Italian clothes sold domestically is high. There are reckoned to be only 700 inhabitants per clothing retailer. Although clothing purchase has grown enormously in Italy since the war, it is still low, by European standards, amongst rural and southern populations.

The Italian clothing industry's export situation is heavily dependent upon a narrow range of destinations. West Germany absorbs half of all the Italian clothing sold abroad; in some branches of the industry the dependence is even greater — 66 per cent for raincoats, 82 per cent for men's shirts and underwear for instance.[17] A supply so markedly centred on one market is bound to cause some concern. But there is a much bigger problem. Both on the domestic market and on the West European export markets, growing imports of cheaper products from Asia and Eastern Europe are hitting the Italian clothing business. This competition is much more strongly felt in traditional types of clothing, mostly manufactured by large northern firms, and much less felt by smaller firms manufacturing fashion and leisure products like jeans, sports kits, skiing and mountain clothing which have benefited from the general diversification of clothing habits since the 1960s. Yet the Italian flair for style in clothing is still important. At a time when national and regional clothes throughout much of the world have succumbed to the Western 'uniform' of jeans, sweaters and T-shirts, foreign buyers in particular look to Italy for something different. In contrast to the high fashion modes of the past (which are still to be found in the most expensive shops in Rome and the big cities), the current Italian style is based on modern, easy-to-wear clothes still made, though on a larger scale than in the past, in the Italian needlework tradition of artistry and craftmanship.

Footwear

Footwear is another traditional Italian industry that has successfully adapted to the modern industrial era, experiencing phenomenal growth in the post-war period. Italian shoe manaufacturers have been very successful in setting stylistic trends for Europe and North America — to the obvious benefit of exports. Since the mid 1960s Italy has been the foremost producer of shoes in the EEC and second only to the USA as a manufacturer of leather shoes.[18] Employment in footwear manufacture expanded by 37.5 per cent during 1971-81, an acceleration over the previous decade (31.9 per cent in 1961-71).[19] Production in 1980 was 45 per cent up on 1970.

Table 6.6 shows the evolution of employment in footwear manufacture for the period 1961-81. The pattern is remarkably similar to that portrayed for hosiery and knitwear (Table 6.5): stagnation or decline in traditional northern regions like Piedmont, Lombardy and Liguria; growth in the north-eastern regions of Veneto and Emilia-Romagna, in most central regions (especially Tuscany, Umbria, Marche and Abruzzi) and in the southern region of Apulia. Lombardy and Piedmont had 26 per cent of footwear manufacturing employment in 1961, but only 15.9 per cent in 1981. Tuscany and Marche, on the other hand, increased their combined share from 26.4 per cent in 1961 to 46.2 per cent in 1981.

Like hosiery and knitwear, footwear is organised into mainly small enterprises: 88 per cent of firms have less than 20 workers; only seven have more than 500. The mean number of workers per enterprise is 10.5, a fall in size since 1971 (17.4) and 1961 (18). Again, therefore, the pattern is one of decline in traditional manufacturing centres in the North, and a restructuring into dynamic, but small, Central Italian firms.

The provincial pattern (Figure 6.7) shows that the regional figures are often based on the dominance of one or two provinces. In Marche for instance, which in 1981 was the most important Italian region for footwear employment, the main provinces are Ascoli Piceno (28,046 employees, 22.2 per cent of the provincial employed population) and Macerata (14,552 employees, 14.4 per cent), yet Pesaro (973, 0.3 per cent) is totally unimportant. Lombardy's footwear industry is mainly in Pavia province, where is to be found Vigevano, the traditional 'shoe capital' of Italy. Here are found not only factories producing shoes mainly for export, but also ancillary industries such as shoe accessories and shoe-making machinery and tools.[20] A speciality of Cornuda (pro-

Table 6.6: Employees in Footwear Manufacture by Region, 1961-81

Region	Number of employees			% change		
	1961	1971	1981	1961-71	1971-81	1961-81
Piedmont-Val d'Aosta	6,391	4,568	3,971	− 28.5	− 13.1	− 37.9
Lombardy	31,132	26,913	26,086	− 13.6	− 3.1	− 16.2
Trentino Alto Adige	32	54	172			
Veneto	15,466	22,603	33,310	+ 46.1	+ 47.4	+115.4
Friuli-Venezia Giulia	2,403	2,235	1,499	− 7.0	− 32.9	− 37.6
Liguria	256	224	252	− 12.5	+ 12.5	− 1.6
Emilia-Romagna	9,844	11,499	12,413	+ 16.8	+ 7.9	+ 26.1
Tuscany	16,622	30,189	40,568	+ 81.6	+ 34.4	+144.1
Umbria	353	776	1,585	+119.8	+104.3	+349.0
Marche	10,884	24,612	46,941	+126.1	+ 90.7	+331.2
Latium	312	1,092	933	+250.0	− 14.6	+199.0
Abruzzi-Molise	339	888	1,644	+161.9	+ 85.1	+385.0
Campania	7,387	8,185	11,625	+ 10.8	+ 42.0	+ 57.4
Apulia	1,388	2,121	6,430	+ 52.8	+203.2	+356.8
Basilicata	3	118	76			
Calabria	24	18	90			
Sicily	1,529	1,425	1,814	− 6.8	+ 27.3	+ 18.6
Sardinia	36	235	29			
Italy	104,401	137,755	189,438	+ 31.9	+ 37.5	+ 81.4

Note: For Trentino-Alto Adige, Basilicata, Calabria and Sardinia the numbers of employees are too small to give meaningful percentage changes.

Source: Cirillo (1974), pp.197-8; 6° Censimento Generale dell' Industria e del Commercio, 1981, Vol. I Primi Risultati sulle Imprese e sulle Unità Locali, Tomo I Dati Nazionali, Regionali e Provinciali, Rome: ISTAT (1983), Table 5.

Figure 6.7: Employment in the Footwear Industry, by Province, 1981

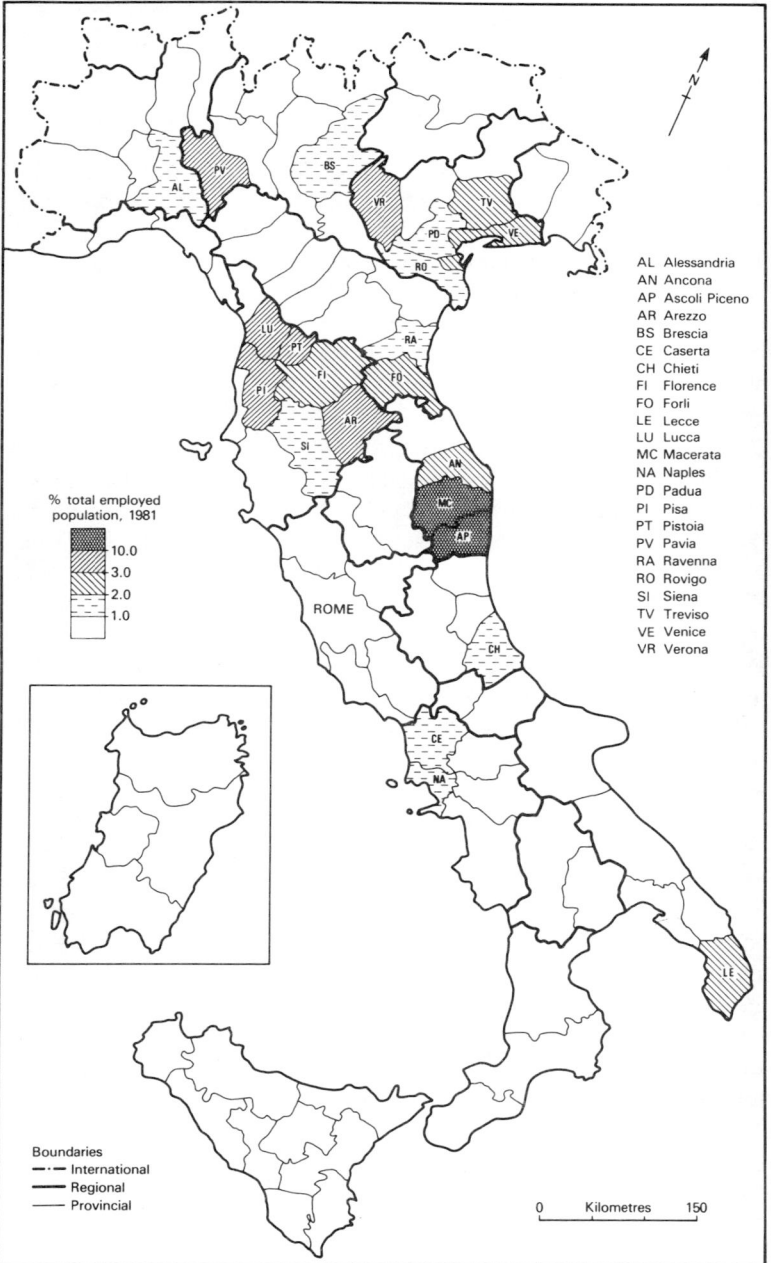

% total employed
population, 1981

10.0
3.0
2.0
1.0

AL Alessandria
AN Ancona
AP Ascoli Piceno
AR Arezzo
BS Brescia
CE Caserta
CH Chieti
FI Florence
FO Forli
LE Lecce
LU Lucca
MC Macerata
NA Naples
PD Padua
PI Pisa
PT Pistoia
PV Pavia
RA Ravenna
RO Rovigo
SI Siena
TV Treviso
VE Venice
VR Verona

ROME

Boundaries
—·— International
—— Regional
—— Provincial

0   Kilometres   150

Source: As Figure 4.1.

vince of Treviso) is the manufacture of skiing and climbing boots, an activity demanding specialised knowledge and skilled craftmanship. Such product specialisation is very characteristic of the footwear industry. Cori's study of the Lower Arno Valley in Tuscany shows that various towns and industrial villages tend to concentrate on one type of product such as sandals (Certaldo), slippers (Monsummano) and military footwear (Fucecchio).[21]

The export of Italian shoes began to develop in the mid 1950s. From 150,000 pairs exported in 1950, the number jumped to 28 million pairs in 1960, 173 million pairs in 1970 and 285 million pairs in 1980. Exports grew by an average of 23 per cent per year between 1962 and 1969, the rate tailing off during the 1970s. Nevertheless, by the 1970s, exports accounted for around 65 per cent of total Italian footwear production, the typical export product being low to medium priced leather shoes. The two main export markets are West Germany and North America, but Italian shoes are widely distributed in most EEC countries and in Sweden and Switzerland.

The relatively successful penetration of export markets stands in contrast to the domestic marketing situation. As with clothing, the fragmentation of retailing limits the efficiency of distribution and sales, and therefore depresses consumption. Figures from ANCI (the Italian footwear manufacturers' association) for 1972 show that 85 per cent of domestic sales of shoes took place through small retailing outlets, with 10 per cent sold by travelling salesmen, 1 per cent by wholesalers and only 2 per cent in chain stores. Although large department stores, some with self-service, have proliferated over the past ten years, Italian domestic sales of footwear are considerably less buoyant than those of most other West European countries.

Now, in the 1980s, even the export position is under threat, challenged by the emergence of efficient shoe industries in countries like Spain, Greece, Brazil and some East European and Far Eastern nations (Czechoslovakia, Taiwan, etc.) with lower labour costs. At home, labour costs have risen steadily since 1970 and the prices of leather and other raw materials have risen. Imports have pushed into the domestic market — 3.3 million pairs in 1970, 27.3 million pairs in 1980. The import penetration comes not only from cheap manufacturers in Brazil, Taiwan, Korea, India, China, etc., but also from speciality footwear manufacturers based in the industrialised West. Italian manufacturers have been slow to spot recent market trends to sporting footwear, and firms like Nike, Spalding and Adidas have recorded booming sales on the Italian market.

The fault lies in the structure and organisation of the industry. In the past, when buyers came to the producers, the industry's fragmented nature was an advantage, for it could quickly respond to fashion trends by providing flexibility and specialisation at even the smallest of scales. Now, the marketing environment has changed. Footwear producers no longer enjoy the luxury of buyers guaranteeing sales: they have to create sales by a much more aggressive marketing policy. An industry split up into a plethora of 'workshop companies' needs help and co-ordination to achieve this. Recently ANCI has been encouraging marketing consortia and group ventures based on an informally agreed division by speciality. If such efforts are not successful, Italy's enviable position in the world footwear trade could become a thing of the past.

Notes and References

1. One official reaction of some interest was the *Legge Tessile* or 'Textiles Law' of December 1971. This was an attempt to provide low interest loans to textile concerns to help them to restructure themselves or to convert to other lines of production. The effect, however, has been relatively marginal: 596 'restructuring plans' were supported, out of a total number of 1,073 applications. Mostly it is the smaller firms that have been able to restructure and hold on to, or even increase, their labour forces. In spite of its feeble impact, the Textiles Law remains one of the few instances of official sectoral-level intervention in Italian private industry. For further details, see Dalla Zuanna (1977).

2. Militerno and Tondini (1979); Picarelli (1977).

3. For more details, see D'Antonio (1977), pp.1056-7.

4. David and Pattarin (1975); Frey (1975).

5. Cafagna (1971), pp.280-1.

6. Mazzaoui (1972).

7. Tremelloni (1937).

8. This account of the nineteenth century cotton industry is mainly based on Cafagna (1971), pp.282-3, 299-300, 311-13.

9. Bellani (1973).

10. Salvatori (1975).

11. Sella (1968).

12. Clough (1964), p.64.

13. 'Hosiery and knitwear' are considered under the 'textiles' heading, whilst clothing is grouped under the umbrella category of 'clothing, household fabrics, hides, skins and footwear'.

14. Zinno (1974), p.802.

15. Houssel (1972), pp.259-66; Solinas (1982). Also useful is David and Pattarin's (1975) study of knitwear production in the Marche.

16. Homeworkers are defined as those who make no use of dependent labour and use either no machinery or only traditional types. Artisans, on the other hand, do employ dependent labour (but only up to the 10 workers and 4 apprentices allowed by Italian law for an enterprise to be classified as 'artisan') and do utilise sophisticated machinery such as automatic power looms or bobbin winders. Large firms contain greater numbers of workers who are, moreover, usually unionised and safeguarded by effectively implemented legislation.

17. Pasini (1974), p.542.

18. Camagna (1971), p.461.

19. This growth is slightly more apparent than real, being based solely on numbers of workers in footwear manufacturing *sensu strictu*. For this, the relevant employment numbers are 104,401 (1961), 137,755 (1971) and 189,438 (1981). This growth in *manufacturing* is partly offset by a dramatic loss of workers involved in made-to-measure shoes and shoe repair: 67,123 in 1961, 3,349 in 1981. Some of this 'loss' is represented by the upgrading of small family workshops into industrial firms using machinery. Outworking in the shoe trade is a disappearing phenomenon — from 12,000 down to 6,000 in recent years. For further explanation of these changes see Cirillo (1974), pp.194-6.

20. Shoes have been to Vigevano what knitwear is to Carpi or shoddy to Prato. Artisans from Milan introduced shoe-making to the town in 1870 when its population was only 18,000. The real period of growth started in the 1950s. Between 1954 and 1960 exports of shoes doubled each year, reaching 13 million pairs, nearly half the national total, by 1960. The boom peaked in 1963 when 14 million pairs were exported, and the same number sold domestically. The town's population had grown to 60,000; 1,300 shoe enterprises gave work to 32,000 people, one-third of whom commuted in from the farms and villages of the surrounding Lomellina plain. Competition from shoe firms in Central Italy then led to decline. One factory in three closed down in the late 1960s; employment contracted to 20,000 by 1971 and to 8,000 by 1981. For more details see Houssel (1972), pp.251-9.

21. Cori (1961), p.174. Similar local specialisation is revealed by Ascoli and Trento's (1975) study of shoe production in Marche.

7 THE METALLURGICAL AND ENGINEERING INDUSTRIES

This chapter deals with what Italians call *metalmeccanica*, a broad term which includes almost any form of metal-working together with all types of engineering. Metallurgical industries, employing just under 200,000 persons in 1981, include the iron and steel industry, the smelting of non-ferrous metals and simple metal working. Engineering is defined as the manufacture of metal base products into more complex items such as ships, machine tools and, most important of all, machines. After a general introduction the chapter will give an account of the metallurgical and historical bases of the engineering industry, concentrating on iron and steel, followed by an examination of engineering under four broad heads: shipbuilding, mechanical engineering, vehicles and electrical/electronic engineering. As with the preceding chapter, the spatial dimension is given a central place in the discussion, with a series of maps of provincial employment in the metallurgical, mechanical, vehicle and electrical products industries.

In spite of historical antecedents such as the Romans' skill in metal working, Milan's development of an armaments industry as early as the thirteenth century and the medieval smelting of iron in the Alpine valleys behind Bergamo and Brescia, Italy was late in developing modern metallurgy and engineering compared to the coalfield economies of northern Europe. Implements, simple arms and parts for machines were fairly widely made in the last century; more sophisticated machinery has only been produced on a mass scale in recent decades. The engineering industry initially developed from the practice of repairing imported machinery; gradually a higher and higher proportion of parts was made locally until entire finished products were turned out. Now Italy has a long list of famous engineering industries, which have played a leading role in the country's rapid twentieth century industrialisation. The speed of development of Italy's engineering industry in recent decades has been matched only by that of France in Europe and Japan elsewhere in the world. Italian engineering output now accounts for roughly one-third of the country's entire manufacturing product.

Table 7.1 shows the shifting composition of manufacturing industry over the post-war period, based on the two criteria of employment and exports. In the early post-war period (1951) textiles were the most important branch of manufacturing exports. Twenty-five years later

Table 7.1: Contribution of Manufacturing Sectors to Total Manufacturing Employment and Exports, 1951-75

Manufacturing Sector	% total manufacturing employment		% total manufacturing exports by value	
	1951	1975	1951	1975
Food, drink and tobacco	10.6	8.3	11.4	4.8
Textiles	33.9	25.4	42.3	17.4
Metallurgical	3.7	5.0	4.0	9.7
Mechanical	24.7	29.8	21.1	40.7
Non-metalliferous minerals	5.5	5.5	2.6	3.5
Chemical and pharmaceutical	5.4	7.4	10.5	14.8
Wood, rubber, paper and plastics	16.2	18.6	8.1	9.1

Source: Militerno and Tondini (1979), pp.626, 633.

textiles had been overtaken on both counts by the mechanical sector, particularly impressive being the approximate doubling of the contribution to exports from 21.1 per cent in 1951 to 40.7 per cent in 1975. The metallurgical and chemical industries also moved in the same direction as the mechanical, whilst food and drink paralleled the downward trajectory of textiles.

The timing of the 'overtaking' of textiles by mechanical industries is interesting: for both employment and exports this took place in the early 1960s, at the end of a period of prodigious growth in the mechanical and metallurgical sectors.[1] The average annual rate of growth of exports of mechanical products was 21.7 per cent during 1955-63, slowing to 8.3 per cent during 1964-72. Over the entire period 1951-75 mechanical exports (by value at constant prices) grew by 20 times, metallurgical by 25. The metallurgical industries took over fourth place in exports from food and drink after 1964. Trends in employment growth have been somewhat less spectacular. Employment in metallurgical industries nearly doubled during 1951-75, but then fell back sharply in the late 1970s. The mechanical industries doubled their employment during 1951-75, the vehicles branch tripling. These trends are also brought out in Table 7.2 which records the figures for employment in metallurgical, mechanical (excluding vehicles), and vehicles for each of the post-war industrial censuses.

This expansion of the metal-using and engineering industries is accompanied by significant structural and spatial changes, notably: (1) a 'deverticalisation' process, especially in the North, whereby formerly

Table 7.2: Employment and Productive Units in the Metallurgical, Mechanical and Vehicle Industries, 1951-81

| | 1951 | | 1961 | | 1971 | | 1981 | |
	units	workers	units	workers	units	workers	units	workers
Metallurgical	1,005	145,071	2,664	202,803	3,837	241,754	3,373	197,415
Mechanical	127,760	803,764	149,760	1,124,432	207,012	1,569,173	165,138	1,726,264
Vehicles	1,054	93,127	1,470	237,976	2,534	334,659	2,428	273,953

Sources: *Un Secolo di Statistiche Italiane: Nord e Sud 1861-1961*, Rome, SVIMEZ (1961), Table 217; *Un Quarto di Secolo di Statistiche Nord-Sud 1951-1976*, Rome, SVIMEZ (1978), Table 96; *6° Censimento Generale dell' Industria e del Commercio, 1981, Vol. I Primi Risultati sulle Imprese e sulle Unità Locali, Tomo I Dati Nazionali, Regionali e Provinciali*, Rome, ISTAT (1983), Table 3.

linked activities are separated to become more specialised, leading to greater operational and organisational flexibility; (2) a corresponding decrease in the mean size of productive unit in the North, counterbalanced by an increasing size of unit in the Centre and South (where mean size remains, nevertheless, well below that of the North); and (3) a concentration of employment growth in the regions of Friuli, Veneto, Emilia-Romagna and Marche — the so-called 'Adriatic Strip'.[2]

Metallurgy and Heavy Engineering before 1914

No great impulse arose for the development of the iron and steel or engineering industries in the pre-Unification period. Railway development was too retarded and uncoordinated. The construction of machinery for other industries did not take place, the limited demand being met by imports from abroad. Repair workshops grew up to service this imported machinery and these were fairly widespread in the northern industrial towns by the mid nineteenth century. By 1855 the Genoa firm of Ansaldo was turning out locomotives assembled from imported parts. The basis of the modest pre-1861 iron industry arose from two sources: the demand for armaments for military quarrels, and the demand for agricultural implements. But the basic problems of lack of iron ore and coal kept the Italian iron and steel industry in a state of small-scale backwardness compared to the same industries in France, Germany and Britain. In 1861 Italy produced 26,500 tons of pig iron, compared to Britain's 3.9 million tons.

State intervention gave iron and steel and engineering a boost in the 1880s. The government intervened with direct support for the industries by instituting privilege quotes for Italian machinery in orders for railway and tramway supplies, assisting the shipyards, and promoting the development of the full-cycle iron and steel works at Terni in Umbria to supply the merchant marine. This promising impetus was then stifled by the 1889-96 depression. The 1889 peak of steel production was not regained until 1904.

More significant advances took place in the period between the end of the depression and the First World War, in particular the remarkable development of the machine industries — machine tools, machine assembly and the birth of the automobile industry. All were founded on the new capabilities made possible by the use of steel. In 1895 Italy hardly had a steel industry: production of steel in that year was only 50,000 tons, compared to 150,000 tons of pig iron. By 1913 the situation had changed dramatically, with 933,000 tons of steel and 193,000 tons of pig iron. Thus by the First World War the Italian economy had entered — just about — the age of steel.

Although the major user of iron and steel products was the mechanical industry, engineering made difficult progress. In order to prosper and progress this kind of industry needed two basic requirements: large industrial markets and a pool of skilled labour, both difficult to come by in the early stages of industrialisation. Despite the protection accorded to the naval shipyards, this branch of heavy engineering did not succeed in dominating the home market; imports of vessels and ships' engines, mostly from Britain, were three times the national production in 1913. National industry did, on the other hand, eventually succeed in securing the monopoly for railway supplies as a result of railway nationalisation in 1905. Even then more than a third of the railway commissions had to be given to foreign companies since Italian industry could not cope with all the supplies needed. Therefore, neither shipbuilding nor the railway industries constituted the real sinews of modern engineering.[3]

Instead the Italian machine industry of the turn of the century became an industry *par excellence* for creating 'new' goods: bicycles, sewing machines, electric motors, internal combustion engines, mass-produced machine tools, agricultural machinery and the like. One of the most important initiatives was the starting up of typewriter manufacture at Ivrea by Samuel Camillo Olivetti in 1911. However, *the* most important branch of industry to be opened up in the pre-1914 period was the nascent development of the automobile industry. This was the most brilliant and effective example of Italy's participation in the new industrial movement of those years. More generally, it was of crucial importance in guiding the development of collateral industries (tyres, components, aluminium, etc.) and in forming the core of a skilled labour force in factory-based engineering.

Two World Wars and After

By 1914 most of Italy's most important engineering companies were already in operation — Fiat, Lancia and Alfa Romeo (cars), Ansaldo (shipbuilding), Breda (heavy engineering) and Olivetti (typewriters). Steel, ships, armaments and the railways all received a boost to their development by the 1914-18 war. Fiat too found that war was good business, yielding bigger profits than public transportation; bus and car production was therefore sacrificed for armoured vehicles and submarine engines.

During the Fascist period the engineering industry was diverted from its natural path of development by policies of autarchy and military expansionism. The Second World War meant both stimulus and destruction for Italian metallurgy and engineering plant. Blast furnaces, steel plants and rolling mills had been so badly damaged that pig iron capacity was cut by 67 per cent, steel by 34 per cent. Half the nation's shipyards were in ruins. Moreover the productive plant that had not been directly hit was badly run down because of lack of maintenance.[4]

'Converting swords to ploughshares is never easy, but Italy needed a vast reconversion in the metal-using industries after 1945. The Italian government recognised that engineering was central to general economic recovery, and gave this sector of industry a large share of American Marshall Aid. Engineering's swelling contribution to industrial exports was dramatic: 6 per cent in 1926, 18 per cent in 1950, 35 per cent in 1965 and 41 per cent in 1975. In short, after 1945 the engineering industry became the most important branch of Italian industrial production — in numbers employed, in value of production, in contribution to the export trade and in capacity for future expansion.

In his book *Italy Chooses Europe,* F. Roy Willis describes the part played by Italian engineering industries in European integration.[5] In spite of raw material deficiencies and the risk of the Italian domestic market being overrun by French and German industrial products, Italy's 'industrial gamble' of entering the Common Market paid off handsomely. Nowhere was this truer than in the production of motor vehicles, dominated by Fiat. Large-scale investment in new models in the post-war period, the establishment of service facilities abroad and aggressive marketing enabled Italian cars to sweep the European market.

A similar situation prevailed in light engineering, where Italian workmanship and ingenuity made similar remarkable advances in the post-war years. Before the war Italy had been known for Olivetti typewriters and calculating machines and for Necchi sewing machines. Both industries received large amounts of American Marshall Aid and were able to modernise production rapidly in the 1950s and 1960s. Typewriter production rose from 74,931 in 1947 to 845,130 in 1967, calculating machines rose from 19,100 in 1947 to 972,469 in 1970 and sewing machines from 88,668 in 1947 to 477,031 in 1967; output then stagnated at slightly lower levels during the 1970s. These well established products were rivalled in importance in the 1950s by new industries catering to the increasingly affluent domestic consumers of Western Europe and North America. After the war it took the domestic appliance industries about 12 years to meet, and defeat, foreign competition; from the the late 1950s on, aided by the Common Market's free trade environment, Italian producers began to conquer Europe, undercutting both French and West German manufacturers in their own markets. A wide range of products was developed, including cooking stoves, toasters, fans, irons, vacuum cleaners, electric razors, and the two staples of the industry, washing machines and refrigerators. By 1965 Italy had become the second largest manufacturer of domestic appliances in the world after the United States. The biggest export, accounting for 60 per cent of the domestic appliance exports by value, was refrigerators, of which nearly a million a year were being exported.

Support for European integration was also expressed by the aeronautical industry, which had ceased production in 1943. Only minimal finance was available for its post-war reconstruction since the government was aware of the high development costs and the restricted nature of the Italian market. It was clear that Italy could not afford to support a national aeronautical industry. Rather than rely on purchases of foreign-made planes, however, it was decided that small and medium sized planes should be produced under licence from foreign manufacturers, mainly for the needs of the air force. Whilst the most fruitful initial collaboration was with the United States and Great Britain, steps have more recently been taken to establish a French-German-Italian aeronautical industry.

In heavy engineering and shipbuilding — both mainly under state control — post-war progress has been even more difficult and these two sectors have been in almost constant difficulty in spite of massive subsidies. War distortion was part of the problem. In the shipyards conversion to civil shipbuilding was hampered by high labour and steel costs. In other engineering sectors the domestic market was not capable of absorbing great increases in heavy engineering products like bulldozers and earth-moving equipment — the direction in which much of the prevous military engineering capacity could most easily be converted. The reconversion process was further constrained by government directives that plants should not be closed down, so that a major restructuring of engineering, with closures and redundancies, was not on the cards. However, heavy state intervention and the deliberate sustaining of industries not economically viable, including the subsidising of marine transport, were directly counter to the philosophy of an integrated European Community. The EEC Commission objected to the subsidies as a falsification of competition, demanding their abolition. Although opposition to the shipbuilding subsidy was later withdrawn, the heavy engineering sector in general was forced to pursue more active policies of re-organisation and loss-cutting.

The Role of State Holding Companies in Metallurgy, Engineering and Regional Development

Like most other major branches of industry, metallurgy and engineering are dominated by big northern firms, some of them members of IRI. Table 7.3 shows the extent to which the state participates in the three main branches of metallurgy (mainly iron and steel), engineering (heavy, mechanical and electrical engineering, but excluding vehicles), and vehicles. In 1970 84 per cent of IRI's total manufacturing sales were in the fields of steel, heavy engineering and shipbuilding. IRI produced 94 per cent of Italy's pig iron, 66 per cent of its steel and accounted for 80 per cent of shipbuilding capacity.

Several IRI *finanziarie* are important in the metallurgical and heavy engineering industries. Finsider (founded in 1937) operates in iron and steel, controlling the main companies of Italsider, Terni and Dalmine. Finmeccanica (1947) is concerned mainly with automobile, electro-mechanical, railway engineering and machine tool production; here the most important concerns are Alfa Romeo (cars), Ansaldo (electro-mechanical branch) and Breda (thermo-mechanical). Fincantieri (1959) controls all the state interests in shipbuilding.

The other main state holding company of relevance to the industries considered in this chapter is EFIM, formed in 1962 to support

Table 7.3: Share of Public Enterprise in Metallurgy, Engineering and Vehicles as a Percentage of National Totals, 1971

Sector	% gross product	% fixed investment	% employment
Metallurgy	40.9	79.8	35.6
Engineering	6.2	14.1	5.5
Vehicles	20.3	53.8	21.1
Total industry	12.2	44.3	7.5

Source: Saibene (1980), p.449.

mechanical engineering. The nucleus of EFIM is the Breda heavy engineering concern; 72 per cent of EFIM's turnover is railway rolling-stock, shipbuilding equipment, cranes, helicopters, light aircraft, engines of various kinds, motorcycles and air conditioning plant. EFIM also controls aluminium processing, including the two main plants (Alsar and Eurallumina) in Sardinia, as well as moving into certain non-engineering activities such as foodstuffs, paper, glass and rubber.[6]

The metallurgical and engineering industries, especially those under state control, have played a vital role in post-war policy to develop the South. Indeed, without the 1957 law compelling IRI, ENI and EFIM-Breda to locate 60 per cent of their new investment in the South (increased to 80 per cent in 1971), the industrial development programme for the Mezzogiorno would never have got off the ground. Figures from the 'Ministry of State Participation' show that this commitment has indeed been honoured, at least initially. By 1972 64 per cent of the industrial investment of these state-controlled firms had been made in the Mezzogiorno.[7] However, in the changing economic climate of the 1970s and 1980s during which IRI and the other holding companies have had to devote resources to rescuing a number of faltering northern firms, the 80 per cent threshold has not been attained.[8]

Iron and Steel

The Italian iron and steel industry evolved during the last few decades of the nineteenth century under an umbrella of high tariffs which were justified by Italian economists on the grounds that the infant industry could not develop in a free market because of Italy's shortage of the requisite raw materials and the limited home market. Even though this rationale can be questioned, there is no doubt that the resulting high prices for steel products had a restraining effect on the entire development of the Italian industrial economy in the first fifty years of national unity.

The main source of Italian iron ore is the island of Elba; other deposits, more costly to extract though sometimes purer, exist in certain Alpine districts and in Sardinia. The germ of the steel industry was the Società Veneta per Costruzioni ed Imprese Pubbliche, a public works company founded in 1872. The real base of the company was railway construction in the Po Valley and, under its energetic president Vincenzo Stefano Breda, the Società Veneta initiated the first steel and rail industry. Breda was able to use his political position (he was elected to parliament in 1876) to secure government contracts, advances and protection for steel development, establishing a model of the politician-industrialist that the most successful post-war industrial *barone,* Enrico Mattei, was to follow eighty years later.

In its early stages the iron and steel industry mainly developed at coastal locations: Piombino (Tuscany) and Portoferraio (Elba) using Elba ore, and Genoa using imported ore. In the interests of military security the government sponsored the establishment in 1886 of a steelworks at Terni in the Umbrian Apennines. By 1889 Terni was producing 70 per cent of Italy's steel, but costs were high because of the inland location. In 1905, one year after the passage of a law favouring the development of the Naples area, work began on the Bagnoli steel plant, for which a quota of Elba iron ore was specially reserved. Older iron-working districts in the Alpine valleys at Lecco and behind Bergamo and Brescia were slowly modernised. With the expansion of engineering in the Milan and Turin areas demand for high-grade steel was rising; new steelworks, using pig iron and imported scrap, and, in time, drawing power from electricity rather than from costly imported coal, grew up in the northern plain. The firm of Falck, already established at Donga in the Alps, built a large new works at Sesto San Giovanni near Milan in 1908. Fiat erected its own steelworks at Turin and the Dalmine works, famous for steel tubes, was built near Bergamo.

Rationalisation in the iron-mining stage also occurred around this time. The Elba iron mines, which were public domain, had originally been leased by the state to various concession holders who sold the ore produced to foreign, usually Belgian, iron manufacturers. In 1899 a new local company, the Elba, acquired the right to use the ore and built its blast furnaces at Portoferraio. In 1902 Count Edilio Raggio (known as 'King Coal' because of his fleet for importing coal) acquired the Società Elba and then merged it with other companies to form Ilva (the Latin name for Elba) in 1906. At first the state allowed Ilva to mine up to 350,000 tons per year, of which 200,000 tons had to go to Italian consumers, but after 1908 the limitation on production was relaxed and output climbed to 850,000 tons in 1916.

The technical development of the Italian steel industry shows interesting peculiarities.[9] The basic technological choice was the decision to adopt the Martin furnace in preference to the Thomas converter. This was the same choice made (for different reasons) in England, but different from the rest of continental Europe. The Thomas process, although more expensive to instal and more complicated to run, was quicker and more economical, but yielded a less homogeneous and adaptable product. The Martin process, being more adaptable, was better attuned to the vagaries of the Italian industrial situation. Above all, it allowed the use of scrap in the production of steel. Finally, locational fragmentation favoured the Martin process. The Thomas plant required an investment at least ten times higher, for a plant five or six times greater, than the Martin plant.

With Italian steel prices running at around 35 per cent above world prices and imports of iron ore, scrap and steel all increasing up to the First World War, a policy of concentration was embarked upon to eradicate some of the organisational quirks of the industry. By 1914 Ilva accounted for half of Italy's steel output and was foremost in forming the Unione Siderurgica cartel to control and regulate production and prices. Helped by the war steel bonanza, Ilva was further reorganised in 1918, bringing under its wing the Siderurgica di Savona, Ferriere Italiane and Ligure Metallurgica companies. It expanded its works at Piombino and Bagnoli, boosted its shipbuilding and shipping interests, developed its munitions business and even manufactured automobiles under the Isotta Fraschini marque. This concentration eliminated harmful uncoordinated overproduction and price wars but failed to get at the roots of the industry's ills. No old plants were closed down; no new plants were opened; and no radical modernisation took place.[10] The industry failed to respond to the Fascist regime's demand for autarchy and the build-up of the armed forces, although further organisational adjustments occurred in the late 1930s with IRI acquiring large proportions of the shares in Ilva, Dalmine, Terni and Ansaldo.[11]

The Second World War left huge scars on the Italian iron and steel industry with two-thirds of pig iron and one-third of steel capacity destroyed. Of the 15 blast furnaces in production in 1939, only 5 remained — those at Cogne (Aosta) and Servola (Trieste). The major plants at Cornigliano, Piombino, Portoferraio and Bagnoli were all out of action.

Recovery, however, was rapid, remarkably so inasmuch as Elba iron ore was running out so that most of the ore had to imported (from Sweden, Venezuela, Brazil, Spain, Morocco and India), as did coal (from the Ruhr and the USA). Italy was surprisingly able to hold its own in the European Coal and Steel Community, which it entered in 1951, and developed an export trade in certain specialised products like pipelines.[12]

A key agent in the post-war steel expansion was Oscar Sinigaglia, president of Finsider and author of the Sinigaglia Plan (1950) for 'integrated' production at certain key coastal sites: Cornigliano, where a new plant was built; Bagnoli which was reconstructed; Piombino, which continued to use Elba ore; and Taranto where an entirely new works — Italy's largest — was built.[13] The greatness of Sinigaglia lay in his proving that a country with little coal or iron ore of its own could produce steel at prices competitive with those countries of Europe possessing coking coal, like Germany, or iron ore, like France. Plant specialisation was also encouraged: Cornigliano in steel plates and castings; Piombino in hot rolled products; Bagnoli in steel rods for reinforced concrete; and Taranto in cold rolled pipes. Other IRI plants and the private steel companies like Falck also tended towards specialisation. IRI's share of national steel output grew from 43 per cent in 1948 to 57 per cent in 1962 but then fell back to around 50 per cent by 1980.

Figure 7.1: Production of Pig-iron and Steel, 1946-80

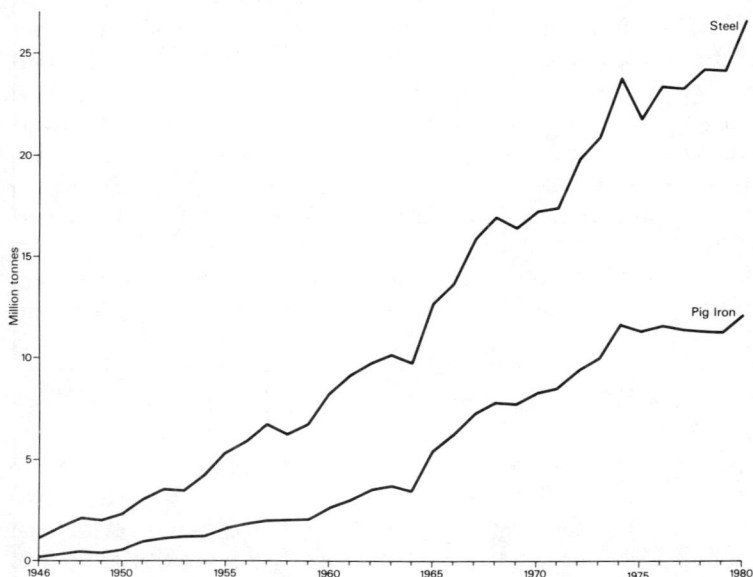

Sources: *Sommario di Statistiche Storiche dell'Italia 1961-75,* Rome: ISTAT (1976), p.95; *Annuario di Statistiche Industriali, 1981,* Rome: ISTAT (1982), p.64.

Figure 7.2: Location of Iron and Steel Industry

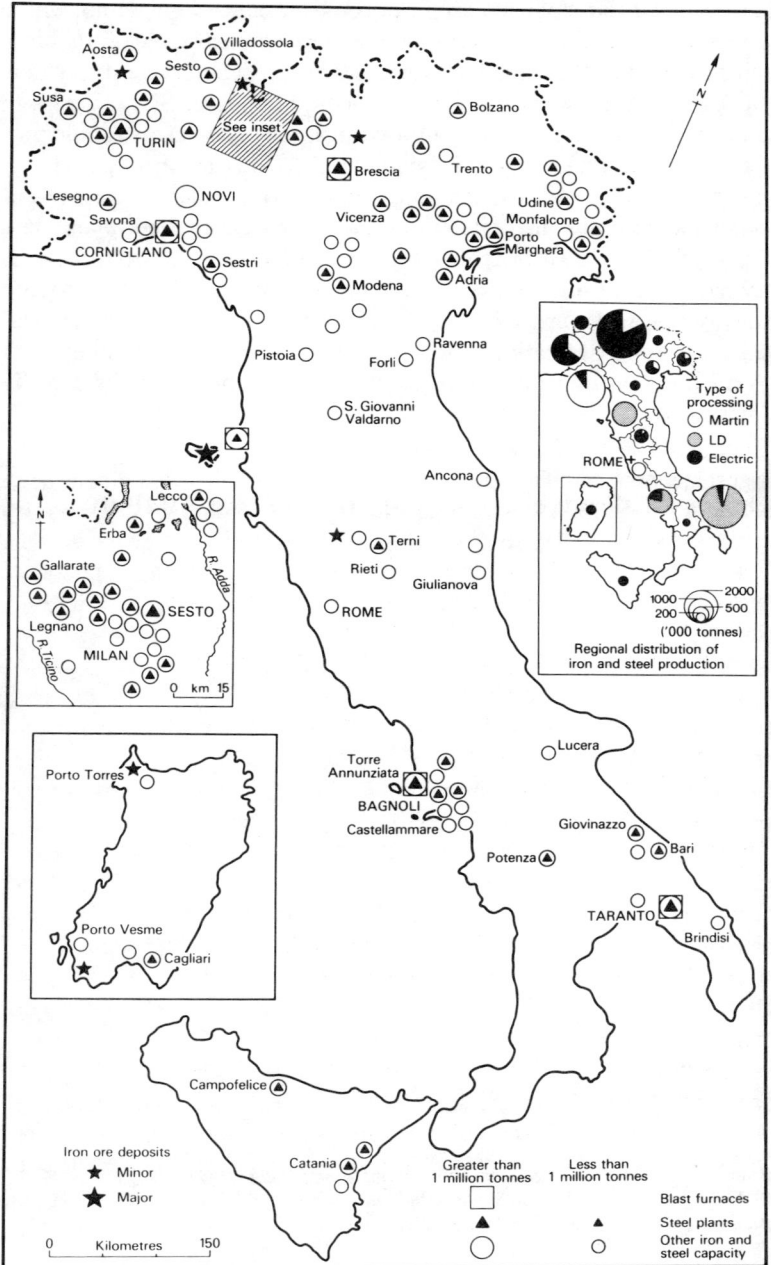

Source: Celant (1980), pp.480-1.

The rapid post-war evolution of steel and pig iron production is charted on Figure 7.1 whilst the spatial structure of the industry is shown on Figure 7.2. After the stagnation of the mid 1970s, Italian steel production at the end of the decade had risen to become second highest in Europe (after West Germany), overtaking Britain, France and the Benelux countries. Steel production figures for 1978 show the following ranking: West Germany 41.2 million tonnes, Italy 24.2 m. t., Benelux 23 m. t., France 22.8 m. t., Great Britain 20.2 m. t. By 1980 Italian production had stepped up to 26.7 million tonnes (Figure 7.1). Apart from concentration at the four integrated works, key elements in this increase were the doubling of capacity at Taranto and the expansion of many small electric-powered steelworks in the North, especially around Brescia. In the world steel rankings, Italy is now fifth behind the USA, USSR, Japan and West Germany.

The single most important post-war development has been the construction between 1960 and 1965 of the huge Taranto works, one of the largest steelworks in Europe. In 1980 it employed 21,000 persons and had an annual productive capacity of 10.5 million tonnes. Taranto is equipped with LD converters; in the North Martin's or electrical processing, based more on scrap, still prevail (Figure 7.2). Taranto's degree of dominance in Italian steel output can be appreciated by examining the following figures for steel production for 1979: Taranto 7.5 million tonnes, Piombino 1.4 m. t., Bagnoli 1.1 m. t., Cornigliano 0.9 m. t., Terni 0.7 m. t., Dalmine 0.5 m. t. In contrast to the four Italsider giants the private sector of steel production is highly fragmented, although there is an interesting spatial concentration in the Brescian Alpine valleys where a myriad of small electric-powered steelworks produces 5 million tonnes, mostly of steel rods.[14]

Italy has not, however, remained immune from the problems of European and world steel over the past decade. Although the Italian steel industry rallied well, in terms of annual production figures, from the mid 1970s crisis, the situation had become near-disastrous by the early 1980s. In 1981 Finsider requested massive government aid — £4 billion — to stave off complete financial collapse. The servicing of interest on mounting losses (£31 million in 1978, £340 million in 1980) and on the accumulated debt (estimated at £6 billion in 1981) has reached the equivalent of 15 per cent of total turnover. In February 1981 Finsider cut salaries by 30 per cent at its Italsider, Dalmine, Cogne and Breda plants. Domestic demand for steel declined 17 per cent in 1980, and prices for steel fell by 12 per cent. The proportion of working capacity utilised dropped from 70 per cent in the mid 1970s to

60 per cent in the early 1980s. Yet imports of steel from abroad increase.

Much of Finsider's financial burden reflects the cost of keeping open the loss-making Bagnoli plant, for which Italsider has recently submitted a modernisation project to the European Community. Bagnoli employs more than 8,000 workers in an area of chronic unemployment and although its heavy losses might have prompted closure in other circumstances, in the Naples area such action is generally regarded as socially and politically unacceptable. Instead a development programme is being instituted to increase the plant's capacity in finished steel products like hot rolled coils, for which Italian demand is high. At the end of the restructuring programme finished steel products will account for 75 per cent of Bagnoli's overall output, compared to the present 40 per cent. This replanning is made more difficult by Bagnoli's cramped site, hemmed in by densely populated residential quarters. Similar problems of congestion and pollution afflict Cornigliano and Piombino, but not Taranto where the steelworks is well outside the town.

The final chapter in the steel story concerns the saga of Italy's proposed fifth integrated steelworks.[15] This plant, initially scheduled for Sicily but then transferred to Gioia Tauro in Calabria in the wake of the Reggio riots of 1970, was a product of the optimism of the early 1970s, when the industry was geared to expand to an annual output of at least 30 million tonnes by 1980. Post-1973 events confirmed that the complex — with a planned capacity of 4.5 million tonnes, possibly rising later to 10 m.t., and with the prospect of 7,500 jobs — had no chance of being viable. The plan was scaled down and then withdrawn, though not before work had gone ahead on constructing a new port. In fact critics had already pointed out that the earthquake-prone Gioia Tauro plain was a highly unsuitable location for a steelworks. The site had no port facilities and was covered with rich olive and mandarin groves, the latter watered with costly irrigation systems already paid for by the Cassa per il Mezzogiorno. A steelworks would thus have gone a long way towards destroying a beautiful and fertile plain, as well as ruining the tourist potential of the coast. But the significance of the decision goes deeper. The aborting of the Gioia Tauro steel project marks the retreat from the 1960s style of southern development planning, and the triumph of local environmental and human sensibilities over grandiose schemes of prestige which owe more to political postures than to technical and economic criteria.

Distribution of the Metallurgical and Engineering Industries

Figure 7.3 shows the distribution by province of employment in metallurgy in 1981. The influence of the iron and steel industry on the pattern is very clear. Virtually all the provinces north of the Apennines have at least 4 per cent of their total employment in metallurgy. Indeed Lombardy alone accounts for 40 per cent of the national employment in this sector, and the three north-western regions (Lombardy, Piedmont and Liguria) have over two-thirds. South of this northern belt provinces with significant metallurgical employment stand out as islands, the most prominent corresponding to the main steelworks of the peninsula — Piombino (Leghorn province), Terni, Bagnoli (Naples province) and Taranto. Indeed Taranto has the highest percentage of metallurgical employment of all the provinces — 23.5 per cent.

Compared to iron and steel, non-ferrous metallurgy contributes little to employment in the metallurgy sector. Lead and zinc working are concentrated in south-west Sardinia (Cagliari province) where there is also aluminium smelting. The Alsar aluminium plant at Porto Vesme is the largest in the country and is the largest metal-mechanical concern in the island, with 1,500 workers and an annual output of 126,000 tonnes.[16] Lead is also processed at Pertusola near La Spezia and zinc is smelted at Vado Ligure and Crotone.

The metallurgical and engineering industries are closely connected with each other; either industry may stimulate a demand for the other. Spatial proximity is often to be observed, therefore. Their location in Italy has not been influenced so much by proximity to raw materials (of which Italy has few) as by accessibility to markets. With the exception of shipbuilding and the engineering activities linked to the big coastal steelworks, the largest centres of engineering are in the northern plain, particularly to the north of the Po and extending into the mouths of the Alpine valleys. Milan is the undisputed centre of the Italian general engineering industry, with many surrounding towns and provinces — Sesto San Giovanni, Legnano, Pavia, Lecco, Brescia, Bergamo, etc. — heavily involved. This loosely structured Lombardian conurbation —the most densely populated and highly industrialised district in Italy —provides the largest market for metallurgical and engineering products, the development of which has historically done much to increase the economic and demographic importance of this region. The earlier development of the textile industry, requiring machinery and equipment, and the intensively cultivated plain, requiring agricultural machinery, are further important factors. The comparative flatness of

Figure 7.3: Employment in Metallurgical Industries, by Province, 1981

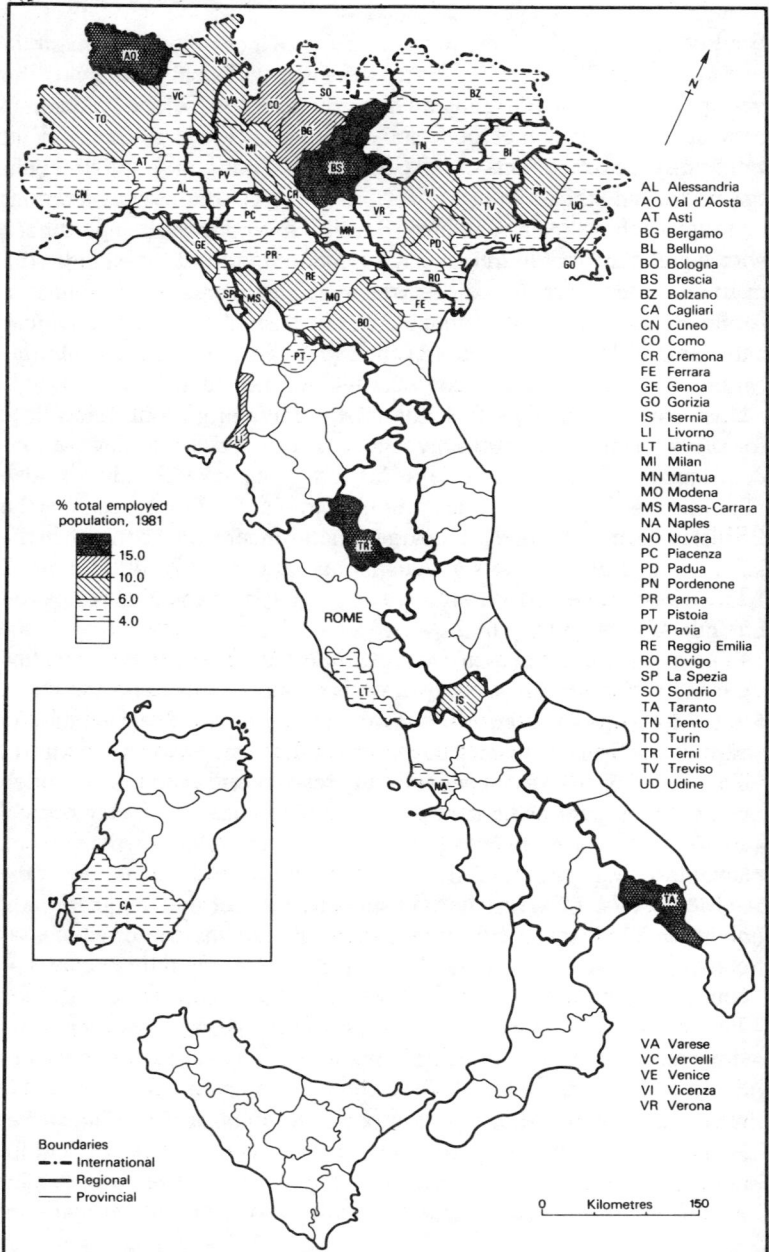

% total employed
population, 1981

15.0
10.0
6.0
4.0

ROME

Boundaries
—·—· International
——— Regional
——— Provincial

0   Kilometres   150

AL Alessandria
AO Val d'Aosta
AT Asti
BG Bergamo
BL Belluno
BO Bologna
BS Brescia
BZ Bolzano
CA Cagliari
CN Cuneo
CO Como
CR Cremona
FE Ferrara
GE Genoa
GO Gorizia
IS Isernia
LI Livorno
LT Latina
MI Milan
MN Mantua
MO Modena
MS Massa-Carrara
NA Naples
NO Novara
PC Piacenza
PD Padua
PN Pordenone
PR Parma
PT Pistoia
PV Pavia
RE Reggio Emilia
RO Rovigo
SP La Spezia
SO Sondrio
TA Taranto
TN Trento
TO Turin
TR Terni
TV Treviso
UD Udine

VA Varese
VC Vercelli
VE Venice
VI Vicenza
VR Verona

Source: As Figure 4.1.

the plain, besides facilitating the transport of raw materials and finished goods, encouraged the development of a dense railway network and the use of cycles and motor vehicles — hence the growth of the rail-linked and motor-engineering industries of the plain. Much the same is true of neighbouring Piedmont except that here the locational separation of metallurgy and engineering is more distinct, the former in the Alpine valleys, including the major developments at Aosta, and the latter on the plain, in and around Turin. Eastwards the expansion of engineering in provinces like Parma, Reggio Emilia, Modena, Bologna, Ferrara, Ravenna and Forlì has been more recent, based on a more diffuse pattern of industrialisation. Nevertheless these provinces dominate the map of employment in the mechanical industries (see Figure 7.4; note that this map excludes shipbuilding and vehicles), and the 'Adriatic trend' continues, in a less dramatic fashion, both northward round the head of the Gulf (Treviso, Padua, Pordenone, Udine, Trieste) and southward down the peninsula (Pesaro, Ancona, Bari, Taranto).

Shipbuilding

The Italian shipbuilding industry has glorious traditions in the medieval arsenals of Venice, Pisa, Genoa, Naples, Amalfi and Palermo. The shipyards of Venice employed 16,000 in the fifteenth century, when they were the largest in the world. The situation in Italy's shipyards today could not be more different: overmanning, spare capacity, lack of planning and a profound structural crisis. The key reason has been a fall in world demand over the past quarter-century and an increasing lack of competitiveness on the part of Italian shipbuilders. Ninety per cent state-owned, the shipyards have been a cross on IRI's shoulders ever since they were put under the management of Fincantieri in 1959.

Most of the big names in Italian shipbuilding were founded in the nineteenth century.[17] Foremost among these was the Ansaldo Company of Genoa. This concern was founded in 1852 on the remains of a company inititated by the English engineer Philip Taylor in 1846. Taylor's successor Giovanni Ansaldo began making steam engines for ships and then moved into shipbuilding, establishing his main yards at Sestri near Genoa in 1886. With orders from the merchant marine (as well as from the railway and military authorities), Ansaldo flourished. By 1889 the company was not only fitting out its own vessels but also making most of the heavy parts and machinery, especially engines, which were also supplied to other shipbuilders. With the founding of

Figure 7.4: Employment in Mechanical Industries (excluding Shipbuilding, Vehicles and Electrical Goods), by Province, 1981

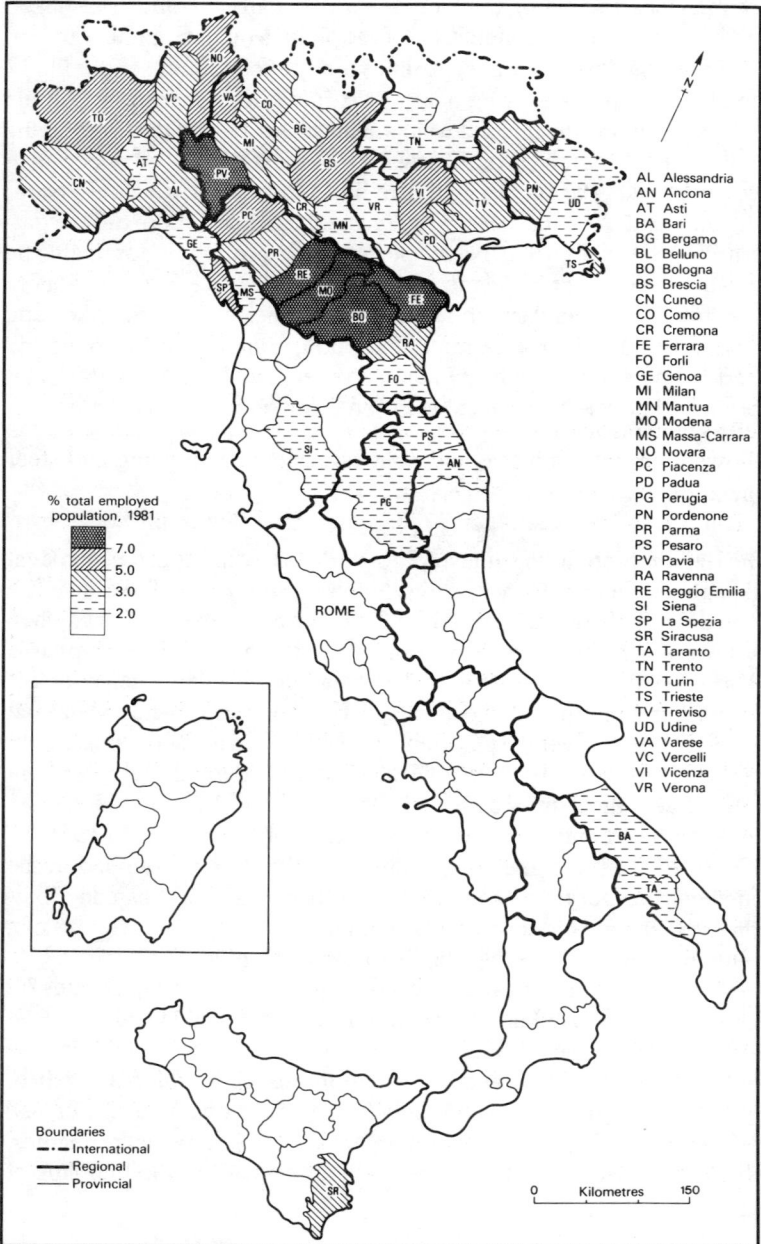

AL Alessandria
AN Ancona
AT Asti
BA Bari
BG Bergamo
BL Belluno
BO Bologna
BS Brescia
CN Cuneo
CO Como
CR Cremona
FE Ferrara
FO Forli
GE Genoa
MI Milan
MN Mantua
MO Modena
MS Massa-Carrara
NO Novara
PC Piacenza
PD Padua
PG Perugia
PN Pordenone
PR Parma
PS Pesaro
PV Pavia
RA Ravenna
RE Reggio Emilia
SI Siena
SP La Spezia
SR Siracusa
TA Taranto
TN Trento
TO Turin
TS Trieste
TV Treviso
UD Udine
VA Varese
VC Vercelli
VI Vicenza
VR Verona

% total employed
population, 1981

7.0
5.0
3.0
2.0

Boundaries
—·— International
——— Regional
——— Provincial

0   Kilometres   150

Source: As Figure 4.1.

Terni and its close association with the Navy (in spite of Terni's inland location), Ansaldo lost part of its profitable business in marine engineering. A brief association with the English firm of Armstrong followed in 1903 (the company taking the name Ansaldo-Armstrong) but new developments, such as the founding of the Cornigliano steelworks and the boost to ship demand given by the First World War, saw Ansaldo regain its dominant position.

Another important shipbuilding dynasty originated with the Orlando family. Luigi Orlando was a Sicilian and heir to a small ironworks. In 1865 the government let him take over the outdated shipyards at Leghorn, which he successfully modernised. The 1870s depression almost finished him but he was saved by Naval Minister Brin who ordered the big ironclad 'Lepanto' from him. By 1881 Orlando was back on his feet and forecasting a great Italian maritime industry based on nationalised steel. Such a self-contained industrial pairing could, he expostulated, redeem Italy from her dependence on the great powers as well as help resolve social problems of unemployment. Orlando's sons followed him into industry and politics, becoming shipping and steel magnates after the turn of the century.

The Florios were another Sicilian industrial family that combined steel and maritime enterprises, although their origins were in spice-trading, tuna fishing and fruit growing. The fishing fleet was the nucleus of the family's shipping interests, which also extended to transporting sulphur, Sicily's principal mineral export. By 1881 the Florios owned 45 steamships and a larger number of sailing vessels. Their combination with the Genoese shipping enterprise of Rubattino in 1881 resulted in the creation of a large, state subsididsed shipping line — the Navigazione Generale — with all kinds of linked industrial activities. Florio began taking part in the steel industry in 1899, at the beginning of that industry's great leap forward. The Orlandos and the Oderos (another important shipping company) came in a few years later, when it became clear that Elba iron ore could sustain a national iron, steel and shipbuilding industry.

So, after about 1885 all the main Italian shipbuilding interests — Ansaldo, the Orlandos, the Oderos and the Navigazione Generale (Florio) — became active in a range of maritime and allied industrial activities, especially those with state backing. Much was achieved in the questionable names of national self-sufficiency, military security and overseas economic expansionism. The key personality in the state patronage of shipping was Admiral Brin who in 1885 saw to it that Italian warships were fitted with locally made rather than imported engines. Two big naval engineering workshops, Ansaldo of Genoa and Guppy of Naples, made the engines, using British plans and technical aid, paying the British firms a 5 per cent royalty on the engines built. The home-made engines performed well, and Italy took a big step towards naval self-sufficiency.

The inter-war period saw the collapse of employment in shipbuilding from 280,000 workers in 1911 to 42,000 in 1927. Between 1926 and 1936 virtually all shipping companies made substantial losses. The proportion of shipbuilding capacity utilised fell to 40 per cent. Foreign competition was difficult to meet because of the high price of steel. By 1932 the main shipping concerns had fallen under control of the major banks. Credito Italiano controlled Ansaldo, Piaggio controlled the Cantieri del Tirreno and the Cantieri Navali Riuniti, and the Banca Commerciale held the reins of the Cantieri Riuniti dell'Adriatico and of the Odero-Terni-Orlando group. Accordingly, when IRI was formed in 1933 to break the hold of the banks over industry and to help ailing enterprises, the shipbuilding and shipping companies were ripe for treatment. By 1937 Finmare had responsibility for over 80 per cent of the national production of the shipyards, a degree of control which certainly facilitated Mussolini's war preparations. From then until 1945 at least half of the shipyards' output was made up of military orders.[18]

The damage sustained during the last war (88 per cent of ships were destroyed and about 60 per cent of shipyard capacity was put out of commission, largely at Naples, Trieste and La Spezia) was quickly made good in the early post-war period. For a decade or so Italy's shipyards enjoyed busy activity sustained by the need to replace merchant tonnage lost in the conflict and by the boom in tanker construction. By the late 1950s, however, the boom was subsiding and more deep-seated structural problems re-emerged: technical deficiencies, too many yards, too much capacity for the internal market's demand for vessels. The problem of conversion from military to civil shipbuilding was made more difficult by the industry's lack of competitiveness in foreign markets — a problem of overmanning and consequently high labour costs, and of high steel costs following the degree of protection given to the nationalised steel industry. A report by a group of experts from Stanford University showed that as early as 1950 the yards were working at only 53 per cent capacity (65 per cent was the break-even point) and recommended that six of the fifteen yards be closed.[19] Yet for social and political reasons IRI, which in 1959 put all shipbuilding industries under the control of a new subsidiary Fincantieri, was committed to keeping all its yards open and to maintaining the labour force, especially in southern locations like Palermo, Naples and Castellammare di Stabia, where the unemployment problem was acute.

This decision to retain shipyard capacity well beyond levels of demand had far-reaching effects. Despite massive state subsidies and several large orders for prestige passenger ships like the Transatlantic liners 'Andrea Doria' and 'Michelangelo', the sector has been in prolonged economic crisis for at least the last 25 years. A general fall-off in world demand and the stiffening of competition from countries like Japan, Korea and Spain have been important external factors for Italian shipbuilders' malaise.[20] With fewer and fewer cargo vessels sliding out of Italian shipyards in recent years the sector has become once again reliant on military orders, either for the Italian navy, currently nearing the end of a ten-year re-equipment programme, or for Third World (mostly Middle Eastern and Latin American) countries. The main military demand has been for medium and small, technologically sophisticated vessels like frigates and corvettes. However, this side of the market cannot be expected to last indefinitely; sooner or later Italian shipbuilders will have to reactivate traditional commercial contracts, for which an upturn in the market is widely forecast for 1985. Other possibilities include the construction of more specialist craft such as submarine-pipeline-layers, drilling vessels and floating industrial platforms. It is also worth mentioning the establishment of Grandi Motori Trieste (a joint IRI-Fiat venture) for the manufacture of diesel engines for vessels. Another new development, almost completely unconnected with traditional shipbuilding, is the phenomenal growth since about 1960 of pleasure craft of various kinds. These vessels — yachts, speed-boats, motor-launches, dinghies, etc. — are produced in a wide range of locations, including the Ligurian, Tuscan and northern Adriatic coasts, and also around the major Alpine lakes.[21] The Rodriguez yard in Messina is a major manufacturer of hydrofoils.

Aside from shipbuilding, considerable numbers of workers are also employed in repair work. In fact, Italy contains over one-third of the Mediterranean's ship repair yards. Over the post-war period Italy has suffered badly from the decrease in repair work, increasingly taken over by other Mediterranean countries like Malta, Yugoslavia and Greece which have cheaper labour forces and larger government subsidies. By 1980, however, the repair sector showed signs of recovery, owing to the increasing number of older ships in existence. Further optimism has been expressed for Italian repair facilities because of, firstly, the widening of the Suez Canal allowing more and bigger vessels into the

Mediterranean from the eastern end and, secondly, the construction of new pipelines (such as the Trans-Arabian pipeline) which will also lead to greater oil tanker traffic operating from the eastern shore. Palermo, specifically equipped to service big tankers, should derive the greatest benefit because of its location close to many tanker routes.[22]

At the 1981 Industrial Census, employment in shipbuilding and repairing had fallen to 46,800 persons, half of whom were employed in eleven concerns. The two main concentrations of shipbuilding activity are at Genoa and Monfalcone-Trieste. In the South the most important facilities are at Castellammare di Stabia and Palermo. Genoa alone accounts for one-fifth of Italian employment in the sector. Other main provinces are Naples (10.6 per cent), Venice (9.5 per cent), Gorizia (9.3 per cent), La Spezia (7.8 per cent), Palermo (7.7 per cent), Trieste (6.1 per cent), and Ancona (4.8 per cent).

Mechanical Engineering

The main consumer of iron and steel products has been the mechanical industries. After the shift to steam vessels took place in the nineteenth century the mechanical industry became closely associated with ship-building and many shipyards fell under the ownership of big northern concerns that were also in the machine trades, like Ansaldo and Breda. Another important contributor to the early development of Italian mechanical engineering, especially in Piedmont, Lombardy and Veneto, was the textile industry. Textile machinery was manufactured at a comparatively early date in Italy; for example, Jacquard looms were made in Milan in 1824, a year before they were produced in Lyons.

In 1861, however, one of the biggest plants in the mechanical field was in the South. This was the Pietrarsa plant in Naples, which had been the main arsenal of the Kingdom of the Two Sicilies. With an employment roll of 1,250 in the 1860s, it engaged in construction engineering and manufactured marine steam engines, locomotives, railway rolling stock, arms and projectiles. Instability of ownership — it shuttled back and forth between state and private enterprise — contributed to its relative demise; after 1885, under the ownership of the Meridionale railway company, it restricted itself to the manufacture and repair of railway equipment, finally passing back to the state in 1906.

Compared to the post-unification stagnation and collapse of many southern engineering concerns, northern firms like Ansaldo and Breda had a more dynamic evolution. Ansaldo's founding father, Taylor, was convinced that Italy needed a machine industry to support its railway building and got aid from Cavour and the Kingdom of Sardinia to build his factory and train Italian machinists. By the 1890s Ansaldo was turning out 50 locomotives a year in addition to a multitude of other mechanical lines. The Breda Company was founded in Milan in 1886 by Ernesto Breda, cousin of the founder of Terni. At first specialised in the manufacture of locomotives and rolling stock, it soon branched into allied fields — steam boilers, tractors and other heavy agricultural and construction equipment, arms, electrical goods and shipbuilding (including submarines during the First World War).

By the First World War these and other, smaller companies, although producing at high cost and failing to satisfy internal demand, had succeeded in building up a corps of skilled workers who could turn their hands to the manufacture of other items as technology and demand allowed. A good example of this is the bicycle industry which started with a number of small factories such as Bianchi of Milan and Rizzato of Padua, and then developed into motorcycles and cars. Linked to this line of technological development was a demand for bearings, and Giovanni Agnelli, founder of Fiat, set up in 1906 the Riv-Officine di Villar Perosa, a ball-bearing factory which has subsequently achieved great commercial success.[23]

Table 7.4: Rates of Employment in Mechanical Industries, by Region, 1881-1971 (per 1,000 Population)

Regions	1881	1901	1911	1921	1931	1951	1961	1971
Piedmont-Val d'Aosta	10.8	12.3	18.2	24.9	32.8	59.7	76.4	94.0
Lombardy	11.5	13.9	22.0	28.0	35.9	56.9	70.9	78.6
Liguria	13.4	25.6	35.3	40.0	42.5	50.3	44.4	43.0
Trentino-Alto Adige	—	—	—	8.1	11.5	16.3	25.0	31.1
Veneto	9.5	9.5	11.6	11.4	14.3	20.8	34.1	42.0
Friuli-Venezia Giulia	4.9	7.5	7.6	16.0	18.5	35.9	41.8	47.9
Emilia-Romagna	8.2	7.7	11.6	11.0	15.3	24.0	36.8	49.2
Tuscany	9.0	9.4	11.6	11.9	15.3	20.2	27.5	32.7
Umbria	7.9	8.9	7.0	11.6	14.4	11.4	21.8	25.7
Marche	8.7	8.1	7.5	7.9	10.5	12.9	20.4	26.4
Latium	8.8	8.7	10.3	9.4	13.9	12.9	18.5	21.8
Abruzzi-Molise	6.6	5.6	5.1	5.0	7.2	8.3	14.3	19.7
Campania	9.6	12.7	13.4	14.6	13.1	14.1	17.0	25.1
Apulia	6.5	8.4	7.6	9.1	11.1	10.5	16.3	20.4
Basilicata	7.7	5.9	5.4	5.3	7.1	8.2	10.6	17.4
Calabria	6.6	4.6	4.6	4.0	6.0	6.0	8.7	15.4
Sicily	7.2	6.6	6.4	7.1	8.7	8.7	12.1	18.0
Sardinia	6.8	6.6	6.8	6.5	8.3	5.8	10.5	14.7
All Italy	9.0	10.0	12.8	14.8	18.2	25.3	34.0	42.2

Source: Golini and Geseno (1981), p.78.

The evolving regional distribution of employment in the mechanical industries between 1881 and 1971 is shown in Table 7.4. Initially, up to 1931, Liguria was the region which relied most heavily on mechanical employment, followed by Lombardy and then by Piedmont. The dominance of Genoa and other coastal towns like Savona and La Spezia over a thinly populated mountain hinterland explains this high Ligurian figure. After 1951 mechanical employment in Liguria stagnated and the dominance of Piedmont and Lombardy was confirmed. By 1971 more than half the workers in mechanical industries were concentrated in these two regions (Lombardy 35.6 per cent of the national total, Piedmont 15.2 per cent). Also by 1971 the mechanical trades had developed strongly in the eastern part of the Po Plain, as the figures for Veneto, Emilia-Romagna and Friuli-Venezia Giulia attest. Central and southern regions have also increased their dependence on mechanical employment over the 90-year period, but not to such a dramatic extent as those northern regions already mentioned. As noted above, Naples was an important centre of the mechanical industry in the late nineteenth century, and in 1901 the region of Campania had the third highest mechanical employment figure. In most southern regions, however, the employment rate stagnated until well into the post-war period (Calabria and Sardinia having lower figures for 1951 than 1881), with significant increases registered only in 1961 and 1971.

Figure 7.4 — the provincial pattern of employment in mechanical industries (excluding shipbuilding and vehicle manufacture) for 1981 — brings the picture more up to date. This confirms the virtual absence of significant mechanical employment in the Centre or South, and the rise to dominance of the newer mechanical industries of North-eastern Italy. However, the data in Figure 7.4 give a slightly false picture to the extent that the statistics for this sector include figures recording the presence of small maintenance workshops and other artisan enterprises which happen to be classified in the mechanical sector. These small-scale traditional forms of mechanical repair become quite important in provinces with large urban centres which do not otherwise have a strong engineering tradition (Bari is a good example of this), and in those central provinces (such as Siena, Pesaro and Ancona) where they provide support for other semi-skilled craft trades. Large-scale manufacturing engineering, as opposed to the servicing of machinery, is much more highly localised in the North, with the main concentration in the Milan-Varese-Como-Bergamo area, with Genoa as the southern outlier, although this city's restricted site has hindered recent expansion of most branches of engineering except those connected to the ailing shipyards. Many towns have special interests — Bologna in railway industries, Legnano in textile machinery, Pavia in sewing machines for instance.

Behind these spatial patterns lies the familiar Italian industrial pattern of structural dualism. More than 92 per cent of mechanical engineering concerns employ fewer than 20 workers, whilst a small number of companies — 1 per cent of the total — employ more than 1,000 workers and account for two-thirds of total production.[24] The limited number of major engineering firms can be gauged from those listed on the Milan Stock Exchange. Apart from Fiat, Alfa Romeo and Olivetti, the engineering sector comprises Franco Tosi, Gilardini, Ercole Marelli, Magneti Marelli, Moncenisio, Nebiolo, Pan Electric, Tecnomasio Italiano Brown Boveri, Westinghouse and Worthington. The last two are subsidiaries of United States parent companies. The myriad of small engineering companies have grown up around a long tradition of artisan workshops, and to this day many enterprises are still artisan-style family concerns. The shortcomings of the Italian stock market system have steered such companies away from share flotation to a mix of short-term credit from local banks and ploughed-back profits to ensure financial survival.

As a whole the engineering industry has felt the impact of the recent recessions rather severely. In addition to falling demand both at home and abroad and the rising costs of important raw materials like steel, energy and water, the engineering employers are faced with the best organised and most militant of the Italian trade unions. The engineering unions were prominent during the 'hot autumn' of 1969 and have spearheaded subsequent campaigns for overall trade union solidarity.

Nevertheless, the various elements of the engineering sectors' structure have felt the economic crisis in different ways. Many state-owned giants have been badly hit, their monolithic size and swollen labour forces a handicap to effective response. Finmeccanica's 89,000 employees have the misfortune to be distributed in three vulnerable branches: cars (Alfa Romeo) and aerospace (Aeritalia, jointly owned by Finmeccanica and Fiat) have been hit by the oil crisis and falling demand, whilst the big electrical engineering conglomerates have come up against internal delays in implementing energy policies and building new power facilities. Among state companies in a stronger position to ride out the storm, thanks to their diversified international activities, are the engineering and plant construction associates of ENI, namely Snam Progetti, Saipem, Nuovo Pignone and Tecneco. The real difference, however, is with the smaller mechanical concerns, for they have been generally able to respond more quickly to changing conditions of costs, prices and demand. The small companies have not been trapped in the past into maintaining large unproductive labour forces but instead have labour flexibility, agile management and a remarkable inventiveness.

A brief look at certain well-defined branches of mechanical engineering concludes this section. In recent years Italy has emerged as one of the world's significant arms exporters; with 3 per cent of the world total it ranks fifth behind the USA (45 per cent), the Soviet Union (24 per cent), France (10 per cent), and Great Britain (5 per cent). In such a sensitive field precise details are hard to acquire; Fiat draws a veil of secrecy over its armoured vehicle division, and little information is forthcoming from the state concerns involved in arms manufacture. However, an estimated 100-150 companies are involved and there is no doubt that the industry is a key element in foreign trade and employment. In certain Alpine districts in Brescia province arms manufacture is the major source of employment. The arms produced go almost anywhere; indeed the lack of control over the manufacture and marketing is disturbing to many, both inside and outside Italy. In recent years Italy has been a major supplier of war goods to both Iran (helicopters) and Iraq (warships). With many armaments produced under licence from foreign, mainly American, firms political constraints sometimes interfere — as in the case of the partial American veto on helicopter sales to Iran. Italy's biggest arms customer, however, lies just across the Mediterranean. The case of Libya also illustrates how arms trading becomes enmeshed in politics, and is probably one of the reasons why Italy is able to maintain reasonably equable relations with a country whose foreign policy is inclined to be volatile.

The textile machinery branch is one of the original foundations of Italian engineering and is still important today, exporting 65 per cent of its output and employing 27,700 (1981), largely in centres of traditional textile activity like Milan, Busto Arsizio, Biella, Prato and Vicenza. As in other countries exporting textile machinery, specialisation has increased: Italy concentrates on spinning machinery, leaving the weaving sector more to West Germany, France and Switzerland. Italy also provides much of the specialised finishing equipment used to dye, bleach, dry, print or coat fabrics after knitting or weaving, and has been responsible for some of the major developments in knitting technology. The main problem faced by the textile machinery industry in recent years has been the decline in activity levels of European textile producers, which has weakened their propensity to re-equip with new machines. Italy has therefore had to look for new markets beyond Western Europe, and these have been fairly successfully found in the Eastern bloc countries and in various parts of the Third World.

A third important branch is machine tools, the manufacture and export of which have remained remarkably buoyant throughout the recent industrial crises. Home sales and exports, which split the production more or less equally, have both continued to rise in recent years, as has employment which reached 37,200 in 1981. With 7.6 per cent of the world export market, Italy now ranks fourth behind West Germany, Japan and Switzerland. The machine tool industry is a product of the rebirth of Italian industry in the 1960s. Being relatively recent it grew up unshackled by the out-of-date equipment and traditions which have hampered the industry in the older industrial countries of Western Europe. The Italian machine tool industry grew up around the needs of the expanding automotive, domestic appliance and electrical industries. Like many other mechanical trades, the production of machine tools is founded on a structure of small to medium sized northern firms. Average firm size is 82 employees, much lower than the United Kingdom (270) or France (188), although there are two giants in Fiat's machine tools division, Comau, which has 11 plants employing 5,800, and the state-owned Innse which was formed out of the merger of Innocenti and San Eustacchio and employs 3,500. Machine tool companies tend to be highly specialised with, in spite of their small sizes, a sophisticated export organisation linked to avid participation in foreign fairs. UCIMU, the machine tool industrialists' association, is trying to arrange a co-operative effort so that the small firms can come together as consortia to produce and export entire manufacturing systems linking together various machine tools, including robotics.[25] It is a symbol of the maturity of the industry that the modern appeal of Italian machine tools lies less in their price competitiveness than in their quality and reliability — qualities which have enabled significant export sales of products like lathes and drilling machinery to be made in the discriminating and competitive markets of northern Europe. The decentralised and fragmented organisation of the industry is in direct contrast to the trend abroad towards ever bigger grouping, and has attracted the attention of numerous foreign industrialists and researchers, anxious to discover so unusual a recipe for success in such difficult times.

The other main sectors of Italian mechanical engineering — vehicles and electrical goods (including domestic appliances) — are dealt with in the concluding two sections of this chapter.

Vehicles

In most large industrialised countries the automobile industry has become the most prominent branch of engineering and the index, if not the mainstay, of production in most other fields of manufacture. Italy is no exception to this. The vehicles industry absorbs, on average, 20 per cent of the rubber goods produced in Italy, 12 per cent of non-ferrous metals, 10 per cent of steel, 6.5 per cent of glass, 5 per cent of electrical goods, 4.5 per cent of precision instruments and 4.5 per cent of plastic goods. No other European country has embraced the automobile revolution with greater enthusiasm. Here the private car is not just a means of transport but a symbol of a way of life and an expression of its driver's personality. These, however, bring their own problems as aggressive driving tactics, chaotic parking and choking urban traffic all attest. In 1981 the vehicles industry employed 273,953 persons. Most of these — 180,585 — were engaged in vehicle production in large firms (numbering 321 for an average size of 563 workers); the rest, 93,368, worked in producing bodies, parts and accessories in much smaller concerns (average size 41 workers).

Vehicle production is dominated by the huge Fiat concern with its base in Turin, where Lancia's factory is also located. Other important centres of the industry are Milan (Alfa Romeo, Innocenti), Brescia (OM heavy vehicles), Modena (Ferrari), Bolzano (Lancia) and Naples (Alfa Sud). Fiat has factories in Argentina and Brazil as well as technical connections in Russia (Lada), Poland (FSO, Polski-Fiat), Yugoslavia (Zastava), Spain (Seat) and Turkey (Tofas). The reputation of Italian design engineers like Pininfarina and Bertone is reflected in automobile design the world over and is locally responsible for several factories specialising in coachwork, especially in Milan, Turin and Modena.

The Italian motor industry had already acquired international importance by 1914. Italy's successful entry into the automotive field so soon after it had been opened up in the great industrial centres of North America and Western Europe is in brilliant contrast to the country's lag in the earlier steam-coal-iron phases of the industrial revolution. The rise of the car industry, together with a whole range of related industries (engines, ball bearings, tyres, electrical parts), in the period between 1898 and 1914 has been seen as 'the qualitative leap that put Italy in a class by herself among the nations of Southern Europe and the Mediterranean'.[26] Undoubtedly there are many reasons for this sudden spurt: technical expertise, the tradition of research in the physical sciences (especially in electricity and magnetism), the new investment and banking systems of the 1890s, low labour costs and hydro-electric power.

As soon as the idea of the internal combustion engine as means of transport gained credibility, a number of car producing companies emerged; 40 were founded between 1899 and 1907. One of the most successful was the Fabbrica Italiana Automobili Torino (Fiat), es-tablished by Giovanni Agnelli in Turin in 1899. Although Agnelli had a technical background, he was not primarily interested in the automobile as a mechanical phenomenon or as a sporting thrill; his main perception was of the car as an industrial good, to be produced for profit rather than prestige. He was successful in persuading aristocrats, financiers and engineers to work together to set up a manufacturing plant in Turin. Agnelli's creations were soon winning trophies in international road races (previously dominated by the French), the most famous being the Paris-Peking race of 1907.

Other manufacturers started in a similar way — Lancia in Turin, Isotta-Fraschini, Alfa, Bianchi and Bugatti in Milan. The initial ten-dency in Italy was not towards the cheap utilitarian vehicle but towards the sports and luxury car, an orientation dictated by the Italian aristoc-racy's love of racing and by the lack of a mass market for cheaper pro-ducts because of the povery of the majority of the population. By 1914 the industry, although well established, was still at the handicraft stage. Less than 25,000 vehicles per year were produced, sufficient to satisfy internal demand (only 3,000 were imported). It was the First World War that led to mass production, fostering the widespread use of trucks and encouraging the development, some years after West Germany and the United States, of the utilitarian cars for which Italy, and especially Fiat, subsequently became famous.

The problems of the proliferation of too many small initiatives were apparent as early as 1907 when a process of concentration set in. By 1929 the automobile sector comprised eleven firms producing engines, chassis and complete vehicles (employing 21,000 workers), together with 80 firms (3,500 workers) making bodies and a further 25,000 persons engaged in the production accessories and in repair work. Annual production at this time had reached 50,000-60,000 vehicles. The inter-war depression led to the further disappearance of many small firms, and Fiat continued to emerge as the dominant force in the industry. Engine and chassis production become more concentrated, but the manufacture of accessories and minor parts (carburettors, radiators, lights, etc.) tended to become more decentralised, with some

200 firms in Milan and 100 in Turin by the late 1930s. By this time annual output of cars had climbed back to 60,000 after a trough of 25,000 during the early 1930s.

The inter-war period saw one further significant development: the takeover by the state of Alfa Romeo. Alfa (Anonima Lombarda Fabbrica Automobili) had been founded in 1910; it ceased production in the war and was then resurrected by Nicola Romeo. It specialised in large and expensive racing cars which achieved success in international races but not in sales. The company was saved for prestige reasons but not without adverse comment from Fiat which claimed Alfa Romeo would receive unfair state sponsorship.[27] Antagonism between the private Fiat and the nationalised Alfa Romeo has continued ever since.

The real quantitative development of the Italian vehicle industry came in the post-war period (Figure 7.5), especially the years between the late 1950s and 1973, when the oil crisis halted a thirty-year period of continuous expansion. By 1957, Italian car manufacturers were accustomed to regarding the home market as their own province, helped by duties of 45 per cent and more on imported vehicles. In that year Italy imported only 5,400 cars but exported 119,000!

Figure 7.5: Production of Cars and Other Vehicles, 1946-80

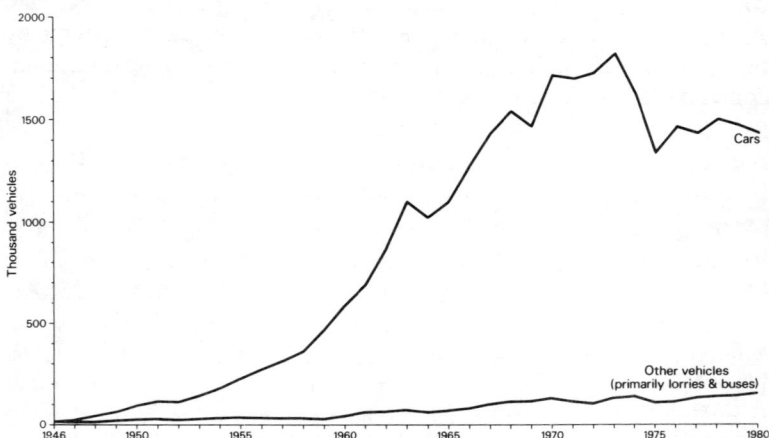

Source: *Sommario di Statistiche Storiche dell'Italia 1861-1975*, Rome: ISTAT (1976), p.97; *Annuario di Statistiche Industriali 1981*, Rome: ISTAT (1982), p.71.

The low rate of car ownership in Italy in the early post-war period (one car per 82 inhabitants in 1950) promised unlimited possibilities for the industry's expansion given the rapidly rising living standards of post-war Italy. By 1962 this ratio had risen to one car per 15 persons but the pattern was very uneven (e.g. one per 59 persons in Basilicata), indicating continuing potential for sales in the South as long as living standards could be improved in the poorer parts of the country. Fiat catered to this growing market very successfully with economical small cars — initially the 500, 600 and 850 models, later the 126 and 127, and most recently the Panda and the Uno. The Common Market enabled these, and other larger Fiats, to penetrate European markets, in return for imports to satisfy Italians' growing demands for consumer variety, especially on larger models with no equivalent local production (e.g. the larger saloons and estates of Mercedes, BMW or Citroën).[28] The market share of imports thus rose from 20.3 per cent in 1969 to 39.9 per cent in 1980; most of the imports are French.[29]

In the post-war period the dominance of Fiat among Italian vehicle manufacturers continues. The company accounts for 80 per cent of Italian cars and about 90 per cent of total vehicle production. It is the eighth largest car producer in the world and shares European supremacy on a roughly equal footing with Renault and Volkswagen. Unlike Fiat which has made its name for specialising in small cars, the remaining companies have specialised in luxury cars such as the fast limousines of Lancia, the sports saloons of Alfa Romeo or the racers of Ferrari and Maserati. Two minor companies, however, also produce small cars: Autobianchi, now a Fiat subsidiary; and Nuova Innocenti, now run by the eccentric Argentinian-born Alejandro de Tomaso after being abandoned by British Leyland in the mid 1970s.

Until the late 1960s there were essentially only three centres of the Italian motor industry: Turin (Fiat, Lancia), Milan (Alfa Romeo) and Brescia (OM lorries). Of these Turin, 'Fiat-city', is by far the most important (Figure 7.6). Fiat has 23 plants in Turin employing 140,000 workers. The plants range in size from the aeronautics factory which has 1,700 employees to the Mirafiori car plant with 23,000. Much of Fiat's workforce is made up of southern migrants who tend to be spatially segregated within the city, either in the run-down tenements of the old city or in soulless public housing schemes out on the periphery. Although some Fiat plants, like the iron and steel works, are situated within the district from which most of the workers are recruited, others, like the railway works and the Mirafiori plant, are out of context with their surroundings and compel workers to make difficult cross-town

Figure 7.6: Employment in Vehicles Production, by Province, 1981

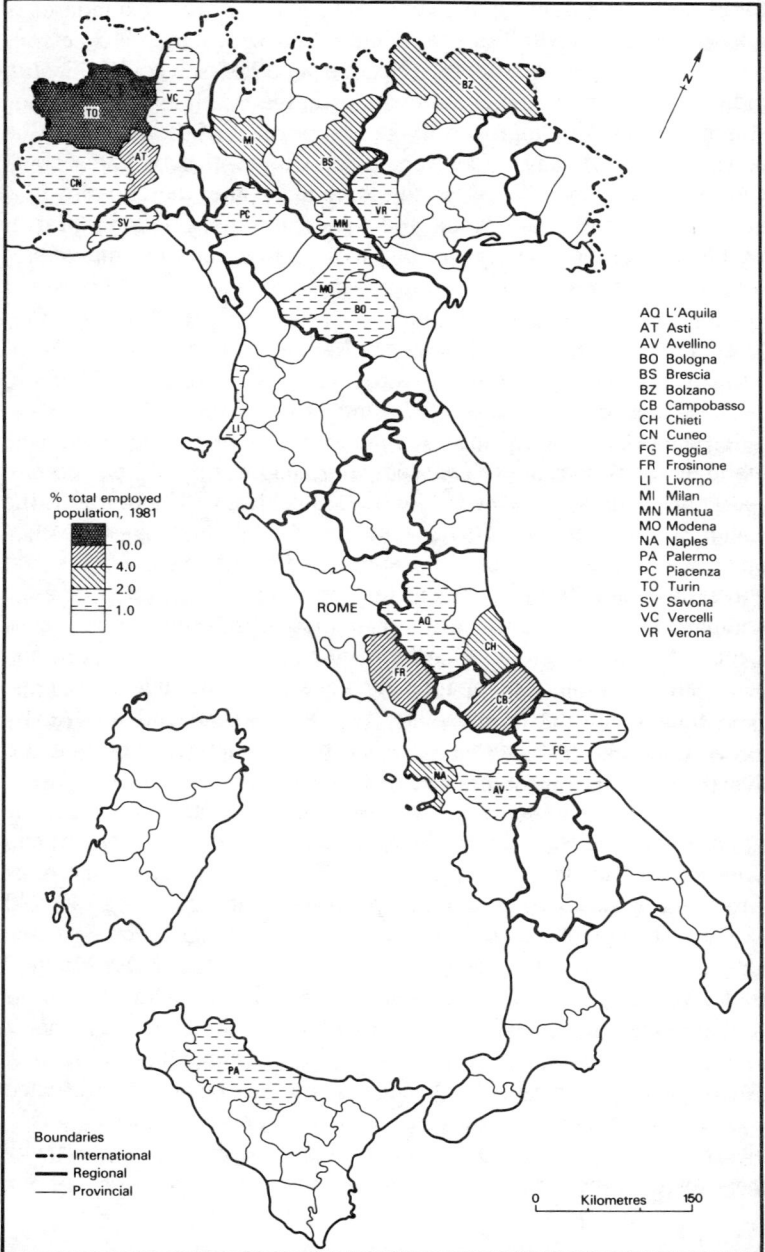

% total employed
population, 1981

10.0
4.0
2.0
1.0

AQ L'Aquila
AT Asti
AV Avellino
BO Bologna
BS Brescia
BZ Bolzano
CB Campobasso
CH Chieti
CN Cuneo
FG Foggia
FR Frosinone
LI Livorno
MI Milan
MN Mantua
MO Modena
NA Naples
PA Palermo
PC Piacenza
TO Turin
SV Savona
VC Vercelli
VR Verona

Boundaries
–·– International
—— Regional
—— Provincial

0   Kilometres   150

Source: As Figure 4.1.

journeys to get to work.[30] The dominance of Fiat over the Torinese economy is almost complete. One authority has estimated that Fiat and its allied industries (metallurgical trades, rubber, glass, plastics, components, etc.) accounted for 69 per cent of the city's industrial employment in 1951, rising to 79 per cent in 1961 and 89 per cent in 1971.[31] In addition to the main concern there are about 8,000 satellite firms which supply Fiat and are in various ways subordinate to the giant. Beyond Turin and its environs, the importance of Fiat to the national economy is hard to overestimate, for its decisions and productive trends affect many other companies both large (e.g. Pirelli, Marelli, Italsider, AGIP) and small. An increase in car production means more tyres, more batteries, more seats, more components, more petrol and so on. A gigantic mechanism is set in motion that affects, certainly, not less than 20 per cent of the entire investments of the country.

Since about 1970 there has been significant decentralisation of vehicles production towards the South. Figure 7.6 shows that vehicle manufacturing employment is of considerable importance in several southern provinces — Frosinone, Campobasso, Chieti and Naples especially. The decision to 'go southern' was first taken by the state-owned Alfa Romeo in 1967. Its Pomigliano d'Arco factory, 20 km north-east of Naples, was built during 1968-72 with a planned capacity of 300,000 cars per year. Under pressure from various sources, Fiat followed suit some years later, locating a range of smaller plants in various parts of the Mezzogiorno. In official parlance 'these enterprises are expected to contribute to the "take-off" of Southern Italy and at the same time check the northward migratory movement with its well-known unfavourable consequences . . . It is thought that the overall investments of the motor industry in the South should be able to create directly not less than 40,000 new jobs, a number which might even be doubled thanks to the induced activities already carried out or about to be undertaken.'[32] Such a view represents an exceedingly optimistic and naïve interpretation of the realities of the situation, as detailed studies by Amin on both the Alfa Sud and Fiat ventures have recently shown.[33] Alfa Romeo's view of the Alfa Sud project reveals very little appreciation of or commitment to southern development policy: the plant was located in the South because CIPE (the interministerial planning authority responsible for vetting big industrial location decisions) refused permission for a second major car plant to be built next to Alfa's headquarters in Milan and because Alfa Romeo was subsequently attracted by the 30 per cent capital grant under the 1965 regional development law.

Amin characterises Alfa Sud as a 'Fordist' plant (i.e. a fully mechanised, integrated style of production dependent on tight control of labour, as pioneered by Henry Ford in the 1920s), and a carbon-copy of the Alfa Romeo plant in Milan. Inasmuch as the plant contained the full cycle of production from the manufacture of parts to final assembly, and therefore was fairly labour intensive (employing 15,000), Alfa Sud was seen as a highly favourable investment for the South. Unfortuately it became a victim of its own timing for it was set up just at the time when, through the labour struggles of 1969-70, the Fordist regime of 'factory despotism' could no longer be made to work. This is the true explanation for the continuous history of labour troubles and absenteeism suffered by Alfa Sud, not the 'uneducated' and 'undisciplined' nature of the southern workforce, as Alfa management would have people believe.

Alfa Sud has failed to make a profit in any of its years of operation. This in spite of the basic market soundness of the idea of producing a smaller, cheaper Alfa Romeo model, for which demand has always been strong. The plant has low labour productivity and almost pathological absenteeism (a major local football match can stop the entire production line) with mean rates of absence exceeding 22 per cent in some years. Absenteeism (which, incidentally, is also high in Alfa Romeo's Milan plant) is, however, merely another symptom of the fundamental cause of Alfa Sud's failure — namely the social and economic obsolescence of plants organised on a technically rigid, assembly line model of production.[34] It remains to be seen what the impact of two new models brought out in 1983 will be: these are the Alfa 33, produced entirely at Pomigliano, and the Arna (a joint venture with Nissan), produced at a new factory (capacity 60,000 cars per year) near Avellino and finished at Pomigliano.[35] What *is* clear is that the induced employment resulting from Alfa Sud has been extremely meagre. One estimate is that Alfa Sud has been worth an additional 2,000 jobs in the South, far fewer than the 45,000 indicated in 1968 when the project started.[36] Moreover, many of the 'extra' jobs which have materialised are in other state-owned companies and are not the result of private industrial enterprise 'responding' to the existence of Alfa Sud. In reality most of the supplies for Alfa Sud originate from the parent plant in Milan or from Alfa Romeo's traditional network of suppliers in the Milan area — firms which are efficient and competitive and which can easily expand supply to cater for the southern plant's needs.

The location of Alfa Sud in the Mezzogiorno brought both moral and economic pressure on Fiat to do likewise. Fiat's expansion into the South was also encouraged by its workers whose unions agreed to postpone the phasing in of shorter working weeks in return for a commitment on the part of the firm to create more jobs in the South (where most of Fiat's workers originate).[34] Yet Fiat's southern initiatives, starting three years after the Alfa Sud decision, and more crucially after the labour crisis of late 1969, were based on very different premises. Fiat was able to learn from Alfa Sud's mistake of creating a large Fordist plant like Fiat's own Rivalta or Mirafiori plants in Turin. Just as Fiat had already opted for the fragmentation of labour power by adopting its industrial 'putting-out' policy in Turin, so too in the South it followed a more dispersed approach, creating a scatter of smaller, more specialised plants in different locations: Cassino (Frosinone province), Termoli (Campobasso), Vasto (Chieti), Sulmona (L'Aquila) and Termini Imerese (Palermo) — all of which show up in the 1981 provincial employment map (Figure 7.6). In its new plants built in the South in the 1970s, Fiat revealed an acute awareness of how best to adapt to the new labour situation. Instead of being set up on the industrial fringes of Naples and therefore drawing on an established and militant industrial proletariat (as did Alfa Sud), Fiat opted for rural areas of high unemployment, recruiting much of the labour force from conservative agricultural backgrounds. Fiat's flexible multi-plant structure (which includes plants in Brazil and Spain) prevents a sudden strike or stoppage holding up overall production, for key products like engines or gear-boxes can be delivered from more than one source. Fiat's pioneering use of robots for labour-intensive tasks like welding and assembly also lessens dependence on labour and, thereby, the risk of unforeseen stoppages. It is, therefore, no accident that Fiat has recovered its profitability in recent years, whereas Alfa Romeo has not.

The stagnation of car output since 1974 at around 1.4 -1.5 million units per year (though other vehicles, including bicycles, motorcycles and motor scooters have enjoyed renewed growth since 1976) is not, of course, a specifically Italian phenomenon. It is part of a demand crisis characteristic of most of Western Europe, and which has been aggravated by the increasing penetration of Japanese cars, accounting for 3.7 per cent of European car sales in 1973, rising to 9.7 per cent in 1982. Italy's fall in annual production of cars over the decade 1972-82 contributes about a quarter of the total European loss of 1.5 million. Yet, compared to some other European countries, demand for vehicles in Italy has held up fairly well, climbing in recent years from 1.45 million in 1979 to 1.72 million in 1981. Italy has now overtaken Britain for the position of third largest market for cars in Europe after France and West Germany.

Labour conditions in the car industry changed in 1980. Until then, unions had successfully prevented the big car firms from reducing their workforces to boost flagging productivity. The situation came to a head in 1979-80 when Fiat sacked 61 shopfloor agitators and announced plans for laying off 24,000 workers. The dispute escalated into a prolonged strike, accompanied by violence on the streets of Turin. The management-union confrontation was bridged by a judicious stretching of the state's subsidised layoff fund, the Cassa Integrazione, which enabled Fiat to shed 23,000 workers and Alfa Romeo 10,000 in the early 1980s. Earlier, the 40,000 strong 'right to work' march by Fiat white-collar employees in October 1980 had signalled an unprecedented defeat for the unions. The fear of job loss has now generated a rise in labour productivity coupled with decreases in absenteeism rates from 14 per cent to 5 per cent for Fiat and from 14 per cent to 9 per cent for Alfa Romeo over the period 1979-83.

Recent years have seen a proliferation of joint ventures with foreign companies. Alfa's arrangement with Nissan was condemned by Fiat as a Trojan horse venture whereby Japan, denied by a strict quota system from exporting many cars to Ialy, could start to infiltrate the Italian market from inside. At present the Arna is only 20 per cent Nissan, and 80 per cent Alfa. In 1981 Nuova Innocenti, uncertain over its continuing links with British Leyland, concluded an agreement with Daihatsu to buy Japanese engines for a new small car. Meanwhile Fiat is collaborating with Peugeot in the production of a new fuel-efficient engine to be installed in medium-range cars in the late 1980s. Fiat already works with Peugeot in the recently-built Sevel light van factory in the Sangro Valley (Chieti province). Finally, faced by mounting import competition, Fiat and Alfa Romeo have put aside ancient hostilities and in 1981 signed an agreement for joint macro-components production to come into effect in the mid 1980s.

Electrical and Electronic Industries

As Bryant[38] points out, Italian entrepreneurs are probably at their best in the light engineering industries, which give them most scope for their designing abilities and innovatory craftsmanship, as well as needing less raw materials and benefiting from Italy's relative wealth of electrical power. The electrical engineering and electronic industries comprise a multitude of activities which can be crudely subdivided into *investment* goods (products which are fed into other industries or constitute infrastructure, such as transformers, generators, transmission lines, etc.) and *domestic* goods (household appliances, televisions, lamps, etc.).[39] The latter group — domestic appliances — has tended to expand more rapidly than the former. 'Investment' products' sales are conditioned by the availability of funds released by the 'demand' industries which are often state concerns like the telephone or energy authorities. Such funds may be cut or delayed by wider decisions or problems, such as the long delays over power station development. Domestic appliance manufacturers, on the other hand, have the possibility of creating and feeding their own markets.

The majority of electrical firms are small in size and fairly widely distributed; this gives a rather widespread pattern of employment, with the exception of most provinces in the 'Deep South' regions of Molise, Apulia, Basilicata, Calabria, Sicily and Sardinia (Figure 7.7). The largest purely electrical firm is Magneti Marelli of Milan, but there are other, bigger firms like Olivetti and Zanussi which bridge the rather hazy divide betwen electrical and mechanical engineering.

Established in 1908 by the Jewish socialist Samuel Olivetti, the firm which bears his name remains a world leader in office equipment and electronics. Based at Ivrea in Piedmont it has 60,000 employees and 21 factories throughout the world. In Italy it employs 34,000. It was also one of the first big North Italian private firms to set up a factory in the South, at Pozzuoli in the 1950s.[40] Typewriters are the traditional backbone of Olivetti's operations, but this product has gradually become less significant with the opening up of other lines, especially in the field of electronics. Italy's annual typewriter production peaked at 845,00 in 1967 since when it has fallen back to a platform of around 600,000 per year. Olivetti claims to hold 18 per cent of the world market for portable typewriters (mainly made in Spain) and 21 per cent of electronic typewriters. Olivetti's switch from purely mechanical to electronic products has been rapid. In 1963 the group was solely involved in the production of mechanical equipment like typewriters, manual calculators and cash registers. By 1969 9 per cent of production was devoted to electronics, rising to one-third by 1972 and two-thirds by 1980. Micro-computers have been a major field of expansion, as well as data and word processing systems. After an abortive attempt during 1955-64 to produce large-scale computers, mainframe machines are now being produced in collaboration with Hitachi of Japan. Big expansions are also under way in the field of telecommunications, traditionally weak in Italy but now

Figure 7.7: Employment in Electrical and Electronic Industries, by Province, 1981

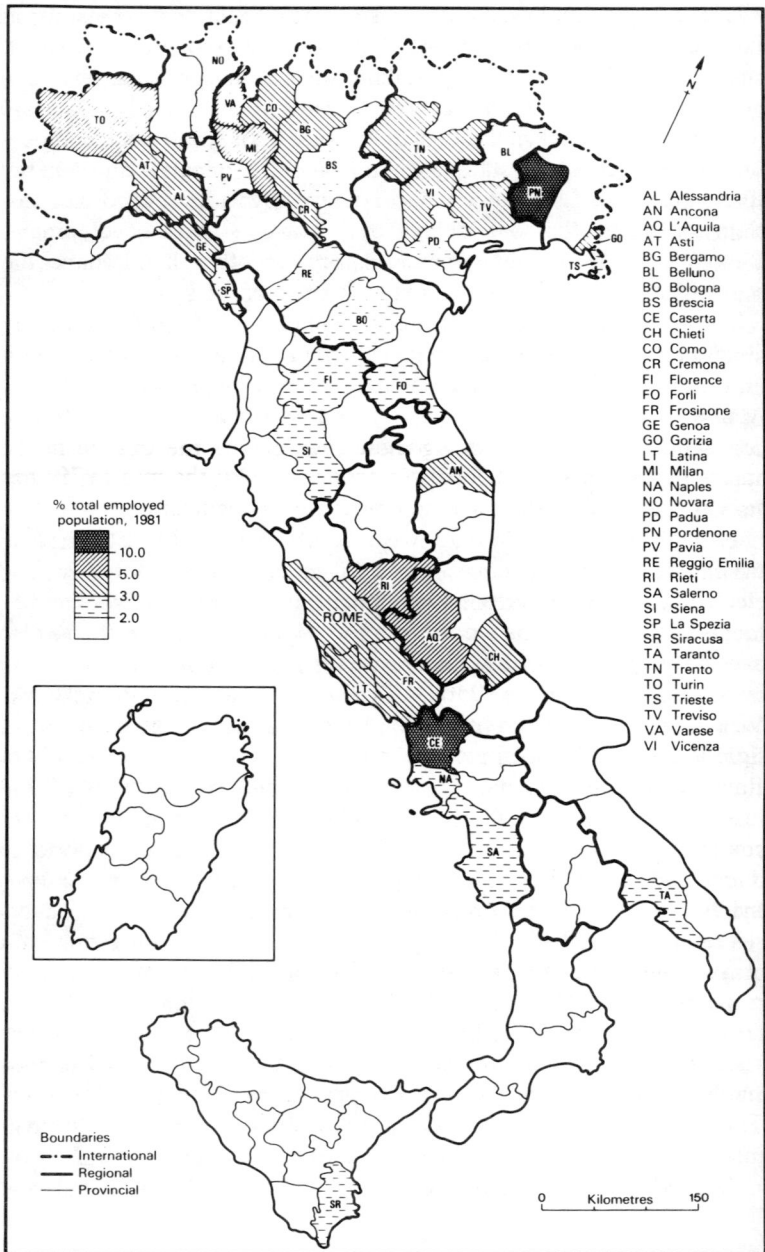

% total employed population, 1981

10.0
5.0
3.0
2.0

ROME

AL Alessandria
AN Ancona
AQ L'Aquila
AT Asti
BG Bergamo
BL Belluno
BO Bologna
BS Brescia
CE Caserta
CH Chieti
CO Como
CR Cremona
FI Florence
FO Forli
FR Frosinone
GE Genoa
GO Gorizia
LT Latina
MI Milan
NA Naples
NO Novara
PD Padua
PN Pordenone
PV Pavia
RE Reggio Emilia
RI Rieti
SA Salerno
SI Siena
SP La Spezia
SR Siracusa
TA Taranto
TN Trento
TO Turin
TS Trieste
TV Treviso
VA Varese
VI Vicenza

Boundaries
–·– International
—— Regional
—— Provincial

0   Kilometres   150

Source: As Figure 4.1.

being bolstered by a 1979 law setting aside £565m of government money to support this sector.

The other main branch of the electrical/electronic industries is domestic appliances, broadly divisible into so-called 'white' goods (refrigerators, freezers, washing machines, cookers, etc.) and 'brown' goods (television sets, sound systems, etc.). Growth in the manufacture and export of these products has been truly remarkable, especially for washing machines and refrigerators. In 1960 Italy was importing half its domestic appliance needs. Ten years later the domestic appliance industry had become the second largest in the world after that of the United States, and exported 64 per cent of its output. A phenomenal and sustained average rate of growth of 15-16 per cent per year was recorded for the 1960s. Further growth occurred in the early 1970s but since the world recession of 1973/4 the industry has encountered a number of problems, and some of the weaker companies have gone out of business or have been 'rescued' by being taken over by their larger competitors. Foremost among these problems is the change in the nature of the market for domestic appliances. By the mid 1970s the Italian and European markets, at least for most 'white' goods, had become saturated, with more than 90 per cent of West European families in possession of a refrigerator, washing machine and modern electric or gas cooker. For the last ten years most of the market is no longer being supplied for the first time, as it was in the 1950s and 1960s, and the replacement market is heavily dependent on general economic trends, especially in the availability and use of disposable income. When times are difficult people tend to make their old machines last a little longer. Under the pressure of inflation, taxation and fiscal drag Italians especially are spending more on day-to-day consumption and less on consumer durables. The result has been a build-up of unsold stocks at the factories and warehouses, followed by suspension of production and the resort to the Cassa Integrazione for varying numbers of the 67,000 people employed in the sector. Annual output of refrigerators fell from 4.5 million in 1976 to 3.4 million in 1980 televisions and washing machines held steady at around 2 million and 3.3 millions respectively, whilst dishwashers (for which the household market is by no means saturated) increased, albeit erratically. With colour television not being available in Italy until 1975, there has since then been a sudden switch from the production of black and white to colour sets. Thus, although the number of sets produced has remained stable, an increasing proportion have been the higher value colour sets.

Nevertheless the Italian domination of the European white goods market remains impressive: 38.5 per cent of refrigerators, 39.1 per cent of freezers, 33.5 per cent of washing machines and 22.5 per cent of dishwashers. The main concerns — Zanussi, Ignis, Indesit, Candy, Merloni — are, quite literally household names. Together these five companies control 85 per cent of Italy's production of white goods. Zanussi is the biggest and most diversified, with an annual turnover of £600 m and 25,000 employees; its headquarters are at Pordenone. Ignis (of Varese) was taken over by the Philips subsidiary IRE in 1973. Indesit has a more scattered production structure with a number of small, specialised plants, including some in the South at Caserta (Figure 7.7). As with many other Italian industrial products which thrived on exports in the 1950s and 1960s, domestic appliances have clashed now with low price products being introduced from cheaper labour countries in Eastern Europe (refrigerators) and the Far East (small domestic appliances)

Notes and References

1. See Militerno and Tondini (1979), pp.626-36 for graphs and more discussion on this.
2. Zanetti (1983), pp.255-60.
3. Cafagna (1971), p.314.
4. Clough (1964), pp.286, 315.
5. Willis (1971), pp.103-18.
6. Keyser and Windle (1978), pp.116-18.
7. Rodgers (1976).
8. Rodgers (1979), p.127.
9. Cafagna (1971), pp.312-14.
10. Clough (1964), pp.88-9; Webster (1975), p.69.
11. For details on this period, including maps of Ilva's holdings, see Avagliano (1976), pp.1131-50.
12. For the early post-war development of the steel industry see Della Porta (1955), Malezieux (1964) and Manuelli (1958).
13. The fourth integrated steelworks was originally proposed for Vado Ligure, a coastal town near Savona and thus close to the main centres of steel consumption in Northern Italy. Taranto was preferred because it satisfied IRI criteria for locating new investment in the South.
14. An interesting set of papers was published in the early 1970s in the journal *Notiziario did Geografia Economica;* see Celant (1971), Floridia (1971), Sica (1972), Simoncelli (1972) and Spinelli (1970).
15. See Rotondo (1979).
16. Paci (1980), p.211.
17. Clough (1964), pp.90-1; Webster (1975), pp.61-2.
18. Avagliano (1976), pp.1158-68.
19. For details of the report see Posner and Woolf (1967), p.29.
20. Japan's share of world shipbuilding rose dramatically from 8 per cent in 1954 to 50 per cent in 1968, a level which held steady right through to 1981. This increase has

been almost exclusively at the expense of West European shipbuilders, whose world market share has fallen from 80 per cent in 1954 to 30 per cent in 1980. The Italian share of world shipbuilding capacity is around 3 per cent. Because of government policies to preserve shipbuilding capacity and employment, the Italian industry has declined more slowly than its European counterparts in Britain or West Germany. In Europe there was a 20 per cent decline in shipbuilding employment during 1975-8; in Italy the fall was 8 per cent, and in the South only 3 per cent. Basilico (1983), pp.12, 15, 27.

21. Manzi (1970).

22. Basilico (1983), p.28.

23. This account of nineteenth century engineering is based mainly on Clough (1964), pp.89-92.

24. Of course most countries exhibit some degree of polarisation in the size distribution of their industrial enterprises, but Italy's is more marked than most, as a comparison with the British mechanical engineering sector shows. In the United Kingdom 66 per cent of companies are under 200 workers, and 9 per cent are over 1,000 workers. In Italy there are only 447 medium-sized firms (6 per cent of the total) operating in this sector; in the UK the proportion is 25 per cent.

25. Girola (1977).

26. Webster (1975), p.93.

27. Avagliano (1976), pp.1151-4.

28. Home-produced cars have increased their share of national output in recent years. During 1976-80 (a period in which annual car production remained static), cars of over 1.5 litres increased their share from 22 to 27.5 per cent of the total. Only 3,000 cars of 2 litres and over were produced in 1976, increasing to over 40,000 in 1980. Cars of less than 1 litre, on the other hand, fell from 39.5 per cent to 27 per cent of total national production. So much for the energy crisis!

29. Nearly 22 per cent of the Italian market is taken up by French cars: Renault 10.5 per cent, Citroën 5 per cent, Simca 4.3 per cent, Peugeot 1.9 per cent. Other significant imported marques are (percentages): Ford 4.6, Volkswagen 4.3, Opel 2.6, BMW 1.9, Audi 1, Mercedes 0.8, British Leyland 0.8, Volvo 0.7. Home produced cars, taking 60.1 per cent of the market, are the made up predominantly to Fiat 44.7 per cent, Alfa Romeo 6.9 per cent, Lancia-Autbianchi 6.8 per cent and Nuova Innocenti 1.7 per cent. All figures are for 1980. Japanese competition does not figure prominently in Italy which, alone of EEC countries, limits this country's exports severely (to 2,000 per year, less than 0.1 per cent of the market). Japanese manufacturers do, however, compete fiercely with Fiat in export markets for small and medium cars.

30. Lusso (1978).

31. Borlenghi *et al.* (1986), p.253.

32. Biscaretti di Ruffia (1973), pp.45-6.

33. Amin (1983; 1984).

34. Amin (1983), p.17.

35. Innocenti (1983).

36. Rodgers (1979), p.156; also Amin (1983), p.14-16.

37. Giugni (1971), p.318.

38. Bryant (1968), p.97.

39. Latis (1976).

40. See Ottieri (1962) for a revealing account by a personnel manager posted down from the North of the setting up of this factory.

8 CHEMICALS

The Italian chemical industry vies with the British for being the third largest in Europe, after the West German and the French. As in other European countries, the outstanding development in the chemicals sector has been the spectacular post-war expansion of the petrochemicals industry with its multiplicity of by-products. Compared to most of the other industries considered so far — textiles, footwear and the metals-based mechanical and engineering industries — chemicals are therefore a relatively recent addition to the Italian industrial family, growing rapidly to become a major employer and revenue earner.

Of all Italian industries, the chemicals sector is one of the most complex and difficult to define. It has a complicated internal structure and overlaps with other major industrial branches. It merges into the extractive industry in the mining of its raw materials, into the metallurgical industry in the production of coke and non-ferrous metals, and into textiles in the production of synthetic fibres. Its products include industrial and domestic chemicals and detergents, paints and dyes, plastics, fibres, rubber and pharmaceutical goods.

The Italian chemical industry consists of two separate worlds: basic or primary chemicals, including plastics and fibres; and secondary chemicals, including paints, drugs and cosmetics.

In basic chemicals, giants prevail. Production is heavily concentrated in a small number of industrial groups, the largest of which, Montedison, is bigger than all the others put together.[1] All these groups are more vertically integrated than their counterparts in other European countries. The vertical link with oil refining has ensured a sufficient supply of refined products even in the darkest days of the 1970s recession.

In sharp contrast to the basic sector, secondary chemicals are one of the most fragmented sectors of Italian industry: 4,000 firms in 1971, of which 3,700 employed fewer than 20 workers and only 10 more than 1,000 workers. Moreover foreign groups enjoy undisputed leadership in this secondary chemicals branch, which is also the most profitable side of the industry.[2]

Another peculiarity of the Italian chemicals scene is that it has always been a highly political industry. There was massive state support for it 70 years ago when its main objective was to provide explosives needed by the army during the First World War. In Fascist times its task was to ensure the country's self-sufficiency in basic chemical production and the firm of Montecatini was handsomely rewarded with a *de facto* monopoly of fertiliser production. Currently public enterprise contribution, largely through the ENI subsidiary ANIC, is also notable: 23 per cent of the chemical industry's fixed investment, 5.8 per cent of its gross product and 4.5 per cent of its employment. ANIC is the second Italian chemicals concern after Montedison and accounts for one-quarter of ENI's total investment and turnover.[3]

In recent years the state has poured enormous funds into chemicals and the industry has been at the centre both of major decisions on industrial policy and of political controversy and scandal. The oil refinery and the chemical plant have become the industrial symbols of tumultuous, uncoordinated growth and of economic corruption. As a result public and private interests in the industry are intertwined in a dense tangle of financial and legal (and illegal!) relationships.[4]

Base Materials and Development of the Industry

Although most of the deposits concerned are modest in size and often inconveniently located, the subsoil of Italy provides a fair selection of chemical raw materials: sulphur and potash from Sicily and Emilia-Romagna; salt from pans at Margherita di Savoia (Apulia), Trapani and Augusta (Sicily) and Cagliari (Sardinia), and from the Miocene rocks of Tuscany and Sicily, which also yield gypsum; and nitrates produced from lignite, from natural gas and by atmospheric fixation. Other useful minerals present include borax (Cecina valley, Tuscany), fluorspar (Trentino), bauxite (Abruzzi) and lead-zinc ores (south-west Sardinia). Reference back to Figure 1.3 and Table 1.2 will provide the location and production totals of some of these minerals.

During the period between Unification and the First World War the Italian chemical industry remained small and restricted to a narrow range of products, prime among which was agricultural fertilisers. Unlike steel and textiles, the chemical industry did not benefit from any protective tariffs. Lack of technical know-how and capital were further handicaps to progress. The demand for fertilisers, however, stimulated the production of sulphuric acid and phosphates. Sicilian sulphur made the country one of the largest producers of sulphuric acid, accounting for 10 per cent of world production by 1913. Copper sulphate, an important fungicide for vines, was produced from 1893, especially by the Società Montecatini. This company, founded in 1888 on the basis of a Tuscan copper mine, expanded its monopoly over many Italian minerals after 1910, extending its control to fertilisers after 1920. Other important companies were founded around this time — Snia Viscosa in 1920, Rumianca in 1921.[5]

Although the chemical industry made steady progress during the first half of the twentieth century, the real progress came after 1950, chemicals, especially petrochemicals, being one of the fastest-growing sectors of Italian industry during the post-war period until 1973. Refined petroleum and natural gas discoveries in the lower Po Valley became major location influences for chemicals processing. The chemical industry and those linked to it — especially plastics and rubber — swiftly made the transition from a carbo-chemical to a petrochemical base.

The discovery of methane in the lower Po Valley was perhaps the largest single raw material factor in the chemical industry's post-war advance. The consequent impact on Ravenna was most striking.[6] Until about 1960 this historic city had been a small coastal town, isolated by the advancing Po Delta from its erstwhile maritime functions. With the discovery of large quantities of methane in the vicinity, it suddenly became the centre of the Italian petrochemicals industry; a new port was opened up in the deltaic mud, and improved communications by river and canal stretched as far inland as Milan. ANIC built a major synthetic rubber factory (much of the output was traded for Soviet oil), as well as complexes manufacturing artificial fibres, resins and fertilisers.

Refining crude oil also became big business after the 1950s. Partly this was to supply Italy's rapidly escalating energy needs, but partly it was linked to the growth of chemical industries. Italian oil production has always had symbolic rather than real value: small quantities were discovered in 1949 at Cortemaggiore (between Parma and Piacenza) and in the 1950s in south-eastern Sicily. Oil refining developed slowly at first, hampered by a lack of capital and technical expertise. The first real spurt in refining activity came in the 1930s with the building of cracking plants like the one at Porto Marghera behind Venice and a network of integrated refineries, mostly in the North. In the early 1950s the refining industry gained further impetus from the rise in Middle Eastern oil production. Italy exploited its geographical location by functioning as a refining intermediary between the new oil producing countries and the major consuming countries of Western Europe. As Italy became the 'refinery of Europe' two distinct locational tendencies emerged

(Figure 8.1). Firstly, there was a tendency to choose centres of consumption as refinery sites. Thus refineries became established at Genoa, Trieste, Porto Marghera, Naples and on the Tuscan coast and at certain inland sites such as Milan, linked by pipeline to Genoa. This was the main tendency in the North, where links were also established with oil-based industries in Switzerland, Austria and southern Germany. Secondly, the location of the larger, newer refineries — including three with an installed capacity of around 20 million tons — tended to shift to the South, closer to the Mediterranean oil tanker routes and where there were attactive fiscal incentives on offer from the Cassa per il Mezzogiorno. By 1977 Sicily had one-third of the national refining capacity (compared to 14 per cent in 1960). Between about 1960 and 1975 several key refinery and petrochemical sites thus developed along the southern coasts: Brindisi, Priolo, Gela, Porto Torres and Sarroch (Figure 81.) By the mid 1970s around 85 per cent of the state products of the chemical industry came from the refining of oil.

Over the long period 1951-73, chemicals exhibited the highest rate of growth of productivity of all Italian industrial branches — more than 10 per cent per annum. The annual average rate of export growth was even higher at 14.2 per cent. The chemical industry thus lends strong support to R. Stern's thesis of the Italian post-war economic boom being export-led.[7] Investment in the Italian chemical industry was greater, in relative terms, than levels in most other European countries. Over the same period (1951-73) Italy made 18 per cent of its total industrial investment in chemicals, compared to only 10 per cent in France and 14.7 per cent in the UK.

Although the current crisis in the chemical — and more particularly the petrochemical — industries is normally thought of as dating from the mid 1970s, signs of strain and imbalance in the linked activities of refining and petrochemicals were apparent several years earlier. During 1964, a year before its merger with Edison, Montecatini drastically cut its workforce by nearly one-quarter, from 41,938 to 31,716. By the late 1960s inflation started to cause financial problems. The refining sector had developed too quickly; demand was levelling off. There were too many refineries (36 in 1970), and both their average capacity (1.5 million tonnes) and their percentage utilised capacity (around 75 per cent, dropping to 60 per cent by the late 1970s), were low by European standards. This inevitably caused prices to rise, even before the quadrupling of oil prices in 1973/4 provided a massive jolt to the whole system. Between 1974 and 1975 (taking average levels for the first nine months of each year) output in the chemical industry fell by 9.6 per cent. The bulk

Figure 8.1: Location of Oil Refineries and Main Chemical Processing Facilities

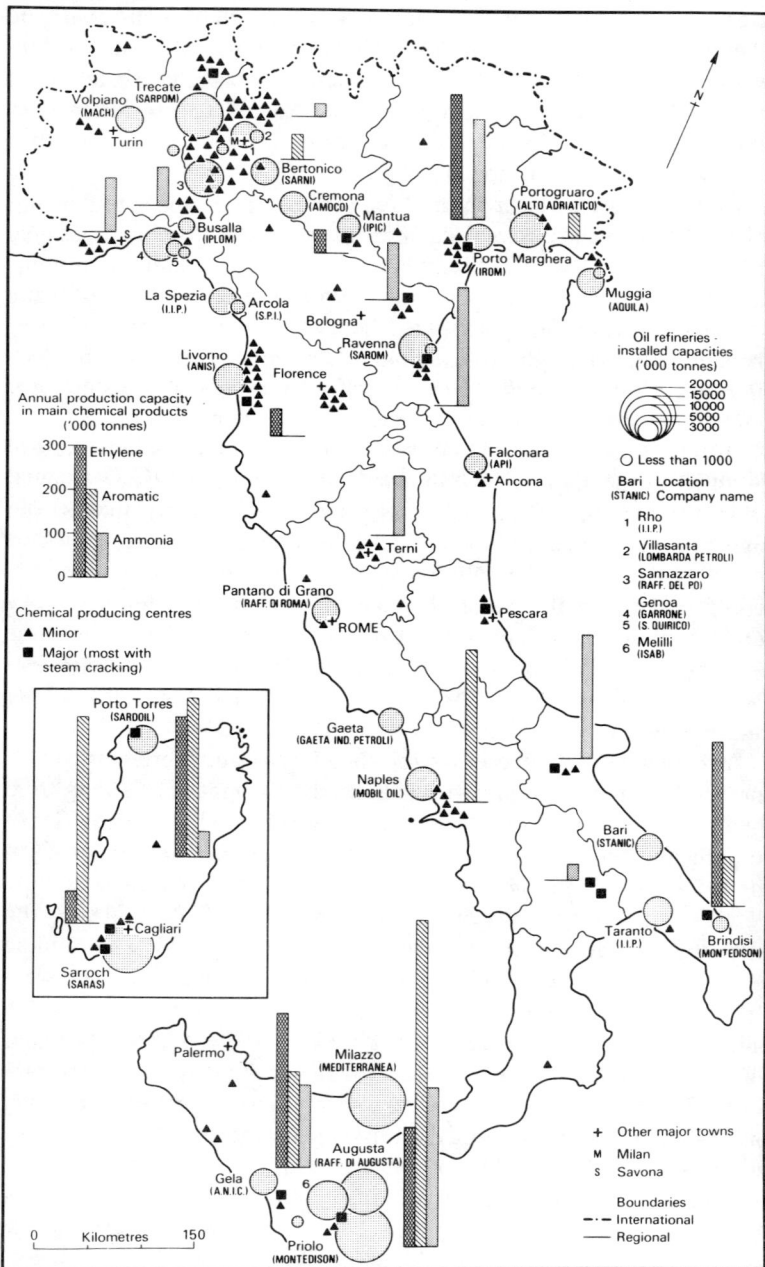

Source: Mariani (1980).

of this was made up by the 18.1 per cent decrease in base chemicals production; secondary chemicals decreased only marginally, by 0.2 per cent. The worst affected branches were synthetic fibres and synthetic resins, down by 29.5 per cent and 28.2 per cent respectively. Not only were output levels dramatically down; the price of base chemicals fell by 23.4 per cent over the same year, whilst labour costs in the industry rose by nearly one-quarter.[8]

Petrochemicals and the Mezzogiorno

The petrochemical industry started during the last war with the production of synthetic rubber and explosives. During the 1950s it continued with cracking for the mass production of organic chemicals. By 1965 organic chemicals products had become more important than inorganic ones. At the end of the decade there were 21 petrochemicals plants operating in Italy, among the most important being those belonging to Montedison (Mantua, Ferrara, Brindisi, Priolo), ANIC (Ravenna, Gela, Pisticci), Ceramica Pozzi (Ferrandina), SIR (Porto Torres) and Rumianca (Cagliari). All but three of these are in the South.

The role of the Cassa per il Mezzogiorno in promoting this development is vital. Up to 1975 (after which the petrochemical boom abated), the Cassa sponsored 653 initiatives in the field of chemicals, accounting for an employment total of 26,805 persons. By 1971 chemicals and rubber employed 60,000 per sons in the South, 7.8 per cent of the region's industrial employment (cf 19,200, 3.3 per cent, in 1951).[9]

Four main locations contain the bulk of the post-1960 petrochemicals development in the Mezzogiorno: Brindisi, the Basento Valley, south-eastern Sicily and Sardinia. Brindisi contains Montedison's propylene, pvc and ethylene cracking unit employing 5,000, as well as a range of smaller firms manufacturing plastics, pharmaceuticals and fertilisers. The Basento Valley chemical plants were developed after the discovery of methane at Ferrandina in 1959. Two main plants were established in 1964: the ANIC artificial fibres and plastics complex at Pisticci Scalo, employing 3,500; and the Ceramica Pozzi (now Liquichimica) plant for industrial chemicals at Macchia di Ferrandina, employing 700. A handful of other firms have set up smaller plants based on ANIC's fibre output, most important being the Penelope textile factory which works acrylic fibres for making up in the textile towns of the North. In the early 1970s Montedison and Pirelli also had plans to set up large plants in the Basento Valley but these have been withdrawn or vastly scaled down.[10]

The major developments, however, have taken place on the islands of Sicily and Sardinia whose 'special autonomy' status enables their regional governments to offer additional financial incentives over and above the standard Cassa package. The islands also possess the advantages of a closer location to Mediterranean oil routes and the existence of many undeveloped coastal sites with flat land adjacent to deep water. Plans to increase the national productive capacity for ethylene (which stood at 1,555,000 tonnes per year after the Brindisi explosion of 1978) by 1,080,000 tonnes by the early 1980s will affect these two islands more than other parts of the country.[11]

Sicily's petrochemicals industry is concentrated at two major sites: Priolo on the Bay of Augusta, and Gela. Although there is a pipeline bringing the heavy local oil in from Ragusa, Montedison's Sincat refinery at Priolo, built during the late 1950s, uses largely imported crude from Libya, unloaded at long jetties spiking the bay. There are four main installations at the Priolo site: treatment of crude; electrolysis from rock salt for chlorine and other chemicals; olefines and aromatic products; and base petrochemicals. The Sincat complex vies with the Taranto steelworks for being the biggest and most important industrial enterprise in the Mezzogiorno.[12] Together with its ancillary industries in chemical by-products and plastics it recruits 6,300 workers from a wide swathe of territory in south-eastern Sicily.

Rather different has been the experience of Gela where the state-owned oil and petrochemical activities remain smaller scale and much more isolated from the regional environment. Hytten and Marchioni title their book on Gela *Industrialisation without Develoment*; they judge that petrochemicals development has acted divisively, providing jobs and better incomes for some — including many technicians and managers from the mainland — but making life harder for the rest through increased costs of living and a spoiled environment. They conclude: 'The presence of industry . . . has accelerated the process of socio-economic marginalisation of the peasant class . . . If state industry wants to be an instrument for the social development of the South . . . it must do more for those who are excluded from the industrialisation itself.'[13]

Much the same conclusion can be drawn for the more recent development of petrochemicals in Sardinia. Here the social divisions drawn by industrialisation have been reinforced by the spatial polarisation of development at the northern and southern ends of the island.[14] In the north the ex-SIR petrochemicals complex, the largest single industrial enterprise in the island, dominates the town of Porto Torres. In 1977 it employed 5,000 workers but since then effective employment has been cut by a programme of short-time work caused by the failure of the plant

Figure 8.2: Sarroch and the Saras Oil and Chemical Plants

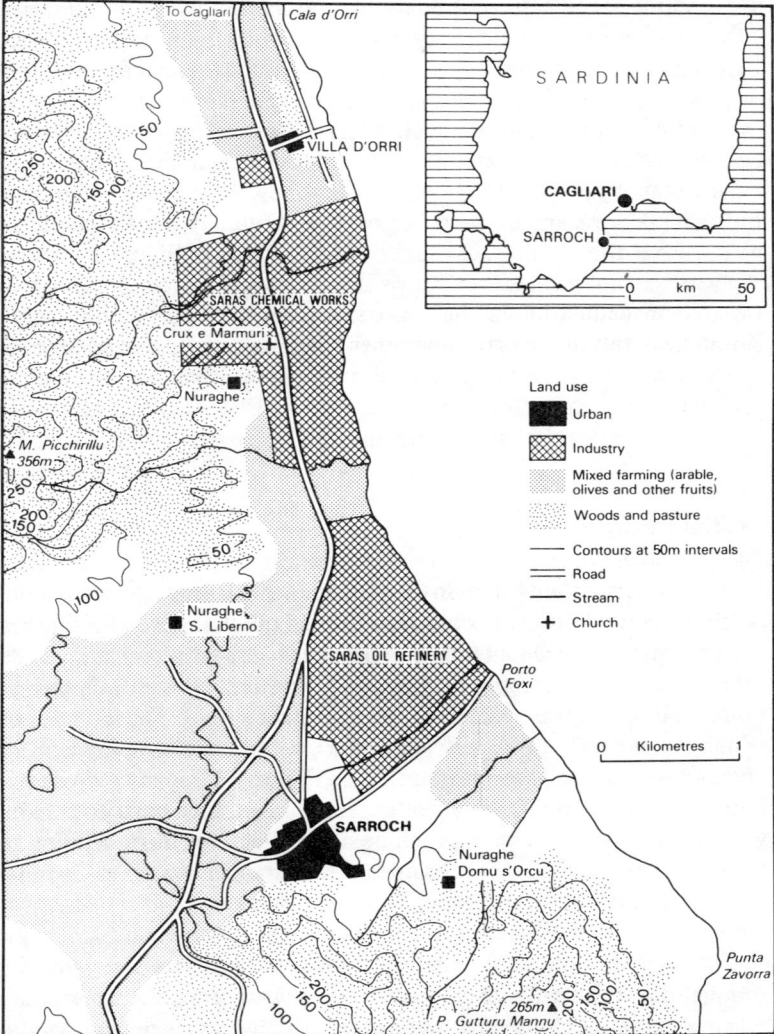

Source: Scaraffia (1975), p.191.

to work at anything like full capacity. The southern pole has two petrochemicals concerns: Rumianca, sited on the edge of Cagliari's saltpans, which produces chemicals, plastics and resins for industrial, household and cosmetic use; and Saras-Chimica, which opened in 1971 as an extension to the Saras service refinery at Sarroch.

Like Gela, Sarroch exemplifies the negative social consequences of the introduction of petrochemicals into the traditional rural south. In a village like Sarroch, previously one of the most poor and isolated in Sardinia, the sudden mixing of people from diverse social and regional origins imposed severe strains on the harmony of the community as well as practical problems of understanding dialects. The social structure has been retextured, but along sharper lines: Saras industrial managers have replaced the feudal landowners as the new 'boss class' of the area. Indeed with Saras buying land for both the oil refinery and the chemical works from the local *latifundista* of Villa d'Orri (Figure 8.2), this replacement has been exact. The purchase of so much sheltered alluvial lowland for industrial use has, moreover, severely curtailed the considerable farming potential of the district — one of the most agriculturally favoured of Sardinia — as well as trespassing on the unique archaeological character of the area, with its Phoenician heritage and its imposing *nuraghi* (Bronze Age megalithic towers).[15]

Spatial Structure of the Industry

Despite the location of so many raw materials in the peninsula and the islands, the majority of processing is carried out in the North. Milan is the headquarters of Montedison and by far the most important centre for the chemicals industry, accounting for virtually the entire production of certain branches like dyes and pharmaceuticals. The province of Milan accounts for 26.4 per cent of the total national employment in chemicals; this fact does not stand out on Figure 8.3 because of Milan's importance in so many other industrial fields. Other northern towns with an interest in chemicals include Turin, Novara, Porto Marghera (Venice province), Mantua, Ravenna, Ferrara, S. Giuseppe di Cairo (Savona province) and Cogoleto (Genoa province); their influence on the pattern of provincial employment (Figure 8.3) is clear.

The northern domination of the chemical industry has been partially tempered by the state-aided expansion of petrochemicals in the South since about 1960. Although the new southern complexes are capital intensive not labour intensive, their influence on patterns of provincial

Figure 8.3: Employment in Chemicals, by Province, 1981

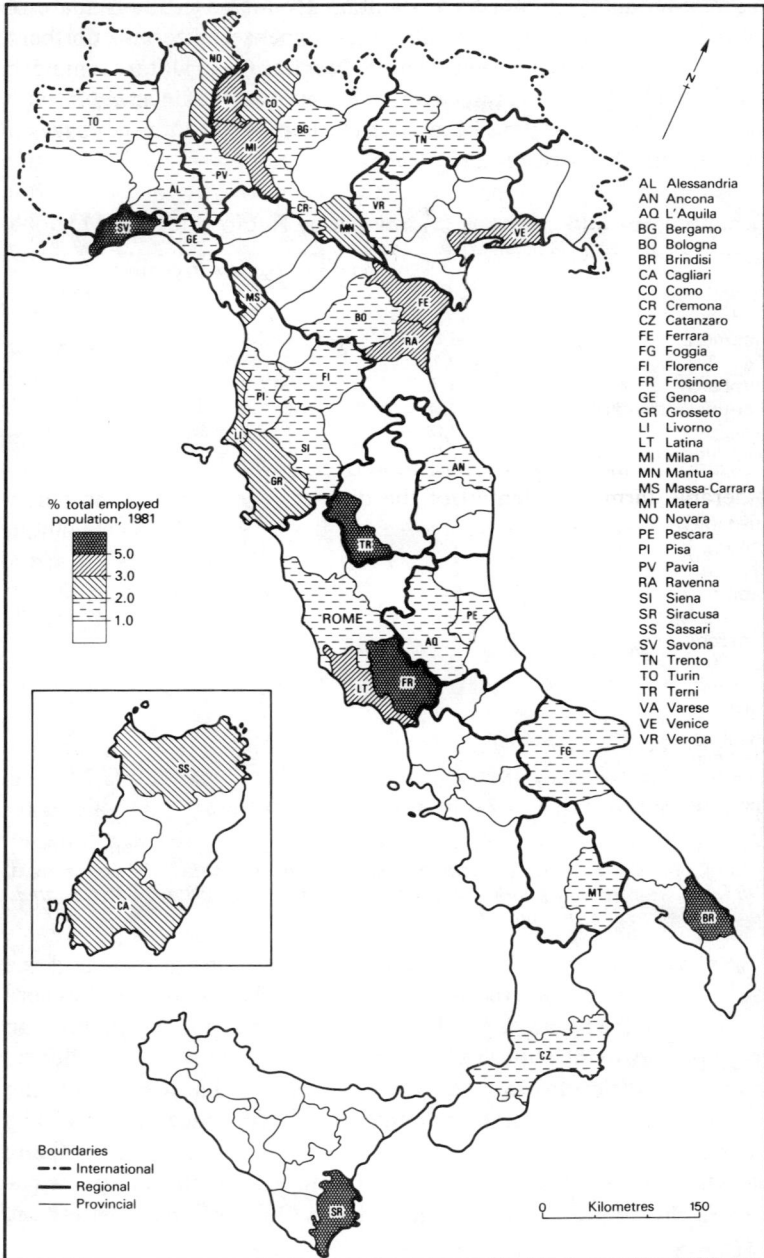

% total employed
population, 1981

5.0
3.0
2.0
1.0

AL Alessandria
AN Ancona
AQ L'Aquila
BG Bergamo
BO Bologna
BR Brindisi
CA Cagliari
CO Como
CR Cremona
CZ Catanzaro
FE Ferrara
FG Foggia
FI Florence
FR Frosinone
GE Genoa
GR Grosseto
LI Livorno
LT Latina
MI Milan
MN Mantua
MS Massa-Carrara
MT Matera
NO Novara
PE Pescara
PI Pisa
PV Pavia
RA Ravenna
SI Siena
SR Siracusa
SS Sassari
SV Savona
TN Trento
TO Turin
TR Terni
VA Varese
VE Venice
VR Verona

Boundaries
—·— International
—— Regional
—— Provincial

0   Kilometres   150

Source: As Figure 4.1.

222   *Chemicals*

(Figure 8.3) and regional (Table 8.1) employment is marked. Regions like Apulia and Sardinia have significantly increased their share of national chemicals employment, at the expense of certain northern regions such as Piedmont and Liguria. Nor has Central Italy remained unaffected by the growth in chemicals employment since 1960, with significant gains in regions both north (Latium) and south (Abruzzi) of the magical Mezzogiorno line.

Table 8.1: Employment in Chemicals by Region, 1961-81

Region	% national employment in chemicals		
	1961	1971	1981
Piedmont	8.5	7.1	6.9
Val d'Aosta	0.1	0.1	0.1
Lombardy	39.7	41.1	38.9
Trentino-Alto Adige	0.8	1.0	0.8
Veneto	8.0	7.7	8.3
Friuli-Venezia Giulia	1.5	0.9	0.8
Liguria	7.2	6.2	3.4
Emilia-Romagna	7.4	6.2	7.3
Tuscany	7.5	6.6	7.1
Umbria	1.0	1.1	1.8
Marche	2.6	1.1	1.2
Latium	6.1	6.7	9.5
Abruzzi-Molise	0.5	0.7	1.3
Campania	3.2	2.8	2.4
Apulia	0.9	2.4	2.7
Basilicata	0.1	0.3	0.4
Calabria	0.7	0.7	0.9
Sicily	4.0	5.6	4.1
Sardinia	0.2	1.7	2.1
Italy (number)	234,516	268,151	264,057

Sources: *Un Quarto di Secolo di Statische Nord-Sud 1951-1976,* Rome SVIMEZ (1978), pp.319, 321; *6° Censimento Generale dell' Industria e del Commercio, 1981, Vol. I Primi Risultati sulle Imprese e sulle Unità Locali, Tomo I Dati Nazionali, Regionali e Provinciali,* Rome, ISTAT (1983), Table 5.

It should, however, be stressed that the provincial map and the regional table conceal the extent to which chemicals employment, especially in the South, is highly concentrated in specific localities: the very opposite to the pattern of diffuse industrialisation noted earlier for footwear and clothing for example. A commune map would show the vast majority of the chemicals employment in the Mezzogiorno to be located in a handful of communes: Naples, Brindisi, Pisticci, Gela, Melilli (Priolo), Porto Torres and Sarroch. Spread effects into neighbouring districts are very slight, as a visit to Gela or Sarroch will show.

The petrochemicals complex, hissing and glinting in the southern sun, is perhaps the best example of that much-vaunted phrase 'cathedral in the desert'.

Chemicals in Crisis

During the recession of the Italian economy in the 1970s, the chemical industry was the one which showed most worrying signs of collapse. Huge losses were incurred by the main petrochemicals giants — Montedison, Liquichimica, SIR and ANIC. This financial crisis tended, however, to overshadow two wider and more important issues. First, the petrochemical industry's crisis has called profoundly into question the entire model of development followed by the Italian economy in recent decades, a model based on cheap oil and mass-produced consumer goods and not on renewable resources and concern for the environment and for the non-monetary aspects of the quality of life. Secondly, the financial crisis obscured the fundamental structural weakness of the chemicals sector — namely the disproportionate development of petrochemicals and base chemicals *vis-à-vis* fine chemicals. The former branch — primary chemicals — requires massive investment yet produces little employment and is uncompetitive in international markets.

The following may be listed as some of the main causes of the crisis in the Italian chemical (especially petrochemicals) industry:

(1) the gaps and imbalances caused by the rapid expansion of the industry in the 1960s;

(2) the oil price increases of the 1970s, and continuing inflationary pressure on raw material and labour costs (hourly earnings in chemicals are higher than in all other major branches of Italian industry);

(3) the stagnation of demand for many chemical products;

(4) the permanent antagonism between the major companies involved in the industry;

(5) the increasingly capital intensive nature of petrochemicals processing, demanded by technological progress and the increasing scale and complexity of plants — including a growing necessity to install anti-pollution equipment;

(6) the high percentage of foreign ownership and share capital in the chemical industry (one-third of the chemical companies operating in Italy have foreign shareholders, accounting for 21.5 per cent of total

chemical share capital), implying a strong external agent in the development (and contraction) of the industry;
(7) the way in which the industry, with its heavy state involvement and large multinational enterprise character, has become an expensive political football, with basically political decisions taken in advance of detailed technical and managerial consultation.

At the simplest, most fundamental level, the crisis is due to a mounting failure to co-ordinate supply and demand in time and space. In this big industry with its monolithic enterprises and massive scale of investment, expansion acquires a momentum of its own which then becomes insensitive to the evidence of stagnation of demand. The best example of this is the frantic continued investment in artificial fibres in the 1970s when the market for such production was already saturated at both Italian and European levels.

Although 'exogenous' factors (such as the recession, the world energy situation, the high rates of interest, and the behaviour of North American and Comecon countries in dumping excess produce on the market) are frequently cited — especially by chemical industry managers — as the main reasons for the chemicals crisis, these in reality are symptoms of the malaise rather than its root causes.[16] The real explanation is to be found much more in the internal nature and contradictions of the industry itself and in the way it operates and is financed: that is to say, in its inert oligopolistic structure and in its politically encouraged overexpansion at the wrong times and possibly in the wrong places. Thus, points (4) and (6) above are particularly relevant in explaining the present state of crisis and conflict in the industry. In fact, for the last 15-20 years the industry has been racked by a ruthless struggle for power and for privileged access to state funds. This struggle for control in the most twentieth century of industries has been waged in an almost medieval pattern like a conflict between feudal barons at war with each other and with a state incapable of imposing its will on them to call them to order. Attempts by the government to introduce a 'chemicals plan' have borne little fruit. ENI, ANIC, Montedison, SIR and Liquichimica continue to plan their development on a largely autonomous basis, expending enormous energy on the kind of political intrigue which still appears necessary to secure access to development funds. Furthermore, a considerable portion of the funds theoretically allocated for investment in chemicals gets channelled elsewhere, into buying shares for instance or into developing other outside interests, of which the most well-known is the purchase of newspapers.[17] The net result of all this dispersal of cash and energy is that the industry has made insufficient efforts in research and development and in the investment necessary to transform the industry away from its current basic chemical and petrochemical base into the more sophisticated and potentially profitable world of fine and secondary chemicals.

Further uncertainties and financial difficulties hit the chemical industry in the late 1970s. A drastic increase in the trade deficit in chemicals constituted a serious warning for the future. Total employment in the chemicals industry, which exceeded 300,000 during the mid 1970s, fell to 264,000 by 1981. National production of ethylene, the most important base petrochemical, fell from 1.45 million tons in 1976 to 1.18 million tons in 1979. Even more worrying for the longer-term evolution of the industry is the slowdown in all capital building programmes. Such investment money as is available is being spent on maintenance and repairs and on energy saving and environmental control systems. Whilst this could be seen as a useful period of consolidation after the chaotic expansion of earlier decades, marking time on new construction could ultimately involve Italy being left behind by its main foreign competititors. Another symptom of the crisis, and a contributor to it, has been the abandonment of petrochemicals enterprises already started. Two examples illustrate this: the cessation of construction of the Montedison-ICI aniline plant at Priolo after protests from local pressure-groups that the chemical induced cancer; and the failure to open the nearly finished ANIC-BP bioprotein plant at Macchiareddu near Cagliari.

Finally, symbol of the more emotive feelings expressed about the Italian chemical industry, with its secrecy, corruption, pollution and external control, is the Seveso explosion of 1976, the biggest industrial tragedy Italy has known. Local authorities were kept ignorant of the noxious nature of the Swiss-owned factory, which only had a licence to manufacture harmless perfume essence. Yet when an overheated reactor yielded, it let out a cloud of trichlorophenols, decomposition products and dioxin, one the most poisonous chemicals known to man. Now to visit this ghost town 20 km north of Milan is to take an eerie glimpse into the doom-mongers' future. In a form, public retribution occurred four years later when terrorists killed the plant's technical director in Monza. But the long-term problems remain: the contaminated soil and buildings; the dormant potential damage to human life which may take years to emerge (many local women had voluntary abortions, afraid of deformities in the children); the question of industrial safety standards; and the morality of externally-owned industry polluting Italian territory.

Positive Signs

After the losses, closures and scandals of the late 1970s, the 1980s were ushered in by a complete reorganisation of the ownership of the main chemical companies and by a commitment by the authorities to intervene at various levels: to boost ethylene production in the South; to rationalise the basic sector and the early stages of petrochemical processing; and to stimulate the development of secondary chemicals which on the whole had lagged.

Montedison, which had tottered on the brink of state ownership for years, has now gone completely private, its shares held by ENI and IRI having been sold off to private industrialists. On the other hand, SIR and Liquichimica, the two other large privately-owned chemical companies of the 1970s, have been taken over by ENI, whose existing chemicals interests are being reorganised to absorb the new arrivals. In 1981 ENI struck an agreement with the American giant Occidental Petroleum to manage the loss-making SIR plants which had been running at minimum capacity for several years. Being relatively modern — indeed in some cases the construction of new units was half-finished since SIR ran out of capital in the late 1970s — the plants represented an ideal opportunity for Occidental to realise its ambition of penetrating European petrochemical markets. Under the new company, Enoxy, spawned by the ENI-Occidental marriage, ethylene production in the South should regain former levels by the mid 1980s. Whether the market will absorb the increased production is another matter.

Whilst the basic petrochemicals branch of the chemicals industry shows signs of profiting from this enforced rationalisation, progress in secondary chemicals has been slow. For some years there has been a wish amongst the unions and certain sections of management to shift the emphasis of the industry from its excessive reliance on petrochemicals to the more labour-intensive and potentially profitable secondary chemical products like paints, pharmaceuticals, biochemicals and agrochemicals. Such a shift, however, requires massive research efforts followed by huge capital investments, and is in the long run dependent on favourable international market outlets: all three are proving difficult obstacles to come to terms with. Symptomatic of the overall problem is the case of the state-controlled ANIC which is trying to lighten its burden of base chemicals and fibres by moving into the more remunerative area of fine chemicals: its efforts have been impeded by the management confusion of its parent ENI (whose director was sacked by the government in 1979 following an oil bribery scandal in Saudi Arabia), and by the decision of the government to saddle ANIC with Montefibre's share of the loss-making fibre plants of Ottana in central Sardinia.

Notes and References

1. Montedison is second only to Fiat as a private enterprise in Italy. The fifth-largest chemical company in Europe and eighth in the world, Montedison accounts for 28 per cent of fixed investment in Italian chemicals and one-quarter of the market (including 40 per cent of petrochemicals, 45 per cent of plastics, 43 per cent of fertilisers and 30 per cent of synthetic fibres). It also has affiliates in pharmaceuticals (Farmitalia Carlo Erba), fine chemicals (Acna) and retailing (Standa chain stores).

2. Significant fractions of the share capital of the secondary chemicals firms are held by ICI, Solvay, Union Carbide, Dow Chemical, Columbia Carbon and Sun Chemical. See Gasperini (1974), p.105.

3. Keyser and Windle (1978), pp.109, 114.

4. For a graphic portrayal of these links — in more ways than one — see Ragozzino (1969), pp.47-63.

5. This early account is based largely on Gasperini (1974).

6. See Gabert (1963).

7. Stern (1967). Some of the figures quoted here are from Allen and Stevenson (1974), p.60.

8. Bracco (1976); Gasperini (1974); Ruocco (1968).

9. Rodgers (1979), pp.48, 143, 147.

10. Coppola claims that, for political and public relations reasons, the large multinational and semi-public firms locating in the South make advance exaggerated claims for the number of jobs they are going to create; then the slightest excuse (the hint of an economic downturn, or some other obstacle, real or imagined) is used to let them off the hook and plans are either revised dramatically downwards or abandoned altogether. In 1971 Pirelli promised 3,600 jobs by 1976 in their new tyre plant in the Basento Valley; by 1980 only 100 were working in a modest enterprise manufacturing caterpillar tracks. Another example is Liquichimica's grandiose (and abortive) plans for a huge fine chemicals complex employing 10,000 workers on the agriculturally, touristically and archaeologically rich Metapontino plain at the mouth of the Basento river. See Biondi and Coppola (1974), p.160 and Coppola (1976).

11. Ruju (1979), p.362.

12. Campagnoli Ciaccio (1971).

13. Hytten and Marchioni (1970).

14. King (1977).

15. For a comprehensive account of the impact of the Saras plants on the local environment and culture see Scaraffia (1975).

16. Rullani and Vaccà (1979).

17. All the main chemical groups have spent heavily in buying control over major newspapers: ENI has a stake in several newspapers, including *Il Giorno* acquired by Enrico Mattei, as well as its own press agency; Eugenio Cefis, head of Montedison in the 1970s, bought control of the principal Rome and Milan dailies, *Il Messaggero* and *Corriere della Sera;* and Nino Rovelli, boss of SIR before his demise, controlled the press in Sardinia where his major plants were located.

PART THREE

REGIONAL PATTERNS OF ITALIAN INDUSTRY

9 NORTHERN ITALY

Regional diversity is an ever-present theme in all writings on Italy's historical, economic and social development. Regional differences in rhythms and styles of industrial development are an important key to understanding Italy's contemporary human geography. From the point of view of industrial geography, three major 'regional formations' can be recognised, and these are the subjects of the last three chapters of this book. First, in this chapter, is considered Northern Italy, the amphitheatre of Italian industrial development since before the industrial revolution and still the dominant industrial region today. The next chapter examines Central Italy, traditionally a region of transitions but now the part of Italy where a new style of industrial growth and organisation is emerging most forcefully. Finally, the concluding chapter will examine the pattern of industrialisation in the South, with its strong overtones of regional development policy.

General Introduction to the North

Northern Italy comprises eight regions (Piedmont, Val d'Aosta, Lombardy, Liguria, Trentino-Alto Adige, Veneto, Emilia-Romagna and Friuli-Venezia Giulia) and 40 per cent of the Italian surface area. It contains a population of 25.4 million, 45.3 per cent of the Italian total. Its general configuration is that of a quadrilateral limited on the north and west sides by the Alpine frontier, on the east by the Adriatic and on the south by the Ligurian coast and the northern Apennine slopes (Figure 9.1). Compared to the fragmented spatial structure of the Italian 'boot', the North is compact and coherent. Its core is the great North Italian Plain, large enough to give continental climatic characteristics; to the north lie the Alps, seamed with long, deep valleys many of which contain an illustrious industrial heritage; and to the south rise, less dramatically, the Apennines, drier, warmer, more 'Mediterranean', especially where they fall to the Ligurian littoral. Although physically heterogeneous, the North is given unity by the sweep of the Alps enclosing the Po Plain; by the close continental connections enjoyed with Central and Western Europe; by the productivity of its agriculture and its industry which furnish a high standard of living; and by the consciousness of its people of being northerners.[1] The broad

Figure 9.1: Northern Italy

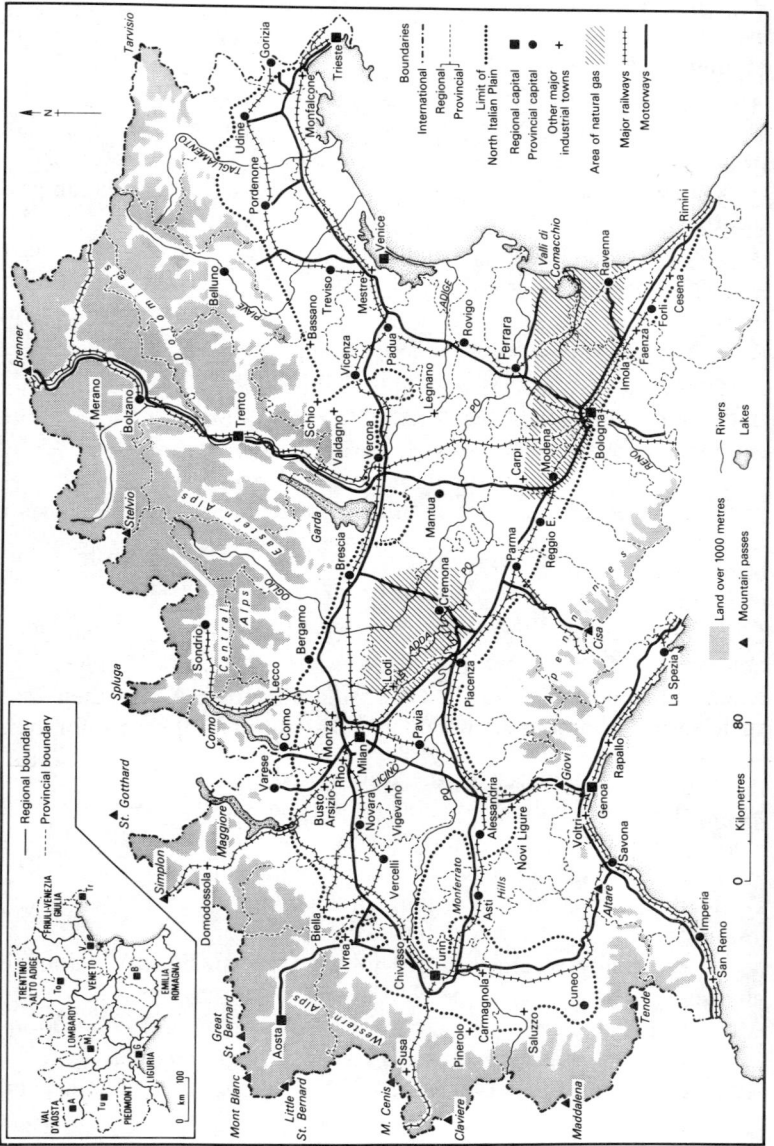

climatic unity of the area is violated by the inclusion of Liguria but this region, with its ports, industries and tourist resorts, is unquestionably part of the northern realm.

The situation of Northern Italy as a 'junction box' between Western Europe and the Mediterranean has conditioned its many important historical developments. If it was Central and Southern Italy that were more intensely developed during the Classical era, by the Middle Ages the North had spawned the development of many powerful commercial towns and seen the formation of powerful political units like the Duchy of Milan and the Republics of Venice and Genoa. The North, sooner than the South, became associated with the main movements of European history — and economy. Lombardy and Venetia were part of the Austrian Empire. Piedmont instigated Italy's own political unity. Turin and Milan led in the creation of modern industry.

The northern pre-eminence in industry, and in economic matters in general, is manifested in several ways. Political decisions may be taken in Rome, but they are often conditioned by the major economic and trade union interests of the North. No one doubts that Milan is the economic capital of Italy, though Turin probably has a more specific industrial function. For millions of unemployed southerners over the post-war period, to get a job in the 'industrial North' has been both a dream and a reality. Economic trends and cultural fashions generally originate in the North, or are adopted there from other European centres of innovation, and subsequently diffuse southwards. Milan, not Florence or Rome, is the principal market centre for Italy's innumerable works of art. In the university world Padua and Bologna are amongst the most distinguished of southern Europe. A pity, then, that such learned traditions are not universal amongst northerners, for their economic supremacy often leads them to make racist judgements about the perceived inferiority of their southern brethren who are often denounced as lazy, inefficient *terroni* ('peasants').

More objective than prejudices are the regional statistics and indices regularly published by ISTAT. These show, for instance, that the North, with 45.3 per cent of Italy's population, generates 56.6 per cent of the gross domestic product (the Centre produces 19.3 per cent and the South 24.1 per cent). In terms of mean *per capita* income the North is still very definitely ahead of both the Centre and South, although the gap has narrowed somewhat in recent years. It remains a significant fact that the seven richest of Italy's 95 provinces are all northern (Milan, Turin, Varese, Genoa, Gorizia, Trieste, Aosta) whilst the seven poorest are all southern (Avellino, Agrigento, Cosenza, Lecce,

Potenza, Isernia, Catanzaro). Milan's *per capita* income is more than three times that for Avellino.

Such disparities in wealth are due largely to the accumulation of industry in the North over the last hundred or so years. Throughout the post-war period, Northern Italy has accounted for over half the factories and over two-thirds of the industrial workers of Italy as a whole. The difference between these two proportions reveals a mean size of factory which is larger in the North than in the rest of the country. The mean number of employees per factory (1981) is 10 for Northern Italy, 6.9 for Central Italy and 4.8 for the South; the national figure is 8.1.

The North's dominance is even more marked in the general field of *manufacturing* industry, for which it contains 70 per cent of the national employees. Within this category the proportion varies by sector or branch, but it is always well above the proportion of population residing in the North. Some examples, all percentages, are food industries 57.5, textiles 76.5, clothing and shoes 56, wood and furniture 59.9, metallurgy 74.9, mechanical industries 76.6, vehicles 83.1, chemicals 70.3, rubber 79.1, paper and printing 70.6. On the other hand the extractive group of industries, with 33.7 per cent of its employees in the North, is under-represented.

These employment figures do not tell the whole story of the North's industrial dominance, for they take no account of the higher levels of investment and productivity in Northern Italy. If value added is the criterion, then even extractive industries rise to 47 per cent of the national total, a proportion more than equivalent to the North's share of national population or area. If crude output figures are taken then several other relevant statistics can be quoted. The North produces 91.4 per cent of the nation's cotton thread, 58.7 per cent of steel, 95 per cent of vehicles, 73.4 per cent of glass, 66 per cent of paper, 78 per cent of nitric acid ... A revealing qualititative indicator of the North's industrial development is the appearance of art, novels and films expressing the alienation of modern man from industrial society: the anomie which is perhaps best seen in the weird and soulless industrial landscapes of the Milan periphery.

The Natural Setting

Natural factors are far from irrelevant to the North's industrial prosperity. In this region, nature has been rather more generous in its gifts than in other parts of Italy. Although it has more than its fair share of high unpopulated mountains and stony, infertile plain, the disposition of mountain and plain has a sharpness and a spatial logic which has acted as a favourable frame for human activity, providing, for example, constant sources of water for irrigation and industrial power. The key to the North's physical geography is precisely this alliance between high mountain and flat plain.

With 35,000 sq. km of Alps and 10,000 sq. km of Apennines, mountains account for 45 per cent of the North's surface area. Medium and low hills are rare: they are limited to the mostly narrow (3-20 km wide) pre-Alpine terraces and moraines on the northern edge of the plain, to the lower slopes of the Apennines and to isolated hilly outcrops within the plain itself, such as the Monferrato Hills near Turin and the Euganean Hills near Padua. Much more important, of course, is the great triangular plain which gradually lowers and widens itself towards the Adriatic: 500 km from Turin to Trieste, 200 km along the meridian of Venice, a total area of around 50,000 sq. km.

The North's natural endowment has facilitated human and industrial development in three broad senses.

Firstly, rapid communication has been possible across the flat plain and along the glacially flattened valleys of the Alps. Railway, road and motorway construction have all forced ahead more quickly in the North than in the peninsula. In 1861, for instance, 1372 of the 1,623 km of railways were in Piedmont, Lombardy and Veneto, then the core regions of Northern Italy. Although these transport networks have developed primarily in response to existing urban and industrial development, rather than being purely a function of physique, relief has not posed the difficult obstacles it has in the more fragmented landscapes of the Centre and the South. Only along the Ligurian coast have transport lines been built with real difficulty. The Alps, in spite of their forbidding altitudes, have always been easily crossed, giving the industrial centres of the Po Plain a considerable advantage in terms of rapid access to all parts of central Europe. The transport network of Northern Italy has also been well served by ports like Genoa, Savona, Venice and Trieste, some of which have hinterlands extending beyond the region. Coastal lagoons, the Po itself and certain of its tributaries form an artery of riverine navigation unique in Italy.

Secondly, the North juxtaposes regions which are physically varied but economically complementary. Before industry became the region's principal activity, capital and labour were already busily engaged in a prosperous agriculture and in lively commerce. Great works of drainage and irrigation mobilised urban capital and led to the dense colonisation of the plain. The mountains were (and of course still are) the domain of forestry and transhumant pastoralism, vines flourished on sunny slopes within the main upland massifs and on the small hills within the plain, and fruit trees grew in sheltered valleys. Such agricultural specialisms have survived and intensified. On the 'high plain' grow cereals such as wheat and maize, as well as specialised tree crops like the mulberry. On the low plain the abundance of water encourages the cultivation of fodder crops and rice. Sugar beet favours the heavy cold soils in the central plain where the climate reaches its most continental character. Along the southern margins, especially in Emilia-Romagna where Mediterranean tendencies begin, various fruits and vegetables establish their specialised domains. Finally, around the Ligurian shore, where the mildness of the winter is assured by the mountain backdrop, olives, flowers and even citrus fruits are grown. This platform of a rich and varied agriculture should not be overlooked in accounting for the region's industrial growth. The food industries themselves have been a vital component in the regional economy, especially in the eastern plain, and abundant local food supplies have been assured for the growth of industrial towns.

Thirdly, the North possesses a number of important industrial resources. *Ferreto* clays are an excellent brick-making material, supplying an industry which is vital in sustaining the prodigious urban growth of the region. The calcareous rocks of the pre-Alps and the Monferrato Hills give rise to many quarries producing lime and chalk for fertilisers and cement. More complex geological formations in the inner Alpine region allow the extraction of marbles and other hard ornamental rocks such as porphyry and coloured granites. The main minerals are iron ore at Cogne, manganese in Liguria, copper in Piedmont, zinc in the Seriana and Brembana valleys and magnesium near Trento and La Spezia. Amongst non-metallic minerals may be mentioned the existence of mines for talc (Val Chisone in Piedmont and Val Malenco in Lombardy), graphite (near Pinerolo) and amianthus (Balangero near Turin). But the North's chief industrial resource is excellent supplies of hydro-electric energy and methane gas, to which must be added the small but locally important source of coal at La Thuile in Val d'Aosta.

Demographic Perspectives

The industrial growth of Northern Italy is closely linked to the region's demography. The region has, for centuries, been an area of relatively high population density. Its population rose from 12.8 million in 1871 to 24.9 million in 1971, an approximate doubling in a century. The present density (215 persons per square kilometre in 1981) is around 15 per cent higher than the national figure, but this means little when there are such marked density contrasts within the North. The Alpine provinces are lightly peopled — Val d'Aosta 34 people per sq. km, Bolzano 56, Trento 69. Even some of the eastern Po Plain provinces are far from densely occupied — e.g. Ferrara 147, Mantua 162. The greatest densities are to be found in the western and higher parts of the lowland, ranging from 344 for Turin province to 1,443 for Trieste (the latter being somewhat exceptional because of its truncated provincial area).

The key to these differences, and to recent intercensal population change, is the existence of large towns and industry. At least until very recent years, there has been an increasing concentration of population in the large industrial cities and an exodus from rural areas, especially those in the mountains and in the North-east. Taking the 1961-71 intercensal period — a decade of rapid spatial demographic change in all Italy — three provinces recorded very marked gains of around 25 per cent: these were Turin (25.7 per cent), Varese (24.8 per cent) and Milan (23.3 per cent). The next biggest gains, Como (15.7 per cent) and Savona (12.6 per cent), were some way behind. Three north-eastern provinces (Belluno, Udine and Trieste) and five in the low plain (Piacenza, Cremona, Mantua, Rovigo and Ferrara) lost population. In the succeeding intercensal period (1971-81) the number of northern provinces experiencing net population loss increased to 13; most of these form a belt along the lower Po axis (Asti, Vercelli, Alessandria, Pavia, Piacenza, Cremona, Mantua, Ferrara), together with three Ligurian provinces (Imperia, Genoa, La Spezia) and the North-eastern provinces of Belluno and Trieste. In the mountains the redistribution of population has had a differentiated character which the provincial figures do not always reveal since many provinces span both upland and plain. The mountainous part of Cuneo province, for example, has lost more than half its population (207,553 in 1881, 102,325 in 1971), much of which has drained to Turin. At the commune level the effects have often been much more dramatic. The village of Briga Alta, near the French border, recorded 1,291 inhabitants in 1861, but only 124 in

1980. Yet there are exceptions to this story of mountain depopulation. Generally these occur where there is development of tourism and skiing (as in parts of Lombardy and Trentino), where there are industrial resources (as in Val d'Aosta), or other special circumstances (such as the high birth rate in Bolzano).

The demographic changes noted above are the combined result of natural increase (or decrease) and migratory transfers. Taking again the 1961-71 intercensal period, when an overall increase of 2,258,819 was recorded in the North, 57.7 per cent was contributed by natural increase and 42.3 per cent by net in-migration. Most parts of the North have the low and falling rates of natural increase normally associated with an advanced industrial economy. But again there are significant exceptions. Bolzano province has already been mentioned, and there are also provinces like Turin and Varese which have seen their native populations rejuvenated by an influx of young adults from other regions. Many rural areas have ageing populations produced by out-migration; at the province level, Asti, Alessandria, Pavia and Vercelli have a significant excess of deaths over births. Liguria also has an old population, due less to the out-migration of the young than the in-migration of the old, for the Italian Riviera, like the French, is an area of retirement migration.

Migratory change can be classified into three types. The most important quantitatively has been local-scale rural-urban migration, mostly within individual provinces and to provincial capitals (which thus increased their share of the total regional population from 19 per cent in 1871 to 34.3 per cent in 1971). Secondly there have been significant long-distance transfers of population within the region, especially from the rural areas of the eastern plain to Milan and Turin, although this pattern has been less marked in recent years. Thirdly, there has been large-scale in-migration from outside the region, especially from the South. This southern migration has largely been of young unskilled workers, many with only a rudimentary education. Such an influx has caused considerable problems of housing, welfare and social relations, yet it is these migrants who, more than anything, have sustained the industrial expansion of the North in the post-war period. These workers are also amongst the first to be laid off during the current recession that is affecting certain branches of northern industry, and are returning to their native villages, thereby upsetting established migratory trends.

The big city communes are thus beginning to participate in the process of counter-urbanisation which has now become well established in the advanced industrial economies of the Western world. Proper documentation of the extent of counter-urbanisation in Northern Italy will have to await the full publication of the 1981 Population Census results, although some provisional results and the annual population registers published for all Italian communes provide some guide.[2] Two trends are fairly clear. First, continued urbanisation in the big cities affects peripheral suburbanised communes more than the city communes themselves, although much depends on where the boundaries of the latter fall. Thus Turin and Milan have experienced declining momentum (respective population increases of 42.6 per cent and 24.2 per cent during 1951-61, 13.9 per cent and 9.5 per cent during 1961-71, and losses of 5.7 per cent and 5.8 per cent during 1971-81). The other big northern cities also lost population during 1971-81: Venice, Trieste, Bologna and Genoa all recorded losses of 6-8 per cent.[3] Meanwhile suburban communes grow spectacularly. The commune of Cinisello Balsamo, north of Milan, is a typical example. A village of 5,158 persons in 1861, it grew steadily to reach 15,336 by 1951, then exploded to 37,699 in 1961, 77,931 in 1971 and 80,484 (estimated) in 1981. The second trend concerns the repopulation of rural areas, both within and beyond urban hinterlands. The annual population registers (which must be regarded as approximations rather than true enumerations) indicate that this process has been going on for at least a decade in most parts of the country, including remote parts of the South. The suggestion is that the trend to a more diffuse pattern of industrialisation is stimulating urban-rural counter-migration, both within the North and from the North to other parts of the country, but return migration from abroad may also be an important factor.

Polarisation of Industry in the North

Although, as we have seen, factors favouring the setting up of industrial activities in the North have been in operation since Roman times, its emergence as the country's major modern industrial region can be traced to the latter part of the nineteenth century when a number of large industries became established in the North, especially in Milan and Turin, giving rise both to the industrial dominance of those two cities and to the oligopolistic structure of Italian industry. Such firms included Edison (electrical industry), Pirelli (rubber), Ansaldo (shipbuilding), Nebiolo (printing), Savigliano (construction engineering), Franco Tosi (mechanical industries), Breda (railway engineering), Ercole Marelli (electrical materials) and Carlo Erba (chemicals). Somewhat later came the big car industries — Fiat (1899), Alfa Romeo

(1905) and Lancia (1906) — followed by Olivetti in 1908. At the 1911 Industrial Census, the dominance of large industry in the North was convincingly revealed: the region had only 49 per cent of the country's industrial enterprises but 58 per cent of those with motive power, 60 per cent of those employing at least 10 workers, 65 per cent of those with more than 100 workers, and 71 per cent of those with over 500. The broad outlines of Italy's regional industrial geography had been fixed.

The first half of the twentieth century did nothing to disturb this trend of spatial polarisation. Fiat, Pirelli and Montecatini consolidated their already powerful positions. Iron and steel and the mechanical industries lent their heavy weight to the process of northern concentration. Fascism had no industrial policy for the South. The Second World War proved more damaging for the South than for the North, for it was in the lower part of the peninsula that the longest and bitterest battles were fought. In the North the bombardments were very trying for the civil population but they did not ravage industry as much as was first thought. Iron and steel and the mechanical industries *were* badly affected but for many other sectors the damage was relatively minimal, no more than 5 per cent of the installations being destroyed. Recovery was complete by 1950 and the country then embarked on the period known as the 'economic miracle' which was almost entirely a northern industrial phenomenon.

The 'miracle' was not merely a period of rapid economic expansion; it represented a profound structural transformation of the Italian economy and way of life — in the North. The agricultural foundations of the regional economy shrunk as new, modern, export-linked industries took over. Government economic policy and the Treaty of Rome encouraged trade liberalism; given Italy's lack of industrial raw materials, it could be argued that there was little choice. Closer to the industrial consumer markets of Western Europe and possessing good supplies of industrially exprienced labour, a well-developed infrastructure and abundant sources of hydro-electricity and gas, the North was ideally placed to draw maximum benefit from the decade-long boom. Of the 32 per cent increase in Italian industrial employment in the 1951-61 period, 73.7 accrued to the North, especially in its fast-growing mechanical and electrical engineering and chemical industries.

The end of the boom in 1961-3 marked the end of the polarisation process. Over the decade 1961-71 industrial employees increased in number by 16.3 per cent nationally; the North contained 61.3 per cent of this more modest increase. During 1971-81 industrial employees increased by 12 per cent nationally, but only 39.2 per cent of this was located in the North. Quite apart from the boom coming to an end, the enhanced spatial dualism which it had given rise to provoked its own backlash in terms both of increasing costs of congestion and pollution in the North and of government policy to develop industry in the South.

The Character of North Italian Industry

With nearly 4.5 m. employees, industry dominates the employment structure of Northern Italy by a wide margin. Table 9.1 highlights some of the features of the region's industrial labour force and output. The diversity of industry and the relative importance of each branch of activity need not be repeated. Statistical data confirm what has already been shown in terms of the historical evolution of northern industry, namely the existence of a wide industrial base supported by three major groups of industries which are particularly strongly developed.

Table 9.1: Industry in Northern Italy, 1951-71

	% industrial workers			% value added		
	1951	1961	1971	1951	1961	1971
Food, drink and tobacco	7.7	7.2	6.3	9.8	8.4	8.9
Textiles	23.3	15.3	11.1	18.3	10.6	8.2
Clothing and footwear	9.2	9.0	8.9	6.9	5.2	5.8
Leather and skins	1.1	1.3	0.9	1.2	1.0	0.7
Wood and furniture	6.9	7.2	6.6	4.0	4.7	4.7
Metallurgical	4.7	5.0	4.9	7.4	8.3	6.5
Mechanical and vehicles	29.4	34.4	40.0	28.8	35.3	39.1
Non-metalliferous minerals	4.7	5.4	4.9	4.1	5.6	4.5
Chemical	6.0	6.5	5.9	9.9	11.7	12.6
Rubber	1.5	1.5	1.8	2.8	2.1	1.9
Other	5.5	7.2	8.7	6.8	7.1	7.1
Total manufacturing	100.0	100.0	100.0	100.0	100.0	100.0
Manufacturing industries	86.3	83.0	83.8	83.3	77.1	75.8
Extractive industries	1.3	0.9	0.6	1.6	1.9	1.2
Construction, public works	10.4	14.3	13.7	9.9	15.0	18.0
Energy and water	2.0	1.8	1.9	5.2	6.0	5.0
Total industry	100.0	100.0	100.0	100.0	100.0	100.0

Sources: Various censuses and other ISTAT publications.

The first group, that which gave birth to industry in the region, is textile manufacture. In 1951 it still accounted for 23.3 per cent of regional industrial employment. It subsequently declined substantially, to only 11.1 per cent in 1971 and 9.3 per cent in 1981. If, however, to the processing of textile fibres are added other activities related to the clothing sector such as dressmaking, shoes, leather and hides, this group accounts for 16.8 per cent of industrial employment and 14.7 per cent of value added (1971) — still an important element in the region's industrial structure.

The second group, which chronologically appeared soon after textiles, comprises metallurgy and engineering. This has now become the region's leading industrial sector, although the metallurgical branch holds a modest position. Northern Italy's industrial power is underpinned by a wide range of manufactured mechanical goods such as motors, electrical equipment, cars and lorries, railway equipment and domestic appliances. This metallurgical and engineering industries group occupied 34 per cent of the regional workforce in industry in 1951 but this had increased to 44.9 per cent in 1971, when it accounted for 45.6 per cent of value added.

The third group, numerically less important, is chemicals, including heavy and refined chemicals, cellulose production for chemical fibres, chemicals derived from coal and petroleum, and synthetic rubber. In combination, these branches contain only 7.7 per cent of the regional industrial labour force but contribute nearly 15 per cent of value added.

This emphasis on advanced technology industries, like engineering and chemicals, or those demanding large amounts of skilled labour, like textiles, clothing and certain branches of engineering, gives the North a virtual monopoly of those industrial products which are most readily exported. Not surprisingly, therefore, Northern Italy commands three-quarters of Italy's export (and import) trade. The diversity of industry also provides flexibility in the regional economy since it tends to even out cyclical fluctuations, while at the same time it permits industrial linkages between complementary and spatially proximate industries.

A further characteristic of the region's industry is the fragmentation of production into a myriad of factories, with only a limited number of large combines. This is a general characteristic of Italian industry as a whole: 98.9 per cent of Italian and 98.4 per cent of Northern factories employ less than 100 workers. Nearly half the workforce — 49.8 per cent — works in factories with less than 100 employees, only 17.8 per cent in factories of over 1,000 workers. Such a structure obviously has many drawbacks since concentration generally permits economies of scale and reduced costs. However, this judgement needs further qualification to take into account the specific character of North Italian industry. In the first place, the crude statistics conceal the heterogeneity of the various sectors. In the case of the northern vehicle and chassis industry, for instance, 94.7 per cent of the workforce are in factories with more than 1,000 employees. Secondly, there are positive advantages to be gained from the existence of a large number of small units. Lacking in capital, they specialise in lightweight products demanding skill and abundant labour. This situation has certain consequences. It strengthens the position of the major firms by giving them access to numerous sub-contractors. In the medium term, it has created employment and fostered the ability to adjust to changing external demands unhindered by the inertia of fixed plant and heavy investment. The disadvantages are evident in the social field of underpaid and insecure labour, in the lack of scientific research, and in an industrial economy too heavily concentrated on consumer goods. Nevertheless, the small firm remains the symbol of the North's industrial stability and prosperity.

Although there are a few 'black spots', such as the murky chaos of Milan's industrial suburbia, the crowded disorder of Genoa and the pollution of Porto Marghera, nowhere in Northern Italy are there to be found the dense industrial conurbations of the older industrial regions of north-west Europe. Italy has no Ruhr, no Lorraine, no Black Country, although a comparison between Lombardy and Lancashire has been attempted.[4] In fact, much North Italian industry is quite scattered, with large areas of essentially rural land use, even within the Turin-Milan-Genoa industrial triangle. Much development, being recent (i.e. post-war), is contained in modern factories surrounded by trees and gardens; its impact on the landscape is thus relatively slight.

Spatial Patterns and Contrasts in North Italian Industry

Northern Italy's early industrialisation was located at the contact point between the Alps and the Po Plain. A belt of factories and workshops follows this break of slope, concentrating on the high terraces and morainic amphitheatres, from south of Turin right round to the Yugoslav border. This locational pattern, clearly evident since the last century, is explained by several favourable geographical factors. By installing themselves on the plain-mountain divide, industries profited from two sets of beneficial influences: from the mountains came wood, mineral resources, abundant labour, the energy of rivers and nearness to major transalpine routeways; the plain offered cheap food supplies, flat land for factory sites and the presence of numerous towns guaranteeing market outlets for the industrial products. This combination of factors has continued to apply until very recently, especially in the east of the region.

This band of industry does not have a uniform intensity or width. It thickens out around Turin and snakes up the lower Alpine valleys, for example to Susa and Ivrea. Narrowing between Ivrea and Lake Maggiore, it broadens again on approaching Milan where it forms its most metropolitan extent. Further east, beyond Brescia, it once again narrows and tends to fragment, isolating industrial nuclei around towns. Outside of this linear zone, the only site of long-established industrial tradition is Genoa.

Twentieth century industrial growth has reinforced this spatial pattern of the pre-Alpine belt, and has also seen the birth of new industrial zones. On the floors of the Alpine valleys towns like Aosta, Domodossola and Bolzano have developed as industrial centres, partly through the survival and rationalisation of traditional mountain artisan trades, notably in iron-working and timber. In the plain and along the Adriatic coast industry has been grafted on to many towns: remarkable in this regard is the line of industrial growth which follows the Via Emilia, with old towns and new industrial estates spaced out like beads on a string drawn tight. Bologna dominates this southern axis. Most recently there has been the diffusion of factories into more decidedly rural areas; the growth of car ownership allows such isolated industries to draw workers from surrounding villages and farms.

The industrial prosperity of Northern Italy is not evenly spread. In addition to those contrasts between urban and rural areas already mentioned, there is a broader regional difference between North-west and North-east Italy. Table 9.2 shows a number of indicators which reveal the relative backwardness of the eastern part of the North up to 1971. The western half — Piedmont, Val d'Aosta, Lombardy and Liguria — is more densely populated, more industrialised, wealthier. This is the region of the famous industrial triangle based on Milan, the economic capital of Italy, Turin the industrial capital and Genoa, the nation's premier port. One should not, however, fail to mention the fact that there are also predominantly rural provinces in this north-western region. Cremona and Mantua have little industry and are not without severe economic problems.

North-east Italy is decidedly peripheral to the industrial triangle, to which its population has long had a habit of migration. The North-east's economy has traditional roots in agriculture and small-scale industry, the former geared more to export than the latter. However the relative nearness of the Lombardian industrial belt has stimulated development in various ways. The western regions have sunk considerable sums of capital in developing first hydro-electricity in the eastern Alps and, second, methane production in the eastern plain. There have also been tendencies for north-western industries to set up branch factories in the North-east, attracted partly by labour supplies, and for local entrepreneurs to develop their own industrial lines as a follow-on. Although Genoa remains the main external link of this industrial triangle, some trade has been pushed through to Adriatic ports which have thus enjoyed some stimulation.

Table 9.2: North-west and North-east Italy: Regional Indicators

		NW	NE
Population in 1961		13,156,710	9,503,507
1971		14,919,311	9,999,725
Population change 1961-71 (%)		+ 13.1	+ 5.2
Proportion of working population	1961 (%)	14.9	28.0
engaged in agriculture:	1971 (%)	7.8	16.2
Composition of Gross Regional Product in 1970:			
Agriculture (%)		5.9	15.3
Industry (%)		53.5	41.1
Other (%)		40.6	43.6
Net revenue *per capita*	1970 (lire)	927,400	724,000
Employees in manufacturing industry	1951	1,850,750	612,975
	1961	2,315,481	888,845
	1971	2,544,455	1,156,279
	1981	2,424,300	1,361,200
Change 1951-61 (%)		+ 25.1	+ 45.0
1961-71 (%)		+ 9.9	+ 30.1
1971-81 (%)		− 4.7	+ 17.7
Average number of workers per factory	1971	15.4	10.0
	1981	12.0	8.9

Sources: Various census and ISTAT publications.

However, there are signs that this situation of a dynamic, prosperous North-west and a peripheral, lagging North-east is changing. Provisional results of the 1981 Industrial Census reveal a decline in manufacturing employment in the North-west of 4.7 per cent over the 1971-81 decade, and the contraction of many key industries in the industrial heartland. By contrast, the North-east has experienced considerable industrial dynamism since 1971, with a 17.7 per cent increase in manufacturing employment (Table 9.2). Put another way, the North-west's share of national manufacturing employment fell from 48.8 per cent to 43.2 per cent, whilst the North-east's rose from 21.8 per cent to 23.9 per cent.[5] As should be clear from previous discussion, this is very much linked to processes of specialisation and deverticalisation in Italian industry. Textiles, clothing, shoes and certain metal and mechanical trades figure prominently in this restructuring. The most important areas, where this restructuring had led to significant industrial growth in the last 10-20 years, are north-eastern and central regions like Friuli, Veneto, Emilia-Romagna, Marche and Umbria. The 'Centre-North-East hypothesis' has been highlighted by Fuà in his studies on backward development, [6] but little in-depth research has been carried out into the origins and mechanisms of change in this 'Adriatic strip' which spans the conventional divide between North and Centre.

Turin, Piedmont and the Val D'Aosta

Turin is the capital of Piedmont as Paris is the capital of France: 'by the pleasure of the prince and the continuity of a dynastic policy'.[7] The prince was Emmanuel-Philibert and the dynasty the House of Savoy. There is another similarity too, for Turin's dominance over the urban hierarchy of Piedmont (ten times bigger than the second city Alessandria) is comparable to that of Paris over Lyons. Turin is one of the few major settlements located on the Po itself, although it is squashed in between the Alpine forelands and the Monferrato plateau, a gap it has watched over since Roman times. Its role as communications centre for the western plain remains unchanged, as the map of railways, main roads and motorways shows (Figure 9.1). The urban renaissance of the Middle Ages passed Turin by but once chosen as the capital of Savoy in the sixteenth century its fortunes waxed. French cultural influence remained strong until the mid nineteenth century. Its progressive leaders were intent on modernising the city even before unification and it probably reached its peak in Italian life when it served as the first national capital for a few years. However, unification of Italy eventually obliged Turin to exchange the role of capital for that of a hard-nosed industrial city. Since the end of the nineteenth century Turin has achieved a twofold demographic growth and a functional transformation from military-administrative to industrial.[8] Its fortunes have risen in parallel with the growth of the motor industry and, remarkable for a city of more than a million inhabitants, it is virtally a company town, a dormitory for Fiat. Two-thirds of the city's labour force is dependent on Fiat, one-third directly and one-third indirectly by working for Fiat's supply industries. Of the 160,000 who work in the Italian motor car industry, 130,000 work in Turin.

Turin's post-war industrial prosperity has been bought at the expense of certain social and economic problems. Not the least of these is the absorption — or lack of it — of over half a million southern migrants, so that Turin has the highest percentage of southern immigrants of any northern city. The prolonged expansion of Turin as a manufacturing city has created a conflict with the need for balanced urban development as firms' expansion and relocation have taken space which could have been devoted to other uses.[9] A high proportion of the industrial activity of Turin is still located within the commune itself (Figure 9.2),

Figure 9.2: Turin

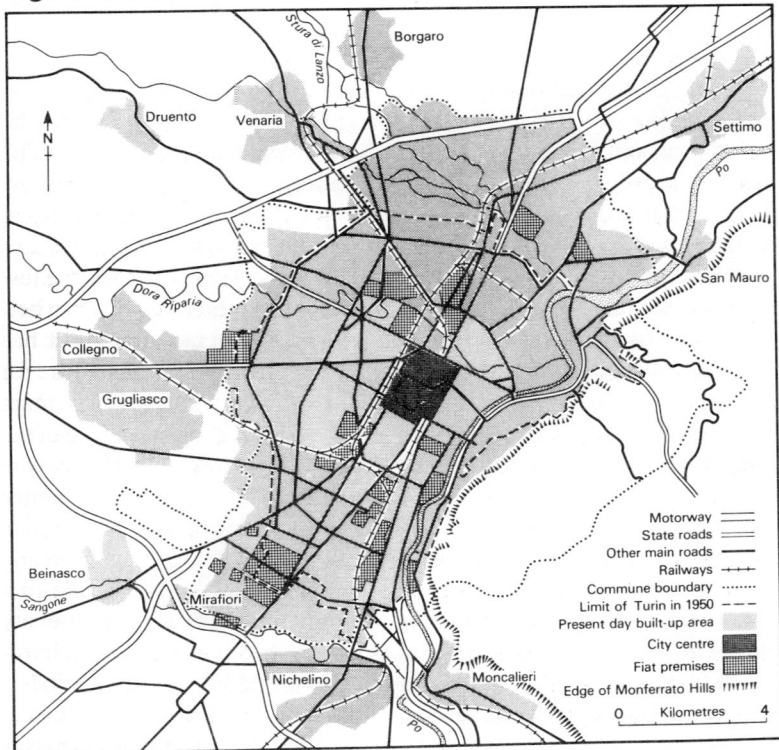

while the population has shifted to the suburbs, some of which are a good way out. As a result there is serious congestion in the Roman grid-iron city centre, despite the construction of peripheral by-passes. The most serious economic problem is the vulnerability of a one-industry, one-firm town. In his book on Turin Pierre Gabert discusses at length the dangers and limitations of expansion based on industry rather than services, on one industry rather than several, and on a single firm rather than many.[10] In the twenty years since Gabert's book the dominance of the car industry and the Fiat empire over the city's industrial structure has, if anything, tended to increase. Of the 90 factories employing more than 500 workers, 74 are in mechanical engineering, with Fiat figuring directly under 10 different entries. Fiat also occurs under different names, such as Lancia, Riv-SKF and Magnetti-Marelli. Furthermore, many other large firms, such as Philips and Westinghouse, work exclusively for Fiat, and the car industry recurs in sectors outside mechanical engineering, like Pirelli and Michelin for tyres. Only 3 of the 90 big factories in Turin remain stubbornly unconnected to the Fiat-mechanical engineering network — two in textiles and one in clothing. The food and drink industry factories, of which the best-known internationally are the Cinzano and Martini-Rossi plants, are all below the 500-worker threshold.[11]

As prosperity migrates eastward from the industrial triangle Turin, with its narrowly based industrial economy, has suffered more than Milan though not as much as Genoa, afflicted by declining marine industries. The current mayor of Turin, Diego Novelli, has said that Turin is suffering a crisis whose duration and outcome are unpredictable, but which will certainly produce a very different city.[12] The recent stagnation of motor car production has had severe repercussions on the city and its auxiliary industries (rubber, bearings, plastics, etc.) which are dangerously overdependent on the vehicle industry. Fiat has trimmed both capacity and output to take account of the shrinkage of the car markets; reabsorption of the 23,000 Fiat workers laid off on generous state redundancy terms in the early 1980s has been slow. The city itself has 92,000 unemployed (1983), nearly half of whom are young people seeking their first job.

Yet Turin's influence over the regional economy and demography of Piedmont remains overwhelming, an inheritance from the French political system of centralism which established a strict division between town and country and a concentration of economic and administrative dynamism in the regional capital. Again following the French model, family size in Piedmont has been low, rural out-migration to the dominant metropolis severe, and a rapidly ageing population structure is common outside the southern immigrant districts of Turin.[13] Dematteis[14] shows the pattern of influence of Turin on the western Alps. A daily commuting distance of 50-60 km extends north and south over the plain and westwards up the lower Alpine valleys. Included in this belt are the many dignified towns of the plain edge like Pinerolo, Saluzzo, Rivarolo and Ivrea as well as valley towns like Susa and Bussoleno. Here a previous pattern of population decline has been arrested as the extension of suburban dormitories repopulates these areas. Further away, in the higher, smaller Alpine valleys and in inaccessible districts in the Monferrato and Langhe Hills, the influence is felt more in terms of permanent residential shifts to the city, so that these areas have continued to lose population rather rapidly.[15]

The industrial belt around Turin now occupies the area between Carmagnola in the south and Chivasso in the north. As it has moved out of Turin (though still centred on the town), industry first reached the banks of the Stura di Lanzo before spreading along the motorway to Settimo and Chivasso (Figure 9.2). The whole system now encompasses 1.6 million people, of whom more than 700,000 settled between the mid 1950s and the mid 1970s.

The regional industry of Piedmont is quite varied and is particularly well-developed in the northern provinces of Vercelli and Novara. Vercelli contains the Biellese woollen area whilst Novara, more under the influence of Milan than Turin, is a notable engineering centre as well as housing the Agostini cartographical publishers. Ivrea, in Turin province, also forms part of this pre-Alpine industrial belt. Piedmont's southern provinces have a weaker industrial tradition, a fact which prompts Bethemont and Pelletier to call them the 'Piedmontese Mezzogiorno'.[16] Alessandria derives importance from its location at the heart of the industrial triangle and therefore as a route centre roughly midway between Milan, Turin and Genoa. Agricultural processing and textiles are its main industries. Asti province lies entirely in the vine-clad Monferrato Hills and is famous for its *spumante*. Cuneo is Piedmont's smallest provincial capital but, like many other towns of the Piedmontese plain, it has benefited from the recent decentralisation of light industry from high-cost and congested locations in Turin.[17]

Although frequently bracketed with Piedmont in tables of regional statistics, the 'special statute' region of Val d'Aosta deserves special mention. Unlike the rest of the western Alps, the francophone Val d'Aosta lies beyond the limit of Turin's influence and has an economic and cultural identity of its own. Industrial resources of note are the anthracite of La Thuile and the magnetite of the Cogne valley; these give rise to the steelworks at Aosta. To this may be added aluminium and electrochemicals at Verrès and Pont Saint Martin, and synthetic fibres at Châtillon. Forestry and, increasingly, tourism are other important economic activities; farming is in decline. Recently the central valley has benefited from the new Mont Blanc tunnel and motorway. In short, local life in this mountain province has survived and prospered to the point that it is now one of the richest parts of Italy, in *per capita* income terms.

Milan and Lombardy

Being a continuation of the Alps and the Po Plain from Piedmont, Lombardy has many features in common with its western neighbour, but some basic differences must be mentioned.[18] Almost half of Lombardy is made up of plain, compared to less than one-quarter in Piedmont; agricultural production is therefore greater. With the exception of the Swiss protrusion of Canton Ticino, the Lombardian Alps are wider than those of Piedmont and in the north they contain a deep longitudinal depression, the Valtellina, which corresponds to the upper basin of the Adda and to the province of Sondrio. The lower ends of several valleys are occupied by lakes, the two largest (Maggiore and Garda) marking the western and eastern limits of Lombardy. Several valleys lead to Alpine passes, the most important being the St Gotthard in Switzerland, easily accessible via the Milan-Como motorway. The plain-mountain divide, rather abrupt in Piedmont, is blurred in Lombardy by a complex zone of calcareous foothills and terraces where are to be found most of the major industrial settlements. South-draining valleys in Bergamo and Brescia provinces (Brembana, Seriana, Camonica, Trompia) have long-established industrial traditions in textiles, metalworking and engineering.

Demographic comparisons may also be made. Although Lombardy is slightly smaller than Piedmont it has nearly twice as many inhabitants; indeed with nearly 9 million people it has a population roughly equivalent to that of Belgium or Sweden. Its employment in manufacturing is also twice as great as Piedmont's, and Greater Milan is twice as large as Turin. Yet Milan does not dominate Lombardy as Turin does Piedmont or Rome does Latium; the ratio between the populations of Milan and Lombardy (1:5) is less overwhelming than those for Turin and Piedmont (1:3.5) and Rome and Latium (1:1.7). And unlike Turin which sucks the blood from its regional corona, Milan collects and redistributes economic functions in a relationship of symbiosis with its surrounding territory.[19]

The southern boundary of Lombardy is the Po River, except for a small triangular projection — the Oltrepò Pavese — into the northern Apennines. The 'low plain', roughly south of the line between Milan and Brescia, is one of the most productive agricultural regions in Italy, a Virgilian landscape of poplars, green meadows, rice, wheat and flax. Dairying around Lodi, Cremona and Mantua gives rise to food-processing industries (Gorgonzola, Galbani, Locatelli) in these and other, smaller towns that dot the flatlands. Vigevano (footwear) and Pavia (sewing machines, chemicals) are more important industrial centres. Natural gas extraction is centred around Lodi and Cremona, the latter of which is also the home of violin-making. Mantua, standing amongst its fens as if floating on a raft, has a recently developed petro-chemicals industry.

The main Lombard industrial region extends from Novara (actually in Piedmont) through Milan to Bergamo, with Brescia as an eastern outlier. The towns of Varese, Como and Lecco mark the northward limit of this dense manufacturing belt, which contains almost 30 per cent of Italy's employment in manufacturing industry (cf. Turin's 9 per cent). Milan is the focal point of this axis. Five provincial capitals (Novara, Varese, Como, Bergamo, Pavia) are within a 40 km radius, all accessible by motorway from the edge of Milan in about half an hour; and five more (Vercelli, Alessandria, Piacenza, Cremona, Brescia) are within 80 km and one hour's travelling (Figure 9.1). The commuting hinterland of Milan thus extends over a wide yet densely populated area.[20]

Although not the capital of Italy, Milan heads the list of Italian cities in many ways: in manufacturing employment, in scale and variety of industry, in *per capita* income, in financial services, in foreign trade and in advertising and public relations. Its annual trade fair, which has been running for 65 years, is the country's principal industrial shop window. Milan is the spiritual home of Italian business enterprise. There is a respect accorded to hard work in the pursuit of business goals, combined with a strong dislike of Roman red tape. Though not officially as large as Rome (whose commune boundary runs to the sea 25 km from the city centre whereas Milan's stops short of its suburbs), the city is the linchpin of a conurbation of 3 million inhabitants (cf. Rome 2.8 million). If more qualitative and cultural aspects are included, there are its newspapers and publishing houses (again, more important than

Rome's), its distinguished educational institutions like the Bocconi University and the Polytechnic, and artistic establishments like La Scala. It is, as Dalmasso points out in the standard work on the city, both the economic and the moral capital of Italy.[21]

The city, its concentric layout so different from grid-iron Turin, has a fairly well-defined functional structure. Industry and residential buildings are virtually non-existent in the centre. The central area, focusing on the spectacularly pinnacled cathedral, has a financial district with the stock exchange and the headquarters of banks and insurance companies, some specialised shopping streets and less distinct groupings of

Figure 9.3: Milan and the Lombardy Industrial Belt

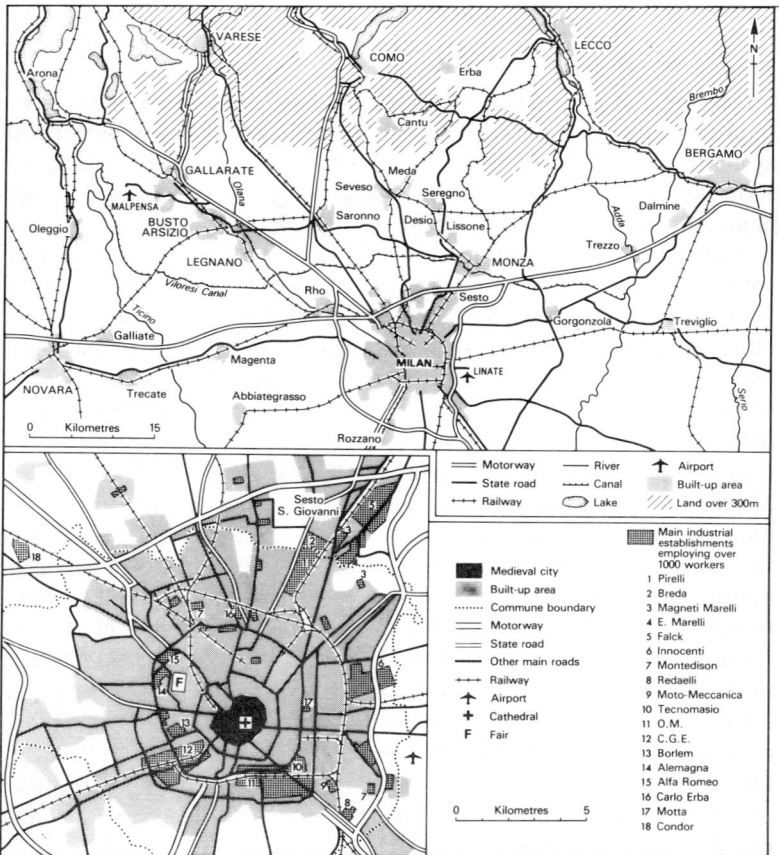

educational, entertainment and public administration buildings. Around this core is a zone of high density residential use which is now losing population steadily, and beyond this the railway ring (Figure 9.3). Many of the older and larger industrial establishments — Breda, Falck, Innocenti, OM, etc. — have locations close to this railway ring or its offshoots. Milan is, above all, an engineering centre but several other important industries are centred here: rubber (Pirelli), oil refining at Rho, the Motta and Alemagna food giants, pharmaceuticals (Carlo Erba) and the ENI research centre of Metanopoli near San Donato Milanese. The last of these symbolises the transition of Milan from an industrial to a tertiary and quaternary city. As factories move out of the city, Milan itself concentrates more and more on laboratories, advanced technology, management and services. Nearly half of Italian firms, in terms of shares, have their headquarters here, a proportion which rises to 70 per cent in chemicals and 75 per cent in rubber and plastics. Milan's transformation into a white collar city of commuters places increasing demands on its slow and outdated railway services. Two improvements are in train however: a third line for the underground system and an integrated regional rail service (the Interpole) linking the eight provincial capitals. Office decentalisation from the city centre is being pioneered by the construction of the Milanofiori trade and business complex south-west of the city at the junction of the ring road with the Genoa motorway. Otherwise the physical expansion of the city is mainly to the north, towards the region most densely packed with other industrial settlements. Modern light industries line the main arteries leading north from the city and many communes have become engulfed by combined residential and industrial expansion in a landscape laced with motorways and high-tension wires. Rho, Bollate, Cinisello and Sesto San Giovanni are without doubt part of Greater Milan and have lost their former identities[22] To the north-east Monza, once a royal residence, has become an attractive dormitory town. Industrial and urban activities predominate everywhere in this belt north of Milan. Rural life has been extinguished. Properties have been fragmented by the proliferation of roads, irrigation networks have been disrupted by urban expansion and the soil polluted by industrial waste as at Seveso. There are perhaps 200 'industrial villages' in this area, scattered betwen the larger towns with their various industrial specialisms — Busto Arsizio in cotton, Lecco in iron and steel, Desio in furniture, Dalmine in steel tubes.

Beyond this belt, Brescia relies mainly on vehicles (OM lorries), metal-working, arms and textiles. Its relative distance from Milan has given it scope to acquire commercial functions of its own and its economic influence extends over a wide area. Brescia claims to have established itself as the third industrial city of Italy. Certainly it is one of oldest and most archetypal. Its worth and progress are measured in the private steel mills which stretch in industrial ribbons up the pre-Alpine valleys behind the city. Brescia is a symbol of the self-made independent ethic which has enabled Lombardy to prosper despite all the untackled problems of the national economy.

Genoa and Liguria

Climatically part of peninsular Italy but historically and economically part of the North, Liguria is one of Italy's most distinctive regions. Sandwiched between mountains and sea, it stretches 250 km round the Ligurian Gulf between the French border and Tuscany. Although only 10-30 km wide, it extends north of the mountain watershed in many areas, notably the Bormida valley behind Savona and the Scrivia valley behind Genoa. The coast is one long urbanised and semi-urban ribbon with three main ports (Savona, Genoa, La Spezia) and dozens of resort towns both large (Imperia, San Remo, Rapallo) and small. Luxury villas with tumbling gardens lend an exotic touch to the scene. Tourism is an important part of the regional economy, with an annual average of 28 million overnights registered in recent years, mostly by Piedmontese, Milanese, Swiss and Germans. British interest in the Riviera has waned, although this nation pioneered the coast's tourist role in the last century. Agriculture, on tiny pockets of alluvium and on steep terraces, takes the form of horticulture, with vegetables, salad crops, olives, vines, citrus and, in the *Riviera del Fiori* between Imperia and the French border, roses and carnations. Only 11 per cent of the region is cultivated. Inland the regime is very different with a poor forestry and pastoralism and decaying hamlets and hill-villages.

The infrastructure for a modern economy has only been provided with difficulty, relief being the main problem to overcome. Extreme ingenuity has been shown in burrowing through mountain spurs to provide a network of railways, motorways and feeder roads. The existence and growth of the three main port towns owe much to their connections inland — Genoa via the Giovi Pass (472 m) to Milan, Savona via the Altare (459 m) to Turin and La Spezia via the much higher Cisa Pass (1039 m) to Parma. All three routes are followed by both railway and motorway so that in spite of the mountain barrier the Ligurian coast is now well connected to its wider regional hinterlands. All three ports are sited on rocky bays with deep water but insufficient shelter, and a dearth of flat land for industrial offshoots. Oil pipelines are another important aspect of these ports' development. Genoa sends its crude oil to Milan, Cremona and Ingolstadt. The terminal at Savona is also connected to this network but more easily supplies the refineries at Novara, Volpiano (Turin) and, within the Alps, Aigle.

Genoa is now the weakest leg of the North's industrial tripod, although regional income statistics do not show this, for the ailing economic and employment situation is financially balanced by an influx to rich pensioners who come to settle along the region's mild and pretty coast. A quarter of Liguria's population are pensioners. Genoa's traditional prosperity is based on its port rather than its industries which are narrow in range and few in number compared to Milan. The port of Genoa is Italy's biggest (handling approximately one-eighth of national port traffic) and, indeed, is one of the great ports of the Mediterranean Basin.[23] It has by far the largest share of the regional freight flow, with 50 million tons per year, compared to 15 m. t. each for Savona and La Spezia. Although it had medieval origins as a great maritime emporium and was, under Piedmont, the port for Sardinia, Genoa's more recent growth has been very much a function of Lombardy's industrialisation, while the development of the Alpine passes has broadened its horizons to include Switzerland and Germany, which now account for more than one-fifth of port activity.

Genoa's European penetration explains why its port function is more important than its role as an industrial centre. However, the possibilities for industrial expansion around the site of the old port are also extremely restricted. For expansion to occur, it was necessary to construct a westward channel to the open sea (completed in 1936 with an extension to Sestri Ponente in 1968). The current work is concerned with the incorporation of the Voltri site to form a continuous port axis of more than 15 km. These successive stages of expansion have enabled Genoa to cope with the increased size of oil tankers. The construction of the sea channel has also permitted the building of both an airport on reclaimed land and the Cornigliano platform containing Italy's second largest steelworks. The steel complex, which includes a blast furnace, a Siemens oven and two rolling mills, supplies a range of associated industries among which shipbuilding is now less important than before IRI's takeover of the Ansaldo yards. Although Genoa received several Finmeccanica mechanical industries to compensate for the run-down of the shipyards, the city's industrial structure remains predominantly heavy and old-fashioned, and heavily dependent on IRI. Lack of space, amongst other things, has discouraged the proliferation of dynamic small and medium manufacturers that characterises Lombardy and other parts of the North. Socially the city is rent by the polarisation between the conservatism of its powerful clergy and old shipping families and its tradition both of old-fashioned union militancy and of new-fangled urban terrorism (the Red Brigades movement originated here). Meanwhile the port suffers from overmanning and outdated practices. Extreme pile-ups at the container depot occur. With its high charges it has been losing trade to Leghorn and Marseilles. Plans under discussion for an integrated regional port system between Genoa (including its sub-port of Voltri), Savona, Imperia and La Spezia have yet to bear fruit.

Of Liguria's other two main ports and industrial centres, Savona (77,000) is rather like a miniature Genoa, but orientated to Turin rather than Milan. Its harbour was first improved in the nineteenth century for the import of English coal, a trade now less important than the piping of oil. Nevertheless the excellent coal installations still support a coking plant and small steelworks. Savona's other industrial interests include some ship-related activities, chemicals, glass and leather. Lack of space on the coast encourages some industrial decentralisation inland to the upper Bormida valley, linked to the rail and motorway routes over the Ligurian Alps.[24]

La Spezia (117,000), an important naval base and centre of the thriving armaments and defence industries, has much more difficult internal links, although it does now have a motorway link to the North Italian plain. Although close to the Tuscan border it has not succeeded in wresting from Pisa (in the Middle Ages) and Leghorn (now) the trade of Florence and the Arno valley towns. Much of its trade is in oil products for and from its refinery, but there is no pipeline inland.

The North-east

East of Lombardy the Italian span of Alpine mountains widens still further in Trentino and northern Veneto, before finally narrowing in the far north-east as the Austrian border encroaches southwards. Trentino-Alto Adige is an entirely mountainous region, with only limited concentrations of industry at Bolzano and Trento, the former being the major industrial centre with vehicles, engineering and electro-metallurgy profiting from the region's abundant hydro-electricity. These two towns are the largest within the Italian Alps; both are located on the main north-south Verona-Brenner-Innsbruck axis which carries railway and motorway along the Adige-Isarco valley system.

The variety of climate and scenery in the eastern Alps is probably unique in Europe. West of Bolzano begins the Triassic domain of the Dolomites, which combines long gentle slopes conducive to pasture and winter sports with steep blocks and rock faces ideal for serious climbers. These features explain the growing popularity of Alpine sports and tourism which are now the backbone of the region's economy. The province of Bolzano, a German-speaking 'window' south of the Alpine crest, attracts many visitors from Germany and Austria. Merano is an important tourist and service centre, with some light industry; Cortina d'Ampezzo, at the northern end of Belluno province, is even better known.

To the south, in Veneto and Friuli, the pre-Alpine industrial belt continues east from Brescia, although the linear conurbation of Lombardy breaks up into discrete units focusing on the main towns and provincial capitals — Verona, Vicenza, Treviso, Pordenone, Udine and Gorizia.

Verona's site at the mouth of the Adige Valley has been very influential in the city's development. To its traditional defensive and commercial roles have been added new agricultural, industrial and trading functions. Its position as a gateway to Austria and the important German food and wine markets has reoriented its land use towards high quality vineyards (Valpolicella and Soave wines) and orchards. Munich is only five hours away on the Adige Valley motorway. The orchards of the Basso Veronese, producing high quality apples, pears and peaches, now link up with those of Emilia south of the Po. This prodigious agricultural intensification, most of which has come about in the last 35 years, has had an effect industrially with the emergence of wineries, cold storage and packaging sheds, commercial back-up services and transport concerns. Verona is also the headquarters of the Mondadori publishing and printing company (the city's largest single employer) and has notable shoe and furniture industries. In spite of its relatively small size (270,000), it is a cosmopolitan place, proud of its Shakespearian and Renaissance traditions and with a fine record of industrial craftsmanship.

This blend of rich agriculture, craft skills and mixed industries continues in neighbouring Vicenza province. Here is to be found an industrial complex equal to that of Lombardy, if not in scale, at least in terms of diversity and degree of local specialisation. In addition to the provincial capital which specialises in engineering, clothing and jewellery, a constellation of small towns and industrial villages provides the setting for a varied and diffuse industrialisation in the north of the province. Valdagno, Schio, Thiene and Breganze specialise in woollen textiles and textile machinery, Bassano in bicycles, Nove in ceramics; Montebelluna (in Treviso province) is a major manufacturer of skiing equipment.

Further east, from Belluno province into Friuli, the quality of agriculture declines. In contrast to the dramatic Dolomites the Friulian Alps are bleak and forbidding, wet and cold. Here rural depopulation has been a long-standing process and has yet to be arrested. There is grazing, some good resources of timber and of course hydro-electricity, but the peripherality of the region preserves a frontier character. Mountain depopulation is linked to a long tradition of foreign emigration which is deeply embedded in the region's culture. Local-scale migration has fed the piedmont towns which derive their livelihood from a more prosperous mixed agriculture and from the recent growth of small and medium industry. Furniture, light engineering, machine tools and electrical equipment are branches of manufacturing which have given a modicum of industrial dynamism to towns like Udine and Pordenone, the latter of which is the headquarters of Zanussi.

Special problems surround Trieste, a place whose economic glories lie more in the imperial past than in the present. Seventy years ago Trieste was the third-busiest port in the Mediterranean; it discharged the maritime affairs of Austria, maintained strong commercial ties with the Middle East and harboured the powerful Lloyd Triestino shipping line. Little now remains of this former greatness except an urban landscape more reminiscent of Vienna or Budapest than Italy. Like its neighbour Gorizia, Trieste is a town cut off from its regional hinterland by the political events of the post-war aftermath when territory was ceded to Yugoslavia.[25] State industry, especially oil-refining, steel and shipbuilding, props up the economy and private interests like Fiat are only there because of special incentives. Much urban activity is associated with frontier traffic and supplying Serbs and Slovenes with products unknown or expensive in Yugoslavia — this trade is reckoned to be twice as lucrative as that earned by the port.[26] Trieste faces strong competition from the neighbouring Yugoslavian port of Rijeka. It has never become the major commercial and industrial centre of the Adriatic to the extent that was expected. Like Genoa, its also has space problems. The population of the city — 270,000 — is declining steadily.

The towns and provinces of the Venetian low plain — Padua, Rovigo and Venice — have different agricultural and industrial patterns to those of the region's Alpine foreland. Throughout the lower plain an intricate network of irrigation and drainage ditches is superimposed on a maze of meandering and dyked rivers. *Coltura promiscua* is widely practised, with maize, soft wheat, fodder, sugar beet, vines, orchards and vegetables. Livestock and poultry rearing reinforce the mixed character of the farming. The Po Delta has been progressively poldered, initially by private consortia, since 1950 by the Ente Delta Padano land reform agency. Rice is the pioneer crop on these newly won fields, giving way to other crops as the soil matures. In the coastal lagoons, shared with Emilia, the traditional occupations are fishing and horticulture; Chioggia is the main port from which the rich fishing grounds of the upper Adriatic shelf are exploited.

Venice, in its lagoon setting, is unique, not only among Italian cities, but also on the world scale. Built on reclaimed land, Venice was the wealthiest commercial power in Europe in the fifteenth century. Entrepôt trade was the foundation of this medieval prosperity; the city was the link between East and West, between Turk and Christian. Venice stagnated after the sixteenth century, the lack of post-Renaissance development preserving its magnificent palaces and churches as well as its humbler, yet equally picturesque, side streets. The causeway carrying the railway to the main island was completed in 1846 and extended port works, now inadequate, were built to revive its trade in newly unified Italy. Apart from shipbuilding (now virtually defunct beyond the gondola yards), Venice has no traditional heavy industry although the medieval glass-blowers, banished to the island of Murano because of the incendiary nature of their trade, represent an early example of industrial zoning. Modern industry, like many Venetians, has migrated to *terra firma* and the estates of Porto Marghera and Mestre.

Porto Marghera is now one of Italy's leading ports. Unlike Genoa and Trieste, it has been able to expand industrially to an impressive extent. Oil-refining, chemicals, non-ferrous metals and engineering make it the leading industrial concentration in Veneto, although it has not escaped the general crisis of these heavy industries. The price of this industrialisation has been high, however. Compaction of the subsoil due to water and methane extraction has been a factor contributing to the sinking of Venice. Pollution of the lagoon by the industries has attacked the physical fabric of Venice's waterline. Further damage is produced by the wash of ships, whilst the dredging of channels upsets the pattern of tidal scour. The slow death of Venice ranks alongside Seveso as a catastrophic environmental by-product of Italy's industrialisation. The future of *La Serenissima* has been a matter of international concern since the disastrous flood of 1966, but only recently has a comprehensive plan been put into operation to save the city. This includes pollution control over the Porto Marghera industries, a halt to artesian water extraction, and the installation of caissons across the entrance to the lagoon to keep out the periodic Adriatic surges. These measures should succeed in keeping the city's head above water but will not necessarily stem the flight of population from a city that seems destined to become only a museum for outsiders to enjoy.[27]

Aside from the problems of the old city, the revival of the Venetian area in recent years has been remarkable. Veneto is now the third industrial region of Italy, with most parts of the region experiencing a rapid increase in industrial employment. The linking of Venice with Padua (an important engineering, commercial and cultural centre with an illustrious university) to form a dynamic regional urban system has provided a counterpoise to the older-established centres of industry to the west. Indeed, with the emergence of the Bologna-Modena node on the south side of the plain, the industrial triangle has become a pentagon!

Emilia-Romagna

This region is roughly comparable in area and population with Veneto, and it has the same solid economic balance between a rich agriculture and a diversified industrial structure based on small and medium sized firms. Politically it is of interest as the 'reddest' area of Italy, the showpiece of the Italian Communist Party after the establishment of the regional governments in 1970. It also has a reputation for good eating and drinking: hence the capital Bologna's nickname of *La Grassa* —the 'Fat City'.

Although unquestionably part of the North, with the Po Plain forming half the region and with good communications to other northern cities, Emilia foreshadows the transition to Central Italy. Its high Apennine wastelands, with poor hill farming (wheat, vines, sheep) on the lower slopes, are repeated in many other regions further south; nor is there any obvious regional divide in the coastal landscapes of tourism south of Rimini. Moreover the southern segment of the Po Plain is different from the northern. The characteristic Lombardy poplars are few and the mulberry almost non-existent. Summer is drier, yet there is little irrigation. Historically Emilia had stronger links with Rome and the

Papal States than did the regions north of the Po. Indeed the strong radical and anticlerical traditions of eastern Emilia, which today find expression in unswerving loyalty to political parties of the left, are often attributed to the area's long experience of Papal maladministration.

But it is in terms of modern industrial development that Emilia-Romagna is most geographically transitional. It is at the core of what has been termed the 'Third Italy', an Adriatic region comprising Veneto and Friuli to the north and Marche to the south.[28] The style of small-scale but very dynamic industrial growth which has characterised these regions in recent years has in fact been called the 'Emilian model',[29] and it is therefore appropriate to discuss this species of industrialisation under this regional heading, even though we shall also find it in parts of Central Italy considered in the next chapter.

The 'Emilian model' is a term which encapsulates three connected features which are held to be at the root of the region's remarkable industrial buoyancy: decentralised production in small and medium sized towns in a rural setting; geographical specialisation of product; and a high degree of sweated labour in small factories and workshops backed up by a sophisticated out-working system. Decentralisation of production is, as we have seen, part of a wider national (indeed European) process in action over the last decade or more. In Italy the increase in union power in the 1960s and the collapse of several big industries in the 1970s encouraged a spatial shift of certain types of manufacturing dynamism to regions like Emilia with an established tradition of small craft-scale industries.[30] Decentralisation has been further encouraged by a change in the pattern of consumer preference away from standardised products towards greater variety. This 'customisation' of demand requires a more specialised and flexible productive structure, more appropriate to small rather than large firms. There is also an obvious connection between small, dynamic industrial enterprises and the use of black labour whereby tax and social welfare payments are evaded and workers paid below minimum wages. *Lavoro nero,* mostly by women, is extremely common in Emila-Romagna. The system of outwork reaches its most 'perfect' form in the knitwear sector, centred on Modena and Carpi, and described in Chapter 6.

From the geographical point of view the most interesting aspect of Emilia-Romagna's 'new' industrial revolution is local specialisation of production. The following industrial districts may be mentioned: Modena and Carpi for knitwear, Parma for food processing, Reggio for ceramics, Piacenza for buttons, Ferrara for linen sheets, Bologna for cycles and motorcycles and Faenza for faience (decorated porcelain and earthenware, named after the town). The existence of these specialised industrial districts does not mean that these activities are the only industries to be found there. Most Emilian towns have a well balanced mixture of administrative, commercial and industrial functions.[31] This equilibrium is especially strong in the case of the regional capital. Bologna's half-million inhabitants derive their livelihood as much from artisanal and commercial activities as they do from the railway works and a diversified range of industries. Modena has an equally impressive range of industries: clothing and knitwear, textile and woodworking machinery, ceramics and vehicles both fast (Ferrari, Maserati) and slow (Fiat tractors).

The combination of diversification and specialisation just described is particularly characteristic of the towns and provinces along the Via Emilia. Along this linear urban axis, paralleled by the railway and the motorway, lie six of the eight provincial capitals in the region, plus other notable towns such as Imola, Faenza and Cesena. It is probably not a coincidence that the two provincial capitals not on the Emilian Way have a different style of industrial development, with bigger plants set up by extra-regional capital. Ferrara has Montedison petrochemical plants and Ravenna has oil, gas and chemical industries, mostly owned by ANIC. With its new canal-port, Ravenna is also the centre for the offshore exploration of the Northern Adriatic gasfields. To the south Rimini is wholeheartedly devoted to the tourist industry and spreads, via ribbon beach settlements of Riccione and Cattolica, down to the Marche border.

Notes and References

1. Walker (1967), p.95.
2. The annual commune data are published by ISTAT each year in the volume *Popolazione e Movimento Anagrafico dei Comuni.*
3. Reyne (1983).
4. Ortolani and Mounfield (1963).
5. See Zanetti (1983), p.259 and his tables 7-12.
6. Fuà (1980).
7. Bethemont and Pelletier (1983), p.122.
8. Gribaudi (1968).
9. Ortona and Santagata (1983), p.70.
10. Gabert (1964).
11. Bethemont and Pelletier (1983), p.126.
12. Quoted in Page (1983).
13. Achenbach (1976).
14. Dematteis (1973).
15. Adamo (1979).

16. Bethemont and Pelletier (1983), p.124.

17. See Vallega (1972) for a detailed study of Cuneo's industries.

18. Cole (1968), pp.181-90.

19. Bethemont and Pelletier (1983), p.127.

20. Turton (1970).

21. Dalmasso (1971).

22. See Rocca (1978).

23. See the detailed but dated studies of Rodgers (1958 and 1960).

24. See the studies by Ferro (1958 and 1969) on the Bormida's industrialisation.

25. Mihelić (1969).

26. Armstrong (1978); and Battisti (1979) for more detailed analysis of Trieste's 'gateway' function.

27. Pacione (1974b).

28. Bagnasco (1977). Also part of the 'Third Italy', but less clearly so, are Tuscany, Umbria, Trentino and Abruzzo.

29. Brusco (1982).

30. In 1971 Emilia-Romagna had only 15 industrial plants employing over 1,000 workers; 66 per cent of manufacturing employment was in firms of less than 100 workers (cf. 45 per cent in North-west Italy). Figures from Coulet (1978).

31. For a good example see Ghelardoni's (1971) study on Faenza.

10 CENTRAL ITALY

South of a line from La Spezia to Rimini Northern Italy gives way to the peninsula. Central Italy, composed of the *regioni* of Marche, Umbria, Tuscany and Latium, is obviously a transitional region between the prosperous, industrial North and the backward, rural South. It has 'northern' features in the long-standing wealth of its vine-growing areas, in its agrarian structure of small farms and stable tenancies and in the splendid urban traditions of its many ancient cities. At the same time there are many 'southern' features — industrial underdevelopment, emigration and land reclamation. But it has its own, original characteristics too. Essentially peninsular and Mediterranean, it is the heart of Italy, and central to the whole Italian experience. It has two cities, Rome and Florence, whose contributions to Western civilisation have been incalculable. It was from the Centre that Rome set its seal on the rest of the country, uniting much of Western Europe and the Mediterranean Basin under one regime. In later centuries the Tuscan cities, themselves heir to a civilisation (the Etruscan) more ancient than that of Rome, led Europe into the Renaissance. It was in the Tuscan towns and countryside, in a setting of Dante, Michaelangelo and Leonardo da Vinci, that the Italian language was perfected. Today there is, arguably, no more immaculately beautiful landscape in Europe, more human in its scale, or more completely right in its proportions and colours.

Physical Setting

While the North can be divided into clear-cut physical regions, the Centre consists of a bewildering variety of topographical units: mountain ridges, interior valleys and basins, hill country and coastal lowlands (Figure 10.1). The Apennines provide the region's backbone, but they are highly complicated structurally and are split up into many sub-units. In the extreme north-west, along the Tuscan-Emilian border, they exceed 2,000 metres but they become lower and narrower south of Florence and in Umbria, widening again in southern Marche as they approach their highest elevation in the Abruzzian Gran Sasso (2,912 m). The main watershed, which does not necessarily follow the highest points, lies closer to the Adriatic coast, giving the two Apennine flanks very contrasting characters, both physically and in terms of the

264

Figure 10.1: Central Italy

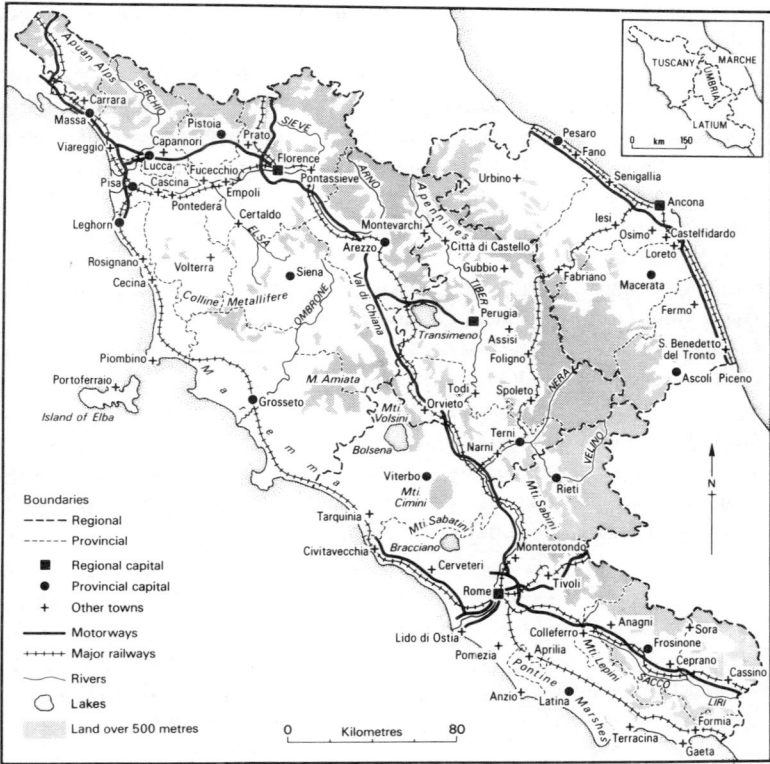

development of forms of settlement and economic activity.

The narrow Adriatic flank has been dissected by consequent rivers into a comb-like pattern of parallel ridges and valleys running at right-angles to the coast. The lower slopes of this hill country, composed of Miocene marls and chalks and Pliocene clays and sands, are easily eroded, to the detriment of farming. Dense settlement is mainly confined to the restricted coastal plain where the main towns are Pesaro and Ancona, although there are some towns both on the interfluves (Urbino, Fabriano, Macerata) and in the valley bottoms (Iesi, Ascoli Piceno). West of the watershed there is a much more extensive area of mountain and hill country, with many longitudinal valleys and two large drainage basins, the Arno and the Tiber.

To the west of the main Apennine spine run other highland areas: in the north the Apuan Alps, in the centre the Colline Metallifere and in the south, in Latium, volcanic plateaux containing many extinct volcanoes, some of them lake-filled (Bolsena, Bracciano). Pliocene hill country occupies the space between the Apennines and the volcanic plateaux. In the upper valleys, especially of the Arno and the Tiber rivers, there are many Plio-Pleistocene lake basins (e.g. Trasimeno) some of which have been drained in historical times. These interior basins are important agriculturally and as the foci of urban settlement, e.g. Florence, Arezzo, Perugia, Gubbio, Terni, Rieti. Since the basins tend to form chains, they are also important as communication axes: the main north-south motorway, the Autostrada del Sole, follows the upper Arno valley and the Val di Chiana trench.

The Tyrrhenian coastlands are made up of several small alluvial plains separated by low, undulating hill country. Since the disappearance of the Etruscans and the decline of the Romans, these coastal lands have become thinly populated, ill-drained and malarial. However, in the present century, successful drainage and reclamation schemes have enabled the settlement of the Pontine Marshes south of Rome and of the Maremma to the north.

The Character of Recent Industrial Growth

As befits its intermediate location, Central Italy is not a region of extremes and in many respects approximates closely to the national average. It has a population of 10,665,000 (1981), equivalent to 19.1 per cent of the Italian total; this proportion is relatively stable, with a diminishing tendency to increase (cf. 19 per cent in 1971, 18.6 per cent in 1961, 18.3 per cent in 1951). The region produces 19.3 per cent of the nation's gross domestic product and it possesses 21.8 per cent of the factories and 18.2 per cent of the manufacturing workers in Italy as a whole.

Industrially, the Centre has little to compare with the concentrations of the North. Only Tuscany could be said to be roughly on a par with the North's less industrialised regions like Friuli and Veneto. Southern Tuscany has some mineral wealth, whilst hydro-electric power is limited to the high Apennines in Umbria and Marche. Over much of the post-war period the Centre has fallen between two stools, not possessing the obvious industrial traditions and advantages of the North, and not qualifying for the governmental package of incentives available in the South.

Since the 1960s, however, this pattern has changed. For the last 20 years many parts of Central Italy have followed the industrial growth trends of Veneto and Emilia-Romagna. In fact the 'Emilian model' described at the end of the previous chapter applies equally well to Marche, Umbria and Tuscany (but not to Latium which is more 'southern' in its socio-economic character). The key to this high growth is the process of 'productive decentralisation' to satellite firms and to cottage industries which are so deeply embedded in the traditional economic fabric of the regions on the northern Apennines. The development of traditional industries (textiles, clothing, footwear, furniture, wood, etc.) in Central Italy has been due to three separate, though linked, mechanisms: the establishment of new firms in the region; the growth of small firms already in existence; and the decentralisation of some production from the north-western industrial 'core' of Italy. In all cases the plants set up in the Centre are small or medium sized with a more elastic organisation of production and lower costs of labour. Spatially, the pattern of industrialisation is diffuse. Helped by their small size, the new and expanding firms have tended to adapt to the existing population and settlement structure which has therefore undergone few fundamental changes. Industrial dispersion has avoided the problems of infrastructural shortage (i.e. of housing, of industrial sites, of water, of waste disposal, etc.) which have been quite severe in the North. It also has avoided the mass concentration of large numbers of wage earners, thereby reducing the conflict between capital and labour.[1]

As a result of these advantages — a broad spectrum of labour-intensive, high value-added industrial processes, territorial dispersion of industry and an abundant and flexible supply of mostly non-unionised labour — the central regions have cushioned themselves more effectively against recession than the regions of the industrial North-west with their heavier industrial concentrations, overloaded infrastructures and inflexible labour forces. The Centre hardly felt the effects of the 1973-4 recession, although some weaknesses did become apparent by the late 1970s. These included a diminution in the supply of marginal labour, economic problems in some of the medium-firm (as opposed to the small-firm) sectors such as textiles, white goods and some branches of engineering, and an increasing difficulty of maintaining export penetration in the face of competition from developing countries. Although these difficulties are pressing, they do not portend the imminent collapse of the system. Indeed, over the period 1961-81 the Centre increased its share of national manufacturing employment from

15.7 per cent to 18.2 per cent.

Marche and Umbria

These are amongst Italy's most rural regions. The historical dominance of stable share-tenancies (*mezzadria*) has given the landscape an open, well-cultivated appearance with much dispersed settlement. Many of the inland towns, such as Urbino, Macerata and Gubbio, were centres of great distinction centuries ago but now they are modest provincial capitals or service centres without much industry. Only one railway, the trans-peninsular line from Rome through Terni to Ancona, crosses the Apennines, while the Autostrada del Sole skirts the western edge of Umbria.

In the Marche, the main concentration of population is along the Adriatic littoral where Ancona (110,000) is the biggest town and the regional capital. Ancona's port handles general cargo and specialises in passenger links with Yugoslavia. Falconara, 10 km north-west of Ancona, receives oil and has a moderate-sized refinery. Other manufacturing centres include Pesaro (furniture, clothing, motor-cycles, pottery), Fabriano (paper, electrical appliance), Iesi (silk), Castelfidardo and Osimo (musical instruments), Loreto (rosaries), Fermo (shoes) and Ascoli Piceno (textiles, shoes). Many of these industries are long-established craft activities: at Fabriano, for example, good quality paper has been made since the thirteenth century. Fishing is an activity shared by most of the coastal settlements; San Benedetto del Tronto is the Adriatic's principal specialist fishing port. The coast is also being developed for tourism, following the Rimini model. Senigallia and Pesaro are the main resorts.

Although modern, large-scale industry scarcely exists in the Marche, this region has experienced Italy's most spectacular growth in industrial employment since 1961 (Table 5.6). As in Emilia just to the north, a new entrepreneurial class has grown from a seed-bed of artisans and sharecropping farmers. Some would trace the process back to 1930 and the establishment at Fabriano of the Merloni Company, which manufactures electrical appliances and furniture under the Ariston brandname.[2] Today Merloni is the region's biggest single employer, with 6,000 workers and annual sales of £250 million, yet it still retains its small company atmosphere. Elsewhere, the region has a patchwork of small industries which now reach deep into rural areas, staunching a flow of depopulation which was once amongst the most severe in the country (half the population left the interior uplands during 1951-71). Textiles, clothing, shoes and furniture are the most typical industries: together these activities account for 53.1 per cent of regional industrial employment. The most dramatic growth has been in the footwear sector where regional employment leapt from 10,884 in 1961 to 46,941 in 1981. Marche is now Italy's main footwear producer, nearly all the region's production coming from the southern two provinces.

Umbria replicates these industrial trends, albeit on a smaller scale. Here there is a relatively greater interest in hosiery and knitwear (2,300 employees in 1961, 7,300 in 1981) than in shoes. Umbria also has, in its provincial capitals, two other well-established and well-known industries, confectionery (Perugia) and steel (Terni).

Perugia (140,000), overlooking the upper Tiber valley, has been a craft centre since the Middle Ages. Nowadays its principal activities are textiles, clothing (Spagnoli knitwear), pottery, paper and confectionery (Perugina). Recent industrial development has gravitated away from the hillside city towards the railway 300 m below, and along the valley to Ponte San Giovanni. Terni (113,000) is a heavy industrial centre whose *raison d'être* is its water power and the former strategic importance of its inland location. Metallurgical industries founded here in the late nineteenth century have been modernised and expanded and now employ 15,000. Other industries in the Terni-Narni industrial node include chemicals, synthetic fibres and paper mills. Foligno (51,000), well-placed on the Rome-Ancona rail and road axis, has become the region's third industrial centre, with woollen textiles, leather goods and food industries. Of the smaller Umbrian towns, Città di Castello has a printing industry, Orvieto is famous for its wines, whilst Assisi has St Francis to thank for its tourist industry.

Florence and Tuscany

Although Tuscany possesses greater historial unity than perhaps any other Italian *regione*, it is composed of two rather distinct parts. South and west of Siena the economy is agricultural with many 'southern' characteristics — lack of industry, large agro-towns, old latifundian estates and a predominance of dry, rolling hill country. By contrast, the north-eastern part of the region, built around the Arno basin, has a dense network of towns and villages with a much more highly developed industrial structure, not to mention a string of provincial capitals — Pisa, Lucca, Pistoia, Florence, Arezzo — with a distinctly prestigious past. This contrast is reflected in provincial population densities: more than 250 persons per square kilometre in the intensively farmed, urbanised provinces of Florence, Pistoia and Pisa; only 49 in Grosseto and 70 in Siena.

The core of industrial Tuscany is the fertile Arno Valley between Pisa and Florence, together with the tributary valleys of the Serchio, containing Lucca, and the Bisenzio, containing Prato and Pistoia (Figure 10.1). This axis contains approximately four-fifths of Tuscany's industrial workers. In the past this valley axis linked up with a coastal belt of industrial activity based on Massa, Leghorn and Piombino. However, recent years have seen the deindustrialisation of the coast (especially Elba, Leghorn and Piombino) which has switched much more to a tertiary economy based on tourism (Viareggio is the main resort). Instead the Arno axis is now extending inland towards Arezzo and the upper tributary valleys.[3]

Although not primarily an industrial city, Florence (population 462,000) contains the region's biggest concentration of industrial employment. Its broad range of craft and manufacturing industries has evolved from a variety of medieval artisan trades, some of which were mentioned in Chapter 2. Today its main activities are textiles, clothing, lace, leather, jewellery, publishing, scientific instruments, agricultural processing and some engineering. The principal industrial districts have developed, since the nineteenth century, towards the west and north-west, notably towards Sesto (now virtually a Florentine industrial suburb) and Prato. In spite of its Apennine location Florence enjoys excellent rail and road links to Rome and the North (via Bologna) and is very much part of the main axis of Italian economic life — a position which is strongly reinforced by the city's commercial, educational, artistic and touristic functions. Florence challenges Venice and Rome for the title of Italy's foremost city of historical and cultural importance.

The many papers by Italian and French geographers on the Arno Valley provide fascinating details of the highly developed local specialisation within the industries of the area.[4] The northern rim generally concentrates on textiles and clothing, with the main centres of these activities at Lucca, Capannori, Pistoia and Prato. Of these Prato, which specialises in 'shoddy', is by far the most important. It is the most important textile town outside of the Po-Alpine region, and accounts for 23.7 per cent of Italy's labour force in textiles (cf. Pistoia 2.5 per cent, Florence 0.7 per cent). Three-quarters of the town's industrial workers are in the textile sector (mostly wool), so that it is almost a mono-industrial town. There are, however, very few big firms in the

Prato area; only 13 have more than 100 workers and only one, Fabriccone, more than 1,000. One other curious fact about Prato is worth a mention: with a population of 150,000 it is the largest town in Italy not a provincial capital, larger in fact than seven of Tuscany's nine provincial capitals (only Florence and Leghorn are bigger).

The southern rim of the Arno basin, along the river itself, has a somewhat different and more varied blend of industries, including glass at Pisa (formerly Tuscany's main port but now 10 km inland), Piaggio motor scooters at Pontedera, furniture at Cascina, shoes at Fucecchio and clothing at Empoli. Here, however, local specialisation rarely reaches the degree of Prato's wool industry. For instance, Empoli's specialisation in clothing (3,000 employees) is diluted by significant numbers working in the glass (2,420), furniture (440) and food (700) industries.[5]

In recent years the industrialisation of the Arno Valley has headed inland, along the main valley to Arezzo and up subsidiary valleys like the Sieve east of Florence and the Elsa south of Empoli. Specialisms of note are hats at Montevarchi, sandals at Certaldo and Chianti-bottling at Pontassieve. However, clothing is the principal and most widespread sector of growth, employing more than half the industrial workers in these upper valley sections. The province of Arezzo, which contains most of the upper Arno Valley, has the highest proportion of industrial employees working in clothing in the country (Figure 6.6).

The north-western corner of Tuscany contains the Apuan Alps, a high (1,945 m) ridge composed of Permian and Triassic limestone and dolomite, locally metamorphosed and famous since Roman times for marble quarrying. Carrara is the main 'marble town', although much of the quarrying goes on at high and remote locations, giving the mountain tops a misleadingly snowy appearance. It is estimated that before the First World War Carrara's quarries employed 10,000 workers but mechanisation — notably the invention of the helical wire cutter — cut this figure drastically to 3,500 in 1955 and 1,500 in 1980. Quarry output, on the other hand, has risen — 350,000 tons in 1955, 1.4 million tons in 1980. Technological change has also meant loss of jobs in the sawmills and workshops: currently there are 700 firms with 5,500 workers, roughly equally divided between the provinces of Massa and Lucca. Recently exports of finished and polished marble have been particularly buoyant to the Middle East where the stone is widely appreciated in the building of palaces, mosques and public buildings. Saudi Arabia alone took 16 per cent of Italy's marble exports in 1980.

Leghorn (Livorno), 15 km south of the Arno estuary, is Tuscany's major port, taking over from Pisa as the latter silted up. Now 60 per cent of Tuscany's maritime freight moves via Leghorn. Its position on Italy's Tyrrhenian coast and its good motorway links via Modena and Verona with North-eastern Italy and the Brenner give it an advantage over Genoa (longer overland haul) or Trieste (longer sea passage) for freight movement between this north-eastern hinterland and North Africa and beyond Gibraltar. Table 5.2 shows that Leghorn is the tenth port of Italy in terms of tonnage handled. Leghorn's industries have developed in association with the port: shipbuilding on the base of the Orlando yards, oil refining at the STANIC refinery, heavy mechanical engineering (notably pumps) and food processing.[6] At Rosignano, 20 km south, is a chemicals industry.

Piombino, on the coast opposite Elba, has Italy's third-largest integrated iron and steel works (after Taranto and Cornigliano). Using foreign coal and a combination of Elba and imported iron ore, it produces about 13 per cent of Italy's steel.[7] The mining of other ores (pyrites at Rovi and Gavorrano, mercury at Monte Amiata, lead and zinc at Massa Marittima, all in Grosseto province) and of non-metallic minerals (e.g. salt, borax and gypsum in the Cecina Valley) is fairly widespread in south Tuscany, whilst near Volterra are to be found sources of geothermal energy tapped for the power stations of Larderello.

Rome and Latium

The shallow volcanic cones and plateaux of southern Tuscany continue into Latium in the old, infertile massifs of Volsini, Cimini and Sabatini, each of which retains one or more crater lakes. Here, in northern Latium, there is little industry. Viterbo is a quiet provincial town standing on a cliff of black tuff, Civitavecchia a modest port with regular sailings to Sardinia. Etruscan necropoli at Tarquinia, Cerveteri and Veio bear witness to a more interesting, if enigmatic past. Inland the province of Rieti has more in common with the high Apennines of the Abruzzi than with the region of Rome, although there has been some attempt to stimulate industry along the Velino valley between Rieti and Cittaducale.[8]

South of Rome and the Tiber valley industrial development is much more widespread, although fairly recent. Rome itself is partially encircled by a ring of small industrial towns established in the 1930s to decentralise industry away from the capital.[9] These comprise Monterotondo, Guidonia, Ponte Lucano and Colleferro inland, and Pomezia and Aprilia on the coastal plain (Figure 10.1). The first group possesses chemical, tyre, armaments and construction material industries, the latter has agricultural, mechanical and pharmaceutical industries. The Colleferro industrial estate, specialising in explosives, employed more than 15,000 workers during the last war; now it employ only half that number.

Special circumstances surround the rapid industrial development of Latium's two southern provinces in the last 25 years. The boundary of the Cassa per il Mezzogiorno does not follow the regional divide between Latium and Campania, the conventional frontier between Central and Southern Italy, but includes the provinces of Latina and Frosinone in the 'South'. This has had the effect of making these two provinces, so close to Rome, very attractive to industrial investors.[10]

In Frosinone province this mushrooming of industries is oriented along the motorway and the railway to Caserta and Naples, both of which follow the long corridor formed by the Sacco and Liri rivers.[11] The Frosinone Industrial Development Area has attracted 253 new industries employing a total of 14,000 workers, mostly in light industries in medium sized units. One of the most important firms to open up in the area was Elicoteri Meridionali ('Southern Helicopters'), employing 1,100; this company has just opened a second factory, manufacturing glass fibre components, at Anagni 20 km north-west of the provincial capital.[12] Other industries (textiles, chemicals, rubber, plastics, metallurgy, engineering, vehicles) have settled in subsidiary industrial nodes at Cassino, Ceprano and Sora, Fiat's Cassino plant being the most important single initiative.

Latina province contains the Pontine Marshes, Fascism's first and biggest land reclamation project, with farmers brought in from Veneto and Emilia-Romagna to settle the newly drained and irrigated land. The area, now one of the most agriculturally productive outside of the North Italian Plain, specialises in cereals, fruits and vegetables and has spawned many agricultural processing industries at and around Latina and Aprilia. The Mezzogiorno 'boundary effect' has added to these food industries a large number of mechanical and light engineering firms (e.g. Massey-Ferguson at Aprilia) which have stimulated population growth in this corner of Latium. Although only founded in 1932 Latina has grown quickly to become the second largest settlement (with 95,000) in Latium after Rome. The coast contains a string of small ports — Anzio, Gaeta, Formia — which have attracted certain industries such as oil-refining and chemicals; Terracina has more explicitly holiday functions.

Finally, there is Rome. In spite of its size — nearly 3 million — and that it contains 60 per cent of Latium's population. Rome is not an industrial city. It made the transition from a pre-industrial city to a city of administrators and tertiary services without ever becoming industrialised, a classic case of urbanisation without industrialisation. With only 32 per cent of its working population in industry Rome is not only less industrialised than the main northern centres of industry like Milan (50 per cent), Turin (61 per cent), Genoa (43 per cent), Bologna (45 per cent) and Florence (40 per cent), but also compares unfavourably with the major cities of the South like Naples (39 per cent), Bari (42 per cent) and Palermo (36 per cent). Yet the problem of Roman industry is not just its quantity but its quality. Of the 20,000 industrial firms in the city, only 120 employ more than 100 workers and only four more than 1,000 workers. Roman industries are small in scale and low in productivity; almost all serve Rome and its immediate region and lack the expansion possibilities deriving from exports; yet they tend to depend on outside sources for raw materials and semi-finished products, there being no major sources of raw materials or power nearby.

Retarded industrialisation in Rome has several causes.[13] What little industry existed in the papal city was eliminated after Unification by the superior political and economic capabilities of the North. Indeed national government policy after Unification sought to discourage Roman industry in order to minimise competition for northern industry and preserve the museum-like character of the city from the possible disruptions of a large and turbulent industrial proletariat. Moreover, Rome has never enjoyed real economic symbiosis with its regional hinterland: the Roman Campagna is a depressed agricultural area of semi-derelict *latifondi* and poor sheep pastures, with only here and there some attempts at agricultural improvement (olives, vines, dairying, etc.). Within the city, industrial development is discouraged by the lack of planning and of appropriate infrastructures (water, power, efficient transportation, suitable land). Potential industrial investors do not consider the ethos of the city conducive to industrial discipline, and generally find Roman real estate much more lucrative.

The dominant industrial sector in Rome, employing 40 per cent of the workers in industry, is construction. Furthermore, much of the manufacturing is geared towards supplying the building trade (wood, glass, bricks, etc.). Textiles, metallurgy and large-scale engineering are virtually non-existent although there is a good deal of mechanical servicing activity and the chemical industry has made some progress. Most other industries simply derive from the presence of the huge local market: food, clothing, printing, furniture, cosmetics, pharmaceuticals, etc. The older industrial quarters are in San Lorenzo east of the city centre and along the Via Ostiense to the south, but new ventures have been sited on the fast-expanding periphery as well as beyond in a ring of small industrial towns, as mentioned earlier.

Although of second rank industrially and commercially, the other facets of Rome's economic geography should not be overlooked. It is the centre of the road and rail networks in the peninsula and possesses the most important airport not only in Italy but of the whole Mediterranean region. The devotion of the Catholic world to the Papal See and the city's magnificent tourist attractions provide major sources of income. Its Cinecittà is the largest complex of film studios in Europe and this is a major contributor to the international character of Roman high society. Above all Rome is a city of bureaucrats, with an estimated 250,000 state employees.[14] They work in public administration at a variety of levels: the commune of Rome, the province of Rome, the region of Latium, the national government. Added to this are the numerous employees in private sector companies and banks and in international organisations like FAO. Rome University, the largest in Italy, has 100,00 students!

Notes and References

1. Arcangeli *et al.* (1980), p. 26.
2. Cornwell (1981).
3. Mori (1977).
4. See the papers by Charnier (1966), Cori (1962), Houssel (1972), Lavoratti and della Capanna (1972), Piccardi (1967, 1968), Pinna (1960).
5. Lavoratti and della Capanna (1972).
6. Gosseaume (1969).
7. For a detailed study of Piombino see Innocenti (1964).
8. Grilloti di Giacomo (1978). The Rieti-Cittaducale industrial node is a north-projecting 'peninsula' of territory in which special industrial incentives are offered by the Cassa per il Mezzogiorno.
9. Attuoni (1959).
10. Mori (1965).
11. Cataudella (1968).
12. Pacione (1982).
13. Fried (1973), pp. 109-10.
14. Bethemont and Pelletier (1983), p. 161.

11 SOUTHERN ITALY

The industrial backwardness of the South has been a recurring theme throughout this book. As a classic 'problem region' the Mezzogiorno has generated a vast literature representing a wide range of scholarly approaches and political interpretations.[1] Throughout a century and a quarter of national life, the *Questione Meridionale* has rarely been absent from the arena of parliamentary debate, although only in the last 25 years has much been done to actively develop industries in the region.

Administratively the South is usually taken to include the regions of Abruzzi, Molise, Campania, Basilicata, Apulia, Calabria, Sicily and Sardinia (Figure 11.1), although the Cassa per il Mezzogiorno's boundary includes much of southern Latium as well as small parts of southern Marche and a few minor Tuscan islands. Taking the former of these two definitions, the South contains 40.5 per cent of Italian territory and 35.4 per cent of the Italian population (19.9 million out of 56.2 million) recorded in the 1981 census.

As a region the South possesses many distinctive and unifying features. For centuries prior to unification it formed a single political unit with Naples as capital. Unification took away Naples' pre-eminence and dealt a severe blow to the city's fledgling industries. Now the city has some of the worst slums and social problems of any urban area in Western Europe, whilst just inland the province of Avellino has the lowest mean *per capita* income in the country.

Although agriculture is more important in the economy of the Mezzogiorno than it is in the North, farming is generally hindered by poor soils, steep slopes and summer aridity. Really productive land is extremely limited. Other elements of the region's economic geography are also unfavourable. The share of national hydro-electric power production is very small, there is now very little mining, and large-scale modern manufacturing is confined to a few places where it has been artificially stimulated since the late 1950s.

Another unifying factor is demography. The South is a region of population surplus. In the 1950s the average annual rate of increase of 1.3 per cent was three times the rate in the North. Population momentum has halved since then but the relative proportions between South and North remain the same: now, as before, the South accounts for roughly three-quarters of the national population increase.

276

Figure 11.1: Southern Italy

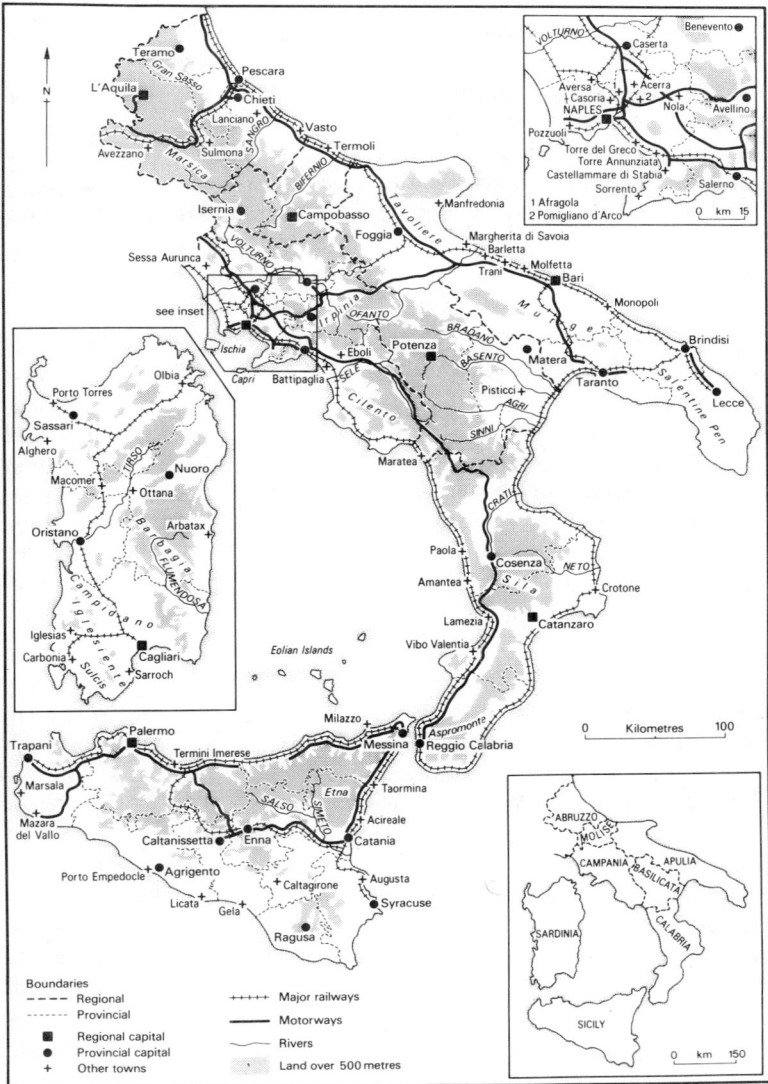

These demographic parameters, when set against a stagnant economic performance, explain the long history of southern emigration which has continued until the present day, although with diminishing force in very recent years. During 1951-61 there was a net loss of 2.1 million persons, most of whom emigrated to other countries. The ensuing decade saw a demographic haemorrhage of similar proportions (1.9 million loss during 1961-71) but principally directed to Northern Italy. Over the last decade falling emigration and a steady stream of returning migrants has held the migration balance close to parity.

A few figures are sufficient to give an impression of the South's economic and industrial backwardness *vis-à-vis* the North in the early 1950s, just before the post-war policy to industrialise the South started. The South, then with nearly 39 per cent of the national population, accounted for only 21.6 per cent of national income and only 14.4 per cent of manufacturing employment, restricted to a few towns such as Naples and Bari and comprising mostly traditional activities like furniture, clothing and foodstuffs. Manufacturing industry only employed 8 per cent of the South's working population, compared to 21 per cent in the North. Southern mean *per capita* income was 46.7 per cent of that of the rest of Italy whilst the poorest province at that time, Agrigento, had an income per head less than one-fifth that of Milan. An official enquiry into Italian poverty found that whilst only 1.5 per cent of the northern population were living in a state of poverty (defined by certain standard criteria), the figures for the mainland South were 28.3 per cent and for the islands of Sicily and Sardinia 24.8 per cent.

Geographical, Historical and Cultural Perspectives on the Backwardness of the South

How far the 'southern problem' stems from the physical environment of the area and how far it is the legacy of deep-rooted historical and social forces will always be a matter of debate, but there is no doubt that the islands and the lower part of the peninsula suffer from many environmental disadvantages when compared with the North. The fragmentation of the region into the long peninsulas of Apulia and Calabria and the two big islands of Sicily and Sardinia has hindered the development of communications and has produced only isolated areas of development, mainly along the coasts. Here there is no equivalent of the Po Plain, or even of the Arno Basin. Relief and lithology impose further handicaps. Only 21.3 per cent of the South is classed as plain and the lowlands (Tavoliere, Salentine Peninsula, Campanian Plains, Plain of Catania, Sardinian Campidano) are limited in extent and scattered in location. Moreover the southern plains are not like the fertile lowlands of the North. Their settlement and development have been retarded by hydrological disorders, malaria, neglect and insecurity. Meanwhile, in the uplands, the combination of unstable rock surfaces, steep slopes and excessive deforestation produces erosion of a ferocity unknown elsewhere in the country. The worst affected areas are the *argille scagliose* or 'scaly clays' of the Apennine flanks, eastern Calabria and central Sicily. Rainfall means drop below 500 mm per year along the south coasts of Apulia, Sicily and Sardinia whilst from June to September little rain falls at all, anywhere, severely limiting agricultural horizons in areas which have not been irrigated. The shortage of regularly available water supplies is an environmental factor which has had a powerful influence over the location of large-scale industry in the South. Finally, whilst it is true that the South possesses the primary industrial resources of sulphur, lead and zinc, these have tended to be exported in a largely unprocessed state. Recently, the mining of these minerals has declined sharply.

Sources of the South's industrial backwardness are also deeply rooted in the past. Dominated by no less than seven dynasties between the end of the Byzantine period and the Risorgimento, the South is a classic example of foreign rule and exploitation. Colonialism meant that a strong tradition of class rigidities was imposed, fostered by the presence of a powerful and oppressive feudal organisation which was, by European standards, late in being abolished. Throughout the history of the dependent South the general rule seems to have been one of regarding taxes as a source of revenue to be maximised from the increasingly impoverished colony. Spanish domination through the viceroys was a period of 200 years of particularly oppressive taxation, draining away capital that might have been used for industrial investment.

After unification the colonial treatment of the South continued in a diluted form. Southern analysts have contended that the South was neglected by the statesmen of the North who led the movement for unification and who controlled the government in the early years after 1861. They have maintained that the South's industrial growth was stunted because southern industries were suddenly faced with competition from state-favoured northern firms, and deprived of adequate tariff protection when the low rates of the Kingdom of Sardinia were extended to the entire country. The classic example of the use of heavy taxation to destroy the competitive position of a southern trade was the silk industry. The 'southernist' argument also claims that governmental expenditure on infrastructures and public works was lower in the South than in the North, and that most of the good positions in public administration went to northerners rather than southerners. These contentions have undoubtedly been exaggerated, but they contain a substantial amount of truth.[2]

Historically the only way the South could have escaped its secular economic subordination by the North would have been by industrialising itself in parallel with the North. But this presupposes substantial capital investment in industry, and the South's pre-capital landowner class preferred to consume or export their wealth in other ways. Furthermore, the general level of poverty amongst the peasantry restricted the consumer market for manufactured goods.

There are also important socio-cultural variables to bear in mind when trying to explain the South's industrial backwardness.[3] Like the historical subjugation of the South by the North, these southern cultural traits have often been overstated, but they nevertheless exist. They include a fierce and emotional loyalty to the family as the primary social unit, an archaic concept of female honour (which has made it difficult to recruit female labour into factories), a tendency to seek security and status rather than financial profit, a relative absence of entrepreneurial initiative and a certain cynicism towards anything that comes from outside the region or that represents officialdom. The real enemy of the South, it has been said, is scepticism and the ironic smile; waiting for someone else to do something is still an accepted posture. Culturally, the southern elite places a relatively low value on industrial activity, preferring instead the roles of landowner and gentleman farmer combined with traditional professions like law, teaching, medicine or the church. Technical education is poorly developed and illiteracy is still relatively commonplace, reaching a high of 15 per cent of the population in Calabria (cf. Italy 4 per cent).

Evolution of Southern Industrial Development Policy

In spite of the over-stated view of the *meridionalisti* that the early northern administration did nothing for the South, the Italian state did demonstrate its concern about the problem of the South by the establishment of a number of parliamentary and other semi-official enquiries at the end of the last century. However, little of a policy-making nature was achieved. A special law for Naples, adopted in 1904, provided hydro-electric power as well as customs and tax exemptions for industries setting up there before 1914. One of the provisions of railway nationalisation in 1905 was that one-eighth of railway rolling stock orders must be reserved for plants to be set up in the Naples area. Some rail industrialists were induced to set up factories in Naples after 1905, but they were soon beset by troubles with an untrained and unruly labour force in an area with strong revolutionary tendencies. An attempt to introduce piecework to raise output led to outright violence in 1908. The 1904-5 measures failed to have any deep effect. The Bagnoli steel plant, built after the special law, remained as an isolated monument to early twentieth century governmental subsidies and good intentions.

The real attempts to foster the industrialisation of the South did not start until the post-war period. Again, the first steps were tentative and feeble. This consisted of efforts to speed up the reconstruction of war-damaged properties and installations, to require government agencies to place one-sixth (after 1950 one-fifth) of their orders for supplies in the South, and to furnish the South with better industrial credit facilities with the hope of bringing down interest rates and making borrowing procedures simpler. In 1953 three important credit institutes were set up: ISVEIMER for the mainland South, IRFIS for Sicily and CIS for Sardinia. Although dating from this 'pre-industrialisation' phase, these three institutes were to play a key role in financing southern industrial growth, providing over the ensuing 25 years 4,000 million of the 10,600 million lire advanced to industries expanding or setting up in the region.

Gradually a more detailed and far-reaching plan emerged for the South. This was the famous Vanoni Ten-Year Plan (1954-64) which had the following two specific southern objectives: to increase the South's regional income by an annual average rate of 8 per cent (cf. 4 per cent in the North); and to create a million new jobs in the South. By these herculean — and unrealistic — measures it was expected that the South would begin to catch up economically with the North, with industry playing the leading role. Few people seriously believed, however, that all the ingrained social and economic differences between North and South could be wiped out in a few years, or that all parts of the South would make similar progress. Nevertheless the plan provided a broad context for more specific programmes and policies which were to follow.

The crucial effort to industrialise the South started in 1957 when the Industrial Areas Law was passed, authorising the Cassa per il Mezzogiorno (which, founded in 1950, had hitherto operated more as a rural development agency) to encourage the establishment of industry in favoured parts of the region. The various incentives offered by the 1957 law to industrial firms locating in the South included exemption from profits tax for industrial capital reinvested in the region, direct grants for plant and machinery, soft loans and customs relief. The combination of direct subsidies on plant and machinery and the very low interest loans (3-6 per cent repayable over 10-15 years) could make up as much as 85 per cent of the total capital invested by a firm settling in the South. At a stroke Italy passed from the position of having no purely regional incentive scheme of any significance to possession of one of the most generous industrial incentive packages in Western Europe.[4] A further important clause in the law compelled the state holding companies to locate at least 60 per cent of their new industrial investment in the South.

More industrial initiatives were taken by the Cassa in the 1960s and 1970s. In 1961 IASM (Institute for the Assistance of Southern Development) was set up, its function to assist the establishment and modernisation of southern industry by preparing technical and feasibility studies. In 1963 a new public shareholding company, IN-SUD, was created, again with Cassa from capital, to enable the government to participate more directly in financing southern industrial development. In 1971 the Cassa was allocated additional funds and a new system of industrial incentives was introduced which included the requirement of the state holding sector to locate 80 per cent of its new investment in the South. As the new regional governments assume responsibility for local industrial planning the function of the Cassa has changed over the past 15 years to that of an advisory body concentrating on special projects, particularly those affecting more than one region, and the furtherance of long-term development prospects through the safeguarding of natural resources. One of the most important 'special' projects is the decontamination of the heavily polluted Bay of Naples. The old Interministerial Committee for the South has been dissolved and southern policy is now the responsibility of CIPE (Interministerial Committee for Economic Planning), aided by a committee of regional chairmen. Private firms above a certain size are required to submit their investment plans to CIPE to ensure that they conform with national planning and, as far as possible, benefit the South.

Some of the most spectacular work of the Cassa has been in the field of industrial infrastructures, especially transport. Where possible and desirable, railways have been modernised, with new lines, double tracks and electrification. Ports have been improved, some of them almost totally transformed for industrial use, as at Taranto and Cagliari. Many, indeed almost too many, new trunk roads and motorways have been built, the main Tyrrhenian and Adriatic coast motorways effectively shrinking the length of the Italian boot, putting many districts in much more direct touch with other parts of the country.[5]

The spatial expression of the operation of the Cassa's industrial policy was the growth pole which in the mid 1950s had many adherents both amongst Cassa staff and researchers of SVIMEZ, a private body dedicated to the promotion of industrial development in the South.[6] Two types of growth centre were established — industrial areas and industrial nuclei. The aim of the former was to concentrate the major industrial initiatives in certain key locations, whilst the latter represented an attempt to diffuse in-growth to more minor centres. In order to qualify for 'area' status a locality had to possess an existing tradition of industry and to be able to supply sufficient labour, land, water and energy resources for further substantial industrial growth. Normally such localities were close to cities or other networks of dense settlement with at least 200,000 people. The aim was to set up at least one major leading industry in each area. The Taranto steelworks and the Bay of Augusta refinery and petrochemical plants are two obvious examples. Less stringent conditions were applied to localities qualifying for 'nuclear' status. Most of these places have smaller populations (less than 75,000) and some have been set up in decidedly rural districts such as interior Abruzzi and central Sardinia. Within each area or nucleus factories were to be encouraged to settle in specially-designated industrial estates *(agglomerati)* where all the necessary facilities were to be provided by the Cassa working in association with local industrial consortia and regional authorities.

The concentration of industrial effort into selected growth areas was in response to the realisation that a major deterrent to large firms locating in the South was the lack of external economies. Spatial concentration of several firms in a suitable area lowers the cost of infrastructure provision and ultimately leads to the creation of a pool of trained and diversified industrial labour. The region as a whole benefits from the spin-off of this industrial development, and other firms are attracted in. Such, at least, was the theory: in practice the spontaneous snowballing of private industries has not really happened, except in one or two areas.

Altogether 48 localities have been granted area or nucleus status. Their locations are given in Figure 11.2. The question immediately arises as to whether there are simply too many nodes to fulfil the original tenet of spatial concentration inherent in the growth pole concept. In fact the 48 areas and nuclei comprise more than one-fifth of the Mezzogiorno's area and contain 60 per cent of the region's population. These are very high proportions.

Figure 11.2: Industrial Areas and Nuclei in the Mezzogiorno, 1980

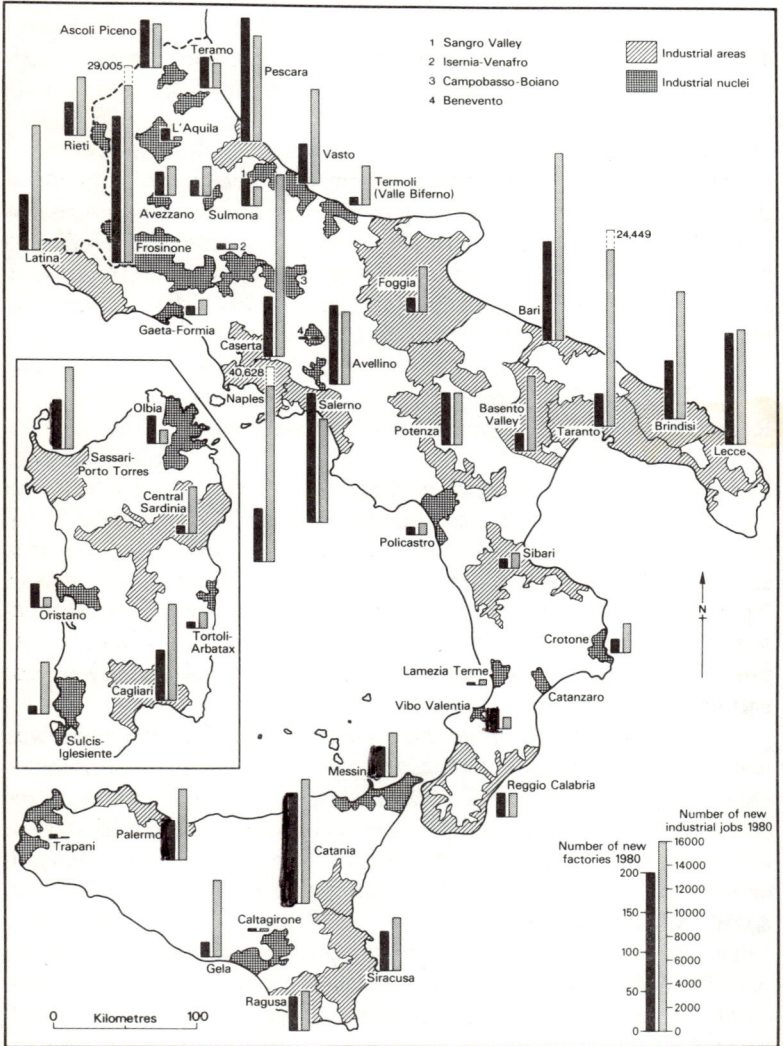

Note: The map does not include the small industrial poles set up by the regional governments in Sicily and Sardinia.

Source: Based on data from *Situazione Insediativa e Infrastrutturale negli Agglomerati Industriali del Mezzogiorno*, Rome: IASM Notizie 12 (1981), 26-85.

The large number of localities selected results largely from southern provincialism and local political influence. For the Cassa to have turned down industrial growth pole status for any applicant locality would have immediately lost votes for the ruling Christian Democrat party in that area. This is why the Cassa is so often referred to as a giant patronage organisation rather than a true regional economic planning agency. It also explains why many 'nuclei' have been upgraded to 'areas', by which they qualify for greater amounts of aid for industrial infrastructures. Many of the smaller industrial nuclei, such as some of those in Calabria and Sicily, have very limited industrial development possibilities. Indeed some virtually exist on paper only, no factories having settled there. They were selected to secure votes in these areas and to give the impression that all parts of the South were being fairly treated.

Results

There is no doubt that the policy of regional incentives has attracted a good deal of industry to the Mezzogiorno over the last 25 years. Among some of the better known establishments are Montedison with its plants at Brindisi, Priolo and Camporeale (Sicily), the Italsider steelworks at Taranto, Olivetti at Pozzuoli, Alfa Sud at Pomigliano d'Arco, Fiat at a range of locations, Pignone with its machine industry at Bari, SIR at Porto Torres, Rumianca at Cagliari, Pittsburgh Plate Glass at Salerno, and many more.

Quantitative information on the increase in manufacturing industries and in industrial employment in the growth poles of the South is provided in Figure 11.2 and Table 11.1. By 1980 2,427 new factories employing a total of over 305,000 workers had settled in the 148 industrial estates belonging to the 48 areas and nuclei. If factories 'planned' and 'under construction' are included the figures rise appreciably to 4,050 factories and nearly 390,000 workers.

These new industrial jobs are highly concentrated in a limited number of industrial sectors. Table 11.1 shows that 72.9 per cent of the employment in factories in operation in 1980 is in the chemical, mechanical and metallurgical branches, mostly in large, capital-intensive units (witness the contrast between chemicals, with a mean of 202 workers per factory, or mechanical industries with 167, and wood and furniture, with only 8). There has been only limited development of small to medium sized labour-intensive units in more traditional

Table 11.1: Industries and Industrial Employment in the Areas and Nuclei of Industrialisation in Southern Italy, 1980.

Industrial branch	In operation		Under construction and planned		Total	
	Factories	Workers	Factories	Workers	Factories	Workers
Food and tobacco industries	270	15,019	205	9,144	475	24,163
Textiles and clothing	107	18,923	74	4,568	181	23,491
Leather goods (inc. shoes)	88	3,419	46	2,395	134	5,814
Wood and furniture	676	5,415	139	3,349	815	8,764
Metallurgy	95	34,835	54	4,390	149	39,225
Mechanical products	729	122,188	561	31,489	1,290	153,677
Non-metallic minerals	343	24,689	98	4,151	441	28,840
Chemicals	324	65,483	173	17,019	497	82,504
Paper and printing	66	6,035	38	1,161	104	7,196
Other manufacturing	36	1,255	54	1,403	90	2,658
Construction and installation	28	2,163	47	1,114	75	3,277
Electricity and gas	58	2,575	11	558	69	3,133
Storage industries	69	1,077	49	631	118	1,708
Transport, communications and other services	38	2,104	24	987	62	3,091
Total	2,427	305,180	1,623	84,245	4,050	389,425

Note: The totals include all factories and employment within the Cassa per il Mezzogiorno region (i.e. including southern Latium, southern Marche, etc.). 'Mechanical' includes domestic electrical goods and vehicles. 'Chemical' includes rubber, plastics and artificial fibres.
Source: Situazione Insediativa e Infrastrutturale negli Agglomerati Industriali del Mezzogiorno, Rome, IASM Notizie, Supplement to issue 12 (1981), pp. 12-13.

branches like textiles, foodstuffs and wood products, although recent legislation (since 1976) gives more weight to smaller firms.

Figure 11.2 shows that there has also been sharp *spatial* concentration of new industrial initiatives in the South. Apart from southern Latium (the Latina and Frosinone industrial areas were dealt with in the previous chapter), the most important developments have been confined to three main districts: the Naples-Caserta-Salerno region, with 64,800 new jobs; the Bari-Brindisi-Taranto 'triangle' with 51,200; and the Catania-Siracusa axis, with 22,100. Moderate increases have been recorded in Pescara (9,000), Vasto (8,000), Lecce (9,850), the Basento Valley (6,500), Palermo (6,000), Gela (6,400), Cagliari (7,900) and Sassari-Porto Torres (7,000). Data on the distribution of Cassa investments reinforce this pattern. More than 80 per cent of the spending has gone to four regions: Apulia (22.5 per cent), Sardinia (22.3 per cent), Sicily (20.8 per cent) and Campania (15.3 per cent). Three regions — Calabria (3.2 per cent), Basilicata (2.2 per cent) and Molise (0.6 per cent) — have received very little. Polarisation within the 'big spending' regions has also been very marked: more than two-thirds of Apulian investment has gone to Taranto, more than two-thirds of Campanian investment has ended up in Naples and Caserta whilst in Sicily Syracuse and Palermo have each absorbed one-third of regional investment.[7]

Industrial development has thus led to sharper regional differentiation *within* the South. At a regional level Abruzzi, Apulia and Sardinia have advanced strongly in general economic terms so that these three regions now have mean *per capita* incomes which are only 20-25 per cent below the national average. In Abruzzi and Apulia one may observe something of the 'Adriatic model' of development discussed in earlier chapters, with recent growth of small firms working in traditional activities. On the other hand personal incomes in the regions of Molise, Basilicata and Calabria are still little more than half the national mean. These three regions have the smallest proportions of their working populations (all less than 10 per cent) employed in industry. Descending to the provincial scale two of the Mezzogiorno's 36 provinces — Taranto and Siracusa (both relatively small provinces with large industrial projects) — have a *per capita* income figure above the national average. The mushrooming of industrial development just south of the Cassa border — in Abruzzi, in the provinces of Latina and Frosinone and along the Rome-Naples motorway — has led to proposals to shift the aid boundary further south or to establish a system of graduated incentives.

The kind of industry which has emerged in the South, overwhelmingly capital-intensive, has been strongly conditioned by the nature of the incentives, based on capital criteria not on labour or value-added or other measures. With large amounts of investment per employee, for each new industrial job in the South double the investment of additional jobs in the North has been required. In the chemical and metallurgical industries, where so much Cassa aid has been directed, each job has cost £100,000. Where firms compete to get state subsidies the results are likely to be different from, and more inefficient than, market competition: plant which is too small and dispersed, in order to increase the number of development grants, or agglomerations which are too big, in order to prevent state funds going to rivals. Amongst chemical companies it has become a favourite ploy to plan a costly plant, pocket the financial assistance and then bankrupt the company.[8]

It is also clear that the South's model of industrialisation is a *dependent* model. Many of the big initiatives are plants belonging to the state giants of IRI and ENI which have had no choice but to move South. Since 1957 the state sector has accounted for over half the new industrial investment in the South, but many of these are branches of northern or foreign companies. Practically none of the important and large-scale industrial initiatives in the South are indigenous. A basic problem with a dependent style of industrialisation is that decision-making is external to the region — it takes place in governmental offices in Rome or in board-rooms in Milan, Turin, Hamburg, New York or even Tokyo. The long-term stability of such a model is always questionable, as the experience of the last decade or more has shown. Industrial recession has strangled the partial industrial take-off of the South precisely at the time — in the late 1960s and early 1970s — when it appeared that conditions for a more rapid and intensive development of manufacturing industry were about to mature, at least in certain areas of the South.

In many of the southern industrial growth poles, particularly those established in predominantly rural areas, the pattern of 'development' has been the same. At least in the initial stages, the majority of managerial and technical workers were northerners who had to be persuaded to move south. In many cases this was done as a deliberate act of company policy, but it also reflected a lack of local industrial managers and technicians available for recruitment. Large numbers of local construction workers were hired but then most of these were laid off on completion of the plants which, being mostly capital-intensive, could not provide permanent jobs for more than a fraction. In this way the type of industrialisation pursued by the Cassa has had a destabilising effect on local labour markets, dislodging rural workers from their farming backgrounds but not giving them satisfactory permanent jobs.

Thus Table 11.1, which chronicles the factories and employment aided by the Cassa's programme and located in the industrial areas and nuclei, gives a rather partial picture. At least two other variables are missing: the possible loss of industrial jobs in the areas and nuclei; and the change in industrial employment outside these poles. Rodgers[9] has presented most interesting data which shed light on these questions. First, taking just the territory of the growth poles, he calculates net manufacturing employment change for these strategic areas using commune data from the 1951 and 1971 Industrial Censuses. For the period 1951-71 he finds a net increase of 234,889 industrial jobs, a figure broadly consistent with the 305,180 jobs recorded in Table 11.1 for 1980 (the extra 70,000 or so jobs coming in the 1971-80 period). However, when individual nuclei and areas are examined notable discrepancies occur. Three industrial poles (Reggio Calabria, Calta-girone and Trapani) recorded net *losses* of industrial employment during 1951-71, in spite of the Cassa's claim of new jobs. In most of the remaining poles the actual increase in industrial employment, as revealed by inter-censal comparison, is somewhat less than the number of jobs induced by the Cassa. This implies that the process of setting up new factories in the South has been accompanied by a simultaneous loss of industrial employment from other industries. Three exceptions to this trend are Latina, Naples and Bari: in these three favoured nodes (one outside the 'conventional' South, and the other two the main regional capitals of the mainland South) spontaneous industrial progress is therefore occurring alongside Cassa policy. Overall, Rodgers found an 81.4 per cent increase in manufacturing employment within the areas and nuclei of industrialisation, and a 16.1 per cent decrease in areas outside the poles. The areas and nuclei accounted for 52 per cent of the South's manufacturing jobs in 1951, rising to 70 per cent in 1971.

Provincial data from the two Industrial Censuses provide complementary evidence for the trends just noted; again the spatial pattern is highly variable. The number of industrial jobs more than doubled in the provinces of Caserta (up by 124.2 per cent), Taranto (148.1 per cent) and Siracusa (101.2 per cent). In Latina province it tripled (213.3 per cent) but, as explained in the previous chapter, there are specific reasons for this. Strong increases (all percentages) were also registered in Chieti (49.4), Teramo (84.4), Naples (51.2), Bari (70.7), Brindisi

(61.4), Matera (78.9), Caltanissetta (56.6), Cagliari (56.8) and Sassari (58.0). But throughout the Apennine spine (Campobasso, Avellino, Benevento, Salerno, Potenza), in the whole of Calabria and in parts of western Sicily (Agrigrento, Trapani) there was a decline in industrial employment between the two census dates. In the three provinces of Calabria and in Campobasso and Benevento provinces this decline was of the order of 20-30 per cent. Clearly, at a time when the North was undergoing its post-war industrial boom, and whilst the major growth poles of the South, at Latina, Naples, Brindisi, Taranto, Syracuse, etc., were generating considerable new industrial employment, the upland backwaters were losing out, and in fact out-migration has continued at a high level from these provinces.[10] The policy of proliferating nuclei, ostensibly a strategy for diffusing industrial development into the interior and other unfavoured parts of the South (but really geared more to electoral campaigning) therefore failed in its stated objectives.

The increasingly imbalanced spatial pattern of industrialisation in the Mezzogiorno is further explored in the next few pages by a regional account of the South's industrial geography.

Abruzzi and Molise

Abruzzi is a transitional region between the Centre and the South. On historical and socio-economic criteria it is part of the South: until 1860 it formed part of the Kingdom of the Two Sicilies, and it has always had a deeply rural character with much subsistence farming and upland pastoralism. Magnificent limestone scenery in the Gran Sasso (now a national park) and Maiella ranges, however, offers little economic anchorage for the younger members of the population and emigration has always been high. Between 1861 and 1961 more than a million people left the region, a figure almost equal to its present population. Before motorways the route from Rome to L'Aquila (the region's capital) was only open in summer and the region was consequently isolated and rather little-known by outsiders. Now Abruzzi lies definitely within the Roman orbit and significant industrial and agricultural progress, especially along the coast, has made it the richest region in the South in *per capita* income terms, although it is still below the national average. Economic development is progressively distancing the region from the traditional southern regions of the Mezzogiorno. Its hydro-electric power, mountain and ski resorts, forests and high natural pastures are reminiscent of the Alpine economy, whilst the expansion of small and medium scale industry makes the region more and more like Marche and Umbria.

The main industrial concentration is along the Pescara Valley where a small conurbation is evolving between Pescara and Chieti, provincial capitals only 10 km apart and linked by a range of new highways. Pescara is a multifunctional town (industry, services, port, beach resort) and is the fastest growing urban area in the South, with a 70.3 per cent growth in population between 1951 and 1971. Moreover, Pescara province has by far the highest rate of net in-migration in the South.[11] When the Pescara Valley industrial area was established in 1962 the employment forecast was for 20,000 new jobs. This figure was subsequently revised downwards to 14,000 and at present a situation of saturation is being reached with around 11,000 workers, mostly in mechanical, building, textile and clothing industries. This saturation is because the urban expansion of Pescara and Chieti within the restricted valley setting leaves little room for further industrial growth.

Of the other industrial poles in Abruzzi, Vasto stands out as being the most important, with 7,400 jobs, most of them in the glass and building products industries. The rest — Avezzano (clothing, textiles), Sulmona (electrical engineering), Sangro Valley (vehicles), L'Aquila and Teramo (both various small industries) — have few large-scale initiatives and only limited employment (all less than 2,500 industrial jobs). An example is the Sangro Valley where the Sevel light van plant (a joint Fiat-Peugeot-Citroën venture) has required considerable infrastructural investment for only 1,500 jobs.

Traditional industries survive in many of the interior towns. Examples of local artisan specialities are copper work at Guardiagrele and sugared almonds at Sulmona. Specialised viticulture has spread over the coastland and lower hill country of Chieti province, giving rise to a thriving wine-making industry. In this province Lanciano is a commercial and market centre of some note, the provincial capital being somewhat peripheral and under the influence of Pescara.

Molise, part of the Abruzzi region before 1964, is even more rural with 48 per cent of its active population working in agriculture. Out-migration has been more intense here than in any other Italian region; as a result the population fell from 406,000 in 1951 to 310,000 in 1973, rising to 335,000 in 1980. The landscape is more open and rolling than that of Abruzzi: wheat is the main crop. The regional capital, Campobasso, has a distinctly 'small-town' air whilst Isernia (19,000) is the smallest of Italy's 95 provincial capitals. If one discounts the network of self-employed village artisans Molise has no industrial tradition, and modern industrial development is modest. Since 1971 sixteen enterprises employing 3,900 persons have settled in the industrial nuclei of Termoli and Isernia (the Campobasso nucleus has no industries as yet). The largest single industry is the Fiat assembly plant at Termoli, employing 3,000 workers; this, however, has completely absorbed the development potential of the Termoli nucleus, blocking plans for a more balanced and diversified industrial structure in this small port town.

Naples and Campania

Thanks to the prodigious fertility of the Naples area and the presence of the country's third largest city, Campania has a far higher density of population than other southern *regioni*: 400 persons per square kilometre, twice as high as Sicily and Apulia, the next most densely populated southern regions, and roughly six times denser than Molise, Basilicata and Sardinia. This is due to the concentration in the small province of Naples of over half the region's population — nearly three-quarters if adjacent thickly populated parts of southern Caserta and northern Salerno provinces are included. The belt between Caserta and Salerno is one of the most densely populated predominantly rural areas of Europe. Towns, large villages and scattered hamlets set in a matrix of intensively cultivated gardens and fields give a landscape halfway between urban and rural. A wide range of vegetables and fruits is cultivated on the fertile volcanic soils, and food processing has a great and long-established importance. North and south of this volcanic belt lie other plains, this time of fluvial deposits. Formerly marshy and malarial, the Garigliano, Volturno and Sele plains have been reclaimed since the 1950s and are now under prosperous networks of small farms set up by the Campanian land reform authorities, providing further large quantities of tomatoes, tobacco, fruits and vegetables for local processing industries.

Around this core of dense urban and rural settlement lies a much more extensive penumbra of mountain country, sparsely populated outside of a few restricted valleys. The Apennines swing across from the Adriatic to the Tyrrhenian coasts, completely shutting out the coastal lowlands by the time the southern part of the region is reached. In these picturesque areas of mountain limestone (the Matese, Irpinia, Cilento) only a meagre agriculture survives, with low-yielding cereals, scrubby forests, poor sheep pastures and scattered plots of olives, vines and tobacco. Industrial penetration into this great sweep of rural poverty and decline has on the whole been feeble.[12] Avellino has the new Alfa-Nissan car plant and a few other industries, a total figure of 6,100 new industrial jobs in 1980. Benevento remains even more of a provincial backwater, notable only for its production of liqueurs and a few foodstuffs. In fact between 1951 and 1971 this province lost more than 2,000 industrial jobs, a fall of 23.8 per cent.[13] It was in these eastern mountains of Campania, statistically the poorest area of all Italy, that the earthquake of November 1980 tragically struck its most severe blows, destroying many villages and causing a death toll of more than 3,000.

The most impressive post-war industrial growth in Campania has taken place in and around Caserta, where IASM figures shown an addition of more than 15,000 industrial jobs by 1980, well diversified across a range of sectors — mechanical, electrical, chemical, food, tobacco and building. The proportional growth of industrial employment in Caserta province (124 per cent during 1951-71) is the highest in the South outside of Taranto. Significantly Caserta was the only Campanian province to experience a net in-migration during the 1970s, and recorded the strongest increase in *per capita* income in the region. This industrial growth may be explained by several factors. First, there is the inherent agricultural productivity of the province, more than half of which is made up of fertile volcanic and alluvial soils, giving rise to a solid platform of food industries and agricultural commerce. Then there are various locational factors. Nearness to the regional capital enables the district to benefit from the Neapolitan labour and consumer markets, as well as being an attractive overspill area for industry fleeing the congestion and high land costs of the coast. Finally, Caserta is extremely handily placed with regard to rail and motorway transport. It is Campania's main railway junction and lies close to the Rome-Naples motorway which, throughout its length, has been attracting industrial development for more than 20 years. In addition to Caserta itself, industrial estates have sprung up near motorway entry points at Marcianise, Santa Maria Capua Vetere, Capua and Sparanise.[14]

To the south, Salerno is a slight outlier of industrial development, isolated from the Naples urban system by the limestone ridge of the Sorrento peninsula, although good motorway links have now overcome this problem. In spite of the growth of new mechanical engineering concerns, the existence of stagnant food and textile industries has limited Salerno's rate of economic growth when compared to that of Caserta, while the tobacco industry of Battipaglia has been periodically stricken by labour unrest. Tourism is an important adjunct to the economy of this part of Campania. Pompeii, Sorrento, Amalfi, Paestum and the Isle of Capri provide a range of attractions for the visitor.

Naples lies at the heart of an urban region of more than 2.5 million people, roughly half of whom live in the city itself. The rest are thickly spread around the shores of the Bay of Naples from Pozzuoli to Castell-ammare di Stabia or clumped in large, crowded towns just inland — Casoria, Afragola, Acerra, Pomigliano d'Arco, etc. Of Italy's four 'million cities' Naples is undoubtedly the most complex in function and form.[15] The characters of the others are well defined: Rome the administrative capital; Milan the economic and commercial headquar-ters; and Turin the industrial city. Naples, on the other hand, is full of contradictions, a complex amalgam of industries and unemployment, riches and poverty, cultural vitality and urban malaise. It is, with its modern office blocks, hotels, universities, splendid new railway station and varied industries, a modern European industrial city. But it is also, with its *casbah*, its underground economy, its corruption and its poor health standards (scene of a cholera outbreak as recently as 1973), a city of the less-developed Mediterranean world. Although unques-tionably the leading city in the Mezzogiorno, with twice as many inhabitants as Palermo and three times as many as Bari, Naples' administrative greatness lies more in the past when it was the capital of a kingdom. One feels that it has never successfully adjusted from the loss of that position, remaining 'the swollen head of a stunted body' still today.[16]

More than any other Italian city, Naples (and its surrounding satellite towns) has a pronounced dualistic industrial structure, with a myriad of tiny, one-person or family enterprises, mostly operating in the older parts of the city, contrasting with a small number of industrial giants nearly all of which are non-local (e.g. IRI-Bagnoli, Alfa Sud, Olivetti, Mobil Oil). The large and small firms tend to work in different sectors, and there is little integration between them. Metal-working, which employs 46.4 per cent of the city's industrial workers, is by far the most important industrial sector, led by the Bagnoli steelworks. Small firms concentrate in the more traditional sectors of industry such as textiles and clothing, footwear, leather goods, and furniture and wood. The division between true industry and artisans can be seen more clearly in a breakdown of the metal-working and engineering sector. The artisan class concentrates on servicing activities such as heating and air conditioning repairs (29 per cent of employment), iron and copper forging (28 per cent) and machinery and electronics repairs (25 per cent), whilst industrial workers are in ferrous metallurgy (40 per cent), electronics manufacture (17 per cent), transport machinery (17 per cent) and other mechanical manufacturing industries (18 per cent).

Industrially the city may be divided into three main areas.[17] The western part is mainly residential and contains almost no industry apart from the Bagnoli steelworks midway between Naples and Pozzuoli and some artisan and service concerns which have grown up to satisfy local neighbourhood demands. The central area contains a massive accumulation of small and very small units working in traditional fields such as footwear, gloves and furniture. Although there is no overall plan of industrial development, there is a high degree of specialisation and integration based on a dense proletarian population and widespread use (and abuse) of female domestic labour. These inner city tenements were badly damaged by the 1980 earthquake so that a proportion of both industrial and residential premises has been rendered unusable. Many small industries, and 50,000 people, were forced to move to a variety of temporary accommodation whilst structural repairs proceed slowly; some are being permanently rehoused in peripheral estates. Finally, the north-eastern area of the city contains the major concentration of larger scale industry, mainly metallurgy, mechanical engineering and chemicals, all of which have extensive plants, many of which cannot expand *in situ* because of encroaching residential development. There is also a significant level of artisan activity in this area.

Of the Naples area's major industries, the Bagnoli and Alfa Sud plants were dealt with in Chapter 7. The Montedison group has a number of plants producing plastics, chemicals, electrical equipment and building materials. Fiat has linked with IRI to establish an aeronautics complex which now forms the heart of the Italian aircraft industry. Traditional industries linked to the port — jute, cotton, rayon and paper mills — have declined or decentralised: their derelict factories and warehouses add little to the beauty of the bay. The rationalisation of Italian shipbuilding has also adversely affected Naples and the yards at Castellammare.

Alone of the southern industrial development areas Naples has become spatially integrated with the national economy. The Rome-Frosinone-Caserta-Naples-Salerno axis, fashioned around long-established urban settlements and the motorway (built in 1962), and aided by the Cassa boundary effect, has emerged as the one southern region to rival the industrial triangle of the North. A revealing indicator of this is that in the two provinces of southern Latium (Latina,

Frosinone) and the three of coastal Campania (Caserta, Naples, Salerno) the growth of industrial employment has exceeded the loss of agricultural employment by 8 per cent whereas elsewhere in the Mezzogiorno (save for a few isolated nodes) the decline in the rural labour force has far outstripped the growth in industrial jobs (the difference being accounted for by out-migration, tertiary sector growth or unemployment). However, whilst there *has* been considerable industrial growth in the Naples-Caserta area, the character of this growth remains distinctly southern and dependent.[18] Of the 235 manufacturing concerns with at least 100 employees operating in the region, only 45 are managed locally; the rest are managed from northern or foreign decision-taking centres.[19]

Apulia and the Southern Industrial Triangle

Apulia provides the setting for perhaps the most ambitious example of industrial planning in Southern Italy: the attempt to create an interlinked industrial complex *ex novo* in a triangle of coastal towns (Bari, Brindisi, Taranto) with little or no industrial tradition. Although the project has not been wholly successful, the results achieved are amongst the most impressive and concrete realisations of the Cassa's southern policy.

Isolated from the Apennines, which impinge on the region only in a corner of Foggia province, Apulia is the only region of the Mezzogiorno whose relief is not predominantly hilly or mountainous. Plains constitute 53 per cent of the region and, apart from the Gargano spur and the lower slopes of the Apennine foreland in Foggia province, most of the upland consists of the karstic ridge of the Murge which forms a low backbone to the region, generally losing height as it fades into the Salentine Peninsula. The plains and wide, undulating benches of this peninsula and of the Terra di Bari provide favourable conditions for the olives, vines and almonds which cover half the region in specialised and well-tended arboriculture. This diffusion of intensive tree-crops, well suited to the hot, dry climate and the limestone soils, dates mostly from the end of the last century; a more ancient latifundian past is evident in the widely-spaced agro-town settlements and the land-use regime of the Foggia Tavoliere which was wheat estates and winter sheep pasture until the 1950s. The widespread distribution of a highly developed commercial agriculture partly explains the lack of a dominant urban concentration. Bari with 357,000 inhabitants has only one-tenth of

Apulia's population and the five provincial capitals together (Foggia, Bari, Brindisi, Taranto, Lecce) do not exceed one million inhabitants, or a quarter of the region's population.

This background of agriculture and settlement types has influenced the distribution of manufacturing activities. As long as artisan crafts-manship prevailed over mass production, industry was scattered widely over the region in a host of small towns and large villages. With the birth of more modern enterprises, larger-scale firms began to concentrate in the biggest urban areas, especially Bari. The establishment of the industrial growth pole policy in the early 1960s furthered this process of spatial concentration. At present the five provincial capitals account for a total manufacturing employment of 56,000 persons, 58 per cent of the region's industrial labour force. If adjacent communes linked to the growth poles are included the proportion rises to 85 per cent. Moreover, with the exception of Bari, this new industrial growth is highly differentiated in terms of sectoral specialisation: food industries at Foggia, metallurgy at Taranto, petrochemicals at Brindisi, clothing and tobacco at Lecce. Another important characteristic of the Apulian industrial scene has been the survival and strengthening of the small firm sector, which has prevented the sad loss of industrial employment that has occurred elsewhere in the Mezzogiorno outside of the indus-trial poles. Instead, in Apulia, there has been steady growth of indus-trial employment outside of the main industrial areas; this has been especially the case in Bari province where there is a dual network of fairly prosperous small towns both along the coast (Barletta, Trani, Bisceglie, Molfetta) and just inland (Canosa, Andria, Corato, Bitonto, etc.).

The Bari-Brindisi-Taranto trio of towns were amongst the first in the Mezzogiorno to be selected as industrial development areas. Following this the European Community designated the triangle as a pole of Euro-pean regional development and in 1962 set in motion studies of the area's economy as a preliminary to drawing up a detailed plan for the region's industrial development. The research, contracted to the Rome consultancy firm Italconsult, involved compilation of a comprehensive input-output table of the region to show the goods and services pro-duced and consumed in all the current productive activities. From an analysis of this table new industries that would find the region's resources advantageous were selected and further feasibility studies made for each of them. In this way a list of over 200 'possibles' was reduced to 30 'probables'. The proposals, made public in 1965, iden-tified a concentration on mechanical industries at Bari and Taranto, and on petrochemical industries for Brindisi.[20]

Meanwhile industrial progress in the area was already under way, stimulated by the Cassa's infrastructural improvements and by the law forcing state industry to locate 60 per cent of its new investment in the South. Bari had already had its port improved and several new mechanical industries were settling in the industrial estate south-west of the town. At the old naval port of Taranto Italsider's giant integrated iron and steel complex was constructed from 1960 on, rising from the olive groves north-west of the town. With limestone the only resource locally available, full use had to be made of the coastal situation, and new jetties, wharves and overhead transporters were built to deal with bulk imports of iron ore from Venezuela and North and West Africa and of coal from the USA.

The Taranto steelworks, one of the largest in Western Europe, is the largest single industrial enterprise in the Mezzogiorno. Construction of the plant severely stretched the financial and human resources of Finsider but there is no doubt that Taranto has put the Italians firmly on the map of world steel production.[21] When the plant first opened it employed 5,000 workers (50,000 applied!) but its payroll has since quadrupled as the capacity of the plant has been enlarged to 10.5 million tons a year, although currently it is running at less than three-quarters of that capacity.

The EEC plan for Taranto proposed the installation of a range of nine major industries (pumps, agricultural machinery, excavators, cranes, machine tools and various domestic appliances) feeding off the steelworks, plus a further 30 auxiliary industries concerned with servicing, repairs, tools, pressing, moulding, galvanising, etc. These numbers were subsequently reduced to eight and 24 respectively. It was hoped that such a functionally interlinked agglomeration would in turn attract other industrial investment, especially from medium sized private firms. Generally this has not occurred, in spite of Cassa infrastructural and job-training aids, higher than average regional incentives and IASM promotional work.[22] Taranto's other main industries are, instead, more basic: a cement works, an oil refinery, a brewery and only a handful of engineeering and light industrial enterprises. Nevertheless the provincial increase in industrial employment during 1951-71 of 148 per cent is the highest in the Mezzogiorno (Latina excepted) and the area has, by southern standards, an air of prosperity.

Bari's industrial development has been less spectacular than that of Taranto but much more diversified. Chemical industries related to rubber production are coupled with mechanical engineering, textiles and an important food processing sector which reflects the city's rich agricultural hinterland. Unusually for the South, many new industries have sprung from local initiatives and some operate independently of the Cassa's incentives. There are 123 Cassa-sponsored new firms employing 15,650 workers (1980 figures), but Rodgers' tabulations indicate 17,230 new industrial jobs already by 1971 for the city's industrial zone, and a net growth in the province of 29,100 manufacturing jobs during 1951-71.[23] Nearly all of the Cassa-sponsored new development is in the large Modugno industrial estate, located between the city and the motorway terminus.[24] The buoyancy of local industrial initiative reflects the city's reputation for business and commercial enterprise built on its outward-looking trading tradition. Bari's annual Fiera del Levante, founded in 1939 when Mussolini used the city as the launching pad for his imperial ventures in the Balkans and North Africa, symbolises the city's mercantile function — it is the Mezzogiorno's window on the world.

Brindisi, on the other hand, conforms much more closely to the typical model of post-war southern industrialisation. Here there are important Montedison refining and petrochemical industries employing 5,000 workers and an active port dealing both in oil products and in passenger and car ferry traffic to Greece.

Developments in the industrial poles attached to the other two provincial capitals have been on a smaller scale. Foggia's industrial development area is spatially extensive but six of the nine *agglomerati* are completely devoid of industries — nor are any planned. In fact this pole represents a good example of the impact of local clientelistic power on industrial location, for it was established expressly to accommodate a single plant, Aeritalia. Foggia also contains a large number of food industries processing the produce of the newly settled and irrigated Tavoliere plains, but these industries would have developed here anyway for they are the natural outgrowth from the improving local rural economy. Manfredonia, also in the Foggia industrial area, has two chemical plants employing 750 workers.

The pattern of industrialisation at Lecce has been more broadly based with 144 firms employing nearly 10,000 workers, mostly in the Lecce industrial estate itself (7,000) but also with significant numbers of industrial jobs created at Galatina (1,200), Nardo (930) and Maglie (640). Here there are many clothing, food and tobacco concerns, but also large-scale plants (Fiat's caterpillar factory at Lecce and laboratories and test track at Nardò).

Basilicata and Calabria: The Deep South

Along with Molise, the regions of Basilicata and Calabria are the least industrialised of Italy. Agricultural improvements, moreover, are limited by an uncompromising physical environment of summer drought, winter cold and storms, poor soils and dearth of flat land. Although standards of living in these 'Deep South' regions have undoubtedly improved over the past 30 years or so of the Cassa's operation, a balanced pattern of economic growth has yet to emerge. The new 'prosperity' is tenuous, based on emigration, pensions, welfare payments and an embryonic tourism.

Although the least densely populated region of Italy after Val d'Aosta, Basilicata is overpopulated; its meagre agricultural resources have consistently failed to sustain a population which has therefore been driven to emigration. Potenza province is entirely upland — two-thirds rugged limestone blocks, one-third badly eroded clay hills. Matera province has further areas of denuded clay hill country, separated by long, parallel trench-like valleys that descend to the Ionian coast. Around this seaboard, in a continuous but ever-narrowing strip all the way from Taranto to the Calabrian border, stretches a fertile, recently resettled plain, the Metapontino. This is the show-piece of the post-war land reform, Italy's 'Little California'. Here thousands of small holders cultivate the sandy alluvial soils with the vital aid of irrigation water from the dams built by the Cassa in the interior hills. Citrus fruits, peaches, vegetables, strawberries, sugar beet and a range of other intensive crops provide the basic inputs for flourishing local agricultural industries such as the sugar and tobacco factories at Policoro and the co-operatively run fruit and vegetable packaging and processing plant at Metaponto. Inland the picture is very different: a bleak, tormented landscape with isolated villages supported largely by emigrant remittances: the southern environment at its worst.

The past 20 years have seen the two provinces of Basilicata evolve with different rhythms and styles of industrial development, although in both cases the total effect has been relatively modest.[25] Before 1960 the only industry of any consequence in the region was the scenically-sited Rivetti textiles plant at Maratea, on Basilicata's short Tyrrhenian coast. Then, the discovery of natural gas at Ferrandina in the Basento Valley south of Matera gave a boost to the development of industry in that province. The Basento Valley industrial area stretches 40 km in a linear fashion along the valley and the railway line between Pisticci and Grassano stations. Most of the factories in this industrial development axis have settled in the original nucleus close to the gas sources between

Pisticci and Ferrandina stations. By 1980 the industrial area contained 24 concerns employing 5,800 people. The main industries are ANIC (synthetic fibres) and Liquichimica (chemicals): both were set up in 1964 and in 1980 employed 3,500 and 700 workers respectively. The build-up of the Basento Valley estate absorbed more than 80 per cent of the Cassa's industrial spending in Basilicata during the period 1961-70. Potenza exhibited little industrial dynamism, concentrating instead on expanding its bureaucratic employment as regional and provincial capital. The ensuing decade saw a switch in both type and location of industry. During the period 1971-81 many small and medium sized firms were established in the Potenza industrial estate, and instead of chemicals and synthetic fibres, the emphasis has been on food, clothing and construction industries.[26] Matera remains the more prosperous of the two provinces, however. This is partly because of its richer farming and partly because it is closer to the more dynamic urban and industrial influences emanating from neighbouring Apulia (workers from much of Matera province are able to commute to Bari and Taranto).

Calabria, the 'South of the South', is the most intractable of the Mezzogiorno's problem regions, retaining the unenviable distinction of coming last in the regional league table on most indices of socio-economic development, from *per capita* income (59 per cent of the Italian average) to illiteracy (15 per cent of the adult population). It is an almost wholly mountainous region, crystalline and metamorphosed rocks introducing into the relief a sharpness not found in the Apennines further north. For most of the 690 km littoral, coastal plains are non-existent: the mountains seem to hang over the encircling sea. To the outsider the region is spectacular and beautiful; to the insider it is tragic and overpopulated, plagued by brigandage in the past and by the Mafia today.

Whilst the Cassa has been unstinting in its efforts to improve Calabrian infrastructure (completing the Autostrada del Sole right down to Reggio, building new cross-peninsula feeder roads, doubling the west coast railway line and contributing to a new airport at S. Eufemia), attempts to industrialise the region have conspicuously failed, in the case of Gioia Tauro farcically so. Foreign capital has shunned the region, with the exception of some Swiss textile plants and a few foreign-owned hotels and tourist villages. New industrial development at Crotone (2,500 new jobs by 1980), Reggio (1,750 jobs), Sibari (1,200) and Policastro (950) has lamentably failed to balance the spontaneous loss of employment from small industries scattered throughout the region. Indeed over the period 1951-71 Calabria suffered a net loss of one-quarter of its manufacturing jobs, evenly spread across all three provinces (4,000-5,000 loss in each). Many industrial initiatives have either failed completely or not lived up to expectations and the promises of politicians: examples are the aborted Gioia Tauro steelworks (which has yielded an unusable port and destroyed 1,000 hectares of orchard land), the railway works at Reggio (2,500 jobs promised but only 350 realised), and the Liquigas bioprotein animal feed plant at Saline near Reggio (built but never permitted to operate by the health authorities and by charges of misappropriation of state funds). The main industrial centre is Crotone on the Ionian coast which has chemical, fertiliser and zinc industries, aided by hydro-electric power from the Sila massif. The three provincial capitals are almost entirely service centres with little industry.

Sicily and Sardinia

The presence of two large islands is a distinctive feature of Italian geography. Sicily and Sardinia share a number of common characteristics but also have their own many unique features. Both received regional autonomy as 'special statute' regions in 1946. Both are isolated from the rest of Italy and, as a result, underdeveloped. This underdevelopment has not been greatly ameliorated by the spectacular expansion of petrochemical industries in both islands in the last 25 years.

These rather superficial similarities contrast with much more fundamental differences. Although the islands are of almost equal size, Sicily has more than three times as many people as Sardinia (5 million as against 1.6 million). Sicily reproduces many of the geographical features already described for the mainland South: summer drought, sedimentary and crystalline mountain chains, Tertiary clay hills, a large volcano and fertile but restricted coastal lowlands. Palermo resembles Naples, Catania is like Bari and Messina, like Reggio, was rebuilt after the 1908 earthquake. On the human side Sicily caricatures much of what is wrong with the country as a whole: the island is addicted to clientelism, corruption and empty rhetoric. Here, more than anywhere else, the lack of an efficient, respected central authority holds back progress. The Mafia is a major social cancer which also takes its debilitating toll of the region's economic life. In spite of this, Sicily has always been an outward-looking region. Its location at the cross-roads of the Mediterranean has caused its enforced participation in most of the currents of the wider region's history. For the most part it has suffered exploitation and domination, but it has also seen the flourishing civilisations of the Greek Empire and Islam. Its external orientation is also linked to the location of most of Sicily's population around the coasts, especially in a strip from Trapani through Palermo to Messina and down to Catania and Syracuse.

The contrast between Sicilian extroversion and Sardinian introspection could hardly be greater.[27] Sardinia's greater distance from the Italian mainland has placed it outside the mainstream of the continent's history. Traditionally its people have turned their backs on the sea, devoting themselves to a semi-transhumant pastoralism that makes best use of the rocky, granite environment. Recent coastal urban and industrial development represents a complete break with the past.

The regional governments of the two islands have offered their own industrial incentives over and above the standard Cassa industrial package. Industries willing to consider an island location have thus received unusually generous aids. There was a massive expansion of oil-based industries in south-eastern Sicily in the early 1960s, and in the following decade this impetus transferred to Sardinia. In addition to the Cassa-ratified areas and nuclei of industrialisation there are in both islands 'regional nodes' of industry sponsored by the regional governments, but generally these have attracted only a few small enterprises.

Sicilian industry has its roots in primary products: tunny fishing on the west coast (Castellammare del Golfo, Trapani, Marsala, Mazara del Vallo), agriculture (especially Marsala wine, pasta, citrus products), construction materials (clay and limestone) and sulphur, potassium, sea and rock salt. Sicily's most important mineral, sulphur, is in decline, annual production falling from 1.3 million tons in the early 1950s to less than 100,000 tons currently. Over the same period sulphur miners have decreased from 12,000 to less than 1,000.

Since 1960 eight areas and nuclei of industrialisation have been designated in Sicily. They are Palermo, Trapani, Messina, Catania, Syracuse (Siracusa), Ragusa, Gela and Caltagirone (Figure 11.2). There are, in addition, regional industrial nodes at Porto Empedocle, Caltanissetta and Enna. The Cassa and the regional authorities have achieved impressive results in infrastructures, although there has also been some waste. The most significant advances have been in transport, with motorways now linking the main urban and industrial areas. The Messina-Catania motorway was built during the 1970s, and by 1978 the important cross-island link, via Enna, was completed between Catania and Palermo. The Palermo-Messina motorway along the north coast is still under construction but will be finished soon. Plans to link Sicily to the mainland by a bridge, much discussed over the years, have yet to show any real signs of coming to fruition.

In spite of the fact that Sicily has received more than one-fifth of the Cassa's industrial spending on the South, the results, at least in terms of employment, have been extremely modest. According to IASM figures the eight industrial areas and nuclei have generated 42,000 industrial jobs. Rodgers, however, finds a net industrial employment increase for the whole of Sicily of only 20,300, indicating grave loss of industrial jobs from interior districts away from the industrial poles.[28]

The most remarkable industrial landscape has emerged in the Siracusa industrial area which stretches north of the provincial capital around the Bay of Augusta.[29] This has become one of the main refining and petrochemicals areas in Western Europe, employing 15,000 people in the manufacture of oil products, chemicals, fertilisers, insecticides, resins, paints, detergents, pharmaceuticals, plastics, synthetic rubber, cement and metal products. The first industrial unit was the Raisom refinery, built during 1949-50 at the north end of the bay. Discovery of oil at Ragusa (1954) and Gela (1956) gave a further fillip to development, although these local supplies turned out to be thick and sulphurous. During 1955-8 the Edison group built the Sincat plant, still the 'giant' of the area. At first Sincat produced inorganic chemicals and fertilisers; later it expanded into various petrochemicals. Like Italsider at Taranto, Sincat encouraged the settlement of other industries in secondary chemicals, building, engineering and maintenance. Montedison's involvement in this area represents the largest piece of private industrial investment in the south of Italy. Between 1951 and 1971 the establishment of the Sicilian petrochemical industry, largely at Syracuse-Augusta but also at Gela where ENI built plants producing fertilisers, polyethylene and synthetic fibres, accounted for 60 per cent of the region's industrial investment.

Although the Bay of Augusta petrochemicals pole contains some of the most significant industrialisation in the Mezzogiorno, the negative aspects of the development need also to be recorded. Chaotic urban growth has sprawled north from Syracuse, swamping the former villages of Priolo and Marina di Melilli.[30] Proper land planning between residential, industrial and agricultural uses has not taken place. Much good agricultural land, previously under vines or olive, citrus and almond orchards, has been destroyed or abandoned. Fishing in the Bay of Augusta is no longer possible, and food processing industries have closed down. The oil and chemical industries remain almost totally divorced from their local setting. Some 95 per cent of all inputs into Sincat come from outside Sicily (85 per cent of this consists of crude oil from Libya and the Middle East), and 92 per cent of the outputs leave Sicily for external markets.[31] All production decisions are taken outside the island.

Very different in character are the two main industrial estates of Catania (400,000), the regional centre for eastern Sicily and a city of some commercial and industrial dynamism. Traditionally the wealth and commercial activity of the city derived from its rich agricultural hinterland on the lower slopes of Mount Etna (lemons, oranges, vines and other fruits) and in the newly reclaimed Plain of Catania (citrus, dairying). This is still the case but new light industries have settled south of the city in the main industrial estate by the airport, and inland along the road to Misterbianco, in all comprising 10,500 new jobs.[32]

Industrial development at Palermo (6,000 new jobs by 1980) has been much more modest, given the regional capital's greater size (651,000). Like Naples, Palermo's wonderful setting around a fertile mountain-backed bay belies its true problems. Based on an unhealthy expansion of tertiary employment, the city has outstripped its economic base. Again like Naples, the inner districts contain appalling slums. Palermo and western Sicily remain the vice-like grip of the Mafia. Recent Mafia assassination victims have included the regional prime minister and Palermo's chief judge. Although there is little hard evidence to support such an assertion, one may suspect that much industrial investment which might otherwise have come to the capital of Sicily has been deterred by fears of Mafia interference. It is no accident that the major industrial projects are clustered in the Mafia-free eastern part of the island.

In Sicily, as elsewhere in the Mezzogiorno, there is widespread realisation that the petrochemicals policy was an expensive mistake. Now there is a greater commitment to promoting tourism, reorganising agriculture and encouraging small and medium industries, based wherever possible on local traditions and resources. The availability of Algerian methane from the newly-built Transmed pipeline should aid light manufacturing, agricultural, fine chemical and electronic indus-tries, whilst further hopes derive from the encouraging explorative finds of oil off the south coast of Sicily. Inland, the revival of mineral-working (especially potash) between Agrigento and Enna has given fresh hope to this squalid part of the island, hitherto neglected by industrial policy-makers.[33] The motor industry in Sicily is represented by a Fiat assembly plant at Termini Imerese and a Pirelli tyre factory at Milazzo, where there is also an oil refinery.

Much the same argument about a misguided model of industrialisation applies to Sardinia where the industrial monoculture of petrochemicals was imported in the late 1960s and the 1970s, only to collapse in disarray with the bankruptcy of SIR in 1979.

Prior to about 1965 Sardinia was very much the forgotten region of the Cassa's southern industrial policy. Between 1953 and 1963 Sardinia's contribution to the gross national product fell from 2.3 per cent to 1.9 per cent, due in no small measure to the decline of mining activities in the south-west (employees in coal, lead and zinc extraction fell from 19,000 in 1951 to 4,300 in 1971).

In Sardinia the infrastructural thrust of the Cassa (new roads, improved port facilities) was given greater coherence by the regional government's *Piano di Rinascita* or 'rebirth plan' which covered the years 1962-74. Four principal objectives were central to the operation of this plan: (a) achievement of a high and stable employment level; (b) a rapid increase in incomes; (c) equalisation of incomes from different sectors of the economy; and (d) transformation from a traditional to a modern socio-economic structure. The main mechanism for the attainment of these aims was to be the rapid development of industry, especially small and medium scale concerns.

Whilst the Sardinian economy *was* transformed in the late 1960s and early 1970s and whilst personal incomes *did* rise appreciably, the mechanisms behind these changes — emigration and the petrochemical 'invasion' — were not those laid down by the plan. The establishment of refinery complexes at the northern and southern extremities of the island (Porto Torres and Sarroch) created isolated, artificial, and ultimately temporary, nodes of prosperity, whilst emigration reduced the working population and led to a rise in incomes which was statistical rather than real.[34] The ex-SIR complex at Porto Torres is the largest single industrial enterprise in Sardinia, employing 5,000 in the late 1970s. The Sarroch refinery has a bigger capacity but is much more a service refinery with only limited downstream development in a small adjacent chemicals plant (1,000 workers overall). The main chemicals initiative on the south coast is the Rumianca complex, built among the salt pans west of the capital Cagliari. Of the other coastal nuclei of industrialisation, Porto Vesme concentrates on electro-metallurgy, Arbatax on paper manufacture from timber imported from the Soviet Union, whilst Olbia and Oristano have smaller-scale clusters of general light industry.

The 1970s saw a remarkable attempt to industrialise the mountain heartland of Sardinia, the Barbagia. These granite plateaux are inhabited by fiercely traditional shepherds whose culture contains disturbingly delinquent tendencies. The social objective of industrialisation in this unlikely environment was to eradicate banditry and livestock theft by providing secure, well-paid factory work.[35] The experiment was a failure. Absenteeism has been high (25 per cent at times) and arguments broke out over which highland communities should be selected for industrial recruitment. By 1980 only 4,800 new jobs had been created. Most of these were at Ottana where three main plants have been established: Chimica del Tirso (terepththalic acid), Fibra del Tirso (polyester fibres) and Metallurgica del Tirso (titanium castings). Further west, Macomer contains the Tirsotex clothing factory. As recorded in Chapter 8, however, the central Sardinia chemical and fibre plants are economically lame ducks and the state has had to intervene to prevent their complete collapse.

The Future of Industry in the South

At present it seems that serious official attempts to industrialise the South have simply been dropped as a result of the industrial counter-revolution which has brought large-scale and especially publicly-owned Italian industry to its knees. The rigidity which has been imposed on the mobility of labour, the sharp increase in the level of industrial wages (faster in the South than in the North), the empirical impracticability of many trade union policies and the fiscal disincen tives on share investments are all incompatible with the much demanded necessity of continuing the programme of industrialising the South.[36] The most spatially equitable policy would be to restructure by concentrating on new industrial enterprises and employment in the South, and pay less attention to preserving jobs in the ailing industries of the North, but given the political realities of Italy this seems an improbable strategy.

Today the South is caught in the competition, on the one hand, of low-labour cost countries outside the EEC for manufactures with easily acquired and transferred technology, and, on the other hand, of the established industrial areas of the North for high technology specialised industries which cannot easily be transferred and for the industrial reconversion programmes which tend to take place *in situ*. The need, nationally, for a change in the industrial structure is widely recognised, but there is very little evidence of linking this primary national aim with the context of the industrial regeneration of the South. And if indusrial growth rates as low as 1 or 2 per cent are accepted, then this allows of virtually no new industrial investment: hence it becomes impossible to help the South.[37]

Nonetheless, there are those who see grounds for optimism in the experience of the last few years. According to this view, there appeared in the late 1970s a self-generating process of industrial development in the South, based on small and medium sized firms operating mainly in traditional sectors — a style of development already described in detail in the centre and north-east regions. Proponents of this view suggest the exploitation of the South's own internal resources as a new strategy for the region, replacing the 'imported development' produced by projects originating from outside the South and carried out by large, often semi-state firms. Although there has been growth in the small firm sector in the South in recent years, particularly in Abruzzi, Campania and Apulia, the characteristics of this growth differ somewhat from the centre-north-east model.[38] In the latter case the small size of productive units and the growth of a complex underground economy were seen as the way to achieve flexibility in the use of the labour force. This process did not run counter to, but rather was accompanied by, the adoption of relatively sophisticated technologies. This permitted growth and fostered product diversification which extended beyond the traditional sectors (textiles, clothing, etc.) to numerous other branches such as mechanical and electrical goods. Diversification has in turn been matched by specialisation amongst individual firms: a change from the production of a product to the production of a component or the processing of one stage of production which has made it possible for small firms to achieve the returns to scale from which they are normally precluded. All this has been accompanied by a geographical grouping of small firms making complementary products or components, as in the manufacture of agricultural machinery in Emilia, and by strong export orientation demanding cost effectiveness, sophisticated market research and flexibility of labour power. In the South, on the other hand, the growth of small and medium firms, where it has occurred, has been very different. Such firms remain concentrated in traditional branches (textiles, footwear, wood products, construction materials) without the evolution to the more technologically based engineering branches. Southern small firm dynamism is also based much more on exploitation of surplus and marginalised labour and the profits are often not ploughed back to improve the enterprise but flow towards the classic southern outlets of real estate, building and commercial speculation. In the wake left by the abortion of the policy of bringing in big industry, the growth of small firms is still a long way from providing the industrial revolution the South needs to become fully integrated economically with the rest of the country and the European Community. The future lies in the development of new industrial activities with a high content of more advanced technology and innovation of products, processes and organisation. To bring about a transformation of the industrial structure of the South in these directions must be the major objectives of an industrial policy for Italy as a whole.[39]

Notes and References

1. King (1971).
2. Clough (1964), pp.164-5; Saville (1968), pp.139-49.
3. LaPalombara (1966), pp.303-9, 314-15; Zariski (1972) p.110.
4. Ronzani (1980), pp.137-8. Other accounts of regional industrial incentives are provided by Cao-Pinna (1976) and Watson (1970).
5. This of course disguises the facts that the South remains peripheral to the main patterns of movement in the country, and that internal linkage within the southern transport system remains far below that achieved in the North. The weak development of port-hinterland relationships is one particular facet of this weak connectivity. See Celant (1976), Elemi and Gambino (1975), Landini (1975).
6. SVIMEZ — the Associazone per lo Sviluppo dell'Industria nel Mezzogiorno (Association for the Development of Industry in the South) — was founded in 1946 and has played an influential role in the debate over development in the South. Its publications are much respected and it has had a strong influence over Cassa policy.
7. D'Aponte (1976), p.261.
8. Wade (1980), p.166.
9. Rodgers (1979), pp.47-9, 62-4; refer especially to Tables 13, 15 and 20.
10. Rodgers (1970).
11. Rodgers (1979), pp.96, 134.
12. There was a pre-unification industrial presence in some of the towns; textiles in Piedimonte Matese, metallurgy in Avellino, food and drink in Benevento (Formica, 1967).
13. Rodgers (1979), p.49.
14. Catudella (1968), pp.365-8.
15. Coquery (1963).
16. Allum (1973b), p.22.
17. Canzanelli *et al.* (1981), pp.344-7.
18. See Biondi and Coppola (1979) and Sciarelli and Maggioni (1975) for detailed survey data.
19. Canzanelli *et al.* (1981), pp.339, 351.
20. For accounts of the background of the 'southern industrial triangle' see Allen and MacLellan (1970), pp.318-27, Allen and Stevenson (1974), pp.205-7, Mountjoy (1966 and 1973), Newcombe (1969) and Watson (1970), pp.53-7.
21. Capanna (1979), p.20.

22. Among the reasons for the failure to live up to the EEC proposals the following may be mentioned: (1) the relatively slow growth of the economy after 1966; (2) the failure of the planners to estimate the degree and nature of technological change and of economies of scale in the industries identified; (3) the neglect of industrial location factors other than those linked to economies of scale; (4) the exaggeration of the responsiveness of local entrepreneurs; and (5) the lack of interest of the state holding sector outside of Italsider. Allen and Stevenson (1974), p.206.

23. Rodgers (1979), pp.49, 64.

24. For a detailed account of the growth of this estate and its effects on the local labour market see Carparelli (1976).

25. For a detailed account of the establishment of the industrial poles in Basilicata see Biondi and Coppola (1974), pp.119-245.

26. A few figures bear this point out. During 1963-71 Matera province secured 80 per cent of Cassa industrial development funds, Potenza only 20 per cent. During 1977-81 Potenza got 55 per cent compared to Matera's 45 per cent. Sectorally, whilst chemicals and synthetic fibres absorbed 62 per cent and food, clothing, shoes and construction industries only 23 per cent during 1961-70, in the following decade, 1971-81, the position was reversed — 32 per cent and 55 per cent respectively. Viganoni (1983), pp.95-6.

27. Bethemont and Pelletier (1983), p.183.

28. Rodgers (1979), p.49.

29. Mountjoy (1970).

30. Under the influence of petrochemicals expansion Syracuse has grown rapidly — 72,000 (1951), 91,000 (1961), 111,000 (1971), 118,000 (1981). See Ruggiero (1975). For interesting sociological studies of the style of development and of the nature of the new workforces see Leonardi (1964), Morello (1962), Parlato et al. (1960).

31. Campagnoli Ciaccio (1971).

32. This figure, from IASM, is in reality an exaggeration since some firms have simply transferred to the industrial estate from the centre of town — see Formica (1970), pp.73-6.

33. Ruggiero (1974).

34. King (1977).

35. King (1975).

36. It is highly significant that strikes throughout a sector (such as the 1979 chemical industry strike) have broken out in both North and South Italy. In the chemical case it was to demand expansion of the industry in the South: a rare example of a *national* protest concerned directly with regional industrial development. Bethemont and Pelletier (1983), p.107.

37. Compagna (1977).

38. See Giannola (1982); Palmerio (1982).

39. Cf. Guantario (1976); Podbielski (1978), p.165.

BIBLIOGRAPHY

Abulafia, D. (1977) *The Two Italies: Economic Relations between the Norman Kingdom of Sicily and the Northern Communes,* Cambridge University Press, Cambridge

Achenbach, H. (1976) 'Studien zur räumlichen Differenzierung der Lombardei und Piedmonts', *Erdkunde, 30,* 176-86

Acquaviva, S.S. and Santuccio, M. (1976) *Social Structure in Italy,* Martin Robertson, London

Adamo, F. (1979) 'Sviluppo regionale, mobilità sociale e residenziale con riferimento al caso piemontese, *Rivista Geografica Italiana, 86,* 3-29

Alberoni, F. and Baglioni, G. (1965) *L'Integrazione dell' Immigrato nella Società Industriale,* Il Mulino, Bologna

Albertini, R. (1959) 'L'industria idroelettrica nel bacino del Noce (Adige) e i riflessi antropico-economici del suo sviluppo', *Bollettino della Società Geografica Italiana,* Ser. 8, *12,* 538-69

Albrecht-Carrié, R. (1960) *Italy from Napoleon to Mussolini,* Columbia University Press, New York

Allen, K. and MacLellan, M. (1970) *Regional Problems and Policies in Italy and France,* Allen and Unwin, London

—— and Stevenson, A.A. (1974) *An Introduction to the Italian Economy,* Martin Robertson, London

Allum, P. (1973a) *Italy — Republic without Government?* Weidenfeld and Nicolson, London

—— (1973b) *Politics and Society in Post-war Naples,* Cambridge University Press, Cambridge

Almagià, R. (1959) *L'Italia,* UTET, Turin, 2 vols

Amin, A. (1983) *Industrial Restructuring, State Intervention and Regional Growth: The Example of Alfa-Sud in Southern Italy,* University of Reading Geographical Papers, Reading, *77*

—— (1984) 'Restructuring and spatial decentralisation in the Italian car industry: the case of Fiat', in R. Hudson and J. Lewis (eds.), *Capital, Accumulation and Class in Southern Europe,* Methuen, London, in press

Ammassari, P. (1969) 'The Italian blue-collar worker', *International Journal of Comparative Sociology, 10,* 3-21

Apicella, V. (1978) 'The evolution of the Italian motorway system', *Review of Economic Conditions in Italy, 32,* 331-46

Arcangeli, F., Borzaga, C. and Goglio, S. (1980) 'Patterns of peripheral development in the Italian regions', *Papers of the Regional Science Association, 44,* 19-34

Archibugi, F. (1960) 'Recent trends in women's work in Italy', *International Labour Review, 81,* 285-318

—— (1978) 'Italian prospects: capitalist planning in question', in S. Holland (ed.), *Beyond Capitalist Planning,* Blackwell, Oxford, pp. 49-68

Armstrong, G. (1978) 'Trieste turns its back on Rome', *The Guardian,* 8 December, p.7

Ascoli, U. and Trento, A. (1975) 'Sviluppo industriale e flessibilità della forza lavoro: il settore calzaturiero', *Inchiesta, 20,* 23-34, 51-3

Attuoni, P. (1959) 'I nuovi centri industriali del Lazio', *Rivista Geografica Italiana, 66,* 322-57

Avagliano, L. (1976) 'Lo sviluppo dei settori IRI e il rapporto stato-gruppi privati (1933-39)', *Rassegna Economica, 40,* 1125-98

Avveduto, S. (1968) *La Società Scientifica*, Etas-Kompass, Milan

Bagnasco, A. (1977) *Tre Italie*, Il Mulino, Bologna

Balella, G. (1972) 'Chemical fibres in Italy', *Review of Economic Conditions in Italy*, *26*, 113-21

Barbagallo, C. (1951) *Le Origini della Grande Industria Contemporanea*, La Nuova Italia, Florence

Barbato, L. (1968) *Politica Meridionalistica e Localizzazione Industriale: della Legge Pastore all' Alfa Sud*, Marsilia, Padua

Barbieri, G. (1959) *I Porti d'Italia*, Istituto di Geografia dell' Università di Napoli, Naples, Memorie di Geografia Economica, *20*

Basilico, R. (1983) 'The shipbuilding industry in Italy and the South', *Isveimer Bulletin*, *31-32*, 11-31

Battisti, G. (1979) *Una Regione per Trieste: Studi di Geografia Economica e Politica*, Università di Trieste, Facoltà di Economia e Commercio, Istituto di Geografia, Trieste, Pubblicazione, *10*

Bellani, F.F. (1973) 'Medium-term evolution of the Italian cotton industry', *Review of Economic Conditions in Italy*, *27*, 313-25

Beretta, P.L. (1968) 'Le autostrade in Italia', *L'Universo*, 48, 209-40, 525-66

Bethemont, J. and Pelletier, J. (1983) *Italy: A Geographical Introduction*, Longman, London

Bevilacqua, E. and Mattana, U. (1976) 'The Po River Basin: water utilisation for hydroelectric power and irrigation', in A. Pecora and R. Pracchi (eds.), *Italian Contributions to the 23rd International Geographical Congress*, CNR, Rome, pp.181-9

Biondi, G. and Coppola, P. (1974) *Industrializzazione e Mezzogiorno: la Basilicata*, Pubblicazioni dell' Istituto di Geografia Economica dell' Università di Napoli, Naples, *14*

—— (1979) 'Il lavoro fuggente: multinazionale e occupazione in Campania', *Orizzonti Economici*, *22*, 109-30

Biscaretti di Ruffia, R. (1973) 'Situation and prospects of the motor industry in Italy', *Review of Economic Conditions in Italy*, *27*, 43-52

Blanchard, W.O. (1928) 'White coal in Italian industry', *Geographical Review*, *18*, 261-73

Bonelli, F. (1969) 'Osservazioni e dati sul finanziamento dell' industria italiana all' inizio del secolo XX', *Annali della Fondazione Luigi Einaudi*, *2*, 257-86

Borlenghi, E., Conti, S., Mazzuca, R. and Serniotti, P. (1976) 'Corporation planning and territorial planning in Italy: the case of some private holdings and state corporations', in A. Pecora and R. Pracchi (eds.), *Italian Contributions to the 23rd International Geographical Congress*, CNR, Rome, pp.249-58

Bracco, F. (1976) 'The Italian chemical industry: prospects and problems', *Review of Economic Conditions in Italy*, *30*, 109-18

Brusa, A. (1964) 'Il decentramento portuale e industriale a Genova', *Bollettino dell Società Geografica Italiana*, Ser. 10, 5, 405-45

Brusco, S. (1982) 'The Emilian model: productive decentralisation and social integration', *Cambridge Journal of Economics*, *6*, 167-84

Bryant, A. (1968) *The Italians: How They Live and Work*, David and Charles, Newton Abbot

Cafagna, L. (1971) 'The industrial revolution in Italy 1830-1914', in C. Cipolla (ed.), *The Fontana Economic History of Europe, vol. 4: The Emergence of Industrial Societies*, Fontana, London, pp.279-328

Cagliozzi, R. (1970) *Prospettive del Traffico Marittimo e Problemi Portuali del Mezzogiorno*, SVIMEZ, Rome

—— (1975a) *Infrastrutture di Trasporto e Sviluppo del Mezzogiorno*, SVIMEZ, Rome

—— (1975b) *L'Ammodernamento delle Ferrovie ed il Ruolo del Trasporto Ferroviario nel Mezzogiorno*, SVIMEZ, Rome

Caizzi, B. (1965) *Storia dell' Industria Italiana del Secolo XVIII ai Giorni Nostri*, UTET, Turin

Camagna, E. (1971) 'The Italian shoe industry', *Review of Economic Conditions in Italy*, *25*, 460-73

Campagnoli Ciaccio, C. (1971) 'Un colosso della zona industriale megarese: la Sincat', *Annali del Mezzogiorno*, *11*, 207-55

Canzanelli, G., Caroleto, E.F. and Corsani, A. (1981) 'Proposals for redevelopment of land and industry in the Naples area', *Mezzogiorno d'Europa*, *1*, 339-55

Cao-Pinna, V. (1976) 'Regional policy in Italy', in N.M. Hansen (ed.), *Regional Policy and Regional Economic Development*, Ballinger, Cambridge, Massachusetts, pp. 137-79

Capanna, A. (1979) 'Steel in Southern Italy', *Isveimer Bulletin*, *21-22*, 11-27

Caracciolo, A. (ed) (1969) *La Formazione dell' Italia Industriale*, Laterza, Bari

Carli, G. (1977) Credit and industry, *Isveimer Bulletin*, *2*, 9-23

Carparelli, S. (1976) *L'Agglomerato Industriale di Bari-Modugno e il Movimento Pendolare della Mano d'Opera*, Facoltà di Magistero dell' Università di Bari, Istituto di Geografia, Bari, Pubblicazione 5

Cataudella, M. (1968) 'Il tronco Roma-Napoli dell' Autostrada del Sole e la localizzazione delle industrie', *Bollettino della Società Geografica Italiana*, Ser. 9, *9*, 357-71

Cavallari, C. and Faustini, G. (1978) 'Labour costs and employment in Italy and the EEC', *Banca Nazionale del Lavoro Quarterly Review*, *126*, 251-70

Celant, A. (1971) 'La siderurgia di Bolzano: il caso di un insediamento volontaristico', *Notiziario di Geografia Economica*, *2* (1-2), 43-60

—— (1976) 'Trasporti e porti del Mezzogiorno nel quadro della politica meridionalistica', *Rivista di Politica Economica*, *66*, 1055-95

—— (1980) 'The steel industry', in M. Pinna and D. Ruocco (eds.), *Italy: A Geographical Survey*, Pacini, Pisa, pp. 477-82

Charnier, J.B. (1966) 'L'organisation de l'espace dans une "aire métropolitaine": le bassin de Florence-Pistoia', *Annales de Géographie*, *75*, 57-83

Ciocca, P., Filosa, R. and Rey, G.M. (1975) 'Integration and development of the Italian economy 1951-1971: a re-examination', *Banca Nazionale del Lavoro Quarterly Review*, *114*, 284-320

Cipolla, C. (1952) 'The decline of Italy: the case of a fully matured economy', *Economic History Review*, *5*, 178-87

—— (1965) 'Four centuries of Italian demographic development', in D. Glass and D. Eversley (eds.), *Population in History*, Arnold, London, pp. 570-87

Cirillo, G. (1974) 'L'industria calzaturiera in Italia e nel Mezzogiorno', *Rassegna Economica*, *38*, 193-222

Clough, S.B. (1964) *The Economic History of Modern Italy*, Columbia University Press, New York

Cole, J.P. (1968) *Italy*, Chatto and Windus, London

Colombo, U. (1980) 'The role of nuclear power in the energy prospects for Italy', *Isveimer Bulletin*, *29-30*, 11-39

Compagna, F. (1977) 'Comment on credit and industry', *Isveimer Bulletin*, *2*, 39-44

Coppola, P. (1976) 'Liquichimica e Metapontino: come liquidare una piana irrigua,' *Nord e Sud*, *23*, 49-66

Coquery, M. (1963) 'Aspects démographiques et problèmes de croissance d'une ville "millionaire": le cas de Naples', *Annales de Géographie*, *72*, 573-604

Cori, B. (1962) 'L'industria del calzaturificio nel Valdarno inferiore', *Rivista Geografica Italiana*, *69*, 162-79

Corna Pellegrini, G. (1973) 'Considerazioni geografiche su alcuni fattori di localizzazione dell' industria italiana nel secolo XIX', *Nord e Sud*, *22* 179-207

Cornwell, R. (1981) 'Marche: happy blend of farming and small industry', *Financial Times*, 13 July, p.13

Coulet, L. (1978) 'La fabrique diffuse en Emilie-Romagne', *Méditerranée*, *34*, 13-25
Dalla Zuanna, U. (1977) 'L'esperienza italiana in materia d' incentivazione industriale: la legge tessile', *L'Industria*, *91*, 99-106
Dalmasso, E. (1964) 'L'industrie électrique en Italie', *Annales de Géographie*, *73*, 450-61
—— (1971) *Milan, Capitale Économique de l'Italie*, Orphrys, Gap
D'Antonio, M. (1973) *Sviluppo e Crisi del Capitalismo Italiano 1951-1972*, De Donato, Bari
—— (1977) 'La diffusione delle industrie manufatturiere nel Mezzogiorno 1970-75', *Rassegna Economica*, *41*, 1045-80
D'Aponte, T. (1976) 'Aspetti geografici della politica di incentivazione finanziaria per lo sviluppo industriale del Mezzogiorno', in A. Pecora and R. Pracchi (eds.), *Italian Contributions to the 23rd International Geographical Congress*, CNR, Rome, pp. 259-71
David, P. and Pattarin, E. (1975) 'Retroterra rurale e condizione operaia femminile: il settore della maglieria', *Inchiesta*, *20*, 9-22
De Cecco, M. (1972) 'Economic policy in the reconstruction period, 1945-50', in S.J. Woolf (ed.), *The Rebirth of Italy 1943-50*, Longman, London, pp. 156-80
Dechert, C.R. (1963) *Ente Nazionale Idrocarburi: Profile of a State Corporation*, E.J. Brill, Leiden
Della Porta, G. (1955) 'Origins, evolution, structure and prospects of Finsider', *Review of Economic Conditions in Italy*, *9*, 553-65
Della Valle, C. (1964) 'Geografia dell' industria,' in *Un Sessantina di Ricerca Geografica Italiana*, Società Geografica Italiana, Rome, pp. 327-46
Del Panta, L. (1979) 'Italy', in W.R. Lee (ed.), *European Demography and Economic Growth*, Croom Helm, London, pp.196-235
Dematteis, G. (1973) 'L' influence de Turin sur les Alpes occidentales italiennes', *Revue de Géographie Alpine*, *61*, 371-90
De Rosa, L. (1973) *La Rivoluzione Industriale in Italia e nel Mezzogiorno*, Laterza, Bari
Di Fenizio, F. (1965) *La Programmazione Economica*, UTET, Turin
Eckaus, R.S. (1961) 'The North-South differential in Italian economic development', *Journal of Economic History*, *21*, 285-317
Elemi, G. and Gambino, R. (1975) 'La posizione del sud rispetto ai sistemi nazionali delle communicazioni', *Rassegna Economica*, *39*, 1227-58
Ferro, G. (1958) 'Le trasformazioni industriali nelle vallate delle Bormide', *Rivista Geografica Italiana*, *65*, 32-51
—— (1969) 'Le possibilità di decentramento industriale nel bacino delle Bormide', *Bollettino della Società Geografica Italiana*, Ser. 9, *10*, 590-625
Flore, V.D. (1972) 'Guidelines for a new Italian port policy', *Review of Economic Conditions in Italy*, *26*, 35-50
Floridia, E. (1971) 'Le attività siderurgiche quale fattore di urbanizzazione di Villadossola e di equilibrio socio-economico nella regione ossolana', *Notiziario di Geografia Economica*, *2*, special issue, 141-61
Fogagnolo, G. (1975) 'Contribution of the Italian nuclear industry to the solutions of the energy crisis', *Review of Economic Conditions in Italy*, *29*, 205-23
Formica, C. (1967) 'I nuclei industriali dell' Appennino campano nelle prospettive di sviluppo del Sud', *Annali del Mezzogiorno*, *7*, 177-95
——(1970) *La Piana di Catania*, Naples: Pubblicazioni dell' Istituto di Geografia Economica dell' Università di Napoli, *6*
Fraenkel, G. (1975) 'Italian industrial policy in the framework of economic planning', in J. Haywood and M. Watson (eds.), *Planning, Politics and Public Policy*, Cambridge University Press, Cambridge, pp. 128-40
Frankel, P.H. (1966) *Mattei: Oil and Power Politics*, Faber and Faber, London
Frey, A. (1975) *Lavoro a Domicilio e Decentramento dell' Attività Produttiva nei Settori Tessile e dell' Abbigliamento in Italia*, Angeli, Milan

Fried, R.C. (1973) *Planning the Eternal City: Roman Politics and Planning Since World War II*, Yale University Press, New Haven

Fuà G. (1965) *Notes on Italian Economic Growth, 1861-1964*, Giuffrè, Milan

—— (ed) (1969) *Lo Sviluppo Economico in Italia*, Angeli, Milan, 3 vols.

—— (1977) 'Employment and productive capacity in Italy', *Banca Nazionale del Lavoro Quarterly Review*, *122*, 215-44

—— (1978) 'Lagged development and economic dualism', *Banca Nazionale del Lavoro Quarterly Review*, *125*, 123-34

—— (1980) *Problemi dello Sviluppo Tardivo in Europa nel Rapporto su Sei Paesi Appartenenti all' OCSE*, Il Mulino, Bologna

Fuga, F. (1976) 'I porti del Mezzogiorno tra Europea e Mediterraneo', in C. Muscarà (ed.), *Mezzogiorno e Mediterraneo*, Istituto di Geografia dell' Università di Venezia, Venice, vol. 1, pp. 47-83

Fuller, J.G. (1977) *The Poison That Fell from the Sky*, Random House, New York

Gabert, P. (1963) 'Le port de Ravenne et sa zone industrielle', *Méditerranée*, *4*, 67-82

—— (1964) *Turin, Ville Industrielle*, PUF, Paris

Gambi, L. (1949) 'Riflessi della seconda guerra mondiale sulle condizioni demografiche dell' Italia nord e centro peninsulare', *Bollettino della Società Geografica Italiana*, Ser. 8, *2*, 124-35

Gasparini, M.L. (1979) 'Elettricità: geografia di un probabile black-out', *Nord e Sud*, *26*, 264-77

Gasperini, L. (1974) *L'industria Chimica nella Storia Italiana*, D'Anna, Messina

Gerschenkron, A. (1955) 'Notes on the rate of industrial growth in Italy, 1881-1913', *Journal of Economic History*, *15*, 360-75

—— (1962) *Economic Backwardness in Historical Perspective*, Harvard University Press, Cambridge, Massachusetts

Ghelardoni, P. (1971) 'Faenza: ricerca di geografia urbana', *Bollettino della Società Geografica Italiana*, Ser. 9, *12*, 20-86

Giannola, A. (1982) 'The industrialisation, dualism and economic dependence of the Mezzogiorno in the 1970s', *Review of Economic Conditions in Italy*, *36*, 67-92

Girola, A. (1977) 'Machine tools: advanced technology for Italian industry', *Review of Economic Conditions in Italy*, *31*, 221-40

Giugni, G. (1971) 'Recent trends in collective bargaining in Italy', *International Labour Review*, *104*, 307-28

Golini, A. and Geseno, G. (1981) 'Regional migration in the process of Italian economic development from 1881 to the present', in J. Balán (ed.), *Why People Move*, UNESCO, Paris, pp. 75-92

Gosseaume, E. (1969) 'Livourne, port industriel', *Revue de Géographie de Lyon*, *44*, 169-93

Graziani, A. (ed.) (1969) *Lo Sviluppo in un'Economia Aperta*, ESI, Naples

—— (ed.) (1972) *L'Economia Italiana 1945-70*, Il Mulino, Bologna

—— (ed.) (1975) *Crisi e Ristrutturazione nell' Economia Italiana*, Einandi, Turin

Gribaudi, F. (1968) 'Functions and physiognomy of Turin', *Acta Geographica*, *20*, 101-11

Grilloti di Giacomo, M.G. (1978) 'Considerazioni geografiche sul nucleo industriale di Rieti-Cittaducale', *Bollettino della Società Geografica Italiana*, Ser. 10, 7, 63-80

Grindrod, M. (1955) *The Rebuilding of Italy*, RIIA, London

Gualerni, G. (1976) *Industria e Fascismo*, Vita e Pensiero, Milan

Gualtieri, H.L. (1946) *The Labor Movement in Italy*, Vanni, New York

Guantario, L. (1976) 'Southern Italy and industrial reconversion', *Review of Economic Conditions in Italy*, *30*, 403-14

Gucciardi, D. (1973) 'Industry and ecological problems in Italy', *Review of Economic Conditions in Italy*, *27*, 305-12

Holland, S. (ed.) (1972) *The State as Entrepreneur. New Dimensions for Policy Enterprise: The IRI State Shareholding Formula*, Weidenfeld and Nicolson, London
—— (1976) *Capital versus the Regions*, Martin Robertson, London
Horowitz, D.L. (1963) *The Italian Labor Movement*, Harvard University Press, Cambridge, Massachusetts.
Houssel, J.P. (1972) 'Lo slancio recente della città manufatturiere dell' abbigliamento nella "Italia di mezzo"', *Rivista Geografica Italiana*, *79*, 241-69
Hytten, E. and Marchioni, M. (1970) *Industrializzazione senza Sviluppo: Gela, una Storia Meridionale*, Angeli, Milan
Innocenti, C. (1983) 'Alfa Romeo: which future?' *Isveimer Bulletin*, *47*, 11-26
Innocenti, P. (1964) 'La città di Piombino: studio di geografia industriale', *Rivista Geografica Italiana*, *71*, 319-403
——(1970) 'L'Italia e la localizzazione di un "terminal" mediterraneo per contenitori: note di geografia applicata', *Bollettino della Società Geografica Italiana*, Ser. 9, *11*, 192-232
Ippolito, F. (1980) 'Italy's position in the current world energy scenario', *Review of Economic Conditions in Italy*, *34*, 9-39
Kalla-Bishop, P.M. (1971) *Italian Railways*, David and Charles, Newton Abbot
Keyser, W. and Windle, R. (eds.) (1978) *Public Enterprise in the EEC, Vol. 5: Italy*, Sijthoff and Noordhoff, Alphen aan den Rijn
Kindleberger, C.P. (1967) *Europe's Postwar Growth: the Role of Labour Supply*, Oxford University Press, London
King, R.L. (1971) *The 'Questione Meridionale' in Southern Italy*, University of Durham, Department of Geography, Durham, Research Papers, *11*
King, R.L. (1975) 'Ottana: an attempt to bring industry to Sardinia's shepherd-bandits', *Geography*, *60*, 218-22
King, R.L. (1976) 'Long-range migration patterns in the EEC: an Italian case study', in R. Lee and P.E. Ogden (eds.), *Economy and Society in the EEC*, Saxon House, Farnborough, pp. 108-25
King, R.L. (1977) 'Recent industrialisation in Sardinia: rebirth or neocolonialism?' *Erdkunde*, *31*, 87-102
Kish, G. (1969) *Italy*, Van Nostrand Reinhold, New York
Landini, P. (1975) 'Il problema dei retroterra portuali nel Mezzogiorno', *Notiziario di Geografia Economica*, *6* (3-4), 1-24
LaPalombara, J. (1957) *The Italian Labor Movement: Problems and Prospects*, Cornell University Press, Ithaca
—— (1964) *Interest Groups in Italian Politics*, Princeton University Press, New York
—— (1966) *Italy: The Politics of Planning*, Syracuse University Press, Syracuse
Latis, M. (1976) 'The electrical engineering and electronic industries', *Review of Economic Conditions in Italy*, *30*, 499-516
Lavoratti, P.L. and Della Capanna, M.L. (1972) 'Empoli: note dia geografia urbana', *Bollettino della Società Geografica Italiana*, Ser. 10, *1*, 419-85
Leonardi, F. (1964) *Operai Nuovi: Studio Sociologico sulle Nuove Forze del Lavoro Industriale nell' Area Siracusana*, Feltrinelli, Milan
Lizzeri, G. (1979) 'Power consumption and industrial development in Southern Italy', *Isveimer Bulletin*, *17-18*, 15-37
Lloyd, E.A. (1925) *The Cooperative Movement in Italy*, Allen and Unwin, London
Lusso, G. (1978) 'Distribuzione delle residenze degli operai della Fiat in Torino', *Rivista Geografica Italiana*, *85*, 43-55
Lutz, V. (1962) *Italy: A Study in Development*, Oxford University Press, London
Luzzatto, G. (1961a) *An Economic History of Italy*, Routledge and Kegan Paul, London
—— (1961b) 'Gli anni più critici dell' economia italiana', in *L'Economia Italiana dal 1861 al 1961*, Giuffrè, Milan, pp. 424-33

—— (1968) *L'Economia Italiana dal 1861 al 1894*, Einaudi, Turin

Malezieux, J. (1964) 'La sidérurgie italienne', *L'Information Géographique*, *28*, 191-205

Manuelli, E. (1958) 'Situation and prospects of the Italian steel industry', *Review of Economic Conditions in Italy*, *12*, 567-79

Manzi, E. (1970) 'Aspetti geografici dell' industria della nautica di diporto', *Bollettino della Società Geografica Italiana*, Ser. 9, *11*, 535-66

Marcelloni, M. (1979) 'Urban movements and political struggles in Italy', *International Journal of Urban and Regional Research*, *3*, 251-68

Mariani, A. (1980) 'Situazione e prospettive della raffinazione del petrolio in Italia', *Rassegna Economica*, *44*, 87-108

Mazzaoui, M. (1972) 'The cotton industry of Northern Italy in the late Middle Ages, 1150-1450', *Journal of Economic History*, *32*, 262-86

Migliorini, P. (1975) 'Note sull' esperienza italiana in materia di localizzazione delle centrali elettronucleari', *Notiziario di Geografia Economica*, *6* (1-2), 17-28

Mihelić, D. (1969) *The Political Element in the Port Geography of Trieste*, University of Chicago, Department of Geography, Chicago, Research Paper *120*

Militerno, A.A. and Tondini, G. (1979) 'Esportazione e occupazione nel settore manufatturiero italiano dal 1951 al 1976', *Rassegna Economica*, *43*, 619-48

Molho, A. (ed.) (1969) *Social and Economic Foundations of the Italian Renaissance*, Wiley, New York

Molino, D. (1972) 'La trazione elettrica ferroviaria in Italia', *L'Universo*, *52*, 1321-68

—— (1976) 'Iniziative e programmi delle ferrovie italiane nel campo delle alte velocità', *L'Universo*, *56*, 9-44

Morandi, R. (1966) *Storia della Grande Industria in Italia*, Einaudi, Turin

Morello, G. (1962) *Industrializzazione della Provincia di Siracusa,* Il Mulino, Bologna

Mori, A. (1965) 'Il limite della zona d' intervento della Cassa per il Mezzogiorno come fattore d'attrazione e localizzazione industriale', *Rivista Geografica Italiana*, *72*, 19-41

—— (1977) 'Aspetti e problemi dell' industrializzazione in Toscana: contributi recenti e considerazioni integrative', *Bollettino della Società Geografica Italiana*, Ser. 10, *6*, 55-66

Mori, G. (1959) 'La storia dell' industria italiana contemporanea nei saggi, nelle ricerche e nelle pubblicazioni giubilari di questo dopoguerra', *Annali dell' Istituto Feltrinelli*, *2*, 264-366

Mountjoy, A.B. (1966) 'Planning and industrial developments in Apulia', *Geography*, *51*, 369-72

—— (1970) 'Planning and industrial developments in eastern Sicily', *Geography*, *55*, 441-4.

—— (1973) *The Mezzogiorno*, Oxford University Press, London

Murrali, L. (1980) 'L'Italia delle autostrade', *Geografia*, *3*, 103-6

Neufeld, M. (1961) *Italy: School for Awakening Countries*, State School of Industrial and Labor Relations, Cornell University, Ithaca, New York

Newcombe, V.Z. (1969) 'Creating an industrial development growth pole in Southern Italy', *Journal of Town Planning Institute,* 55, 157-61

Nice, B. (1976) 'Il ruolo delle autostrade nell' organizzazione territoriale dell' Italia', in A. Pecora and R. Pracchi (eds.), *Italian Contributions to the 23rd International Geographical Congress*, CNR, Rome, pp. 203-17

Ortolani, M. and Mounfield, P.R. (1963) *Lombardia e Lancashire: Saggio di Geografia Industriale Comparata*, Università di Napoli, Istituto di Geografia, Naples, Memorie di Geografia Economica e Antropica, 2

Ortona, G. and Santagata, W. (1983) 'Industrial mobility in the Turin metropolitan area, 1961-77', *Urban Studies*, *20*, 59-72

318   *Bibliography*

Ottieri, O. (1962) *The Men at the Gate*, Gollancz, London
Paci, M. (1973) *Mercato di Lavoro e Classi Sociali in Italia*, Il Mulino, Bologna
Paci, R. (1980) 'L'industria metalmeccanica in Sardegna', *Quaderni Sardi di Economia*, *10*, 205-32
Pacione, M. (1974a) 'Italian motorways', *Geography*, *59*, 35-41
—— (1974b) 'The Venetian problem: an overview', *Geography*, *59*, 339-43
—— (1976) 'Italy and the energy crisis', *Geography*, *61*, 99-102
—— (1979) 'Natural gas in Italy', *Geography*, *64*, 211-15
—— (1982) 'Economic development in the Mezzogiorno', *Geography*, *67*, 340-3
Page, C. (1983) 'Prosperity migrates from the Industrial Triangle', *The Guardian*, 15 November, p. 8
Palmerio, G. (1982) 'Some reflections on the gap between the North and South in the economic context of today', *Mezzogiorno d'Europa*, *2*, 157-67
Panunzio, V. (1978) 'The Italian ports and their problems', *Review of Economic Conditions in Italy*, *32*, 27-40
Parlato, V., Mazzarino, M. and Peggio, E. (1960) *Industrializzazione e Sottosviluppo: Il Progresso Tecnologico in una Provincia del Mezzogiorno*, Einaudi, Turin
Pasini, G. (1974) 'Situation and prospects of the clothing industry in Italy', *Review of Economic Conditions in Italy*, *28*, 537-53
Pasquino, G. and Pecchini, U. (1975) 'Italy', in J. Hayward and M. Watson (eds.), *Planning, Politics and Public Policy*, Cambridge University Press, Cambridge, pp. 70-92
Picarelli, A. (1977) 'The Italian textile industry: problems and prospects', *Review of Economic Conditions in Italy*, *31*, 43-68
Piccardi, S. (1967) 'Il Valdarno Superiore: studio di geografia industriale', *Rivista Geografica Italiana*, *74*, 157-222
—— (1968) 'Industrie e centri abitati lungo l'Arno e la Sieve a monte di Firenze', *Rivista Geografica Italiana*, *75*, 65-91
Pinna, M. (1960) 'Aspetti geografici dell' industria dei mobili nel Valdarno Inferiore', *Rivista Geografica Italiana*, *67*, 31-54
Podbielski, G. (1978) *Twenty-five Years of Special Action for the Development of Southern Italy*, SVIMEZ, Rome
Poncet, J. (1969) 'Sous-développement et facteurs naturels: l'exemple du Mezzogiorno', *Méditerranée*, *10*, 63-79
Posner, M.V. and Woolf, S.J. (1967) *Italian Public Enterprise*, Duckworth, London
Prodi, R. (1973) *Sistema Industriale e Sviluppo Economico in Italia*, Il Mulino, Bologna
Ragozzino, G. (1969) Una mappa del grande capitale in Italia, *Rassagna Sindacale*, Quaderno *23*, 37-73
Rapp, R.T. (1976) *Industry and Economic Decline in Seventeenth Century Venice*, Harvard University Press, Cambridge, Massachusetts
Repaci, F.A. (1960) 'Le spese delle guerre condotte dall' Italia', *Rivista di Politica Economica*, *50*, 695-713
Reyne, G. (1983) L'évolution démographique récente de l'Italie d'après les résultats du recensement d'octobre 1981, *Méditerranée*, *9*(4), 19-26
Rocca, G. (1978) 'Sesto San Giovanni: un centro satellite della conurbazione milanese', *L'Universo*, *58*, 609-36, 705-36, 937-1000
Rochefort, R. (1960) 'Le pétrole en Sicile', *Annales de Géographie*, *60*, 22-33
Rodgers, A.L. (1957) 'The role of the state in the industrial development of the port of Genova', *Papers and Proceedings of the Regional Science Association*, *3*, 290-300
—— (1958) 'The port of Genova: external and internal relations', *Annals of the Association of American Geographers*, *48*, 319-51
—— (1960) *The Industrial Geography of the Port of Genova*, University of Chicago, Department of Geography, Chicago, Research Paper *66*

Bibliography 319

—— (1970) 'Migration and industrial development: the southern Italian experience', *Economic Geography*, 46, 111-36

—— (1976) 'Southern Italy: the role of governmental location policy and practice in the development of industry in an underdeveloped region', in C. Muscarà (ed.), *Mezzogiorno e Mediterraneo*, Istituto di Geografia dell' Università di Venezia, Venice, vol. 4, pp. 47-81

—— (1978) 'Mediterranean Europe', in G.T. Trewartha (ed.), *The More Developed Realm: A Geography of Its Population*, Pergamon, Oxford, pp. 79-97

—— (1979) *Economic Development in Retrospect: The Italian Model and Its Significance for Regional Planning in Market-Oriented Economies*, Winston-Wiley, New York

Romeo, R. (1963) *Breva Storia della Grande Industria in Italia*, Cappelli, Bologna

Ronzani, S. (1980) 'Regional incentives in Italy', D. Yuill, L. Allen and C. Hull (eds.), *Regional Policy in the European Community*, Croom Helm, London, pp. 134-56

Rotondo, W. (1979) 'Note siderurgiche sul Mezzogiorno', *Rassegna Economica*, 43, 1261-81

Ruggiero, V. (1973) 'I porti industriali del Mezzogiorno', in *Problemi Geografici dell' Industrializzazione in Europa*, Pubblicazioni dell' Istituto di Geografia Economica dell' Università di Napoli, Naples, 10, 187-216

—— (1974) 'Un asse di sviluppo per il riequilibrio territoriale della Sicilia centro-meridionale', *Annali del Mezzogiorno*, 14, 149-77

—— (1975) 'Siracusa nuovo centro coordinatore della Sicilia sud-orientale', *Rivista Geografica Italiana*, 72, 21-86

—— (1980) 'Air transport: evolution and prospects', in M. Pinna and D. Ruocco (eds.), *Italy: A Geographical Survey*, Pacini, Pisa, pp. 366-72

Ruju, S. (1979) 'Dinamica, contraddizioni strutturali e prospettive di sviluppo dell' industria petrolchimica', *Quaderni Sardi di Economia*, 9, 333-68

Rullani, E. and Vaccà, S. (1979) 'Miti e realtà della crisi petrolchimica italiana', in P. Ranci and S. Vaccà (eds.), *L'Industria Petrolchimica in Italia: Anatomia di una Crisi*, Angeli, Milan, pp. 17-49

Ruocco, D. (1968) *Il Petrolio nel Vicino Oriente e L'Industria Petrolifera Italiana*, Scientifiche, Naples

Saibene, C. (1980) 'The Italian industrial system', in M. Pinna and D. Ruocco (eds.), *Italy: A Geographical Survey*, Pacini, Pisa, pp. 441-51

Salvatori, F. (1975) 'Crisi tessile nella media e alta Val Seriana', *Notiziario di Geografia Economica*, 6(3-4), 25-39

Saraceno, P. (1959) *Ricostruzione e Pianificazione, 1943-1948*, Laterza, Bari

—— (1975) *Il Sistema delle Partecipazioni Statali nell' Esperienza Italiana*, SVIMEZ, Rome

Sarti, R. (1971) *Fascism and the Industrial Leadership in Italy, 1919-1940*, University of California Press, Berkeley

Saville, L. (1968) *Regional Economic Development in Italy*, Edinburgh University Press, Edinburgh

Scaraffia, L. (1975) 'Trasformazione del territorio e stratificazione sociale di Sarroch (Cagliari)', in L. Scaraffia and D. Testa, *Le Industrie del Sud*, Angeli, Milan, pp. 155-274

Scattoni, P. and Williams, R. (1978) 'Planning and regional devolution — the Italian case', *The Planner*, 64, 38-40

Sciarelli, S. and Maggioni, V. (1975) 'Un' industria acèfala: primi risultati di un' indagine svolta in Campania', *Rassegna Economica*, 38, 1493-1514

Scimone, J. (1964) 'The Italian miracle', in *Studies in Economic Miracles*, Institute of Economic Affairs, London, pp. 169-220

Secchi, B. (1973) 'Sviluppo della rete dei trasporti e distribuzione territoriale degli insediamenti in Italia', *Urbanistica*, 61, 88-93

Sella, D. (1968) 'The rise and fall of the Venetian woollen industry', in B. Pullan (ed.), *Crisis and Change in the Venetian Economy in the Sixteenth and Seventeenth Centuries*, Methuen, London, pp. 106-26

Sica, A. (1972) 'Fattori geografici nella crisi della siderurgia lecchese', *Notiziario di Geografia Economica*, 3(1-2), 15-42

—— (1973) 'L'assetto regionale dell' industria e dei livelli di reddito in Italia', *Notiziario di Geografia Economica*, 4(3-4), 18-31

Simoncelli, R. (1972) 'Siderurgia camuna e insediamento umano nel bacino dell' alto fiume Oglio', *Notiziario di Geografia Economica*, 3(3-4), 1-46

Solinas, G. (1982) 'Labour market segmentation and workers' careers: the case of the Italian knitwear industry', *Cambridge Journal of Economics*, 6, 331-52

Spinelli, G. (1970) 'La siderurgia della Val di Susa, *Notiziario di Geografia Economica*, 1, 13-26

—— (1980) 'La struttura regionale dei consumi di elettricità in Italia', *Notiziario di Geografia Economica*, 11, 60-4

Stern, R. (1967) *Foreign Trade and Economic Growth in Italy*, Praeger, New York

Surace, S.J. (1966) *Ideology, Economic Change and the Working Classes: The Case of Italy*, University of California Press, Berkeley

Sylos-Labini, P. (1964) 'Precarious employment in Italy', *International Labour Review*, 89, 265-85

—— (1972) 'Sviluppo economico e classi sociali in Italia', *L'Astrolabio*, 10(3), 18-31

Tagliacarne, G. (1955) 'Italy's net product by regions', *Banca Nazionale del Lavoro Quarterly Review*, 35, 215-31

—— (1973) 'The regions twenty years later: socio-economic dynamics of the regions between 1951 and 1971', *Review of Economic Conditions in Italy*, 27, 127-61

Tarulli, E. (1973) 'Interventi nel settore dei trasporti in Italia', *Urbanistica*, 61, 76-86

Tosco, E. (1964) 'Economic policy in Italy 1949-1961', in *Economic Policy in Our Time*, North Holland, Amsterdam, vol. 3, pp. 138-286

Tremelloni, R. (1937) *L'Industria Tessile Italiana*, Einaudi, Turin

—— (1947) *Storia dell' Industria Italiana Contemporanea*, Einaudi, Turin

Turton, B.J. (1970) 'The western Po Basin: a study in industrial expansion and the journey-to-work', *Town Planning Review*, 41, 357-71

Vallega, A. (1972) *Il Cunese: un Territorio di Nuova Industrializzazione*, Pubblicazioni dell' Istituto di Scienze Geografiche dell' Università di Genova, Genoa, 20

—— (1977) 'La proiezione marittima dei porti: il caso di Genova', *Bollettino della Società Geografica Italiana*, Ser. 10, 6, 401-30

—— (1980) 'The problem of transport in Italy', in M.Pinna and D. Ruocco (eds.), *Italy: A Geographical Survey*, Pacini, Pisa, pp. 351-61

Vannutelli, C. (1962) 'Labour costs in Italy', *Banca Nazionale del Lavoro Quarterly Review*, 63, 355-81

Vedovato, G. (1973) 'Situation and prospects of the Italian extractive industry', *Review of Economic Conditions in Italy*, 27, 225-35

Viganoni, L. (1983) 'La politica d'incentivazione industriale in Basilicata: considerazioni sugli effetti territoriali', *Rivista Geografica Italiana*, 90, 93-109

Viterbo, D.D. (1975) 'Acqua e industria nel Mezzogiorno', in *Atti del XXII Congresso Geografico Italiano (Salerno, 18-22 Aprile 1975)*, pp. 214-23

Votaw, D. (1964) *The Six Legged Dog: Mattei and ENI — A Study in Power*, University of California Press, Berkeley

Wade, R. (1980) 'The Italian state and the underdevelopment of southern Italy', in R.D. Grillo (ed.), *Nation and State in Europe*, Academic Press, London, pp. 151-71

Waley, D. (1978) *The Italian City-Republics*, Longman, London

Walker, D. (1967) *A Geography of Italy*, Methuen, London

Watson, M.M. (1970) *Regional Development and Policy in Italy*, Longman, London

Webster, R.A. (1975) *Industrial Imperialism in Italy 1908-1915*, University of California Press, Berkeley

Willis, F.R. (1971) *Italy Chooses Europe*, Oxford University Press, New York

Wiskemann, E. (1971) *Italy since 1945*, Macmillan, London

Zanetti, G. (1983) 'The industrial structure and efficiency of the Italian economy: trends and planning prospects', *Review of Economic Conditions in Italy*, *37*, 249-300

Zariski, R. (1972) *Italy: The Politics of Uneven Development*, Dryden, Hinsdale, Illinois

Zinno, F. (1974) 'L' industria delle maglie e delle calze in Italia e nel Mezzogiorno', *Rassegna Economica*, *38*, 795-820

INDEX